THE LOST HISTORY
OF THE CAPITOL

*The Hidden and Tumultuous Saga
of Congress and the Capitol Building*

EDWARD P. MOSER

Guilford, Connecticut

An imprint of Globe Pequot, the trade division of The Rowman & Littlefield Publishing Group, Inc.
4501 Forbes Blvd., Ste. 200
Lanham, MD 20706
LyonsPress.com

Distributed by NATIONAL BOOK NETWORK

British Library Cataloguing in Publication Information available

Library of Congress Cataloging-in-Publication Data

Names: Moser, Edward P., author.
Title: The lost history of the Capitol : the hidden and tumultuous saga
   of Congress and the Capitol building / Edward P. Moser.
Other titles: Hidden and tumultuous saga of Congress and the Capitol
   building
Description: Guilford, Connecticut : Lyons Press, 2021. | Includes
   bibliographical references and index. | Summary: "An account of the many
   bizarre, tragic, and violent episodes that have occurred in and around
   the Capitol Building, from the founding of the federal capital city in
   1790 up to contemporary times"— Provided by publisher.
Identifiers: LCCN 2021016242 (print) | LCCN 2021016243 (ebook) | ISBN
   9781493055906 (cloth) | ISBN 9781493055913 (epub)
Subjects: LCSH: United States Capitol (Washington, D.C.) —History. | United
   States. Congress—History. | Washington (D.C.) —Buildings, structures,
   etc. | Washington (D.C.) —History.
Classification: LCC F204.C2 M67 2021 (print) | LCC F204.C2 (ebook) | DDC
   975.3—dc23
LC record available at https://lccn.loc.gov/2021016242
LC ebook record available at https://lccn.loc.gov/2021016243

∞™ The paper used in this publication meets the minimum requirements of American National Standard for Information Sciences—Permanence of Paper for Printed Library Materials, ANSI/NISO Z39.48-1992.

Also by Edward P. Moser:

The White House's Unruly Neighborhood: Crime, Scandal and Intrigue in the History of Lafayette Square

The Two-Term Jinx!: Why Most Presidents Stumble in Their Second Terms, and How Some Succeed: Volume 1, George Washington–Theodore Roosevelt

Foundering Fathers: What Jefferson, Franklin, and Abigail Adams Saw in Modern D.C.! Second Edition

A Promise for Life: The Story of Abbott (as writing consultant to the biomedical company)

Secure Internet Practices: Best Practices for Securing Systems in the Internet and e-Business Age (coauthor)

The Politically Correct Guide to the Bible

The Politically Correct Guide to American History

To explorers and travelers of all kinds,
who overcome any obstacle to reach their journey's goal.

CONTENTS

Preface

THE CAPITOL BUILDING IS THE HANDIWORK OF MASTERS OF ARCHITEC-ture and design who worked across more than two centuries. Among their number are Benjamin Latrobe, William Thornton, George Hadfield, Charles Bulfinch, Montgomery Meigs, Thomas Walter, and Frederick Law Olmsted and the many craftsmen and laborers who worked for them. The grand structure and grounds they devised are among the world's most impressive man-made creations. Most years, upward of six million visitors stroll its landscaped lawns, or take the fine if brief public tour of the interior or the more individualized excursions provided by the staff of the members of Congress.

A tourist may be generally aware of the history of the place and the famous figures, events, and accomplishments associated with it. However, a deeper look at the Capitol and its surroundings shows that since the start of its construction 230 years ago, it has witnessed an astonishing amount of turmoil, bloodshed, and controversy. A locus of so much power and wealth inevitably leads to considerable bad along with the good. Stepping behind its magnificent façades reveals a place that has been marked by bombings, race riots, deadly duels, mammoth protests, criminality, espionage plots, terror attacks, corruption, hangings, and assassinations. The Capitol has even been burned to its foundations by foreign invaders, only to rise up larger and more impressive than before.

Take a trip back to the secret history and wild past of America's Capitol Building and Congress, and to the men and women who have inhabited the locale. Spend time with its heroes, villains, heroines, and femme fatales—the human architects of its downfalls and achievements alike.

ACKNOWLEDGMENTS

A GREAT MANY ARCHIVES AND RESEARCH INSTITUTIONS ARE AVAILABLE for anyone seeking to explore the rich and intriguing history of the Capitol Building, Congress, and Capitol Hill. The author drew on the knowledge of many organizations, including the Library of Congress, Cultural Tourism DC, the Architect of the Capitol, the National Portrait Gallery, the National Archives, the archives of the US House of Representatives and US Senate, Congressional Cemetery, Oak Hill Cemetery, and the White House Historical Association. Among the particularly useful publications and blogs were *American Heritage*, *Smithsonian*, the archives of the *National Intelligencer*, the *Streets of Washington*, the *Washington Post*, the *Washington Examiner*, and WETA's *Boundary Stones*, as well as *JSTOR* and *Find a Grave*. The collections of the Washington Historical Society deserve special praise. As do leading authors on relevant subjects, such as Anthony Pitch, Mary Kay Ricks, Tom Lewis, Candace Millard, Robert V. Remini, P. J. O'Rourke, Garrett Peck, Peter Schweizer, and Joanne Freeman, among many others.

The book is based heavily on research the author performed for stories he tells in his capital region travel events: The Lafayette Square Tours of Scandal, Assassination, and Spies, as featured on TripAdvisor, Meetup, Airbnb Experiences, Eventbrite, Travel Curious, the Mayflower Hotel, and Atlas Obscura.

The author would like to heartily thank all lovers of history, culture, architecture, and art, who provide the inspiration and support for his books, articles, and travel excursions.

And also the thoughtful and thorough work of editor Ellen Urban and publishing manager Eugene Brissie, so easy to work with.

And a vigorous nod to the author's hard-laboring, book-loving parents. *The Lost History of the Capitol* was completed in very busywork weeks in the midst of the worldwide viral outbreak that originated in Wuhan, China. But to quote an oft-used family phrase: "Hard work never hurt anyone."

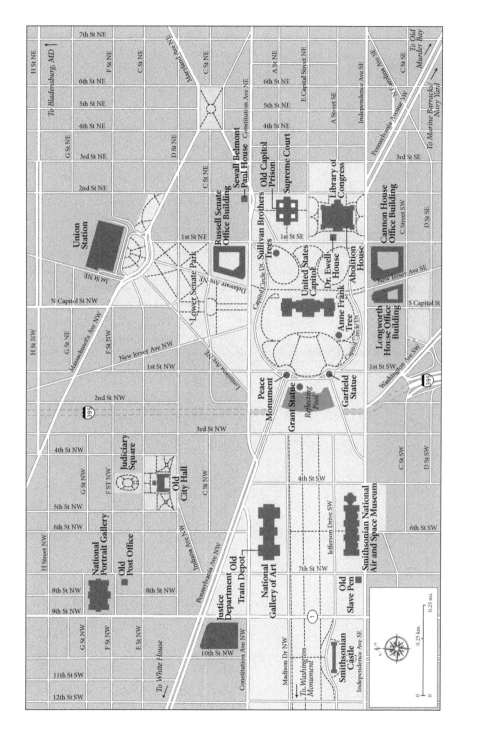

I have used this [bribe] where it will produce most good.
—Congressman Oakes Ames

When crime and criminals are thrust before us, they are to be met by all the energies that God has given us by argument, scorn, sarcasm and denunciation.
—Senator Charles Sumner

CHAPTER ONE

L'Enfant Terrible:
The Capital Designer's Fall from Grace

New Jersey Avenue, south of the Capitol Building and north of the Longworth House Office Building

IN NOVEMBER 1791, THE FEDERAL COMMISSIONERS OVERSEEING THE construction of America's new capital city were shocked. And stunned most of all was Daniel Carroll of Rock Creek.

THE DISAPPEARING MANSE
The officials were visiting the southern fringe of Jenkins Hill, which the city's planner, Pierre L'Enfant, had selected as the site of the future Capitol Building. They went along a rude path near what would become New Jersey Avenue. They approached the home of Carroll's nephew, Daniel Carroll of Duddington.

Or what was left of it. Daniel of Duddington was the largest landowner in the area, and owner of the land that would become Capitol Hill. He had been building his new house there: not on the land slated for the public buildings, but on his own property.

To their astonishment, the commissioners confirmed what L'Enfant's two deputies, Isaac Roberdeau and Benjamin Ellicott, had done. Roberdeau was the son of a provisioner of George Washington's army during the American Revolution. Ellicott was the brother of Andrew Ellicott, charged with surveying the boundaries of the new city.

Roberdeau and Ellicott had directed a team of men to take apart the unfinished house. They had ripped off the roof and stripped away its stone foundations.

THE BEST MAN FOR THE JOB

The commissioners could hardly believe what they saw. Less than a year before, when President George Washington had selected L'Enfant as the city's designer, the Frenchman had seemed an excellent choice. A master of the arts and of science, he'd moved to America to help it win its independence. He served with the Marquis de Lafayette as a military engineer, rising to the rank of major. A skilled artist, he sketched portraits of General Washington.

After Washington was sworn in as president, L'Enfant grandly redesigned what became Federal Hall in New York City, the federal government's first capital. The Hall was the first meeting place of the US Senate and House of Representatives, and home to the offices of the president.

However, problems cropped up of the kind that would plague L'Enfant in his later endeavors. His designs for the Senate and House chambers were showy and expensive. Some saw them as suited more to a House of Lords than a democratic republic.

In 1790, the first Congress passed the Resident Act, that compromise of Washington's Treasury secretary, Alexander Hamilton, and secretary of state, Thomas Jefferson, to place the permanent capital in a new city. They had struck their deal in "the room where it happened," a dining hall in the temporary capital of New York. They chose the border land of Maryland and Virginia, in between the Northern and Southern states, and in the backyard of the Virginian Founding Fathers.

In March 1791, at Suter's Tavern in the bustling seaport of Georgetown, L'Enfant met with Washington, Ellicott, and the landowners and merchants of the region. They began to thrash out an approach for building the capital.

But from the start, L'Enfant's ambitious aims differed from some in the government. The Washington Administration was under a constitutional mandate to establish a functioning capital city by early 1800. Jefferson, who was Washington's point man for the project, suggested L'Enfant plot out a small government town just east of Georgetown.

Yet like Jefferson and Washington on other matters, L'Enfant figured that, if you dream, you should dream big. The Frenchman proposed a grand, if grandiose, scheme. His creation would stretch from Rock Creek, northeast of Georgetown, through an expanse of woodlands, ridges, and marsh. Its terminus was a full five miles away, at the Potomac's Eastern Branch, as the Anacostia River was then known.

He proposed a humongous presidential mansion, measuring about 230 yards across, three to four times more spacious than the future White House, which itself would be the largest residence in the nation. He took Jefferson's notion of a wide boulevard open to the people and sketched out what would become the National Mall. And he proposed putting the houses of Congress atop the steep, forested Jenkins Hill, even though its cliffs and woods made construction difficult. L'Enfant, thinking such a promontory made for a majestic view, notably termed it a "pedestal awaiting a monument."

Power Brokers

In going about his work, it was in L'Enfant's interest, if not his nature, to cultivate good relations with the politically powerful city commissioners.

They were: David Stuart, the stepfather of Martha Washington's son from her first marriage, and thus a relative of L'Enfant's boss President Washington; Thomas Johnson, the first governor of Maryland, and in time a US Supreme Court justice; and, quite importantly, as it turned out, Daniel Carroll of Rock Creek, of Maryland's leading family, perhaps best known for Charles Carroll of Carrolton, the only Catholic signer of the Declaration of Independence as well as John Carroll, the founder of Georgetown College, later Georgetown University, established in 1789, the same year Washington became president. Daniel Carroll of Rock Creek had been a major player at the Constitutional Convention that had established the new Congress and presidency.

There were so many important Carrolls that, to differentiate themselves, they called themselves after their localities, such as Rock Creek, Carrollton, and Duddington.

This was the very clan that L'Enfant irked with his building deconstruction!

Biting the Hand That Feeds

Even before the Carroll home's dismantlement, L'Enfant courted trouble. His very ambitious plans, not surprisingly, fell behind schedule. The commissioners had to coax him into hiring 150 workmen, including many slaves, to start building the President's House, or President's Palace, as it was originally called. L'Enfant and the commissioners squabbled over whom was the ultimate authority for the city's construction. Further, Congress was stingy with appropriations.

In autumn 1791, L'Enfant had a major falling out with the commissioners over what seems a minor thing. Namely, whether to print copies of his map of the city's layout, including the land lots that investors might purchase. This was his famous chart that organized the capital in a grid of parallel and intersecting streets, with diagonal boulevards shooting out between them. These included a broad Pennsylvania Avenue to connect the President's House with the Capitol Building. His notion of diagonal streets was creative, though even today they take lost visitors on lengthy tangents across town.

To spur land purchases in, and development of, the new city, the commissioners wanted ten thousand copies of the map engraved and distributed. Many government officials were themselves speculating on land in the federal city, and thus had a vested interest in its success. George Washington himself owned a swath of turf in Georgetown and bought several lots just north of the future Capitol Building.

L'Enfant, however, was convinced publishing the map would lead to speculators buying up land in the city outskirts, thus undermining sales in the key areas around the President's House and the Capitol Building. After much bickering back and forth, Washington admonished L'Enfant to follow the wishes of the commissioners.

Then came the imbroglio over the Carroll house. It had seemed at first a compromise would be worked out. Ellicott, the surveyor, assured the owner, Daniel Carroll of Duddington, that L'Enfant had told him the new roadway could be adjusted to steer clear of his home. But L'Enfant told Carroll the house had to go. So Carroll decided to take legal action. He went to a chancery, or court record office, in Annapolis, the capital of Maryland. That state still had jurisdiction over the land.

His uncle, Daniel Carroll of Rock Creek, wrote to then-Congressman James Madison about his nephew's action: "Mr. Carroll [of Duddington] apprehending that [L'Enfant] would not wait had gone to Annapolis . . . he obtained an injungtion [*sic*] in Chancery to stop proceeding [with the demolition] with a Summons or Subpoena. . . ." Madison wasn't pleased about the whole mess.

When Carroll of Duddington returned from Annapolis with the court order, he was shocked, like the commissioners, to find that most of his house had been removed.

But Carroll had friends in very high places. He fired off an angry missive to Washington. The first president was mortified. He worried L'Enfant's precipitous action would embarrass, or even imperil, the fledging federal city. It could provide ammunition to politicians who wanted to keep the capital in Philadelphia. It could tarnish the administration's reputation.

In a letter, the president informed L'Enfant the demolition could render the Frenchman legally liable for damages. Washington also wrote Carroll of Duddington, stating he regretted L'Enfant's "zeal" that "carried him too fast," and that the government could reimburse him for the house.

Things simmered until early in 1792. Washington and Jefferson came down squarely on the side of the commissioners. But L'Enfant and his aides refused to acknowledge their authority.

In January, the commissioners fired Roberdeau, L'Enfant's deputy. When he continued to work on the Capitol Building's foundation, the commissioners placed him under arrest.

The following month, L'Enfant himself was fired. Jefferson, in a curt, if lawyerly letter, and with the concurrence of Washington, and Madison, wrote L'Enfant: "[It] is understood that you absolutely [*sic*] decline acting under the authority of the present Commissioners. If this understanding of your meaning be right I am instructed by the President to inform you that notwithstanding the desire he has entertained to preserve your agency in the business the condition upon which it is to be done is inadmissible and your services must be at an end."

A DESIGNER IN DECLINE, THEN A LASTING COMEBACK

From that point, L'Enfant's career took a downward path. Alexander Hamilton, an early proponent of American manufacturing, invited him to be a chief engineer for the new, model industrial town of Paterson, New Jersey. But L'Enfant's complex and costly scheme of waterworks for its mills fell flat, and he was let go. He also labored in Philadelphia, where he designed an ornate mansion for the very wealthy Robert Morris, "the financier of the American Revolution." As with the federal city and Paterson, however, L'Enfant's construction fell behind schedule and went over budget. Further, Morris's investments went belly up; the once wealthy man wound up in debtor's prison. Again out of a job, L'Enfant first declined, then accepted, a post as an engineering instructor at West Point. Later, after the War of 1812, he was a supervisor in the rebuilding of Fort Washington, a mammoth, Potomac River bastion destroyed during that conflict. But he soon departed that position as well.

The federal city, in the meantime, its early real estate investments gone bust, remained for the rest of its designer's life a small and swampy place. L'Enfant's association with it was practically forgotten. Falling into poverty, he died at age sixty-five in Chillum, Maryland, just north of the city he envisioned, in the backwater of Prince George's County. His surviving possessions, including maps and surveying devices, were worth less than $50.

But like many noted artists, L'Enfant proved a visionary. By the late 1800s, his tiny town had grown into a major city with paved boulevards and many public attractions. In 1902, the Senate-sponsored McMillan Commission, which beautified the center of Washington while expanding its parkland, revived some of the Frenchman's notions. Given special attention was his idea of a large public park, the National Mall. In 1909, at the behest of the French ambassador, L'Enfant's remains were disinterred and placed in state at the Capitol Building.

Three years later, with President William Howard Taft presiding, the soldier and engineer of the American Revolution was rendered a place of honor at Arlington National Cemetery. His remains are on a ridge just below the Arlington House mansion, the former home of George Washington Parke-Custis, the step-grandson and adopted son of L'En-

A map of L'Enfant's plan for the city of Washington, as modified by surveyor Andrew Ellicott

fant's former boss, George Washington—and near the site of the future, hallowed grave of the slain president, John Kennedy.

And thus, for all eternity, the spirit of L'Enfant gazes down upon the bustling metropolis he envisioned.

CHAPTER TWO

Gridlock in the House: One of the Wildest Elections in US History

North wing of the Capitol, the Senate, then the temporary quarters for the House

REP. JAMES ASHTON BAYARD OF DELAWARE WAS FEELING BIG-TIME pressure. If he made the wrong decision, the federal government, just eleven years old, could collapse. Mobs might storm the Capitol Building, and torch it. Civil War, between the Northeast and the Southwest, might erupt. An ancient republic had ended with the assassination of Julius Caesar. The new republic was rife with rumors of murder plots against high-ranking politicians.

The thirty-three-year-old Bayard and 104 other congressmen were attending the very first meeting of the House of Representatives, in the new, partly built Capitol Building. The initial gathering could hardly have been less auspicious.

A rare blizzard in the Border-South town had legislators sliding and slipping to work. And, on that February 11th of 1800, the House didn't have a house yet. The southern wing of the Capitol, which was to host the House of Representatives, wasn't built. So, the representatives had to share the northern wing with the thirty-eight senators from the sixteen states that then made up the Union. And with the half-dozen justices of the Supreme Court, and the staff members and bookshelves of the Library of Congress. Neither the Court nor the Library would have its own building for generations.

When the House of Representatives assembled for the first time in Washington, to decide the winner of the 1800 presidential election, it met in the Senate wing of the unfinished Capitol Building.

Instead of getting down to legislative business, the House had to deal with an Executive Branch crisis that threatened to rip the nation to shreds.

ADAMS, JEFFERSON, HAMILTON, BURR

There are many contenders for the wildest presidential election of all. The 2020 campaign, for instance, with its backdrop of virus-sparked shutdowns, nationwide protests and riots, and post-election charges of voter fraud, followed by the Capitol Building Riot. Also, the "hanging chad" ballots of Florida, in 2000. The election of Sen. John Kennedy in 1960 over Vice President Richard Nixon may have been pilfered, by dubious vote counts in Texas, and especially Chicago, Illinois. The same for the 1876 race, where Rutherford Birchard Hayes took the White House after

Electoral College votes from decisive Southern states were denied his rival Samuel Jones Tilden.

And there's the 1860 election, which had nominees from four major parties: a Constitutional Union Party; a Democratic Party riven in two, with much of it spinning off into the Southern Democratic Party that formed the Confederacy; and the winner, the new Republican Party of Abraham Lincoln's. The electoral aftermath: the Civil War.

But civil conflict also loomed in 1800, after that year's tumultuous race. It pitted former, and future, friends, President John Adams of the Federalist Party, and his vice president, Thomas Jefferson of the Republican Party, as rivals for the Executive Mansion.

Yes, the president and vice president were from opposing parties back then, which was a big problem. Jefferson's "Republican" Party was the faction which over much time turned into the Democratic Party, while Adams's Federalist Party eventually morphed into the Republican Party. Also, Jefferson's Republican Party was also then referred to as the Democratic-Republican Party. Clear enough?

Modern-day Americans may be surprised to learn the early political contests were also vicious. The Jefferson camp hired a slanderous muckraker, James Callender, to accuse the stolid John Adams of having a "hideous hermaphroditical character." (Callender later turned coat, accusing Jefferson of fathering children with an enslaved house servant, Sally Hemings.)

For its part, the Adams campaign portrayed Jefferson's supporters as "given to murder, robbery, rape, adultery, and incest . . . openly . . . taught and practiced." Even as Adams was accused of being in the pocket of the Brits, Jefferson was derided as a stalking horse for the French and mocked as a supposed atheist. Devout Federalists, fearing Jefferson would confiscate their Bibles, hid their scriptures in backyard gardens.

Behind the waves of invective, the two sides fought over issues of real importance. Much of Adams's term had been taken up with the Quasi War, an undeclared naval war with France. This very real and bloody conflict led to the founding of the US Navy. It also influenced the president to sign the Sedition Act passed by Congress. It authorized the federal government to jail those speaking out against the war for criticizing government officials. Republicans like Jefferson raged against this infringement on free speech, especially as the courts, under the Act, targeted Republican reporters and advocates. For their part, the Federalists accused their opponents of traitorously taking the side of a foreign enemy in a time of war.

However, along with fighting the Quasi War, President Adams also pushed for peace. He sent his secretary of state, John Marshall, the future Supreme Court chief justice, to Paris to negotiate. In fall 1800, too late to affect the election, which was back then spread out over the election year, Marshall returned with a peace agreement.

For the 1800 election campaign, the Federalists had again chosen Adams as their presidential nominee. For Adams's vice-presidential running mate, the party picked South Carolina's Charles Cotesworth Pinckney, the brother of Adams's running mate in 1796, Thomas Pinckney. Choosing a man from Massachusetts and from Carolina lent the ticket regional balance.

The Republicans echoed the Federalists by again selecting their candidate from 1796, Jefferson. For the Virginian's number two, a Republican caucus chose Aaron Burr of New York, a war hero from the Revolution: as with Pinckney, for regional balance, and election impact.

For Burr had set up a very efficient political machine in the "swing state" of New York. It had seized political power from the Federalists there, and from their leader, Alexander Hamilton, the archrival of Burr and Jefferson. For the

This portrait of Aaron Burr as vice president hints at the man's intelligence and guile.

presidential election in the Empire State, Burr had skillfully recruited an impressive Electoral College delegate slate. It boasted such luminaries as Revolutionary War general Horatio Gates, a commander at the Battle of Saratoga, and the skillful former New York governor George Clinton (not Bill Clinton, and definitely not the other George Clinton, of the musical band Parliament-Funkadelic).

As savage as the brawl between Adams and Jefferson that year was the internal bloodletting in the Federalist Party, between Adams and Hamilton. Hamilton, who lusted for war with France, felt Adams had been far too conciliatory toward Paris. He also seethed that Adams had ousted from his Cabinet men sympathetic to him.

Hamilton penned scathing letters to ranking Federalists against the president of his own party. A Republican newspaper got hold of one, and gleefully published it in October 1800. Hamilton had written Adams has a "jealousy capable of discoloring every object . . . and through vanity . . . is very apt to fall into the hands of miserable intriguers, with whom his self-love is more at ease, and who . . . by flattery, govern him. . . ."

A POPULAR LANDSLIDE, FOLLOWED BY A TIE

In the 1796 election, Adams had beaten Jefferson by a narrow Electoral College margin, seventy-one to sixty-eight. The 1800 election was also close in the Electoral College, with the winner and loser reversed. Jefferson's ticket got seventy-three votes, while Adams and his running mate got sixty-five. Jefferson-Burr handily won the small popular vote of the time, garnering 61 percent of the sixty-nine thousand ballots cast. In the elections then, both the presidential and vice-presidential candidates of a ticket got the same number of Electoral College votes, one each for each ballot cast.

Both parties knew this could lead to confusion, or rivalry among the men on the same ticket, or worse. So both parties arranged for one of their vice-presidential electors to vote for someone other than the vice-presidential pick. Thus a Federalist elector voted for New York governor John Jay instead of for Pinckney. However, due to an unbelievable slip-up, none of the Republican electors voted for someone other than Burr. Thus Jefferson and Burr wound up even.

According to the Constitution, in the event of a tie, the House of Representatives, which acts as the Electoral College, "shall chuse" the president.

The Republicans had won a smashing victory in the congressional races of 1800. In modern parlance, they "flipped" the House. Whereas the Federalists had controlled it, sixty to forty-six, the Republicans gained a large majority of sixty-eight to thirty-eight. So, their congressmen would easily elect Jefferson, their party's clear standard bearer, right? Wrong.

For the new Congress wouldn't take office until December 7, 1801. (Things were so much slower then, with very long summer recesses.) The old Congress, controlled by Federalists, who hated Jefferson, would pick the president!

MANEUVERINGS AND MACHINATIONS

Many possibilities presented themselves to the lame-duck representatives entering the Senate chamber in February 1801. They could delay a vote for months and block a Republican from taking over the presidency. Another option was to vote for Adams, to re-elect him as president. Or, if they delayed past Inauguration Day, March 4, Adams would stay as president until someone else was picked. That scenario was improbable, as Adams was unlikely to seek such a "usurpation." Such a move might also ignite civil war. And some Federalists believed Jefferson, as the election's biggest vote getter, should in fairness get the nod.

Hamilton for his part sought to engineer the selection of Pinckney, Adams's running mate. He figured he'd have influence over the South Carolinian.

But many in his party were inclined to strike a blow against Jefferson by striking a bargain with Burr. The former senator, after all, was thought to be "flexible" in his views. And as Burr hailed from New York, a commercial hub, some thought he might be more amenable to the policies of the Federalists, the party of banking and business.

Yet Jefferson, who had watched Burr efficiently line up New York for their ticket, at first spoke highly of his running mate. "The Federalists were confident at first," he wrote his daughter, that "they could debauch Colo. B. from his good faith by offering him their vote to be President, and have seriously proposed it to him; his conduct has been honorable & decisive, and greatly embarrasses them."

By December 1800, however, Jefferson seemed less confident about Burr's fidelity. In writing to the New Yorker, he dangled a carrot, hinting his vice-presidential duties would be substantial, unlike Adams under President Washington. In reply, Burr took pains to "disclaim all competition."

Weighing in against Burr was Hamilton. President Washington's former "right-hand man" had much to dislike in him, much of it personal. Burr had won a US Senate seat in 1791 by beating Philip Schuyler, Hamilton's father-in-law. Burr had crushed Hamilton in the 1800 contest to win New York's electoral votes, thus unhorsing him as New York's leading politico. (In a duel later in 1801, a New York Republican ally of Burr's, George Eacker, would kill Hamilton's oldest son, Philip Hamilton.)

In correspondence with fellow Federalists, Hamilton tore into Burr, branding him a "unprincipled . . . voluptuary," a plunderer, a man "without Scruple." In his verbal assault, Hamilton seemed to anticipate Burr's alleged future conspiracy to set up a nation of his own in the West:

"His public principles have no other spring or aim than his own aggrandizement . . . I take it he is for or against nothing but as it suits his interest or ambition . . . He is sanguine enough to hope everything—daring enough to try anything—wicked enough to scruple nothing . . . if we have an embryo Cesar [*sic*] in the United States it is Burr."

At the same time, Hamilton lobbied the influential Representative Bayard. As the only Delaware congressman, he personally controlled its vote. Hamilton now urged Bayard to cast his ballot for Jefferson, the bane of Hamilton's party. In the ultimate of backhanded compliments, Hamilton opined the Virginian was the clear lesser of evils, though nonetheless in his opinion evil: "I admit his politics are tinctured with fanaticism . . . that he has been a mischievous enemy to the principle measures of our past administration, that he is crafty & persevering in his objects, that he is not scrupulous about the means of success, nor very mindful of truth, and that he is a contemptible hypocrite. . . ."

Talk about feuding Founders!

In December, Hamilton had written more charitably about Jefferson, compared to Burr at least, to his successor as Treasury secretary, Connecticut's Oliver Wolcott Jr. "There is no doubt, but that, upon every virtuous and prudent calculation," stated Hamilton, "Jefferson is to be preferred. He is by far not so dangerous a man and he has pretensions to character." He urged his fellow Federalists to reach an accord with the putative president-elect in which Jefferson, in return for the office, would promise to retain key Federalist policies such as a Navy and a federal bank.

For once, President Adams agreed with Hamilton, according to *Smithsonian* magazine. He contacted his vice president, informing Jefferson that acceptance of such a deal would assure his election. At first, at least on the surface, Jefferson demurred, stating he "should never go into the office of President . . . with my hands tied by any conditions which should hinder me from pursuing the measures" he favored. With Jefferson seemingly unwilling to budge, the Federalist caucus in the House warmed further to Burr.

Burr himself, with the presidency seemingly within his reach, seemed to warm to the prospect. In December he wrote to a colleague of Jefferson, Maryland representative Samuel Smith. He stated that if the presidency became available to him, he would accept it, and keep it, instead of promptly resigning.

Bayard informed a horrified Hamilton that, "By persons friendly to Mr. Burr, it is distinctly Stated that he is willing to consider the Federalistes [*sic*] as his friends & to accept the office of President as their gift."

CLIFFHANGER BALLOTING

On February 11, 1801, the House assembled in its chambers to vote on the selection of a chief executive. Per the Constitution's rules, in the event of an Electoral College tie each state's delegation constituted one vote for president. To win, a candidate needed a majority of at least nine out of the sixteen states.

Seven states with Republicans in control voted for Jefferson. The majority of these were in the South, Jefferson's base of support: Kentucky, New Jersey, New York, North Carolina, Pennsylvania, Virginia, and Tennessee. Georgia's Federalist congressman bucked his party and voted for his fellow Southerner, giving Jefferson the Peach State, and eight states in all.

Six states controlled by Federalists, with their base in New England, voted for Burr: Connecticut, Bayard's Delaware, Massachusetts, New Hampshire, Rhode Island, and South Carolina.

One state, Vermont, was evenly split between the two parties, and cast a blank ballot. Maryland had five Federalist congressmen to just three Republicans, but one of the Federalists voted for Jefferson, for a four to four tie. Therefore Maryland abstained as well.

The tally was eight to six to two. Jefferson fell one vote short of the needed majority.

The House tried again, and got the same result. And tried again, and again.

After nineteen ballots, it was still deadlocked. At three o'clock in the morning of February 12, the exhausted legislators ended the session. Shivering, they went back along icy, unpaved paths to their lodgings.

Over the next three days and into the weekend, the House held fourteen more votes. Each time the tally was the same, eight to six to two.

Meanwhile there was much pressure on the House to act, and to not undercut the presumed president-elect. Crowds gathered in Washington City to demand the legislature not block Jefferson from becoming chief executive. Lawmakers heard a pro-Republican mob had taken up arms in Philadelphia. With approval from their state governors, militias in Pennsylvania and Virginia assembled, and threatened to march on the capital. Some in Virginia, foreshadowing events sixty years thence, threatened to take the Old Dominion out of the Union. Some in the Republican congressional caucus demanded a second constitutional convention. A Jeffersonian newspaper editorialized: "Usurpation must be resisted by freemen whenever they have the power of resisting."

The almost president-elect and the incumbent president corresponded on the crisis. Jefferson wrote Adams that Republicans angry about a "legislative usurpation" of the election might attempt to break up the country. In the White House, President Adams, waiting to return to his native Massachusetts, was also deeply worried. He thought a "civil war was expected."

Historians have often portrayed Hamilton's savage attacks on Burr as pivotal to swinging the House vote to Jefferson. In fact, Hamilton's campaign may have had little effect on most Federalist congressmen. The ex–Treasury secretary had damaged his reputation with his verbal assaults on President Adams, to whom many Federalists felt loyal.

The Federalist Speaker of the House, Theodore Sedgwick of Massachusetts, favored continued outreach to Burr. Believing Burr could be trusted, he paid the New Yorker his own backhanded compliment: "His very selfishness prevents his entertaining any mischievous predilections. . . ."

Feeling the heat from the congressional Federalists, from Hamilton, and from the Republicans was Bayard. Along with determining his own state's vote, he had influence over the representatives from the two states, Maryland and Vermont, that kept voting to abstain.

Bayard quietly opened up a back channel of communication with colleagues of Jefferson, including Virginia's Rep. John Nicholson. Through the intermediaries, Jefferson was asked whether he would keep some of the Federalists', and Hamilton's, key initiatives. Namely: the recently established Navy; "neutrality" in the wars between France and Britain, which to Hamilton meant a bias toward London; and Hamilton's Bank of the United States, a sort of early version of the Federal Reserve. Bayard also wanted Jefferson to retain Adams appointees in his government.

Maryland representative Samuel Smith also approached Jefferson at Bayard's urging. Smith may have urged Jefferson to keep the Federalist officials at the Delaware and Pennsylvania customs offices that collected the tariffs on imports.

Publicly, Jefferson later claimed he made no deal. The Virginian is sometimes depicted as having been passive in this process. That seems unlikely. Jefferson was, with Madison, the cofounder of the two-party system. He was a highly skilled politician and behind-the-scenes operative. According to Bayard, on Saturday, February 14, Jefferson let his intermediaries know such a compromise was acceptable. Bayard figured he had an agreement.

On Sunday, February 15, Federalist representatives conferring in the Senate learned Bayard would abstain in the next vote, paving the way for Jefferson's election. They were not happy.

On hearing the news, Federalist lawmakers shouted out, "Traitor! Deserter!" The "clamor was prodigious," Bayard remembered, "the reproaches vehement. . . ."

The Federalists were irate Bayard hadn't consulted with them first, that he had made up his mind without hearing back from Burr, and that Jefferson hadn't given him concrete assurances.

Bayard buckled. He agreed to wait for Burr's response while trying to get a firmer reply from Jefferson.

On Monday morning, however, Jefferson again communicated through a third party. According to Bayard, he asserted the conditions "corresponded with his views and intentions, and that we might confide in him."

That afternoon, the Federalist congressmen received eagerly awaited correspondence from Burr. His response was disappointing, falling short of what Jefferson may have agreed to. Speaker Sedgwick sadly admitted, "the gigg is up."

Bayard was himself disappointed his negotiations hadn't yielded further gains, according to the *Smithsonian*. He lamented: "Burr has acted a miserable paultry [*sic*] part. The election was in his power." Still, Bayard was relieved civil strife would be averted.

Hamilton was also relieved. He wrote that "I should consider the execution of the plan" of the Federalists to cooperate with Burr as "signing their own death warrant. Mr. Burr will probably make stipulations, but he will laugh in his sleeve while he makes them and will break them the first moment it may serve his purpose." No wonder the two men later took to pistols.

On Tuesday, February 17, the House held its thirty-sixth ballot on the presidency. Delaware voted to abstain. Following Bayard's lead, the Federalist congressmen from Maryland and Vermont did likewise. The Republican congressmen from those states voted for Jefferson, giving him a winning majority of ten out of the sixteen states.

The crisis was over, just two weeks before Inauguration Day.

Three weeks after his inauguration, a pleased Jefferson wrote a political ally, seventy-eight-year-old Samuel Adams, the one-time "firebrand of the American Revolution," and a cousin of John Adams. The new president told the relative of the old president: "The storm is over, and we are in port."

POLITICAL FOLLOW-UP

Thomas Jefferson went on to become the first two-term president to reside in the new capital city. His impact on the District was marked.

He chose or influenced all the city's early architects, including those for the Capitol Building; he founded Eastern Market on Capitol Hill; he extended Pennsylvania Avenue to spin off President's Park, now Lafayette Square, from the President's House; and he had poplar trees planted along the Avenue—which proved popular.

If a deal with Bayard was struck, did Jefferson keep to its terms? Only to an extent. He retained a Navy, but mothballed its major ships, frigates like the USS *Constitution*. He kept Hamilton's federal Bank of the United States, but his ally and successor as president, James Madison, allowed its charter to lapse. Some historians stress Jefferson retained Federalists in his administration. Yet he also dismissed many. He and his personal secretary, Meriwether Lewis, of Lewis and Clark fame, carefully went through the roster of Army officers. Strident Federalists were let go; more centrist ones stayed.

Further, the new president's Republican Congress passed legislation that ousted the Federalist "midnight judges" that President Adams had appointed just before leaving office. The jurists put out of work included Bayard's own father-in-law, Delaware governor Richard Bassett. As for neutrality abroad, in effect a tilt toward Britain, Jefferson's great achievement, the Louisiana Purchase, resulted from skillful diplomacy with his preferred foreign power, France.

As for Burr, his quiet machinations for the job of chief magistrate alienated him from the new president. In 1804, he fatally alienated himself from the Federalists, by killing Hamilton in their infamous duel.

Congress was elated at having sidestepped a civil war during the very first meeting of the House of Representatives in Washington. For perhaps the first time in history, a peaceful transition of power between rival parties had taken place in a large, democratic republic. And in 1804, the House and Senate approved the Constitution's Twelfth Amendment. Thereafter, instead of leaving things to chance, the delegates of the Electoral College spelled out their choice for president and for vice president.

CHAPTER THREE

Capital Crime: Washington's First Hanging

*Southwest edge of the Capitol grounds, near the President
Garfield statue*

IT WAS A PUBLIC ENTERTAINMENT OF SORTS, MET WITH HORRID FASCI-
nation. The young town had no playhouses, no concert halls, just a handful of hotels and taverns. Because most members of Congress and the
administration were hundreds of miles from their homes, few wives or
lady friends were on hand.

Yet the novel event offered a spectacle, and something new to the
Capitol Building, whose Senate and unfinished House of Representatives
had officially met in town just two years prior.

A LOCUS OF DEATH

On October 10, 1802, workmen set up a gallows on the Capitol Building
grounds. The apparatus was for the first criminal to be executed in Washington City. It was the talk of the town.

The wooden scaffold was placed on the western fringe of the legislative edifice, then much lower in height. The hanging grounds were at the
crossing of Maryland Avenue with 1st Street N.W.

The area became a locus of deathly imagery. The gallows stood less
than a hundred yards south of the future Ulysses S. Grant Memorial,
unveiled in 1922. As part of it, sculptor Henry Shrady crafted a self-portrait of himself trampled to death by Union army horses. And the scaffold stood near the future statue of President James Garfield, assassinated

in 1882 at a railway depot six blocks to the west. (See the chapters on the Grant statue and the Garfield assassination.)

But in autumn 1802, high-profile death was still new to the citizens of Washington. They gathered by the thousands to watch the macabre event.

The lead actor in the drama was an Irish immigrant bricklayer, James McGirk (also spelled *McGurk*). He and his wife had lived on 12th and F Street, N.W, four blocks east of the spanking-new White House.

McGirk was a violent man who drank himself, and his family, into oblivion. When inebriated, he would beat his wife. Worse, he continued beating her after she'd become pregnant, with twins. In August 1801, his spouse had delivered two stillborn boys. Remorseless, relentless, McGirk kept abusing his wife. In January 1802, at age twenty-three, she died from the pummeling.

Washington City was so new it had no prison. After his arrest, McGirk was held in a small, temporary jail on 4 1/2 Street N.W. He complained of the cramped space and lack of ventilation.

He was tried before the federal Circuit Court of Appeals. The Court was so new it had no courthouse. Its proceedings were held in a room inside the Capitol Building.

There was no doubt of McGirk's guilt. The trial judge was the Harvard-trained, John Adams–appointed William Cranch. Cranch stated McGirk's "offence was much aggravated, by the deceased having been his wife, who ought rather to have received protection at his hand, than such barbarous treatment as to occasion her death."

AN APPEAL FOR CLEMENCY

The town, then as now, brimmed with lawyers. One of them, Augustus Brevoort Woodward, represented McGirk. Although his client's case was seemingly hopeless, Woodward pushed for clemency, perhaps because he had friends in the highest of places. Woodward was close to the one man who could pardon McGirk, or commute his sentence from hanging to imprisonment: President Thomas Jefferson.

Woodward and Jefferson were friends, and birds of a feather. They were both tall, lean, and informal in dress to the point of careless-

This reputed depiction of Augustus Woodward reveals an attorney of a most striking aspect. A friend of President Jefferson, he tried to save the life of his client, accused murderer James McGirk.

ness. Skilled in languages, both knew ancient Greek and Latin. Both wished to reform the criminal justice system, and to abolish medieval punishments such as flogging and public stockades. As a Virginia assemblyman, Jefferson had restricted the number of crimes punishable by death. Woodward and McGirk pinned their slim hopes on the president.

With his attorney's help, McGirk wrote a letter to Jefferson in April 1802 that pleaded for deliverance. He wrote of his impending doom, "unless Prevented by the interference of your Excellency, in whose benevolence only depends the excistance [sic] of the Unfortunate wretch James MGurk who will be hurried into eternity and meet that alwise Judge Unprepared—Death is a terror to the human heart, but more so, to Such a wretch as I am. . . ."

It might be noted, in looking over McGirk's spelling, that the use of American English would not be standardized until twenty-six years later, via the dictionary of an ardent patriot, Noah Webster.

The execution was set for August. That month, Woodward rushed to Monticello, where the president spent his summers, to deliver his plea. Jefferson likely had no intent of altering McGirk's ultimate fate. But he did gift the condemned man a two-month stay of execution.

The delay led to a political spat.

Jefferson's foes in the Federalist Party, which represented national strength and public order, attacked the stay of execution, and accused the chief executive of being weak on crime. Worse, they charged him with political favoritism toward McGirk. It was alleged the felon had in 1799 assaulted a colleague of the Federalists' leading publicist, John Fenno. A noted journalist, Fenno had been hired by Alexander Hamilton, Jefferson's archrival, to advance his party's cause. But it turned out the man in question was another Irishman named McGirk, who had no relation to the convict.

On the morning of the execution, lawyer Woodward petitioned the president one last time for clemency.

He received no reply.

LEAPS INTO THE UNKNOWN

McGirk was taken from his dank cell over to the Capitol grounds. The large crowd there watched him climb up to the scaffold. Some looked on with eagerness, some with dread.

The hangman readied the rope. Officers of the law stood next to McGirk. The condemned man was full of nervous energy.

The executioner placed the rope around the murderer's neck.

A Catholic priest tried to console McGirk. The prisoner seemed filled with guilt. He stated: "When a man's character is gone, his life is gone."

Then, to everyone's shock, he pushed away the hangman, and leapt off the platform.

He was trying to hang himself!

For a moment, his body hurtled through space. Then the rope grew taut.

But his neck didn't snap. Instead, McGirk, gasping, and alive, swirled from the rope in midair.

The spectators were thunderstruck. The men on the scaffold struggled to reel him in before he choked to death. They hauled McGirk back onto the platform.

As the killer caught his breath, a fresh rope was brought out. For the second time, the hangman placed the noose around his neck.

The crowd watched once more with anxious expectation.

Then McGirk broke free from the officers again! He jumped from the platform.

He hurtled through the air. But this time the plunge broke his neck. His form went slack. In a sense, by taking control of the execution, he cheated the hangman.

A grisly superstition next came into play. After the rope was taken from McGirk's bruised and broken neck, the spectators rushed over, and plucked away pieces of the cord. Some believed a hanging rope had the power to allay headaches and other maladies.

The capital city's first gallows execution was over.

A MOVEABLE CORPSE

One might think the murderer's grisly demise would have ended his story. Not so.

When he died, the town's largest burial ground was Holmead Cemetery. It was located above today's Dupont Circle, one block from the Washington Hilton where President Ronald Reagan was nearly assassinated in 1981. Friends of McGirk laid him to rest there, next to the grave of a woman. But the deceased woman's mother grew furious on learning a despised killer had been buried near her daughter, violating her sacred space.

So one night she and some relatives went to the gravesites. They unearthed the body of McGirk, and brought it over to the "Slashes," a deep ravine close by. They buried it there.

McGirk's friends were upset over the removal. One evening, they went over to the Slashes. They uncovered their dead friend's decomposing body, brought it back to Holmead's, and buried it in the same place.

This further distressed the mother. She and her friends and relatives returned once more to the gravesite, unearthed McGirk for the third time, and carried his body back to the Slashes. To make sure there'd be no more disinterring, they sunk the deceased in a bog, thorn bushes all about it.

And there he stayed, one might have thought, never to be disturbed again.

Except that, forty years later, a man digging in the ravine stumbled upon McGirk's skull.

The bones and tortured spirit of the wife and baby killer were fated it seems, to never rest in peace.

CHAPTER FOUR

The Worst Day in the City's History: Invaders Burn Down the Capitol

Albert Gallatin Home/Sewall-Belmont-Paul House/National Women's Party, 144 Constitution Avenue N.E.

THE HAUGHTY YET SKILLED REAR ADMIRAL, GEORGE COCKBURN, AGE forty-two, and the brave, chivalrous major general, Robert Ross, forty-eight years old, were weary but confident.

THE CONQUERORS

In the twilight of a baking-hot day, they and their sailors and Royal Marines paused outside the Sewall-Belmont house, then the stately home of their foe's Treasury secretary, Albert Gallatin, on land once owned by Daniel Carroll of Duddington. The commanders were only two blocks from the Capitol Building.

The hundred or so light infantrymen of the invading British force looked like "flames of fire, all red coats . . . the stocks of their guns painted with red," noted Michael Shiner, an enslaved worker and chronicler at the nearby Navy Yard.

In the open land in front of the officers loomed the two linked wings of the legislature, the House and the Senate, that had been waging war on mighty Britain since the conflict's declaration there on June 17, 1812.

That day, August 24, 1814, had already been quite eventful. The commanders' army of four thousand soldiers were hardened veterans of the wars against Napoleon. It had crushed a poorly led and barely trained force of seven thousand militiamen, regular Army troops, and US Marines and sailors. The battle, which happened just nine miles to the northeast, at Bladensburg, Maryland, had flung open the door to Washington.

In the melee, Cockburn and Ross had nearly been killed, according to Anthony Pitch's classic *The Burning of Washington*. The admiral had watched a British Marine die from a bullet intended for him. General Ross, who had a horse shot out from under him, was bruised from four spent bullets that had smacked into his uniform.

After a violent but brief fight, most of the Americans had run from the battlefield, except for a stalwart force of US Marines and seamen led by Capt. Joshua Barney. Crippled by a leg wound, Barney had fallen into British hands. But Cockburn and Ross, impressed by his valor, had paroled him, letting him go free.

For hours, the routed Americans had been streaming through Washington, fleeing up to the Georgetown hills and beyond. A soldier on horseback raced past the Capitol Building and cried out, "Fly! The ruffians are at hand! . . . For God's sake send off your wives and daughters!"

At Pennsylvania Avenue and 6th Street, N.W., the head of the city's militia, ex-congressman and future city mayor, Gen. Peter Van Ness, took pity on the retreating militiamen. At a grocery, he handed over $25 in cash for a barrel of whiskey, which he gave to the thirsty soldiers.

President James Madison, once the leading legislator in Congress, had himself fled from the battlefield to northern Virginia, his Cabinet members tailing alongside. It had been a trying war for him, and his Treasury secretary, Gallatin, then in Belgium trying to negotiate peace. The conflict had emptied his Treasury, forcing it to persuade Congress to raise taxes on imported goods, carriages, salt, and moonshine whiskey.

Since 1813, a fleet of the invincible Royal Navy had been raiding and burning towns throughout the Chesapeake. Its ships ranged from Havre de Grace in the northern fringe of Maryland to Hampton in southern Virginia. Far to the north, multiple US invasions of British Canada had collapsed. An exception was a successful seizure and burning of York, Ontario, today's Toronto, then the capital of British Canada. Retaliation for that act was the reason for the British march on Washington. Yet

Congress had been sanguine, even smug, about the threat. A House committee stated that military "preparations are, in every respect, adequate to the emergency. . . ."

Outside the Gallatin residence, Cockburn and Ross knew from their spies and advance parties there was little American resistance in the capital. Two hours before, at 6:00 p.m., their advance guard had fired into the windows of the Capitol Building. No Americans had fired back.

The admiral and the general had disagreed on what to do with the city after seizing it. Cockburn wanted to burn the whole place down, government and civilian buildings alike. Ross, who preferred to leave everything alone, stressed their orders, which were to only destroy federal government properties.

THE SHOTS IN THE CITY

Suddenly, shockingly, as the two gazed toward the impressive if unfinished Capitol, shots rang out. From the Gallatin house, and perhaps elsewhere.

One or two Britishers were killed, and several were wounded. A bullet just missed Ross, and hit his horse. The bay mare was killed, with the general tumbling off it, shaken yet unhurt. Another bullet killed the horse of his trumpeter.

According to some sources, several Maryland militiamen had fired from inside the Gallatin residence, then scurried off into the rough countryside behind it.

Believing otherwise was Martha Parke Custis Peter, a granddaughter of Martha Washington, and then matron of Georgetown's lavish Tudor Place estate. She insisted the shooter was a longtime barber for Congress, a high-spirited man named Dickson. An Irishman, he had no love for anything British.

Some English officers later reported the gunfire came from more than one house, and perhaps even from the Capitol Building.

Indeed, the day before, a regiment of Virginia militia had arrived in the city. It had about 750 men—but no muskets, flints, nor bullets. In a fruitless search for supplies, these latter-day Minutemen spent the day marching over to the White House and War Department, and then out to the Eastern Branch (the Anacostia River), and then back to Capitol Hill. Its frustrated commander, Col. George Minor, bedded his men down for the night in a deserted House of Representatives. It was one of only three times in US history that troops bivouacked in the halls of Congress. The others were at the start of the Civil War, when Union soldiers took up quarters there due to a feared Confederate attack, and when National Guard soldiers stayed there after the Capitol Riot of 2021.

The next day, while the fight at Bladensburg raged, the regiment spent frustrating hours at Greenleaf Point armory. Today it's the site of Fort McNair, across a Potomac inlet at the District's southwest edge. A youthful bureaucrat there insisted on painstakingly handing out guns and ammo himself to each man. As a result, the regiment missed the battle.

Later in the day, as American troops fled past the Capitol Building, Colonel Minor, spoiling for a fight, assembled his soldiers near it. Knots of cavalrymen were also gathering, based on hearsay the Americans might make a stand at the massive complex. Indeed, the overmatched secretary of war, John Armstrong, had briefly thought of turning the stone edifice into a fortress. But then word came to hightail it into Maryland. The Virginians left, but some of them may have taken parting shots toward Cockburn and Ross.

BONFIRES OF THE PROFANITIES

Whoever was responsible for the fusillade, Admiral Cockburn was enraged. He ordered the Gallatin house burned down. Five British sailors rushed inside and torched the place.

General Ross sent for reinforcements. And, if there had been any doubt, Cockburn commanded the destruction of the sixty-seven-foot-high Capitol Building.

The British soldiers rushed toward the houses of Congress. To their left was a hotel, a site where Congress would make its temporary quarters, and where much later the Supreme Court Building would stand.

The Royal Marines broke open the doors on the east front of the Capitol. They swarmed into the House wing on the south side. The red-curtained chamber had the shape of a compact, slanted octagon, bracketed by Greek columns.

An official portrait of the vain, yet very capable, Rear Admiral George Cockburn. He preens in front of the city he burned.

Mounting the House Speaker's podium, Cockburn was like a fiery preacher addressing his flock. He harangued his men with a challenge, with words like the following:

'Shall this harbor of Yankee Democracy be burned? This Mobocracy, this insult to our King? All for it will say, 'Aye'!'

"Aye!" shouted the troops.

His invincible army suffered a temporary setback, however. The Marines couldn't set the House on fire.

Its architect was Benjamin Latrobe, "the father of American architecture." Latrobe had so skillfully constructed the place with sturdy materials, such as marble, copper, zinc, and iron, that it wouldn't catch. Next, the invaders readied their Congreve rockets, which had terrified the militia at Bladensburg. They fired them up into the roof. The missiles scorched its wood and shattered its imported English glass but failed to ignite the sheet iron.

So the Marines, egged on by Cockburn, made a great pile of mahogany furniture, slaked it with gunpowder from their remaining missiles, and lit a bonfire.

This blaze caught. The chamber's twenty-six-foot-high Corinthian columns smoked and cracked apart. Among the artifacts destroyed was a twelve-foot-wide figure of an American eagle rising above the canopied Speaker's rostrum. (Tuscany sculptor Giuseppe Franzoni had modeled the bird on an actual, preserved eagle that Latrobe acquired from artist Charles Wilson Peale.) Also lost was a large statue of Liberty, her foot stepping on an overturned crown representing the despotic English monarchy.

Yet the bonfire worked too well. The blaze grew so hot the British had to quit the House of Representatives. They were unable to further stoke the fire, and the fire gave out, sparing the House's west side. Latrobe's brick supports saved other rooms.

But not before a crowing Cockburn picked up a souvenir, a gilded, leather-bound book inscribed, "President of the U. States . . . RECs & EXPENDS U S FOR 1810." It was President Madison's own copy of his government's budget. It contained a $1,000 line item for testing a weapon, developed by inventor Robert Fulton and others, that might have proved useful against Cockburn's fleet: an underwater torpedo. The admiral would gift the volume, according to *The Burning of Washington*, to his brother, the royal governor of Bermuda.

An even more important document went up in smoke: a record of the House's spending for the current year. It had been in the locked drawer of the clerk of the House, Col. Patrick Magruder. He'd been off fighting with city militia at Bladensburg.

In contrast to Cockburn, some Brits were glum, not gleeful, about the destruction. One captain later recalled he had "no objection to burn arsenals, dockyards . . . etc. [But] we were horrified at the order to burn elegant 'Houses of Parliaments'."

THE SENATE IS SMOKED, THEN REBORN

The still-new Capitol then had no central dome, just a wooden walkway connecting the two wings. From the House into the northern, Senate side went the rampaging Brits. There they wreaked even more destruction, as they had more readily combustible material: the original Library of Congress, and its three thousand volumes, then located in an upstairs chamber of the Senate.

The Marines little cared that many of the books were by British authors, and about British law. The volumes were mixed with busted-up furniture and gunpowder, and another great blaze was set. The thirty-six-foot-high Library room, made of timber, burned fiercely. The Senate's marble columns collapsed.

By 9:00 p.m., the glow from the burning Senate and House could be seen as far away as Baltimore, thirty-eight miles to the northeast. From the Virginia side of the Potomac, a US Navy administrator viewed the conflagration as a "sight so repugnant to my feelings, so dishonorable, so degrading to the American character . . . [it] almost palsied my faculties. . . ."

Still, Latrobe's keen handiwork provided another firebreak, which saved the Supreme Court chamber. Like the Library, the Court was then housed in the Senate. Latrobe, disdainful of the shoddy original, had in 1808 redone its first-floor space. He added a multi-vaulted ceiling and a bayed arcade independent of the original walls. The architect, an apostle of the Greek Revival style, supported the arches with thick, Ionic columns. It resembles a flying buttress from a medieval cathedral shrunk in

The magnificent, sturdily constructed Supreme Court chamber survived the British conflagration of 1814, and still stands.

size and applied to an ornate courtroom. The masterpiece survived the conflagration and endures to this day.

His creation had come at a stiff price, however. During its construction Latrobe's chief aide, John Lenthall, the clerk of the works, removed the vault's wooden props. This caused some of it to collapse. Lenthall was fatally buried under a tumble of wood and stone. It's said his spirit curses the place. If so, the hex took full effect in 1814.

After the British invaders departed Washington, Latrobe reconstructed the entire Capitol Building. In 1818, he handed the project off to Boston architect Charles Bulfinch. The latter supplied the finishing touch of the Capitol's original dome. A phoenix rose from the ashes even better than before.

A help in the redo was retired President Jefferson. Perhaps he felt guilty over claiming a wartime conquest of British Canada would be a mere "walk in the woods." America's leading bookworm sold his private library, the largest in North America, to Congress to replace its lost Library. For $23,950, the Senate wing got 6,487 volumes that spanned the arc of human knowledge, from ancient Athens to the French Enlightenment.

The inestimable Benjamin Latrobe, the "father of American architecture," built the Capitol Building, then rebuilt it after the rampaging Royal Marines set much of it ablaze.

ARTIFACT EVACUATIONS

More of the Capitol Building's contents would have been lost, if not for intrepid House and Senate workers in the days before the invasion. In the House, two assistant clerks, Samuel Burch and John T. Frost, managed to cart away some valuable papers. But they were hamstrung by a dire shortage of wagons, packing material, and beasts of burden. This was due to panic among the populace and the agencies of government which, faced with the Britons' approach, seized almost all the means of transportation.

Wrote an out-of-town observer: "Stages, hacks, carts or wagons cannot be procured for love or money. They are all pressed for the military." Burch and Frost later lamented: "Every thing belonging to the office, together with the library of Congress, we venture to say, might have been removed in time, if carriages could have been procured."

A House investigative committee agreed. In late 1814 and early 1815, it concluded that "due precaution and diligence were not exercised to prevent the destruction and loss," and noted the "neglect to provide the means of transportation." The supervisor of the two assistant clerks, Magruder, felt compelled to resign.

Workers at the Senate had more luck, but only through great exertions. A clerk there named Lewis Machen had a job tracking the amendments of bills. As the British threatened, Machen "borrowed" a wagon. With the help of a Senate messenger, an African American named Tobias, he loaded up the conveyance. The trove had documents containing the identity and rank of every US serviceman, as well as the minutes of secret Senate sessions. On the way into Maryland, a wheel broke, so the two "borrowed" a wheel from a blacksmith. The overloaded cart overturned, but they repacked it. They hauled their cargo thirty-five miles into the countryside, safe from the clutches of the foe.

A NAVAL DILEMMA

As the torch-bearing British rushed toward the House and Senate, another military leader got ready to ignite a massive blaze. For him, however, the job presented a dreadful prospect.

Just a mile southeast of the Capitol Building is the Washington Navy Yard, and Thomas Tingey was its portly, sixty-four-year-old commandant. Tingey was a veteran of the undeclared naval brawls of the 1790s with Britain and France. He had then bravely faced down a British man-of-war that demanded the "impressing," or kidnapping, of American sailors to supplement its own crew.

Recently widowed, Tingey proudly ran the busy Navy Yard and the hundreds of Washingtonians and military personnel working there. Back in 1801, President Jefferson, accompanied by the commandant of the US Marine Corps, had ridden over to the site. The two had selected the location of the Yard, the Marine barracks, and the Marine commandant's home, just up 8th Street. Architect Latrobe had designed the Yard's wharves, workplaces, and its imposing entrance, as well as the home of its commandant.

But on the day of the British invasion, Tingey found himself without a force of Marines or sailors with which to fight. The Yard did contain two first-class warships. Unfortunately, they were still under construction. These were the forty-four-gun frigate the USS *Columbia*, and the eighteen-gun USS *Argus*.

At 2:00 p.m., in the wake of the Bladensburg debacle, Tingey got a grim directive from Secretary of the Navy William Jones. "You will make the necessary preparations," stated Jones, "for destroying the public shipping and all the naval and military stores and provisions at the Navy Yard. . . ."

Tingey set a deadline of 8:30 p.m. to carry out the order, unless he learned the enemy had decided against occupying the city. Meanwhile, he ordered his men to place firebombs with fuses on vessels and installations.

The commandant tried putting off a decision until the last moment. He realized a prevailing southwest breeze could carry sparks from fires in the Yard to nearby homes. He went out to personally warn residents of the danger. But that ignited a panic, according to *The Burning of Washington*. Frightened women lined up to implore him to spare the Yard.

Throughout that afternoon and evening, Tingey sent out riders, including his tireless chief clerk, Mordecai Booth, to scout out Washington for the approach of the Brits. At 8:00 p.m., a half hour before the deadline, Booth and another scout reported back. The British were at the Capitol Building, a fifteen-minute march from the Yard.

The commandant had no choice. At about a quarter past eight, he sent Navy Department personnel about the facility to light the fuses and trails of gunpowder leading to powder kegs. The big ships were set afire. Also ignited were oared galleys, and small scows outfitted with powerful cannons. For Tingey, the destruction of the *Columbia*, a world-class warship to be, was wrenching. The frigate was just ten days from launch, and from taking on the British fleet. The deliberate destruction was, according to the wife of the Yard's chaplain, "the most suicidal act ever committed."

Tingey yelled at his workers to spare the nimble, six-gun schooner the USS *Lynx*. For some reason, the British would spare it too. It would later spend six years fighting pirates in the Mediterranean and Caribbean, but it seemed cursed. In 1820, the ship and its forty-seven crew members, while sailing off Jamaica, were lost.

The Navy workers also ignited the infrastructure for the construction of ships. Up in flames went work sheds, nautical instruments, building tools, blacksmith and painter shops, gunneries, and a sawmill, as well as warehouses filled with rigging, timber, and sails. Tingey ordered that two heavily laden gunboats be cast off, in hopes they could make it down the Eastern Branch. But one sank from the weight of its provisions, and the other, stocked with ammo, beached, its contents looted by locals.

The commandant's men ignited the Yard's stock of munitions as well. Residents throughout the region were awed by the resulting flames shooting skyward, and the thunder of explosions. Not until Pearl Harbor did the US Navy suffer a more distressing day.

Tingey was a marked man to the British, and his staffers urged him to flee. He shoved off on a rowboat with one of his scouts, Marine captain John Creighton, who earlier had blown up the Eastern Branch bridge adjacent to the Yard. The commandant weighed spending the night on the river, to keep watch on his beloved installation, then thought better of it. Heartsick from watching the fires consume the place, he boated downstream to Alexandria, Virginia, to spend the night. (Days later a British flotilla seized that town, which surrendered without a fight, while offering up many merchant ships and many barrels of tobacco and whiskey.)

A DOCTOR'S SURPRISE GUESTS

That evening, more drama broke out at a fine townhome, at 1st Street and A Street, S.E., at the site of the future Library of Congress. Across from the southeast edge of the Capitol Building, it afforded a ringside seat for the congressional inferno. Its owner was a physician, Dr. James Ewell, age forty-one, from one of the region's most prominent families. His father-in-law was Benjamin Stoddert, the first secretary of the navy. (His hulking townhouse in Georgetown, built in part by Pierre L'Enfant, had underground cisterns that escaped slaves may have later used as part of the Underground Railroad. Benjamin Stoddert's grandson, Richard Stoddert Ewell, would be a Confederate general at Gettysburg.)

Dr. Ewell, who had sent his wife to safety, was one of the few to not flee the city. He had stayed to care for an ill patient, according to the book *When Britain Burned the White House*. He was horrified at the destruction of the Capitol Building across from him, and of the Navy Yard, a spinoff of his father-in-law's work. "Never shall I forget my tortured feelings," he later wrote of the Capitol, "when I beheld that noble edifice wrapt in flames, which, bursting through its windows and mounting far above its summits, with a noise like thunder, filled all the saddened night with a dismal gloom."

The physician was worried about his house, his family, and his person. He grew even more concerned when British officers knocked at his door, telling him his house had been requisitioned as a temporary headquarters. He became even more worried when he realized, in all the confusion, that someone, a British soldier he thought, was stealing things from his home. He demanded the officers put a stop to the larceny. To his embarrassment, he found out one of his servants was the thief.

Poor Dr. Ewell. It turned out his home was requisitioned by none other than Admiral Cockburn and General Ross!

The two commanders rode over to talk with him. They assured Ewell they would end any thievery. Ross rather tenderly told him: "I am myself a married man, have several sweet children and venerate the sanctities of the conjugal and domestic relations." Cockburn, less tenderly, told Ewell it had been foolish to leave one's possessions in the safekeeping of a servant.

Ewell was impressed by the chivalry of Ross, and by the professionalism of both men. He knew their presence would turn his endangered home into the safest in Washington. He made a virtue of necessity. He insisted Ross take his own bedroom as his sleeping place. Cockburn informed Ewell his abode was now safe enough for his wife and children to return, and they did.

Follow-Up Mayhem

Even with the Capitol Building burnt, Ross and Cockburn had plenty of other devastation in mind that evening. They directed a column of about two hundred Royal Marines down dusty Pennsylvania Avenue to their next targets. One would be Gallatin's Treasury Building. They found it disappointingly bereft of gold and government bonds, as the Treasury was nearly bankrupt from the war. The other would be the President's House, as the White House was generally known before it was burned, then covered with whitewash. There Dolley Madison and friends and servants had spirited away a Gilbert Stuart painting of George Washington and a copy of the Declaration of Independence. But Dolley did leave behind food and wine intended for her husband and aides, which the famished British officers happily devoured.

One might have thought Cockburn and Ross would have been sated by the dinner, and by their burning of the Capitol and President's House. Around midnight, they and their exhausted if triumphant raiding party returned up Pennsylvania Avenue to their encampment near the ruined Capitol Building, and their headquarters at Ewell's home. But on awaking, early on August 25, they were ready to wreak more havoc.

At 8:00 a.m. they sent a raiding party to the Navy Yard, to destroy anything Commandant Tingey had left unscathed. The destruction took just less than half an hour.

When they departed, a round of looting broke out. Locals scurried through the Yard, picking up things the Americans and the English had failed to burn or smash. Thieves broke into houses, carrying off furniture and fixtures. They made their way into Tingey's very own home.

Yet Tingey boldly returned by boat soon after the British left. He made a lightning inspection of the Yard, and his commandant's house, saving his most valued items from the felons. Tingey later wrote his daughter: "I was the last officer who quitted the city after the enemy had possession of it, having fully performed all orders received . . . I was also the first who returned and the only one who ventured in on the day on which [the British] were . . . masters of it."

That morning, the British also made a return visit to the White House neighborhood. Their Light Brigade pranced down Pennsylvania Avenue. Its cavalrymen and skirmishers torched the offices of the War Department and the State Department. Going up in smoke was a list of all the US soldiers recruited in the prior two years. Still, the employees there had carted to safety some valuable artifacts, such as British flags captured in the American Revolution.

Glumly watching the new immolations was Dr. William Thornton. A renaissance man, the fifty-one-year-old native of the British Caribbean was a physician, an inventor, the local justice of the peace—and an architect. He had designed the Capitol Building that Latrobe, with an assist from another architect, George Hadfield, had made a reality. The previous night, Thornton and his wife Anna Maria had watched the fires claim his Capitol creation, from the vantage point of Martha Peter's Tudor Place mansion, which Thornton had also designed.

PLEAS TO SAVE THE TREASURES OF MANKIND

Among his many roles, Thornton was the superintendent of the Patent Office. It then stood on 7th Street inside the so-called Blodgett's Hotel, an elegant, three-storied brick structure replete with four large chimneys and light-colored pilasters. It was later the site of the General Post Office, built in the 1840s, and across the street from a future Patent Office, which is now the National Portrait Gallery.

Thornton learned the British intended to burn his Patent Office, just as they had ignited his Capitol Building. He dashed over to Blodgett's Hotel to try to head off another catastrophe.

He knew the hotel had a checkered past. When the City of Washington was founded, the sale of its building lots disappointed. Few businesses moved into town, and few residents, except for its seasonal denizens: members of Congress and the administration. In a novel bid to jumpstart the economy, merchant and land speculator Samuel Blodgett Jr. set up a lottery—the first "D.C. Lottery"—that aimed to raise funds for construction in the city. Blodgett offered up a deluxe prize: a mansion, or hotel as the French style it, named for the sweepstake's impresario. The lottery, like the local economy, was a bust. But Blodgett's Hotel remained.

The federals took it over, and employed it as a storehouse, a sort of early Smithsonian, for such prized possessions as Native American headdresses and Revolutionary War muskets. And more practically, to store the models for the inventions registered by the Patent Office, such as Robert Fulton's model of his steamship. It was a treasury of invention.

Thornton hurried up to the Patent Office just in time, as columns of Britishers were rushing up to burn the place. He confronted the soldiers' commander, a major named Waters. A handful of locals crowded about Thornton, eager to watch the face-off.

The Patent Office chief launched into a stirring appeal to the Brits, with words to this effect:

'Are you not men? Are you barbarians instead? Like the Turks who burned the ancient library of Alexandria, Egypt?! An action condemned by all upright nations. In front of you lies a repository of creations, not for any one country, but for every nation on Earth, for all of mankind! And for all time! Are you barbarians? Like the Vandals and Visigoths who pulled down Rome? Or are you civilized men?!'

A jack of all trades, and master of many, Dr. William Thornton designed the original Capitol Building, and saved the original Patent Office from British marauders, while treating wounded Americans and Britishers alike during the 1814 invasion.

Then employing more down-to-earth rhetoric, Thornton informed the officer in charge that the patent models had been contributed by private citizens, not government agencies. Thus the officer, by wrecking the building, might be disobeying the standing orders to spare private property. Thornton added that, if government property were found within, it would be wise to take it outside to burn. An internal fire could spread to the entire building, and all the items inside, both private and public. (Along with all his other roles, Thornton would have made a good lawyer.) The polymath also had a personal concern: The edifice contained his own patent-pending model for a stringed musical instrument.

Swayed by Thornton's oration, Major Waters ordered his troops to hold off. Taking Thornton in tow, he strode over to Pennsylvania Avenue, with the smoldering Capitol in plain sight, in search of his commanding officer, a colonel named Jones. The colonel heard Waters out, then told him to spare the Patent Office. A clerk there locked the place up to bar looters, and for safekeeping gave its door key to a British trooper.

Congress would be grateful for Thornton's quick action because, with the Capitol burnt, it would convene at Blodgett's Hotel for fifteen months. With the President's House burnt, James and Dolley Madison would move into the Octagon House, a nearby mansion that was designed by—William Thornton.

On Pennsylvania Avenue, Thornton watched another debate over burning down a building. These were the offices of the town's leading newspaper, the *National Intelligencer*, published by Joseph Gales, an ardent supporter of the war. Ordering Royal Marines to burn it was an irate Admiral Cockburn. He had reason to be miffed. For months, as his fleet ravaged the towns of the Chesapeake, the paper's editorials had lambasted him, "the Ruffian," for all manner of outrages. And in their editorial meetings, they had, like most locals, pronounced the hated admiral's name, not properly as CO-burn, but as COCK-burn.

Thornton watched several local women whose homes were next to the *Intelligencer* approach Cockburn. They pointed out that a fire could spread and inflame their own abodes. As Thornton looked on with surprise and relief, the admiral acted chivalrously, for these damsels in distress. He ordered the Marines to put down their torches.

And to simply tear the building apart, stone by brick, and haul down its wooden walls with rope.

Near the Capitol Building, at 2nd and Pennsylvania Avenue, S.E., the British were ready to burn another private property. This was the three-story, Federal-style home of Elias Boudinot Caldwell, the clerk of the Supreme Court. Caldwell had a longtime grievance against the British. During the American Revolution, a British soldier had shot his mother to death. The prior day, at the Battle of Bladensburg, he'd been a captain of volunteer cavalry.

Cockburn's men found a store of cartridge boxes in his home. The house also contained the Supreme Court's library of books. After the battle, Caldwell had hurriedly moved the books from the Capitol Building. The British were about to torch the place when Caldwell's friend and neighbor, none other than Dr. Ewell, intervened. He urged a British captain to spare the home as private property, and as the residence of a fellow officer. The captain checked with his superior, General Ross, and the house was saved. In later years there, Caldwell would entertain the most prominent "hawks" in Congress, Henry Clay of Kentucky and John Caldwell "C." Calhoun of South Carolina, who had pushed for the war with Britain.

ARSENAL AGONISTES

Still, even with almost everything federal from the Navy Yard to the White House in ashes, the British were determined to add to the toll. Cockburn and company sent a force of about seventy-five men down to the Greenleaf Point arsenal. There the British found scores of American cannons. They turned one of the big guns on the others and blew them up. They also came upon more than 125 barrels of gunpowder.

Accounts differ whether the Americans had thrown the barrels into a deep well, to deny them to their foe, or whether the British did so. Accounts also differ on what caused the resulting, massive explosion. It blew apart storehouses, threw a great cloud of debris into the air, and left a crater twenty feet deep and forty feet wide.

It also blew to bits some thirty Royal Marines. Soldiers were buried alive under the rubble. About fifty men had their limbs blown off or were otherwise maimed. According to *When Britain Burned the White House*, a US officer who later inspected the installation noted "the horrible spectacle of legs, arms, and heads protruding from the mounds of earth thrown up by the explosion."

Perhaps a Royal Marine had dropped a match down the well or let drop a spark from a torch. Or maybe the barrels of high explosive ignited from rubbing against each other in the high heat of that day.

Many of the maimed Marines were brought back to Dr. Ewell for surgery. Dr. Thornton also treated wounded soldiers, both British and American, per agreement with Cockburn and Ross. When the invaders departed, some Washingtonians lambasted Ewell and Thornton for aiding the enemy. They were merely being chivalrous, and humane.

The Washington Typhoon

The arsenal disaster was a sign the luck of the British was turning. In the early afternoon of that sultry summer day, one of the worst storms in Washington's history smashed into town. It had the force of a hurricane, and aspects of a tornado. Cold, torrential rains carrying hailstones the size of softballs tore into the streets.

The downpours had effects both bad and good on the smoldering buildings. The chilly waters cracked the simmering stones of the foundations. At the same time, they doused the remaining flames.

The storm peaked with a freak cyclone. It knocked horse soldiers off their mounts. It blew three chimneys off the Patent Office, on the same day Thornton saved it. "Roofs of houses" were "whirled into the air like sheets of paper," reported one of Cockburn's junior officers. Swirling about the National Mall, it hoisted captured American cannons into its funnel, then twirled the guns to the ground, where they smashed near Americans and Britishers alike.

Meteorologists now view the maelstrom as part of an unusually wet and cold decade. Giant volcanic eruptions in South America and elsewhere poured enough sunlight-deflecting dust into the atmosphere to make the weather colder and damper worldwide.

This was reflected in some of the epic battles of the era. In 1812, the coldest winter of the century, Napoleon's Grand *Armée* dissolved in the snows outside Moscow. In 1814, Napoleon's attempt at a comeback failed when rain and mud slowed his rebuilt forces near the battlefield of Waterloo. In 1815, the year after the sack of Washington, another British army met unseasonably cold weather in the runup to its crushing defeat at the Battle of New Orleans.

In the District, even the steely Cockburn was affected by the hurricane's gusts and sheets of rain. During the downpour, he shouted to a local woman: "Great God, madam! Is this the kind of storm to which you are accustomed in this infernal country?!"

The plucky lady was not intimidated. She responded sharply, with what some have called, "The Curse of the Washington Woman": "No, sir, this is a special interposition of Providence to drive our enemies from our city!"

Although Cockburn, as usual, had a retort: "Not so, madam. It is rather to aid your enemies in the destruction of your city!"

Still, Cockburn and Ross may have figured enough was enough. Certainly they knew they'd accomplished their mission. With the federal city in cinders, and awash in mud, they determined to pull their forces out. After dark on August 25, less than thirty hours after riding up to the Gallatin house, the two leaders marched their host back to Bladensburg and then to the Chesapeake Bay.

By then, Washington's ubiquitous looters were aware of a complete absence of authority. They swarmed about the Capitol Building, Navy Yard, and adjoining houses, carrying off the items that remained. In the aftermath even the *National Intelligencer*, the newspaper ravaged by Cockburn, opined: "No houses were half as much plundered by the enemy as by the knavish wretches about the town who profited at the general distress."

However, William Thornton again rose to the occasion. In his guise as justice of the peace, he placed guards at the Capitol, the Navy Yard, and the President's House, sparing them further insult.

Triumph After Disaster

After reaching the Chesapeake, Cockburn and Ross found, whether through a woman's curse or not, that the great storm had damaged their fleet. The need for repairs delayed their planned attack on Baltimore.

That gave Charm City time to prepare. To throw up earthworks and to muster an Army and militia force of ten thousand. And to bring into its ranks adept commanders such as Joshua Barney, the brave soldier whom Ross and Cockburn had chivalrously freed.

Everyone knows about the failed British cannonade of Fort McHenry, documented lyrically by that lawyer and amateur poet, Georgetown's Francis Scott Key. But fewer know of the land battles at North Point and Hampstead Hill, where the Americans turned the tables on the Bladensburg debacle, and checked the conquerors of Napoleon.

The invaders lost more than a battle. At North Point, American fighters succeeded at what they had failed to do outside the Gallatin manse. A Maryland militiaman with a deadly aim shot and killed General Ross.

Ross was revered by his men; they longed to give him a fitting burial. But how to preserve his body? His soldiers placed the deceased Irishman in a barrel—filled with 129 gallons of Jamaica rum.

He rests, like any Celt should, awash in liquor.

Cockburn, who was absent from the Baltimore fight, went on to a distinguished career. Over time he reformed the Royal Navy, helping to phase out corporal punishment. He pushed to replace the sails of ships with steam. He even served in Parliament and was granted the great trust of placing the defeated Napoleon into lasting exile on a remote South Atlantic island.

If you're going to lose a battle, and your capital, you might as well lose to the enemy's best, be they chivalrous or eccentric.

CHAPTER FIVE

The First Attempted Presidential Assassination: Old Hickory Faces Death

The Capitol steps, east side, between the House and Senate sides

IT WAS APPROPRIATELY GLOOMY FOR A FUNERAL. CLOUDS AND MIST enveloped the capital that January 30th of 1835.

SICKLY AND UNPROTECTED

A gaunt, sixty-seven-year-old president, Andrew Jackson, was attending the requiem for Rep. Warren R. Davis of South Carolina. Old Hickory, his stooped shoulders draped by a cape, paid his respects to Davis, a former political foe and fellow Southerner. At the end of the ceremony, the president, accompanied by lawmakers, well-wishers, and some military officers, moved down the East Portico, the columned steps on the Capitol Building's hilltop side.

The president's health was poor. A bullet from a duel three decades prior was still lodged an inch from his heart; at times the slug inflamed his lungs. Three years before a surgeon had removed another bullet, from the president's left shoulder, a token from an 1813 brawl with Thomas Hart Benton, who'd become a Missouri senator. Jackson also ailed from migraines and bad eyesight. His behavior was somewhat erratic, perhaps due to the lead- and mercury-laden compounds with which his doctors plied him.

There was then no Secret Service; Jackson had no formal guards at all. But few were worried. Beginning with George Washington, no one had posed a serious physical threat to a president. An attempt on the life of the chief magistrate, who traveled freely about the capital of the republic, was unthinkable.

A SURPRISE ATTACK

Yet as Jackson descended the Capitol steps, a wild-eyed man suddenly emerged from behind a marble pillar.

Thirty-five-year-old Richard Lawrence gripped two single-shot derringers. He pointed one of them square at the president's chest. He pulled the trigger.

Its percussion cap crackled. But the gunpowder did not ignite. The gun misfired!

President Jackson reacted in a way that reflected his explosive temper, and uncanny courage. Brandishing his hickory cane, the aged ex-general rushed at his assailant.

Lawrence, startled by the quickness of his prey, grasped the second pistol of brass. He pointed it toward Jackson's heart, at point-blank range. He pulled the trigger. Again the percussion cap loudly sounded. The second gun also misfired!

The president was furious.

"Let me alone!" he cried to his handlers. "I know where this came from!"

Raising his hickory cane, he struck Lawrence savagely. And raised his stick again, and brought it down with a crushing blow. Several men rushed over to restrain Jackson, saving the assailant from serious injury. One of the men was a Navy lieutenant, a Thomas Gedney. Another was a congressman from the president's home state of Tennessee. Like Jackson a valorous man of the West.

It was Davy Crockett, the legendary pioneer!

The president was hustled into a carriage. His attacker was arrested. Andy Jackson had miraculously survived the first assassination attempt on a president.

Jackson's former blood enemy, Senator Benton, later wrote: "The pistols were examined, and found to be well loaded; and fired afterwards

SCENE AT THE CAPITOL.

Providence seemed to intervene for President Andrew Jackson in 1835 at the Capitol's East Portico, when both pistols of his would-be assassin, Richard Lawrence, misfired.

without fail, carrying their bullets true, and driving them through inch boards at thirty feet."

One hundred years later, in 1935, the Smithsonian possessed the two guns. It had ballistic experts test the pistols.

Both fired perfectly.

The Smithsonian estimated the odds of both weapons misfiring at 1 in 125,000.

No wonder Jackson's supporters were certain the hand of Providence had spared him, and that their hero was indestructible.

The weather, along with the Deity, may have been responsible. It's thought the mist and damp of that day moistened the gunpowder, preventing it from igniting. Further, the pistols of that era were notoriously unreliable in less-than-ideal conditions. (Participants in the 1813 fight of Jackson's with Benton had only escaped grave injury when four of their pistols had misfired.)

Conspiracy Theories

Jackson himself thought the attack was part of a conspiracy. Richard Lawrence was a house painter who'd worked some months before on the Washington home of Mississippi senator George Poindexter. The senator was an enemy of the president's in the bitter fight over the Second Bank of the United States. With great controversy, Jackson had in 1833 shut down the Bank, shifting its deposits to state institutions. The Bank's head, Nicholas Biddle of Philadelphia, had actively tried to prevent Jackson's re-election. Congress was enraged at the president's action. (Some of its members doubly so, as they had received payoffs from Biddle's Bank.) In 1833, the Senate formally censured Jackson, the only time that's happened to a chief executive.

The president had in turn raged at Congress. The story went he'd ordered the newly rebuilt Treasury Building next to the White House raised to a height that blocked his view of the Capitol Building, and of his antagonists working there. Out of sight, out of mind.

After the assassination attempt Jackson believed, without evidence, that his political enemies had put Lawrence up to it. He thought Senator John C. Calhoun was involved. The former War of 1812 hawk had turned into the president's bitter foe by backing nullification, the voiding of federal law by a state. In the Senate, however, Calhoun flatly denied any link to Lawrence.

Jackson also accused Senator Poindexter of being in on the conspiracy. He recalled the senator had physically threatened his vice president, Martin Van Buren, over the Bank issue. For protection, Van Buren had armed himself with pistols. The president also made public the testimony of two men who claimed they'd witnessed Lawrence entering Poindexter's house. But on examination, the stories of these two accusers fell apart. Still, Jackson's allegations led to Senator Poindexter losing his re-election bid.

The Lone, Lunatic Assassin

Three months after his attempt on the president's life, Lawrence went on trial at the federal court in Judiciary Square. The prosecution was led by Francis Scott Key, a political ally of Jackson's.

Defense attorneys produced witnesses who admitted Lawrence was violent, but also showed him to be indisputably insane. Lawrence had once threatened to kill a house servant and had tried to batter his sister with a lump of metal. But Lawrence was also convinced he was King Richard III, the medieval English monarch chronicled by Shakespeare. In his delusions, Lawrence believed he owned estates in America for which the US government owed him money. And that Jackson's closing of the Bank of the United States had prevented the government from paying what he was due. Lawrence was gripped by a fantasy that if he killed Jackson, thus making Vice President Van Buren the president, Van Buren would reestablish the Bank, and Lawrence would get his money.

It took the jury but five minutes of deliberation to declare Lawrence crazy. Recalled Senator Benton: "Hallucination of mind was evident, and the wretched victim of a dreadful delusion was afterwards treated as insane." Spared the gallows, Lawrence was packed off to an asylum. He lived until 1861, dying in a sanatorium that would become a noted District institution, St. Elizabeth's Hospital. (Some historians believe Lawrence was driven to insanity by ingredients, such as arsenic, mixed into the paints of the time.)

POSTSCRIPT

An odd sequel involves the man who'd helped save Lawrence from Jackson: Davy Crockett. As a congressman, Crockett opposed the president on a tragic issue, the expulsion of Indian tribes to beyond the Mississippi, along the so-called Trail of Tears. But the lawmaker's stance was unpopular in Tennessee, long the battleground of Indian wars, and Crockett lost his bid for re-election.

So, he left town for the far southwestern frontier. Crockett got up caught up in the movement for Texas independence. And he found himself, in 1836, at an old Spanish mission.

The Alamo.

Where he died with his boots on, fighting to the death with his knife and his rifle butt.

CHAPTER SIX

Don't Mess: The Founder of a Sprawling Republic Raises Cane

B Street (Constitution Avenue), just north of the Capitol Building

THE FORMER US SENATOR FROM TENNESSEE, AND FORMER GOVERNOR of the same, was still steaming. That Friday the 13th, he was walking with friends along Pennsylvania Avenue, north of the Capitol Building's squat dome. Eleven days prior, on April 2, 1835, his good name had been slurred, and within the very halls of Congress where he'd served. To make the humiliation worse, a coward, as he saw it, had slandered him.

On the floor of the House of Representatives, Congressman William Stanbery—a federalist foe of President Andrew Jackson—had made a highly charged accusation against the man.

A NATIVE AMERICAN TRAGEDY

The issue in question was, along with the tariff and slavery and the Bank of the United States, another running sore between the federalist Northeast and the anti-federalist Southwest: what to do with the Indian tribes.

The Northern states had settled the matter decades, sometimes generations, before. During the War of 1812, the US Army and state militias had crushed the Native Americans of the old Northwest, stretching from Ohio to Minnesota. Long before, in New England, the Indians had been killed off, assimilated, consigned to segments of land, decimated from disease, or driven out of the region.

But American Indians in large numbers still peopled the heart of the South, from Tennessee to Georgia. Five of these nations had become "civilized." They'd given up their roving ways, and taken up farming, built churches and schools, and some even owned slaves. But they sat on a vast expanse of land for which American settlers, and precious metal prospectors, lusted. And, from the perspective of the whites, the Indians' savage form of frontier war, complete with scalping and enslavement of female war captives, was fresh in memory.

The ex-senator had himself fallen prey to the "savages," with possibly dire effects on his romantic life. At the War of 1812's Battle of Horseshoe Bend, he'd served with General Andy Jackson's army. It smashed the fierce Red Stick tribe, thus opening up Alabama and Mississippi to massive settlement. But he'd fallen wounded with an Indian arrow—in his groin. He survived, but an unhealed, putrefied sore remained on his manhood. Some believe his wound horrified his first wife, Eliza Allen, leading to their separation after just three months of marriage. (Others deem it more likely the precocious, eighteen-year-old Eliza had been in love with another man.) Oddly, the man had inflicted a similar injury, in an 1826 duel outside Franklin, Tennessee, against War of 1812 veteran Gen. William A. White. In the duel, White's bullet missed, while the man shot White in the groin. A grand jury indicted the duel's winner, but the state's governor declined to press the case.

Despite the arrow wound, the fellow in question did not despise Native Americans. In fact, he served as an agent and envoy for the Cherokees. He sometimes wore their traditional attire, and he'd wed an Indian woman from the Oklahoma territory. (His friend President Jackson, that fearsome Indian fighter, had adopted a Native American boy.)

And now this canard about the "Indian removal" issue.

President Jackson had determined, with the support of most in the South, and to the consternation of many in the North, especially among missionary folk, to expel from the Southland the five "civilized tribes": the Cherokee, Chickasaw, Choctaw, Creek or Muscogee, and Seminole.

These native bands could be terrific fighters. The Cherokees, later the horse-mounted warriors in the Great Plains of the Wild West; the Creek, Jackson's bitter foes in the War of 1812; and the Seminoles, who took on a generation of US Army troops from their strongholds in the Florida Everglades.

Jackson's administration, and that of his successor, President Van Buren, would send many of these Native Americans all the way across the Mississippi to the dry-bone Oklahoma Territory. That trek, on which thousands lost their lives, became infamous. On route, they'd be watched over by federal troops, and provisioned from federal storehouses. That effort would be marked by lax administration of the government supplies.

A Slanderous Charge

In the House, the hefty, forty-four-year-old Congressman Stanbery was a foe of the planned expulsion. A supporter of the Bank of the United States that Jackson had closed, he was an investor in real estate that Jackson's policy had undermined. Stanbery was from Newark, Ohio, and originally from another Newark: Newark, New Jersey. He was originally a Democrat, but he voted like a federalist, backing the construction of canals to spur commerce, and supporting a federally subsidized National Road that would run through his old hometown of Newark. After Jackson was elected president in 1828, he switched over to the "Anti-Jackson" faction of Congress.

Stanbery knew the ex-senator he targeted was a friend of Jackson's. And that like the president he was an anti-federalist Democrat.

The congressman also knew that New York's Rep. Robert Rose had tried to enrich himself from the Indian removal. He did this by inflating the price of goods that a contractor sold to the government for provisioning the Indians. And that the former senator himself had tied to obtain a profitable, no-bid contract for supplying the same.

In Congress, Stanbery lambasted the ex-senator for allegedly trying to profit from this shady contracting, of selling the Treasury and the Indians, in effect, a bill of goods. The charge was a stretch. And the former senator, instead of enriching himself with past "public service," was then penniless.

Congressional Contretemps

To the man accused, a frontier brawler and War of 1812 soldier, Stanbery's accusations were fighting words. His ire increased when he read Stanbery's remark reprinted in a newspaper. He strode over to the House of Representatives to confront him.

Worried colleagues in Congress headed off a clash and led the forty-two-year-old back to his residence near the Capitol. Still angry, he had an intermediary, Tennessee representative Cave Johnson, hand Stanbery a note demanding an apology, or a duel. The representative declined.

The man now deemed Stanbery a coward as well as a liar.

Stanbery, knowing the rage he had engendered in the man, as well as the fellow's martial reputation, went about Capitol Hill heavily armed. On his person he carried two pistols and a dirk, a long thrusting knife.

The congressman stated: "I expected every time I went out of, or came into the Capitol, to meet him, and I was prepared for such an event."

Washington City was then a largely rural village of under twenty thousand residents, with hardly any places of entertainment. Thus it was big news when a theater opened close to the north side of the Capitol Building.

STREET FIGHT

The man in question, like many in town, made plans to see a show there. On Friday, April 13, the stocky former senator was strolling with companions to the emporium, located at the corner of B Street, as Constitution Avenue was then called, and New Jersey Avenue N.W., near today's statue of Ohio senator Robert A. Taft.

As the former soldier and his friends approached the theater, he caught sight of his tormentor, who happened to be exiting his lodging.

The eyes of the former legislator opened wide. He grasped his stout hickory cane. He'd actually crafted it out of wood from the Hermitage plantation of Jackson, "Old Hickory" himself.

He strode across B Street, and up to the congressman.

In a deceptively quiet voice, he asked: "Are you Stanbery?"

"Yes," came the reply.

The man exploded: "Then you are a damn rascal!"

As Stanbery watched in shock, the man smashed his hickory cane onto his head. Stunned, Stanbery tried to get away, but the man tackled him. They wrestled around in the dirty, unpaved track that was B Street.

Raising his stick again, and again, the man unleashed savage blows against Stanbery's wrists and ribs.

The legislator, though pummeled, was able to pull one of his pistols out of a pocket. He pressed it square against his attacker's chest. He pulled the trigger. The flint struck and sparked. But the gun failed to discharge!

His assaulter continued to lambaste him with the cane.

Then, as the whimpering congressman lay dazed and bleeding on his back, his attacker added an extra punishment.

Perhaps he thought back to the terrible wound he'd received at Horseshoe Bend.

He parted Stanbery's legs and caned the lawmaker in the groin.

Finally, he stopped. Leaving the bloodied congressman on the street—with a concussion, bruises, and a busted wrist. Then he and his companions continued to the theater.

Washington City was shocked.

Because of the violent attack on a congressman.

And because the attacker was a nationally known statesman.

A man thought to be a logical successor to President Jackson.

The man was Sam Houston!

The future founder and president of the Republic of Texas. And later still one of the first two federal senators from Texas.

Years before he became president of the Republic of Texas, former Tennessee senator Sam Houston administered a savage caning to Ohio representative William Stanbery, who'd slurred Houston before the House of Representatives.

JUDICIAL JOUSTS

From his sick bed, Stanbery wrote the Speaker of the House that "he had been waylaid in the street . . . attacked, knocked down by a bludgeon, and severely bruised and wounded by Samuel Houston, late of Tennessee, for words spoken . . . in the House of Representatives."

The House voted 145–25 to direct federal magistrates to arrest Houston. He was charged with "breaching the privileges of the House." A trial, before the House of Representatives itself, was set for six days after the assault, on April 19.

From a modern perspective, it was an open-and-shut case.

But Sam Houston, unlike Garth Brooks, had friends in high places.

One was powerful Tennessee representative and fellow Democrat James Knox Polk. That year, Polk was elected Speaker of House. Later, as president, Polk would acquire the Pacific Northwest and the American Southwest, through the kind of grand westward expansion that Houston dreamed of.

President Jackson was another ally. Wishing Houston to look his best at the trial, Jackson bought him a suit of clothes. He also picked a top-flight defense attorney for his friend: Francis Scott Key, soon to be the city's district attorney.

The House convened to put Houston on trial.

Newspaper coverage was extensive and public interest keen. For three weeks, Washingtonians in fine apparel packed the House gallery to watch the legal battle on the floor below.

Houston appeared before Congress in a buckskin coat while grasping his hickory cane, according to author Roger Busfield Jr. He was permitted to cross-examine Stanbery, the man he'd assaulted! The reporting of the trial was bowdlerized to spare female readers accounts of the caning of Stanbery's groin.

Houston's friends in the legislature helped thwart a formal censure. Instead, he was found in contempt of Congress, a lesser offense. (He surely had contempt for Stanbery.)

Angry at such a weak punishment, Stanbery took Houston to court. The judge in the case was sixty-six-year-old William Cranch, the same jurist who'd presided over the murder trial of James McGirk. (See the chapter on the District's first hanging.)

The legal proceedings found Houston guilty of assault. However the court declined to impose a prison sentence. Instead, it fined him $500.

Houston refused to pay it.

President Jackson refused to collect it.

Houston said of Stanbery: "His vices are too odious to merit pity, and his spirit too mean to deserve contempt."

Meanwhile Stanbery himself was censured by the House, in an act of partisan revenge, for rather mildly proclaiming that the House Speaker had undue presidential ambitions. He also failed to get the federally supported National Road, beloved by federalists, to run through his hometown of Newark, New Jersey. With his clout in Congress slipping, he failed to win re-election. Stanbery spent the rest of his life as a lawyer in Newark—Newark, Ohio, that is.

A Startling Second Career

Among some, Sam Houston's stock actually rose for his aggressive role in an "affair of honor." In Washington, however, his political future was cloudy, having alienated Stanbery's colleagues, who made up a significant chunk of Congress.

In such a situation, what was an ambitious man from the Southwest to do?

To move further South by Southwest—like the music festival in the state with which he was to become synonymous.

Like Davy Crockett, Houston ended up in the Texas Territory to become the militant leader of the settlers from his native Tennessee and other Southern states, a boisterous crew who threw off the yoke of Mexican president Santa Anna. The caner of Congress became the leading light of the new Republic of Texas.

His late-career dream was the union of Texas with the United States, a feat he accomplished with the Lone Star Republic's admission in 1845, with Houston as a US senator.

When Texas seceded from the Union in 1861, then-Governor Houston was aghast. His life's great accomplishment was at risk. He was one of the few statesmen in the South to denounce joining the Confederacy. As a result, he was pushed out of office. Ever adamant in his views, Houston passed away in 1863, at the height of the Civil War he despised, his prophecy of disunion as a disaster for Texas and the South soon proven correct.

Ironically, the brother of his old foe William Stanbery, one Henry Stanbery, served as a defense attorney for that staunch proponent of the South, President Andrew Johnson of Tennessee, during his 1868 impeachment trial before the Senate. Henry Stanbery got Johnson acquitted by one vote.

Don't mess with Texas—and especially not with Sam Houston.

CHAPTER SEVEN

A Star-Spangled Race Riot, a Labor Strike, and a First Amendment Brawl

Judiciary Square, 5th and D Streets, N.W., and Mt. Vernon Square, 7th Street and New York Avenue, N.W.

WHO DO YOU CALL?

Yes, who do you call upon? When the city you are charged with protecting faces ruin from vandals?

That was one of the headaches facing fifty-six-year-old Francis Scott Key, long since the lyricist of the "The Star-Spangled Banner," and now in 1835 the district attorney, the chief law enforcement officer, of the city of Washington and its twenty thousand troubled inhabitants.

CLASS AND ETHNICITY

The crises that summer began at the Washington Navy Yard.

There the "mechanics," manual laborers, for the most part Irish working men, had sought better pay, lunch benefits, and ten-hour workdays. They were fed up with the dawn-to-dusk shifts then customary. Theirs was one of the first instances of labor unrest in US history.

But rejecting the demands was the stern commandant of the Navy Yard, sixty-two-year-old Commodore Isaac Hull, a hero from the War of 1812. The Connecticut-born Hull was more concerned with the arduous task of converting his installation from a shipbuilding yard to a maker of naval armaments.

The mechanics responded with a work stoppage. On July 29, 1835, some 175 of them walked off the job.

The standoff that followed was much worsened by race. Many of the free African-American laborers at the Yard, some of them recently enslaved and most of them poor, were anxious to keep working and getting paid. They declined to strike.

Many strikers saw themselves as competing for jobs with the free blacks, who were paid low wages, as well as with the Yard's enslaved laborers, whose owners often compensated them with food and clothing alone. Further, the number of black workers at the Yard had recently swelled with the arrival of African-American ship caulkers from Baltimore.

The white mechanics would take their ethnic and workplace grievances to the downtown streets of Washington.

There, one of the city's restaurants was the grandly named Epicurean Eating House: Epicurean, as in an epicure, a lover of the good things in life. As its name suggested, the business specialized in the sumptuous seafood of the Tidewater region.

It was smartly sited, between the Capitol Building and the White House, on 6th Street along the town's main boulevard, Pennsylvania Avenue. Congressmen, reporters, Capitol Hill staff, and officials and clerks from the Andrew Jackson Administration frequented it. (The Capital Grille restaurant is there today, a steakhouse serving the lobbyists and job seekers still plying for government's favor.)

By the mid-1830s, about half the African-American population of Washington was made up of free men and women. Around the time of the city's founding in the 1790s, a number of the region's major slave-owners, notably George Washington and Lord Fairfax, had freed their slaves. Some who remained enslaved were hired out for wages. If a slave could save enough of such earnings, he might purchase his own freedom. In Washington, things were getting better for many blacks.

But the underlying tensions were great, partly from the fears of whites at the growing numbers of free blacks. And partly due to terror over the Nat Turner slave rebellion in southern Virginia just four years prior. During that revolt, led by a black man convinced he was a modern-day Moses leading his people from bondage, about fifty whites were massacred, before the rebellion was crushed, with the deaths of about one hundred blacks. For generations, the South was gripped by fears of a repeat of the Haiti slave revolt of the 1790s, which had toppled the French government there and led to the death of thousands of whites and blacks.

In 1835, many in the North mailed to Southern officials and institutions thousands of publications demanding restrictions on slavery. These missives so upset Southern members of Congress that they clamped down a gag order forbidding debates over slavery. At the same time, rumors flew of a potential slave revolt in Mississippi, the center of King Cotton and its burgeoning slave plantations.

Terror in the Night

In Washington, the owner of the Epicurean Eating House was himself a "free man of color," Beverly Randolph Snow. Like many figures in early civil rights matters, he was a proud man of mixed ancestry. His white father and black mother had hailed from Lynchburg, Virginia. With a middle name of one of Virginia's aristocratic families, he built up a lucrative business. Snow offered delectable cuisine to a rustic town starved for fine dining, or for classy establishments of any sort. His menu boasted of roasted partridge and steamed turtle. His thriving enterprise was just two blocks away from the house of the esteemed Anna Thornton.

Thornton was, with Dolley Madison, one of the city's grand dames. Sixty years old, she was the widow of Dr. William Thornton, the designer of the Capitol Building who'd faced down British Marines seeking to burn down the Patent Office Building. (See the chapter on the British burning of Washington.)

Originally a Northerner of abolitionist sentiment, Thornton had adapted to the culture of his adopted Southern town and purchased some slaves as household servants. His wife continued this practice after his death.

Late on the night of August 4, at her fine townhouse on 8th Street, up from Pennsylvania Avenue, Anna Thornton got the fright of her life. Awaking with a start, she saw in the dim light of her bedroom the figure of Arthur Bowen, her eighteen-year-old servant. Bowen was holding a hatchet. He'd obviously been drinking heavily. And he muttered slogans, gleaned from abolitionists, calling for an end to slavery.

Thornton was doubly startled, for she had known Bowen, a person of mixed ancestry, since he was a young boy. He and his mother had long been Thornton's slaves.

Terrified, Anna Thornton cautiously got up from her bed. The situation was doubly unnerving, as Anna shared the bedroom with her mother as well as Arthur's mother. Bowen remained there, drunk, the ax in the crook of his arm, muttering angrily. According to author Jefferson Morley, Thornton silently stepped around him, and out of her house.

Then Arthur's mom, Maria Bowen, woke up. She too was shocked at the sight of her son, standing in the bedroom with the ax. She pushed Arthur away, shouting: "Get out, get out!"

Arthur left, then pounded on the back door, shouting: "I've got just as much right to freedom as you do!"

Anna Thornton hurried to her next-door neighbor, who happened to be, like her late husband, a doctor. In fact, he was President Jackson's physician. The doctor sent for the town's peace officers. A lengthy search commenced. Four days later, on Saturday, August 8, Bowen was arrested.

Word spread about the violation of Mrs. Thornton's boudoir by an inebriated young slave. Many assumed Bowen had been mulling a sexual assault, or a murder. The *Washington Globe* opined Thornton had barely "been saved from butchery in her own chamber." The likely punishment for such was the gallows. Unless a lynching happened first. Under heavy guard, Arthur Bowen was taken to a tiny cell at the crumbling city jail.

Word also spread about a supposed instigator of Bowen's rage.

This was Reuben Crandall. He was a young resident of Georgetown disliked by many Washingtonians for his antislavery views. Many disliked Crandall's "notorious" Connecticut sister even more. Three years before, Prudence Crandall, a Quaker, had admitted a black teenager into her private school for young women. This ignited a firestorm whereby Connecticut banned education for blacks from outside the state. Those wary of abolition worried Reuben Crandall was spreading his sister's "radical" notions into their own town.

Francis Scott Key, the D.A., shared these concerns. Key was a man in the middle on slavery. He owned slaves, freed some of them, helped set up the African nation of Liberia for free blacks, and strongly opposed immediate abolition.

Key arranged for police to search Crandall's home on High Street, today's Wisconsin Avenue. In a trunk, they found stacks of abolitionist publications, including *The Liberator*, published by William Lloyd Garrison of Massachusetts. Key had Crandall arraigned. He was clamped into the same jail as Bowen, and denied bail by the Circuit Court in the old City Hall at Judiciary Square.

WILD IN THE STREETS

Meanwhile, the striking workers at the Washington Yard closely followed the news about Bowen and Crandall. It deepened their anger at blacks over the labor strike. Their rancor only rose with a rumor that restauranteur Beverly Snow had made insulting remarks about the wives and daughters of the mechanics.

It was August, when Washington is humid and hot, when brittle tempers are liable to fray. The white laborers decided to seek revenge.

On August 12, a large angry group of working men, from the Navy Yard and other neighborhoods, assembled in downtown Washington.

Their first targets were the city jail, and the nearby City Hall. Mostly, they wanted to get to Bowen and Crandall before a court could. According to African-American diarist Michael Shiner, the enslaved Navy Yard worker, the mechanics "swore they would pull the jail down . . . to get [Arthur Bowen] and hang him without judge or juror." Soon hundreds of laborers surrounded the jail and City Hall, baying for blood.

Francis Scott Key, charged with keeping order in the city, watched with alarm. Washington then had precisely ten constables, and no federal police. His gendarmes were no match for an out-of-control mob.

Who do you call, when your city is verging on chaos?

Key figured he knew. He sent word to the Marine Corps commandant, in his quarters near the Navy Yard, to call out his troops.

Soon a full company of Marines with fixed bayonets came pouring out of their barracks. It was located, then as now, on 8th and I Streets,

S.E., near the Washington Navy Yard. The soldiers quick-stepped along the edge of the Capitol Building, then turned down onto Pennsylvania Avenue. They came up to the mob.

Faced with a professional fighting force, the throng of mechanics hesitated, then dissipated, and disappeared.

WHITE ON BLACK
However, the horde reassembled the next day—at the Epicurean Eating House, just blocks from the prison. The black-run private business made for easier prey.

Restaurant which formerly stood on the northwest corner of Sixth street and Pennsylvania avenue, where the Snow riot of 1835 occurred.

The Epicurean Eating House on Pennsylvania Avenue down from the Capitol was the pride of African-American restauranteur Beverly Snow, the target of Irish laborers who rioted against black businesses.

The mob of about 350 people smashed the restaurant's windows, and wrecked the tables, chairs, and kitchen within. They fell upon the liquor supply. According to Shiner, "the mechanics drank all Snows [*sic*] stock of whiskey and champagne."

Facing a lynch mob, the owner of the Epicurean Eating House fled for his life. Aided by white friends, Snow slipped out of his bistro, and rode for fifty-six miles up to Frederick, Maryland. He implored the sheriff there to place him in protective custody. Snow made a public plea: "Do me the honor to look back at my past conduct, as a citizen, for the last six or seven years. If anything can be produced against me, let the world know it."

The entrepreneur soon moved to Canada, part of the British Empire, which had abolished slavery two years before. In Toronto, he started up a cafe and taverns. His Eating House in the District was later acquired by another free man of color, with the evocative name of Absalom Shadd.

With the restaurant of the Epicureans wrecked by Philistines, the rioters swarmed on to Snow's residence. They broke inside and, frustrated at not finding the restauranteur, smashed up the place.

Meanwhile Washington's mayor and town council fretted about the safety of their municipal properties. They authorized a veteran officer from the War of 1812, and about fifty citizen volunteers with muskets, to guard City Hall.

The city's pro–Democratic Party newspaper, the *National Intelligencer*, knew the workers made up part of its faction's base of support. Yet even it was shocked at the violence. The paper editorialized: "We could not have believed it possible that we should live to see the Public Offices garrisoned by the clerks with United States troops posted at their doors, and their windows barricaded, to defend them against the citizens of Washington."

Checked at some places by the volunteers and the Marines, the rioters rushed toward other black establishments.

Prominent among these was Union Seminary, a one-room schoolhouse run by a cleric and civil rights advocate, the Reverend John Francis Cook Sr. Rev. Cook was a nephew of the remarkable Alethia Browning Tanner, a mixed-race slave who, in running a profitable grocery business in Lafayette Square, had bought her freedom and those of over a dozen relatives, including Cook. Rev. Cook operated a debating club that discussed issues like abolition. Arthur Bowen had attended some of its sessions.

The mob rolled into Cook's schoolhouse. It damaged the walls and wrecked its library. Rev. Cook managed to escape by borrowing a friend's horse and hightailing it to Pennsylvania, where he stayed until things calmed down.

Six years later, Cook would found the nearby First Colored Presbyterian Church, today the influential 15th Street Presbyterian Church. At the end of the Civil War, Cook's successor as church rector spoke before Congress as it passed the constitutional amendment banning slavery.

The rioters sacked the institutions, homes, and tenements of other blacks. A school managed by Mary Wormley, evidently the mother of James Wormley, another noted black restauranteur, was looted. For good, or bad, measure, a house of prostitution was burned to the ground as well.

Fortunately, in three days of turmoil, no one was killed.

Meanwhile the labor walkout continued, but Commandant Hull wouldn't bend. On August 15, the mechanics ended their strike. With no improvement in their job conditions, they glumly went back to work with the black laborers.

With grim humor, townsfolk nicknamed the disturbances the "Snow Riot," after Beverly Snow, and the unlikelihood of snow in the high heat of a Washington summer.

A TIME OF TRIAL

As for the D.A., Key moved against those whom he saw as responsible for the trouble: first of all, the rioters. He prosecuted their leaders for destruction of property and for disturbing the peace.

Reflecting the politics of his Tidewater town, and his own fears, Key prosecuted two other men in federal court.

One was Arthur Bowen. The youthful slave was charged with attempted murder and attempted burglary. His trial took place in the Circuit Court. In the proceedings, a neighbor of Thornton's gave damaging testimony. He said the slave had called out for violence while slamming his ax into the door of Thornton's home.

The court convicted Bowen and sentenced him to be hanged. The death penalty was to be served early the following year, on February 26, 1836.

Giving up hope, Bowen blamed his fate on liquor. He wrote out rhymes, published by a local newspaper, stating: "Brought up I was by parents nice/Whose commands I would not obey/But plunged ahead foremost into vice/And into temptation's dreadful way."

His longtime owner, Anna Thornton, was distraught. At the time of the riot, Thornton had written: "Oh I am grieved indeed at this business. The people are incensed against Arthur as he is thought to be one of a party instigated by some white friends to raise an insurrection. . . . Oh God protect us." At the trial, she testified in Bowen's favor, believing he hadn't meant her physical harm. According to the author Morley, the affair likely reminded Thornton of her minister father. He'd been hanged for forgery, in trying to provide money for the poor.

Some historians suspect, without hard evidence, that Bowen may have been the illegitimate son of William Thornton. His mother, Maria Bowen, was a servant in the Thornton household when Arthur was born.

In any event, Anna Thornton determined to help Arthur Bowen. She wrote out a petition asking for a presidential pardon, and got thirty-four well-connected friends to sign it. She buttonholed an acquaintance, Vice President Martin Van Buren. She also lobbied a future vice president, Kentucky anti-federalist Richard Mentor Johnson. He was then in political hot water for having a black woman as his common-law wife.

Most importantly, Thornton wrote President Jackson a letter, seventeen pages long. In it she characterized Bowen as a scapegoat: "The recent alarms & agitations," she wrote, "may have had an unconscious influence in determining the expediency of seizing the first occasion to make a severe and terrifying example. . . ."

Further, she got a former US senator from Kentucky and friend of Jackson's to argue Bowen had been seized with "temporary insanity" in entering Thornton's bedroom. (Astonishingly, the killer of Francis Scott

Key's son, Philip Barton Key II, would use the same defense in his 1859 murder trial.)

Anna Thornton was a good woman to have on your side.

At the last minute, Jackson moved to answer her entreaties. On the night before the scheduled hanging, long after Bowen had prepared himself for the end, the president issued a stay of execution, to last until June of 1836.

That month, Key faced an awful tragedy of his own. His son Daniel, who was the same age as Bowen, was serving with the US Navy. After he and another seaman exchanged angry words, they agreed to settle their dispute at the dueling grounds of Bladensburg, Maryland.

In the ensuing firefight, Daniel Key was slain. His death nearly unhinged his father.

It was, perhaps, the time to proffer some mercy.

Andrew Jackson soon wrote out a directive: "Let the Negro boy Arthur Bowen be pardoned." The presidential directive took effect on the Fourth of July.

Although now free, Bowen remained a marked man in Washington. Thornton, having saved his life, sold him for $750, clearing his way to begin a new life. He lit out for Florida to labor for a new master. There Bowen obtained work on a steamboat, through the intervention of Jackson's former secretary of war.

"Public Order" vs. Individual Liberty

Yet Key's other high-profile legal target was Reuben Crandall, the possessor of the antislavery tracts. To make an example of him, the D.A. indicted Crandall for sedition.

At his trial, in a packed US Circuit Court, Key accused abolitionists of the "most horrid principles, whose means of attack upon us are insurrection, tumult and violence." Crandall defense attorney Joseph Bradley cleverly retorted by reading an eloquent critique of slavery—then noting the words were Key's. Thirteen years later, Bradley's black butler would help plan the *Pearl* slave escape from the very shadow of the Capitol. (See the chapter on the largest slave escape.) The defense lawyers succeeded in painting Key as a prosecutor with conflicting views.

The D.A. himself countered with a racially charged appeal to the jurors:

"Are you willing, gentlemen, to abandon your country; to permit it to be taken from you, and occupied by the Abolitionist, according to whose taste it is to associate and amalgamate with the Negro?"

The defense lawyers themselves countered by noting Key's legal precedent, the Sedition Act of 1798, had lapsed, and no longer had the force of law. Attorney Richard Coxe also warned against setting an ill precedent in restricting freedom of speech, lest "tyranny . . . fly to the remotest parts of this once free land."

The stout defense persuaded the jury. After less than four hours of deliberation, Crandall was declared not guilty.

But tragically, during his eight months of imprisonment in the dank conditions of the city jail, Crandall came down with tuberculosis. He never recovered and died two years later. His trial and detention were surely the worst episode in his life, and possibly Key's as well.

Washington had survived, but was tarnished by its first race riot, and by its persecution of an abolitionist.

Chapter Eight

Rifle Duel!: The Fatal Face-Off Between Members of Congress

Capitol entrances, West and East Porticos

At the west end of the Capitol Building, James Watson Webb grasped his sturdy cane. The youthful publisher of the hard-hitting *New York Courier and Enquirer* was eager to hand out a beating. He toted a horsewhip along with his hickory stick.

Pugilistic Publishers

The structure in front of him, that May 6, 1830, was grand. Just the year before, architect Charles Bulfinch had finished a decade and a half of reconstruction and expansion, following the British burning of the place in 1814.

The nattily dressed, twenty-eight-year-old Webb was confident. As an Army lieutenant, he'd relished pistol duels and bare-knuckle brawls.

And Webb's antagonist, Duff Green, publisher of the Washington-based *United States Telegraph*, was scrawny. The New Yorker figured Green, age thirty-eight, from frontier Missouri by way of Kentucky, had no chance.

Yet he may have underestimated his foe. Green was a veteran of the War of 1812 and of battles against American Indians.

On the platform at the top of the Capitol's steps, Webb's eyes widened as he spotted his prey. Duff Green stood right in front of him!

Webb and Green were at war over politics. In 1828 Webb's editorials had helped Andrew Jackson win the presidency. Then he had turned against Old Hickory. But Green mostly stuck with the president.

The personal merged with the political. Green falsely opined that Webb had left the US Army due to scandal. After Green's newspaper branded Webb a "base calumniator," a liar, Webb vowed to avenge the slight. Webb rushed down to the capital, where Green covered Congress.

Webb strode over to Green. He brandished his cane high in the air, ready to strike.

But Green had been expecting Webb's arrival, after getting a letter that warned Webb would give him a horsewhipping.

So, as Webb drew near, Green pulled out a gun.

Stunned, Webb stopped short. Then recovering somewhat, he told Green: "Throw away your pistol. And I will throw away my cane. And give you a damned whipping."

Green's response was firm, and rather formal. "I do not intend to be whipped by you. Nor will I put myself in a position to invite attack from you."

Below the Capitol's new dome, the two men continued their unusual dialogue.

Webb told Green, "Are you not a coward to draw a pistol on an unarmed man?" Green didn't mention Webb was armed with a cane and a whip.

Webb added, less than politely: "You poor, contemptible, cowardly puppy . . . I will throw away my cane, and only pull your nose and box your ears!"

Green replied curtly: "I have no time to waste with you." Fingering the gun, he added: "You must march out of my path."

"I will not," Webb countered.

"You shall," answered Green.

He cocked his pistol and pointed it.

Then, according to the accounts of both men, discretion overtook the outgunned Webb's valor. The journalist scampered up the steps into the safety of the House of Representatives.

The astute observer of America, France's Alexis de Tocqueville, pegged a typical American editor of the time. He wrote that such a man engaged in "an open and coarse appeal to the passions of his readers; he abandons principles to assail the character of individuals, to track them into private life. . . ."

A Frontier Culture

The Webb-Green clash was the kickoff to the Capitol Building's most violent decade. The 1830s witnessed the first assassination attempt on a president, the brutal caning of a congressman by an ex-senator, and the city's first race riot. (See the chapters on Andrew Jackson and Richard Lawrence, on Sam Houston, and on the Snow Riot.) And the only killing of a congressman by another congressman.

The issues of the day were vital, often violently argued, and at times settled with violence. America was then a frontier nation whose legislators often hailed from districts marked by foreign invasion, Indian raids, and gunfights out of a Wild West movie. Intemperate language was the norm. Words were often met with demands to uphold one's honor by cane, whip, dueling pistols, or even deadlier ordinance.

The 1830s emerged from a wild 1828 presidential election in which the opponents of the winner, Jackson, had distributed "Coffin Handbills" illustrating his many duels, some of them fatal, some of the information false. His presidency had begun with an affair between his secretary of war John Eaton and a Georgetown tavern worker named Peggy O'Neil Timberlake. It led to the resignation of almost the entire Cabinet, and with Eaton threatening the life of a Cabinet member. The president's departing vice president, John C. Calhoun, had returned to his native South Carolina to back the movement to nullify federal laws, a dress rehearsal for civil war that Jackson faced down.

The nullification issue in turn almost led to Duff Green being beaten to death. Green was a supporter of states' rights, including South Carolina's asserted right to void federal legislation. Two years after his face-down of Webb, Green lambasted South Carolina representative James Blair for opposing nullification. He branded Blair's ilk as "Tories," referring to those who supported King George during the American Revolution. Green had practically called Blair a traitor.

Green might have chosen a different target. Whereas Green was slender, Blair measured six feet, six inches tall, and weighed 350 pounds. He was also addicted to morphine and given to fits of violence. Once, at a Washington theater, he fired his pistol at an actor on stage.

On Christmas Eve 1833, Representative Blair spotted his accuser, not far from the Capitol on Pennsylvania Avenue. Rushing up from behind, he caned the publisher to the ground. (Green later described the weapon as a large club.) Blair then kicked his enemy into the gutter. Blair, all 350 pounds of him, leapt up and down on Green like a professional wrestler. He left his victim with a broken leg, a broken arm, a busted collarbone, and broken ribs.

Still, the publisher was plucky. From his recovery bed, he eloquently denounced the attempt to "suppress the voice of truth and to silence the press by brute force." He sued Blair for $300 in damages in a District court. He won the case and obtained another $350 via a lawsuit in Blair's native South Carolina.

Those who live by the cane, sometimes die by the gun. On April Fool's Day, 1834, Representative Blair was in his District lodging. He was sitting with a friend, the governor of Alabama, when he got a letter from his wife intimating a romantic affair with the governor. According to a diary entry of former president, and then-Rep. John Quincy Adams, Blair took out a pistol—and shot himself to death.

FALLOUT AND FURY

Eight years after his face-off with Duff Green, Webb was the instigator of a fatal Capitol Hill confrontation.

By 1838, Webb was an influential member of the Whig Party. It was a descendant of Alexander Hamilton's Federalist Party, with its support of a national bank, protective tariffs to bolster domestic industry and to fund canals and roads, a powerful Army and Navy, and a strong federal government generally.

Opposing it was the Democratic Party, a descendant of Jefferson's Anti-Federalists. It opposed a federal bank, sought tariff cuts, and was skeptical of federal support of transportation projects and of an overreaching federal government generally. The two factions were growing further apart on slavery, with the Whigs more critical and the Democrats more supportive, though that dispute wouldn't burn white-hot until the 1850s.

The Whigs were strongest in the Northeast, and the Democrats in the Southwest. However, the bloody matchup between congressmen in 1838 happened between a Whig from the Border South, and a Democrat from the far Northeast.

The affair was in part blowback from the epic brawl in the early 1830s between Jackson and the Second Bank of the United States, abbreviated as BUS. Ugly feelings over the issue persisted for years. In early 1838, the Washington reporter for Webb's newspaper made charges about contractors bribing members of Congress. In response, first-time representative Jonathan Cilley, from Maine, rose before the House to accuse Webb of having taken $52,000 in payments from the BUS during the debates over it. (Cilley's name was pronounced "Silly," which seemed apt, given the farcical, if tragical, events, that followed.)

The prickly Webb was irate. And even more than usual because, though his editorials had backed the BUS, he hadn't pocketed bribes. He thus demanded a pistol duel with Cilley.

Like most Northern politicians, including Northern Democrats, the thirty-five-year-old Cilley saw duels, and caning and fisticuffs, as outdated and barbarous. In fact, New England had long instituted harsh punishments to deter personal duels. By the American Revolution, authorities would execute the winner of a duel, then drive a stake through his heart and leave his body out to rot.

Cilley also saw it as beneath him, a congressman, to respond to a challenge from a mere journalist. After asking friends and fellow legislators for advice, he turned a deaf ear to Webb's demand.

Although a New Yorker, Webb looked favorably on dueling, and with some sophistication. He saw a pistol fight as "a conservator of the public peace—a check on the arrogance of the strong—a bridle on the tongue and the passions—a substitute for brutal rencontres, and secret assassinations." Given that the alternative for men like Webb was a caning or a beating, his attitude made a kind of sense.

Webb responded to Cilley's cold shoulder by drawing on his contacts in the Whig Party. On February 21, 1838, in the House chamber, he approached a political ally and Kentucky congressman, William Graves. His last name would also turn out to be apt. Webb asked Graves to personally deliver a note to Cilley that demanded an explanation of his criticism of Webb. Graves did so. Cilley declined to accept the message.

Some sensed that, instead of ending the matter, trouble was only beginning. Cilley's old college chum, Sen. Franklin Pierce of New Hampshire, the future president, advised Cilley to arm himself for protection. And indeed, political intrigue came into play.

Power Plays and Negotiations

The leaders of the Whig Party thought they could play the tiff between Cilley and Webb to their advantage. The head of the Whigs was Graves's fellow Kentuckian, Henry Clay, then a US senator.

Clay was the sponsor of a Federalist-style "American System," with its strong governmental role in what we today would call "infrastructure projects," such as national roads bankrolled by tariffs. Senator Clay was still smarting from the closure of the BUS, and from his defeat by Jackson in the election of 1832.

On the Webb-Cilley matter, Clay met with prominent Whigs. They were Graves; the hot-headed Rep. Henry Wise of Virginia, later the state's governor; Rep. Richard Menefee of Kentucky; and respected Sen. John Jordan Crittenden, also of Kentucky. Crittenden was later attorney general for three presidents: William Henry Harrison, John Tyler, and Millard Fillmore.

Other congressmen weighed in, as the Cilley and Graves camps engaged in much back and forth. In the end, several dozen congressmen took part in the discussions.

No Clay Pigeon

Henry Clay was himself the veteran of several duels, one of which was with a fellow congressman. After the War of 1812 revealed weaknesses in the federal military and banking systems, Clay adopted many Federalist stands, and headed up the Whigs. As such, he had run-ins with a staunch Anti-Federalist from Virginia, Rep. John Randolph. The two differed on politics and even more on personality. In trying to maintain order as a new House Speaker, Clay was miffed when the rustic, aristocratic Randolph insisted on bringing his hunting dogs into the House sessions!

Then came the bitterly contested presidential election of 1824. Andy Jackson took the popular vote, but John Quincy Adams took the election when he won over the electoral votes controlled by Clay. Adams then made Clay his secretary of state. In slamming this so-called "corrupt bargain" before the House, Representative Randolph labeled Adams, of devout New England beliefs, a "Puritan," and Clay a "blackleg," that is, an animal with anthrax. Even worse, he accused Clay of cheating at cards, a cardinal sin on Kentucky's steamboats and horserace tracks. Jackson also savaged Clay, stating the "Judas of the West has closed the contract and will receive the thirty pieces of silver." An irate Clay challenged Randolph to a duel.

Dueling was illegal in Washington City but, instead of going to Prince George's County, Maryland, where it was allowed, the two congressmen went out to Great Falls, Virginia, where it was not. Because Randolph had insisted, "If I am to spill my blood, if must be on the soil of my native land, Virginia."

At the firefight Randolph, who insisted he didn't want to make a widow of Mrs. Clay, threw away his fire, that is, fired into the air. Clay did shoot at Randolph, but in a way calculated to teach his antagonist a lesson, not harm him. He fired a bullet through Randolph's loose, flowing coat. When each man realized both were unharmed, they rushed together to express affection and relief.

And Randolph quipped to Clay: "You owe me a new coat!"

That was the way a duel was supposed to end. No blood spilled, honor upheld, relationships repaired. But sometimes things didn't turn out that way.

A comic-opera duel took place in 1826 between boyish-looking Virginia senator John Randolph and then–Secretary of State Henry Clay, the former House Speaker. Randolph threw away his fire, while Clay sent a bullet through Randolph's jacket, leaving both statesmen unhurt.

When Representative Cilley declined to respond to Webb's letter, Clay and the other big Whigs met with Representative Graves. Graves was persuaded to ask Cilley to write out the reason for his refusal to answer Webb, and to explain his verbal attack on Webb in the House.

Once again, Cilley declined to respond. And he stated he would not respond to any requests for explanations.

Graves also gave Cilley a reworded note about the Webb matter. Clay probably ghostwrote the letter. Further, Graves insisted Cilley state he had no "personal objections to Colonel Webb as a gentleman".

The Whigs figured Cilley, as a Northerner, would shy away from a physical altercation. The congressman would seem a coward, with the Whigs scoring political points. On the other hand, some lawmakers felt Cilley shouldn't be held responsible for statements made during a congressional debate, where congressmen had the privilege of free speech.

Cilley refused the letter of Graves. In so doing, he stressed he meant no offense to his fellow congressman. He further stated he did not want to correspond with Webb, nor get involved in a dispute over the publisher's character.

Remarkably, it was Representative Graves who now took offense. He saw Cilley's refusal to accept the messages he passed along as an insult to *his* honor.

As a result, on February 23, 1838, he challenged Cilley to a duel! Even though he and Cilley barely knew each other and had previously borne each other no animosity.

An Affair of Dishonor

Cilley was an unlikely candidate for a gunfight. He'd been a teacher, enjoyed raising flowers, and was fascinated by beekeeping, according to the New England Historical Society.

Yet he was also principled, and outspoken in his beliefs. Faced with a challenge from a fellow congressman, as opposed to a lowly journalist, Cilley felt compelled, despite his disdain for duels, to accept. In addition, he thought backing down in the face of a threat would set a bad precedent for confrontations between Southerners and Northerners. He stated: "It is an attempt to browbeat us, and because they think I am from the East (New England) I will tamely submit."

Yet a betting man would have bet against Cilley. He had no experience with guns. Graves, on the other hand, was a good shot. For the upcoming contest, he readied his nine-inch English dueling pistols.

However, as the person who'd been challenged, Cilley got to choose the weapons. To even the score, the Cilley camp decided to fight—with rifles.

To us, this conjures up an image of two men blasting away with heavy weaponry from a few feet away. Which actually happened in some duels. But Cilley and his seconds, his companions for the duel, weren't stupid. The rifles of the time were inaccurate, the odds of hitting an opponent low. Moreover, as the person challenged, Cilley also got to set the distance between the two duelists.

He and his team set it at one hundred yards! On the day of the fight, the distance was reduced some, to ninety-four yards. Still, it was unlikely that even a skilled rifleman could hit his target at that distance with a single shot. And Graves, though handy with a pistol, had no experience with long-barreled weaponry. Indeed, not owning a rifle, he had to borrow one from one of Cilley's seconds.

It seemed the Cilley camp had turned the tables and stacked the deck against Graves. In fact, Graves's colleague Representative Wise labeled the terms of the duel "unusual and objectionable." When he told Clay this, Clay shot back that Graves "is a Kentuckian, and can never back from a rifle."

A dozen years after Clay's bloodless duel with Representative Randolph, dueling was still illegal in Washington, yet legal in Maryland. Therefore Cilley, Graves, their seconds, and their doctors—in case either was wounded—rode out to the dueling grounds of Bladensburg, Maryland, six miles from the District line.

That place was filled with ghosts: from those killed in duels, such as the valiant Navy commodore Stephen Decatur, mortally wounded there by a fellow officer in 1820, and from those killed in war, the scores of Americans and Britishers who fell at the War of 1812 battle there.

Graves had three men as his seconds, all of them Whigs who'd advised him on the duel. They were Representative Menefee, Senator Crittenden, and Representative Wise. The latter was the Virginia legislator who objected to the use of rifles. Loud and combative, the gaunt, clean-shaven Wise had been, like Webb, a Jacksonian who'd broken with the president over the BUS.

Cilley also had three men as seconds, all Democrats from the West and South. It was as if the Maine lawmaker was lending "regional balance" to his duel. His colleagues were Rep. George Wallace Jones of Wisconsin, Rep. Jesse Bynum of North Carolina, and a friend of Jones, Col. James Schaumburg. The latter was a Louisianan who'd fought sword duels on horseback!

At three o'clock in the afternoon of February 24, 1838, the two groups assembled on the broad, rolling lawn of the killing field.

The rules were the men would fire at one another during a count of four. After each shot, if the duelists were in a condition to continue, their seconds would consult on whether the contest should resume.

On that cold, windy day, Graves and a nearsighted Cilley took up their positions ninety-four yards apart. As they stood, they swiveled their hips at an angle to present a narrower target.

Both men had elegantly made, breech-loading rifles. Graves wielded a forty-five-inch-long gun of .44 caliber. (In the United States, caliber refers to the width of the barrel's interior in inches.) It was manufactured by the Derringer company of Philadelphia, better known for its pistols. Cilley's rifle was smaller: a .38-caliber that was thirty-five-and-a-half inches long. Both weapons had glossy, maple stocks, as well as motifs that strangely reflected their users' personalities. Graves's gun had tiger stripes, Cilley's a floral design.

With tense expectation, the seconds, the physicians, and a few spectators watched the lawmakers line up.

The two congressmen pointed their rifles at each other.

There was silence, as Representative Jones called out the count.

"One, two, three, four—."

Two shots went off. Holding their breaths, observers looked to see if either man had been hit. But both shooters had missed their mark. In fact, Cilley, that inexperienced gunman, had misfired.

The seconds gathered for a discussion. Sometimes, after the first shot of a duel, the contest would end. Cilley's men argued the exchange of shots had satisfied Graves's honor. They pressed their case, stating Cilley had no ill sentiment toward Graves. But Graves's men, according to the book *The Field of Blood*, noted that Cilley declined to apologize. They insisted the duel continue.

The distance between the two men was shortened to eighty yards. They reloaded their single-shot weapons.

Again, the congressmen steadied themselves, and again the onlookers tensed. Again, came the count to four.

Two shots rang out.

Cilley stood unhurt. Graves appeared to stagger, leading some to think he'd been shot. Then he steadied himself. He later explained his gun had gone off by mistake, throwing him off balance.

Both men were evidently still getting used to rifles. It seemed the strategy of the Cilley camp was working.

The seconds met for another talk. Once more they considered ending the duel. But partly because Graves had misfired, his seconds wanted to continue. Representative Wise fiercely argued for continuing as a point of honor. He recalled later "they would not and could not leave the ground under the accidents which would have caused misapprehension and perhaps ridicule."

Once again, the congressmen pointed their long-barreled guns at one another. Again, the spectators tensed.

The call went out:

"One. Two. Three. Four—."

Twin shots echoed down the lawn.

Graves was unhurt.

But Cilley reached both hands to the top of his leg. Blood spurted onto them.

"I am shot!" he called out.

He sank to the ground.

His seconds and his doctor crowded around. The bullet had struck at the very top of his leg, near the groin. It had hit his femoral artery, the main channel of blood to the leg.

Within a few minutes, Cilley bled to death.

After instigating a deadly firefight between Maine representative Jonathan Cilley and Virginia representative William Graves, publisher James Watson Webb moved about the Capitol heavily armed.

AFTERMATH

Congress and much of the nation were shocked by the killing of one congressman by another. A House committee investigated. At first, it voted four to three to expel Graves. Later he ended up censured, while avoiding expulsion. However, Graves decided against running for re-election. He never returned to Congress.

Politics colored the reaction to the duel. Cilley had been a Democrat, and Democratic president Martin Van Buren and his Cabinet attended his funeral, which took place at the House of Representatives, then controlled by Democrats. Out of protest at Cilley's death, the Supreme Court, with six of its members appointed by Van Buren and Jackson, declined to attend. The Democrat Jackson had been an eager duelist for much of his life. However, from retirement at his Hermitage estate in Nashville, he said Congress had stained its halls with blood.

Whigs were more supportive of Graves. Publisher Webb, who had brought on the duel, was very supportive. Heavily armed, he took a long and deliberative walk down Pennsylvania Avenue, daring critics of the duel to assault him.

At least the death of Congressman Cilley was the last of its kind. In 1839, an Act of Congress forbade its members from issuing a challenge to a duel or taking part in one.

The final word on the incident might go to a famed wordsmith, New England author Nathaniel Hawthorne. In 1825 he'd graduated from Maine's Bowdoin College with Cilley, and with poet Henry Wadsworth Longfellow. In a postmortem opinion piece, Hawthorne called the duel "a shadowy pretext" that had "overstepped the imaginary distinction which . . . separates manslaughter from murder."

CHAPTER NINE

Lincoln's Lodging: Abductions and Underground Rails

101 Independence Avenue S.E., now the site of the Library of Congress, Thomas Jefferson Building

"ABOLITION HOUSE" WAS A BEACON OF LIBERTY THAT JANUARY OF 1848. For years, the brick boardinghouse, just across the southeastern lawn of the Capitol Building, had hosted congressmen and public speakers calling for restrictions and bans on the "peculiar institution" of slavery.

The lodging was part of a handsome row of five three-story structures, originally dubbed Carroll's Row, after Daniel Carroll of Duddington. He was the local magnate who'd granted what became Capitol Hill to the federal government. It was his house that city designer Pierre L'Enfant had dismantled without Carroll's permission. (See the chapter on L'Enfant.)

Since the 1830s, the buildings had been owned by Duff Green, the publisher, entrepreneur, and staunch states-rights advocate. It was Green who'd confronted New York City publisher James Watson Webb, and who had been beaten up near the Capitol Building by Rep. James Blair of South Carolina. (See the chapter on the duel between Representatives Cilley and Graves.)

The two dozen lodgers at Carroll's Row included a very tall, rail-thin, rookie congressman from Illinois: Abe Lincoln, then thirty-nine. He was known for his plain attire, and for his humorous tales that diffused political spats among the boarders. In Congress, even some staunch defenders

Carroll's Row, across the street from the Capitol Building, contained the lodgings of Rep. Abraham Lincoln and other abolition-minded congressmen.

of slavery admired him. Georgia senator Alexander Hamilton Stephens said Lincoln "always attracted the riveted attention of the House when he spoke; his manner of speech as well as thought was original. He had no model. He was . . . an earnest man." An Honest Abe, you might say. His wife Mary Todd Lincoln and their young sons Robert and Edward sometimes stayed with him at the hostelry.

Like the other congressmen living there, Lincoln was a Whig. His political party was named, not after the powdered wigs of the Founding Fathers, but after a reform faction in England. For many Whigs, a key reform was to end the District's slave trade—the buying and selling of slaves. Partly due to the wild events in 1848 in the boardinghouse, and on the other side of the Capitol Building, the Whigs would morph into the Free Soil Party opposed to the extension of slavery in the western territories. Eventually they'd turn into the Republican Party demanding outright abolition. Nine Whig congressmen lived at Carroll's Row.

Different Paths to Liberty
A previous occupant, Massachusetts-bred orator Theodore Weld, was a lobbyist for the American Anti-Slavery Society. Weld counseled congressmen such as Pennsylvania representative Thaddeus Stevens about

abolition. Later Stevens would push a President Lincoln toward full emancipation.

Weld was a character, someone who would have fit in with a later era's obsession with fitness. A vegetarian, he exercised daily by running back and forth for an hour on the Capitol's East Lawn. Afterwards he might snack on the healthy new food introduced by the Reverend Sylvester Graham, the Graham cracker.

A current resident, Rep. Joshua Giddings of Ohio, was the most prominent abolitionist in Congress. Since the early 1840s, he'd helped run a congressional select committee on slavery. Its command center was in Abolition House. (Giddings was a law partner of future Ohio senator Benjamin Wade, who would give future President Lincoln grief for his more deliberate approach toward abolition.) The fifty-two-year-old Giddings had collaborated with congressman and former president John Quincy Adams, in their years-long battle to end the House "gag rule." The gag rule was not a ban on humorous behavior in the Capitol Building (such a restriction would be impossible), but a prohibition on debating the issue of slavery. It is remarkable in retrospect that Congress long forbade even talking about the most pressing issue of the time.

Stalwart abolitionist Rep. Joshua Giddings of Ohio helped overturn the House's "gag rule" on debating slavery, and may have taken part in the city's Underground Railroad.

Back in 1842, the House had censured Giddings for violating the gag rule over the *Creole* ship incident. American slaves being transported on that brig from Richmond, Virginia, to New Orleans had rebelled. After seizing control of the ship, they sailed it into the British Bahamas. There they were free, as the British Empire had ended slavery.

Giddings argued before the House that the US government should neither compel the British to return the slaves, nor pay compensation to their former owners. In the end, Giddings won. The slaves stayed free, the gag rule was thrown out, and the congressman was triumphantly re-elected by his constituents.

Giddings knew of, and may have aided, the capital's Underground Railroad. This was the secretive collection of safe houses, individuals, and transit routes that moved escaped slaves from the South to the free states of the North. At a minimum, the congressman and fellow abolitionists at the lodging corresponded with former slaves who had fled the District to freedom.

The boarding home's landlady, despite public professions to the contrary, seemed to echo the views of her lodgers. Forty-eight-year-old Ann G. Thornton Sprigg was the widow of Benjamin Sprigg, a House of Representatives clerk who died in 1833. To support her family of five children, Ann managed the hostelry. (It seems she was unrelated to Anna Thornton, the widow of Capitol Building designer Dr. William Thornton.)

In 1820, Benjamin Sprigg had owned eight slaves. By 1840 Ann, who had inherited her husband's servants, had only free black workers residing at the house. At times she did employ slaves. But she only hired slaves who were earning wages to buy their own freedom. One reason for this was that enslaved servants with no prospect of altering their plight tended to run away. Still, under Ann Sprigg's tutelage, Abolition House had transformed into a kind of freedom house.

As mentioned before, and paralleling the decline in the region's once-dominant tobacco industry, quite a few enslaved persons were obtaining their freedom. For that reason, Washington City was from early on a center of African-American life. In the thirty years before the Civil War, the percentage of slaves in the city plummeted, from 12 percent to just 3 percent.

However, many slaveowners had "surplus" slaves, whom they were tempted to sell to the new and very profitable cotton plantations in the Deep South. Slaves fearing such a fate had added incentive to flee the city for the North.

Ann Sprigg had once employed a freed African American, Thomas Smallwood. Smallwood and white abolitionist Charles Torrey had helped run a major local branch of the Underground Railroad. The duo funneled hundreds of escaped slaves from the region to the free states, according to author John O'Brien. In fact, New York Rep. Seth Gates had referred an enslaved waiter at the Sprigg lodgings to Torrey and Smallwood for his escape north. After Maryland authorities in 1844 arrested Torrey, William L. Chaplin, a transplanted New Yorker, took over as the chief manager of the District's Underground Railroad.

ABDUCTORS AND GUARDIAN ANGELS

One of the slaves working his way to freedom at Sprigg's was Henry Wilson. He was a waiter there, and his wife Sylvia, a "free woman of color," was a maid in Sprigg's employ. (Henry Wilson happened to have the same name as a future abolitionist senator from Massachusetts.) Wilson had an agreement with his owner, a local woman, to buy his freedom from her for $350. As 1848 began, he had just $60 left to pay off.

But then came the horrific night of January 14, 1848. Wilson's owner had decided to renege on their deal—and sell him instead. And at his full price of $300, after already collecting most of that sum!

Three slave traders with pistols burst into the Sprigg boardinghouse. They seized Wilson by the throat and handcuffed him, according to Kenneth Winkle's book *Lincoln's Citadel*. As his wife Sylvia watched in horror, they pulled the waiter outside and hustled him into a getaway carriage. "Poor Sylvia," noted Rep. Giddings, "was overwhelmed with grief."

Giddings wrote that he "could not sit down quietly in the midst of so much distress." He and another Sprigg lodger, Rep. Abraham McIlvaine of Pennsylvania, rushed over to Williams Pen. This was a jail for slaves, owned by a man named William W. Williams. It was sometimes called the "Yellow House" from the color of its walls. The overseer there was a dreaded slave trader named James H. Burch (sometimes spelled *Birch*).

Williams Pen was located at Maryland Avenue and 7th Street, S.W., south of the Smithsonian Castle and near today's L'Enfant Plaza. Its two-floor brick building stood next to a stockade: a yard with a tall wooden fence to block prying eyes. Slaves or, at times, free persons of color who'd been kidnapped, were kept there under watchful guard. Foes of slavery might sardonically remark Williams Pen was similar to the name of, but the opposite to the beliefs of, abolitionist Quaker William Penn, of namesake Pennsylvania.

Washington, DC, had a number of such slave jails. Several were on 7th Street on either side of the National Mall. In fact, the city's commercial hub was the Center Market on 7th and Pennsylvania Avenue, N.W. Other slave pens were in the basements of hotels. One was at the United States Hotel at 3rd Street and Pennsylvania Avenue, near the western edge of the Capitol Building. In that hotel Burch maintained thirty-six-foot-long slave cells, complete with manacles and metal rings on the walls.

Enslaved African Americans were kept in such places before being sold or shipped elsewhere for resale. They were often sent first to Alexandria, Virginia, the nearby riverport town which had been part of the District until 1846. Whole families of slaves might be broken up and sold and sent by foot or ship to the large slave market in New Orleans, and then to the cotton fields.

Giddings noted the atmosphere of Williams Pen was predictably grim. "The whole contour of the buildings and grounds appeared in harmony with the piratical vocation to which they were appropriated," he stated. "Its inmates, both slave dealers and victims, appeared to be isolated from all sympathy and association with the moral world around them, as they were separated physically from all other buildings of the city."

Reps. Giddings and McIlvaine met with two of Williams's slave traders and inquired about Wilson. To the congressmen's dismay, they were told: "The negur has gone. We took him immediately onboard ship at Alexandria, and he has sailed for New Orleans." Giddings reacted that "we were in a barbarous land, controlled by barbarous laws," according to the blog Bytes of History.

Many would have given up at that point, but not Giddings. Several days later, on the House floor, at the site of today's Statuary Hall, he denounced the abduction in general and the slave trade in general. He stated that the "colored man had been employed in [Sprigg's] boarding-house for several years, had become well and favorably known to members of this House, had married a wife in this city, and under a contract to purchase his freedom for the sum of three hundred dollars, had by great industry paid that sum within about sixty dollars . . .

"Outrages like the foregoing," the representative continued, "have been of common occurrence in this district, and are sanctioned by the laws of Congress, and are extremely painful to many of the members of this House, as well as in themselves inhuman."

Even more to the point, Giddings met with the owner of Mrs. Sprigg's boardinghouse, the ubiquitous Duff Green. Although a slave-owner himself, the tough, kinetic Green, then fifty-six, had reason to be upset over the abduction. He owned the premises where the violent seizure had occurred. He took his meals at Mrs. Sprigg's table with its congressmen. He personally knew Giddings, Sprigg, and Wilson, and was even related by marriage to Mrs. Lincoln.

The owner of Rep. Abraham Lincoln's boardinghouse, journalist and entrepreneur Duff Green, acted decisively to free a servant at the lodging from unscrupulous slave traders.

Green may have also thought the incident put the institution of slavery in a bad light. It was true he was no abolitionist: His daughter had married a son of South Carolina senator John C. Calhoun, the apostle of secession residing up the street at the Old Capitol boardinghouse. A residence for Southern lawmakers, it was a counterpoint to Abolition House. (See the chapter on the Confederate jail.)

Whatever his motive, Green sent the owner of Williams Pen a letter seeking Wilson's return. Williams replied he would sell Wilson back—for $700! Green rejected the overpriced offer. He threatened to enlist the city's district attorney against Williams, according to *Lincoln's Citadel*. Green wrote Williams again, stating that if Wilson's return was "not done immediately, we will take efficient measures to compel his return, and to do all that is in our power to prevent the recurrence of a similar outrage."

Wary of Green's influence in town, Williams backed off, and responded through a legal intermediary. The attorney, a member of the city council, informed Green that Wilson's owner was willing to part with him, in return for $180: the $60 that Wilson had remaining to pay off, and the $120 or so she had already spent, she said, from what Williams had paid her for the sale. Green branded the greedy woman a "Jezebel," an evil queen of ancient Israel. However, he agreed to the deal.

A relieved Giddings then organized a unique fundraiser to make up the $180. He passed the hat in Congress. The congressmen in the Whig caucus, including Lincoln, chipped in $5 each. "Jezebel" got her money. In February, six weeks after the abduction, Giddings was overjoyed to greet Wilson, now a free man, outside the doorway of the Abolition House.

A PEARL BEFORE SWINE

The District before emancipation could be a terrifying place for blacks, enslaved or free. For some it was intolerable. Three months after the Henry Wilson episode, unfree blacks, with the help of sympathetic whites, undertook a daring attempt at mass emancipation.

If Congressman Lincoln had walked out from Abolition House on the cloudy night of April 15, 1848, and crossed the Capitol grounds to its western side near the Mall, he might have noticed something unusual: individuals and small groups of people walking quickly, and furtively, past the Capitol Building toward the Anacostia River wharf at the end of 7th Street, one mile south, the site of today's renovated Wharf district. Some were riding there by horse or hack cab.

Lincoln might have noticed that all the people on the move were African American. They moved fast, for they needed to get to their destination before 10:00 p.m. That was when the city-wide curfew kicked in. Any black person outdoors after that hour had to have a special pass of permission. Otherwise the penalty for missing the curfew could be ten heavy lashes of a whip. The travelers, who included thirteen children, numbered seventy-six people in all (some accounts peg the tally at seventy-seven). If Representative Lincoln had tried greeting any of them, they would have silently kept going, fearful of attracting attention.

Before 10:00 p.m. the walkers and riders reached their goal. A fifty-four-ton masted schooner, the *Pearl*, was waiting at a secluded spot on the wharf. On board were two white seamen: the pilot and part-owner of the ship, Edward Sayres, and the leader of the expedition, forty-six-year-old Daniel Drayton. The latter was a veteran skipper of many voyages, legal and illegal, in the Chesapeake region. Just the autumn before, Drayton had aided an enslaved woman and five children in bondage to depart for freedom in the North. Chaplin, the Underground Railroad "conductor," was an organizer of the *Pearl* scheme. He paid Drayton and Sayres for their task. It was a daring and dangerous one.

To co-captain the largest planned slave escape in American history.

The escape emerged from the conundrum faced by Daniel Bell, a free African American and a blacksmith at the Navy Yard. Daniel was married to a woman named Mary with whom he had many children. On the death of her owner, Mary Bell had been freed, and the term of her children's enslavement had been limited. But the owner's widow reneged and took the Bells to court. The court ruled the owner could retain the Bells' children as slaves for life. Stymied by the law, Daniel and Mary Bell determined to flee north with their brood.

Chaplin arranged with Drayton and Sayres to take the Bells up north by ship. At some point Drayton informed an abolitionist in town, perhaps Representative Giddings, that the *Pearl* could take on board many people. The word went out among the African-American grapevine, and the number of escapees grew considerably.

Some of those fleeing were inspired by the rhetoric of freedom in the air. In spring 1848, democratic revolutions were breaking out throughout Europe, from Ireland to Russia, inspired in part by the American republic. In a speech near the White House acknowledging events abroad, anti-abolitionist Sen. Henry Foote of Mississippi, without irony, declared the following: "The age of tyrants and of slavery was rapidly drawing to a close . . . the universal emancipation of man from the fetters of civic oppression [progresses] . . . the great principles of popular sovereignty, equality, and brotherhood was at this moment visibly commencing."

The greatest slave escape of all needed a lot of planning, and funding. The scheme was probably financed by New York abolitionist Gerrit Smith. And Chaplin got help from the local Underground Railroad, an important member of which was Samuel Edmonson. He arranged to have five of his enslaved brothers and sisters depart on the *Pearl*. They included Mary and Emily Edmonson, ages fifteen and thirteen, respectively. Remarkably, the former manservant for President Madison, Paul Jennings, now free, was one of the plotters. A US senator, noted orator Daniel Webster of Massachusetts, may have been involved as well. (Webster had purchased Jennings for the purpose of him buying his own freedom.) Chaplin spoke to Representative Giddings of the plot, likely at the Sprigg house, the night before the *Pearl* set sail.

Pursuit on the Potomac

With seventy-eight hopeful souls aboard, including the skippers, the *Pearl* slipped from its berth. Its voyage was slowed at first by a contrary tide and a calm. Then the ship, its sails billowing, cruised down the Potomac to where the broad river turns north into the mighty Chesapeake. At that point, strong and contrary gusts forced Drayton and Sayres to make for safe harbor. The stop was unfortunate for, back at the federal city, word of the escape had leaked out.

The morning after the departure, some forty-one slaveowners throughout town noticed many of their charges were missing. Servants were absent from kitchens, gardens, and hotels. Rumors spread, soon confirmed by facts. Some of the news was conveyed by a Judas, a black hack driver named Diggs. He'd driven escapees to the *Pearl*, while still upset over a failed love match with Emily Edmonson. Aware of the ship's mission, he betrayed the escape to the authorities.

An influential citizen owned some of those who'd fled. That was Francis Dodge Jr., co-owner with several other slaveholders of a large Georgetown warehouse for tobacco, the plantation crop which had made that town's fortune.

Dodge acted fast. His family owned one of the quickest ships on the river, a steam-powered craft, the *Salem*. A posse of thirty or more men carrying muskets boarded it and readied two small cannons on the deck.

Led by police official W. C. Williams, the craft raced down the Potomac in pursuit of the *Pearl*.

The posse had almost given up its search as the *Salem* neared the mouth of the Chesapeake. It was daunting to trace a boat in the vast Bay. But suddenly, Williams's men spotted the *Pearl* berthed along shore.

The slaves had been singing hymns of deliverance, to be unfulfilled. Some of those fleeing wanted to make a fight of it, but they had no weapons. Drayton and Sayres, their cause hopeless, surrendered the ship. The *Salem* towed it back to the Anacostia wharf.

On the District waterfront, Officer Williams placed a manacled Drayton and Sayres at the front of the group of prisoners. The male slaves were bound and marched in double file. The women and children tramped behind them, with policemen carefully watching. All were accompanied by a howling mob, enraged at the attempted escape. Its size and ferocity increased during the trudge back into town.

As the procession neared the National Mall, it passed one of the slave markets, called Gannon's after its owner. Gannon himself raced over and lunged at Drayton with a knife.

"Lynch them!" screamed the crowd. "Damn villains!" they cried, according to author Stanley C. Harrold Jr.

Outside the United States Hotel, where Burch had his slave pen, some in the throng cried: "Shoot the hell hound! Lynch them!"

A man tried to assault Sayres, according to the Historical Society of Washington, DC, before a policeman slammed the assailant to the ground.

The peace officers feared the crowd would tear the co-captains to pieces. They hustled them into a hack, which took them to the city jail, a dank, blue-painted prison, nicknamed "the Blue Jug," three blocks northwest of the Capitol Building in Judiciary Square. An angry crowd milled outside the place. The captured African Americans were thrown into cells as well.

As he had with Wilson, Representative Giddings rose to the occasion. He spoke before Congress, questioning why the escapees had been jailed without formal charges. He visited Drayton and Sayres in prison, assuring them they would get defense counsel. He also visited the slaves, as the mob raged outside.

Someone in the crowd procured a key to open the prison gates. About three dozen men rushed inside and milled menacingly around a stairway near Giddings. The congressman managed to leave unscathed. Back at the Sprigg boardinghouse, persons upset over Giddings's support for the escapees pushed angry notes under the door to his room.

A Publisher Under Siege

More turmoil spun out from the *Pearl* incident. On Tuesday, April 18, after the ship's capture, an angry crowd surrounded a two-story brick building containing the offices and printing press of an abolitionist newspaper, the *National Era*. It stood eight blocks from Congress near the site of the old General Post Office Building, today's Monaco Hotel. Rioters, hoping to destroy the print works, smashed up the publication's windows and doors. They demanded its earnest publisher, Gamaliel Bailey of Ohio, get out of town.

Bailey had seen this kind of trouble before: In Cincinnati, pro-slavery mobs had twice wrecked his printing press. Still, he was determined to bring the emancipation message to the capital city. Chaplin, as he had with Representative Giddings, gave Bailey advance word of the *Pearl*'s escape. It's unclear whether Bailey had a hand in the planning, but many Washingtonians thought so.

The city's first police chief was J. H. Goddard; his formal title was Captain of the Auxiliary Guard and Night Watch. He'd been appointed years before after a physical assault by Whig partisans on President John Tyler. He was charged with protecting Bailey's offices from the mob.

Goddard and his men, wielding long hickory bludgeons with iron tips, pushed the crowd away. They were aided by some prominent private citizens, some of whom disagreed with, but liked, the affable Bailey. The crowd retreated. A drenching storm sent the remnants of the trouble-makers home.

However, a larger group returned the next evening. It included out-of-town slave traders and numbered anywhere from five hundred to four thousand people, according to differing newspaper accounts. Fortunately, some civic leaders diverted the throng from the *National Era* to the steps of the Patent Office (today's National Portrait Gallery) one block away, for a public meeting. Wags eyeing rioters grasping rocks joked the gathering was just a "stone's throw" from Bailey's publication. Ruffians also threatened Bailey personally, at his nearby home at 8th and E Street N.W. Several congressmen spirited Bailey's wife and five children safely away to the mayor's home.

Echoing the mob, city potentates urged Bailey to get out of Dodge, and to take his printing press with him. The publisher was a short and thinly built man but possessed considerable nerve. He responded to his critics with an elegant defense of freedom of speech: "You are demanding from me the surrender of a great constitutional right. . . . How can you ask me to abandon it and become a party to my own degradation?"

From the White House, President James Knox Polk followed the turmoil. Though a slaveholding Tennessean, Polk forbade government employees from taking part in the rioting. He also arranged to have up to one hundred marshals supplement the small city police force guarding the newspaper. After a few days, the crowds dispersed, without any-one seriously harmed. Many Washingtonians, and some in Congress, congratulated themselves for defusing the matter without widespread destruction.

THE *PEARL*'S POSTSCRIPT

Abolitionists and advocates of free speech in Congress pushed for an inquiry into the causes of the riot. But the House tabled the notion by a large margin of 130–42. Even Lincoln, viewing an investigation as futile, voted with the majority.

Some of the language in the debate was violent. New Hampshire senator John P. Hale would be the nominee that year of the Liberty Party, the first party to stand explicitly for abolition. Hale called for legislation making the city liable for damages from public disorders. Senator Foote, who'd waxed eloquently about liberty in Europe, replied brutally. Foote stated that if Hale traveled to his home state he "could not go ten miles into the interior, before he would grace one of the tallest trees of the forest, with a rope around his neck."

The city government put the crew of the *Pearl* on trial. A court charged Drayton and Sayres with seventy-six counts of theft and set their bail at $76,000 (about $2.5 million in 2020 dollars). But Giddings was good to his word about finding an effective defense attorney, namely, lawyer and educator Horace Mann of Massachusetts. And now a congressman too, as Mann had been elected to fill the House seat of the deceased John Quincy Adams. Mann had been part of the Adams legal team that in 1841 famously freed rebellious slaves aboard the *Amistad* ship.

In the *Pearl* case, Mann got the more serious charges of thievery dropped. He argued persuasively that men trying to bring other people to freedom could not be considered thieves. Yet Mann failed to stop Drayton and Sayres's conviction on illegal transportation. The court sentenced them to prison at the Blue Jug. (President Millard Fillmore of New York, a former House leader and a Whig, pardoned the pair in 1852.)

The outlook for the captured slaves was grim. Their masters, deeming them untrustworthy, sold them off to new owners via the Bruin and Hill

After their failed escape aboard the *Pearl* schooner, Rev. Henry Ward Beecher arranged to purchase the freedom of slaves Mary and Emily Edmonson, while Beecher's sister, Harriet Ward Beecher Stowe, went on to pen *Uncle Tom's Cabin*.

slave trading company in Alexandria. The Bells' children were sold to a slave trader in Baltimore. Lincoln would later brand such flesh merchants as "a sneaking . . . class of native tyrants, known as the 'SLAVE-DEALER' . . . instinctively shrinking from the snaky contact." Even many slaveowners despised such men.

Within days of the failed escape, fifty slaves were chained together and marched down Pennsylvania Avenue from their jail to a train depot, then located west of the Capitol Building. Most of the unfortunates were shipped to New Orleans. When a yellow fever outbreak hit Crescent City, some were sent back to Virginia. Most wound up with new owners in Louisiana or Georgia.

A lucky few were spared a lasting exile. Local landowner Thomas Blagden gave Daniel Bell the money to purchase the freedom of his wife and one of his children. Further, the young Edmonson sisters became cause célèbres among abolitionists. A noted one, the Reverend Henry Ward Beecher, from Brooklyn Heights, New York, took up a collection among his congregation. It raised $2,250 to buy the freedom of the sisters through Bruin and Hill. (Union marshals would confiscate its slave pen in the Civil War.) Three other Edmonson children were also bought and freed. Moreover, their story lent inspiration to Rev. Beecher's sister, a lady named Harriet Ward Beecher Stowe.

With slave escapes and abductions as inspiration, she penned the abolitionist novel *Uncle Tom's Cabin*, a smashing bestseller, and the origin of the term Uncle Tom. Gamaliel Bailey excerpted it in the *National Era*. His newspaper kept publishing, riot-free, until the dawn of the Civil War.

AN UNDERGROUND GROUND UNDER

In the short run, the failure of the *Pearl* escape spurred many slaveholders in the District to sell their slaves to new owners in the Deep South. The incident terrified Border-State communities about a slave rebellion. It dried up funds for the region's Underground Railroad. And it pushed city police to shut down Chaplin's local version of the Railroad, in spectacular fashion.

In August 1850, Chaplin was transporting two escaped slaves named Garland and Allen in a carriage to the edge of the District. It was the start of their freedom ride to the Northern states. However, police chief Goddard learned of Chaplin's plan. The very man who'd guarded Bailey's newspaper was also in charge of running down escapees.

Goddard had had run-ins with "conductors" before: He once searched the home of Underground Railroad operator Smallwood for a fleeing female slave. Smallwood had fooled Goddard by hiding the woman in his back garden under a pile of corn.

For Captain Goddard and his posse of five slave catchers, the two escapees with Chaplin were of special interest. For they were owned by two US senators, both from Georgia. Garland belonged to Sen. Robert

Toombs, and Allen was a slave of Senator Stephens, the legislator who admired Lincoln. The two senators were fierce defenders of slavery and, in time, of secession. Toombs would serve as the Confederacy's first secretary of state, and Stephens as its vice president.

When Chaplin's hired carriage reached Silver Spring, Maryland, a wild fight erupted. Goddard and his slave catchers stopped the conveyance by shoving a wooden rail into its wheels. The slaves were desperate, and armed, and one or both fired at the deputies, then fled from the hack. Goddard's men fired back, wounding both of the slaves. Allen was captured, and Garland escaped, according to the Historical Marker Database. The posse seized Chaplin and beat him. Garland surrendered to authorities after a few days.

TROUBLE AFOOT

The events of 1848–1850 were reflected in the Senate's Compromise of 1850, an act passed one month after the Chaplin shootout. Rancorous sessions in Congress highlighted the North and South's stark slavery divide. Lawmakers fearing violence attended the sessions armed. Kentucky's Sen. Henry Clay, author of the Missouri Compromise of 1820 over the same issue, led a last-ditch effort for another accord.

At the time of the congressional debates, Senator Foote had taken issue with the influential senator from Missouri Thomas Hart Benton. Benton was the lawmaker who'd keenly commented on the 1835 assassination attempt on President Jackson. Benton had grown increasingly dubious of slavery. Foote had publicly attacked Benton in personal terms, and the latter hinted a duel was in order.

At a Senate session, Benton eyed Foote, threw his chair aside, and rushed down the aisle toward his antagonist. In response, the Mississippian pulled out a long-barreled horse pistol. He nervously aimed it at Benton. The Missourian, a US Army veteran of frontier brawls and fights with Andy Jackson, little feared the diminutive Foote. With contempt, Benton opened his jacket and thrust out his chest, shouting: "I have no pistols! . . . Stand out of the way and let the assassin fire!"

Foote, gun in hand, pondered pulling the trigger. For a moment, it seemed a senator would kill a fellow senator, and in the halls of Congress.

Lawmakers watched in horror. Then a third senator took the weapon away from Foote, and stashed it in a drawer.

Cartoonists gleefully mocked the episode. One illustration showed terrified spectators fleeing the Senate gallery, as Senator Clay cautioned calm:

"It is a ridiculous matter. I apprehend there is no danger on 'foot'!"

To appease slaveowners worried about their servants going on the lam, the Senate passed a strengthened Fugitive Slave Act as part of the Compromise. It enabled lawmen to enter Northern states to bring back escaped slaves. Northerners, not to mention slaves, hated that. However, the new law also handed the residents of Abolition House a major win. It banned the slave trade in the District: the buying and selling of slaves at pens like the Yellow House.

That time of tumult had a major impact on a lodger of the Abolition House, Rep. Abraham Lincoln. In early 1849, he made a proposal to Congress to abolish slavery in the capital. It was a relatively modest measure. His ban would take place gradually, would have to be approved by local referendum, and owners would be compensated for the market value of their slaves.

As expected, Lincoln's notion went nowhere. Yet it had the outlines of the scheme he employed for the city after he was elected president. A year before his Emancipation Proclamation went in effect for much of the country, the Great Emancipator ended slavery in Washington—by buying out its slaveowners. The action is celebrated in the District every year as Emancipation Day.

In 1864, a year after his Emancipation Proclamation, President Lincoln penned a much less famous missive. It was to his Treasury secretary, asking he grant the elderly Ann Sprigg a job as a clerk.

Lincoln wrote that Sprigg "is a most estimable widow lady, at whose house I boarded many years ago when a member of Congress. She now is very needy; & any employment suitable to a lady could not be bestowed on a more worthy person."

With that sterling recommendation, Sprigg got the position, and worked there until her death in 1868.

In a city, and a nation, free of slavery.

Chapter Ten

Raising Cain and the Specter of War: The Worst Attack by a Congressman on a Congressman in Congress

The Senate chamber, north side of the Capitol Building

THE NATION, THE CITY, AND THE SENATE WERE TENSE THAT HOT afternoon of May 22, 1856. The telegraph wires were transmitting word the town of Lawrence, in the new territory of Kansas, had been sacked by pro-slavery men. It was two years after Congress had passed the Kansas-Nebraska Act, which had split up a great chunk of the Great Plains into two territories that would soon apply for statehood. Groups for and against slavery had been moving into the areas in hopes of making the turf their own.

CLOUDS BEFORE THE STORM

That January, with the Kansas issue as background, a deadlocked House of Representatives had taken 132 votes to elect a new Speaker. To the consternation of the South, the House finally chose Nathaniel Banks of Massachusetts, a "free-soil" advocate in favor of banning slavery in any new lands. But not before Rep. Albert Rust of Arkansas had caned *New York Tribune* publisher Horace Greeley, just outside the Capitol Building, for questioning Rust's motives in trying to block Banks. For good measure, Rust later that day assaulted Greeley with his fists, outside the publisher's National Hotel lodgings down Pennsylvania Avenue. Fearful of another attack, Greeley noted he was "too sick to be out of bed, too crazy to sleep . . . surrounded by horrors." To protect themselves, Washington reporters and congressmen headed to work at the Capitol with pistols and knives tucked within their clothes.

Another fault line in the nation's politics had been revealed two weeks before, at the Willard Hotel near the White House. Rep. Philemon Herbert, of California by way of Alabama, and a staunch slavery advocate, had flown into a rage over a waiter's failure to provide him breakfast. A wild fight ensued in which the two men had thrown knives and crockery at each other. Herbert cursed the waiter's Irish ancestry—and then shot him to death. As the congressional Democrat had support from the mostly Northern Know-Nothing Party opposed to Irish-Catholic immigration, the slaying had undertones of the growing nativist vs. immigrant divide. Alternatively, some Northerners attributed Herbert's mayhem to his Southern, secessionist views, and a politics of violent intolerance.

A DC federal court would try Herbert for manslaughter. The prosecuting attorney was Philip Barton Key II. But Key was sympathetic to Southerners, and the jury was packed with Know-Nothings, and Herbert walked.

The grand meeting place of the Senate in antebellum days.

Then came The Speech: Sen. Charles Sumner's oration, "The Crime Against Kansas." A five-hour stemwinder delivered from memory over two days, to transfixed lawmakers and packed galleries in Benjamin Latrobe's Old Senate Chamber.

SLAMMING THE SLAVE POWER

The speech was delivered by a vain, learned, stubborn, and brave man from Massachusetts, the forty-five-year-old Sumner. Six-foot-four, lanky, with a powerful upper body, Sumner was then a leading advocate of abolition.

He'd attended Harvard Law School, where he'd come under the wing of Joseph Story, a long-serving US Supreme Court justice. It was Story who wrote the opinion in the *Amistad* case. Its 1841 verdict ordered the freeing of slaves who'd entered an American port after they staged a successful revolt aboard their slave ship. (It's the subject of a 1997 Steven Spielberg film starring Anthony Hopkins as John Quincy Adams.) During a trip to France, Sumner took note of talented black students at the Sorbonne. He concluded: "It must be then that the distance between free blacks and whites among us is derived from education and does not exist in the nature of things."

Entering the US Senate in 1851, in his maiden speech he savaged the Compromise of 1850 and its Fugitive Slave Act. On that occasion, an opposing senator from the Deep South shrugged off Sumner's talk with mild derision: "The ravings of a maniac may sometimes be dangerous, but the barking of a puppy never did any harm."

Sumner aimed his Kansas philippic at a national audience. Before he spoke, he had its 112 printed pages typeset for publication. With it, he targeted the Kansas-Nebraska Act, which hadn't banned slavery in those territories. Instead, it had left it up to settlers to decide, under the doctrine of "popular sovereignty." The hands-off approach touched off a scramble between pro-slavery and antislavery groups to lay claim to the regions. As the assault on the town of Lawrence, Kansas, showed, it was a recipe for carnage.

Sumner was deliberately provocative. He termed pro-slavery Kansas settlers the "drunken spew and vomit of an uneasy civilization." Henry

Wadsworth Longfellow noted Sumner spoke "like a cannoneer ramming down cartridges."

The Massachusetts senator launched broadsides at three men. One was Virginia senator James Mason, the grandson of George Mason, and unlike his ancestor an advocate of slavery's expansion. The second was powerful Illinois senator Stephen Arnold Douglas, the prime proponent of popular sovereignty. Sumner was not known for diplomatic language. In private, he termed Douglas a "brutal, vulgar man" who "looks as if he needs clean linen and should be put under a shower bath." In his speech, he referred to Douglas as a "noise-some, squat, and nameless animal."

But Sumner's main fire was reserved for the sickly, fifty-nine-year-old Sen. Andrew Butler of South Carolina. Butler had coauthored Kansas-Nebraska.

Sumner compared his fellow lawmaker to a hypocritical knight errant who takes slavery as his prostitute. "The senator from South Carolina," he stated, "believes himself a chivalrous knight with sentiments of honor and courage. Of course he has chosen a mistress to whom he has made his vows, and who, though ugly to others, is always lovely to him; though polluted in the sight of the world, is chaste in his sight—I mean the harlot, slavery. . . ."

As he listened in on the speech, Douglas said of Sumner that "this damn fool is going to get himself killed by some other damn fool."

AN AVENGER AND HIS ALLIES

But far more upset than Douglas was Butler's cousin: two-term South Carolina congressman Preston Smith Brooks. Butler had suffered a stroke and couldn't defend himself. The thirty-five-year-old Brooks figured he'd defend his relative instead.

The personal echoed the political. Brooks believed in a kind of "domino theory" about Kansas: that if it became a free state, the free-soil movement would spread to the slave states of Missouri and Texas. Further, the volatile Brooks had a past marked by violence. He was kicked out of college, from the future University of South Carolina, for brandishing a gun at an officer of the law. In an 1840 duel with a prominent attorney, he'd shot his foe in both legs, and had himself been shot in the leg. The wound left him with a permanent limp, and a need for a walking stick.

In that era, when a man of standing, especially a Southern man, felt his honor was impugned, he'd often challenge the man who crossed him to a duel. After Sumner's verbal assault on Butler, Brooks consulted with two other congressmen from the South on what action he should take.

One was Rep. Lawrence Keitt, a fellow South Carolinian, from present-day Calhoun County, named after the apostle of Southern rights, John C. Calhoun. Then in his second term, Keitt was one of the "fire-breathers" already calling for South-

This illustration of South Carolina representative Preston Brooks captures the bellicosity of the man who nearly beat a fellow legislator to death.

ern secession. Brooks's other advisor was four-term representative Henry Alonzo Edmundson, a major landowner in Virginia's fertile Shenandoah Valley. Both of these counselors, like Brooks, were apt to settle disputes with violence.

During an 1854 debate over Kansas-Nebraska, Edmundson had threatened a congressman from Ohio, before the House sergeant-at-arms broke things up. (The sergeant is the lead official for law enforcement and protocol.) Two years later, during the raucous debate over the new House Speaker, Edmundson threatened ardent abolitionist Rep. Joshua Giddings, the defender of the *Pearl* slave escapees. Giddings, channeling Shakespeare, had mocked Edmundson's temper: "Go, show your slaves how choleric you are/And make your bondmen tremble."

In 1860, in a weird follow-up to the Brooks-Sumner affair, Edmundson would strike Pennsylvania's Rep. John Hickman with his cane as Hickman departed the House down the Capitol steps. Hickman had derided Edmundson's home state over its fear of a slave rebellion. Rep.

John Cabell Breckinridge of Kentucky, the future vice president of the Confederacy, happened by, and he led Hickman away before Edmundson could injure him further.

In 1856, Representative Keitt would be at the center of the worst brawl in congressional history. It happened during an angry debate over a proposed, pro-slavery state constitution for Kansas. Rep. Galusha Grow of Pennsylvania, a free-soil Republican, had wandered over to the Southern side of the aisle. (In an echo of the French Revolution, the Democrats, making up the more "radical" party, then sat on the left side of the legislature, while Republicans, the more "conservative," pro-business faction, camped out on the right side. We still use the terms *Left* and *Right* in politics today.)

Keitt called the abolitionist Grow a "black Republican puppy," and demanded he go back to his party's side of the aisle. Grow retorted: "No negro driver shall crack his whip over me." Keitt rushed over and went for Grow's throat, according to the *Saturday Evening Post*. Hell broke loose. About fifty representatives from both sides fell into a bedlam of punching, grabbing, and clawing. Two Republican congressmen from Wisconsin, John "Bowie Knife" Potter and Cadwallader Washburn, tore the wig off of Rep. William Barksdale, a Mississippi Democrat. A mortified Barksdale retrieved his hair piece—and put it on backwards. Seeing this, the rioters doubled up with laughter. The donnybrook ended, with none seriously hurt.

In the discussions that followed Sumner's speech, Keitt advised Brooks that the New Englander was "no gentleman." Thus, under the arcane code for duels, it was beneath Brooks to challenge him to a pistol fight. Further, Brooks and his handlers knew that, since the 1838 killing of Rep. Jonathan Cilley by Rep. William Graves, it a was a federal crime for a congressman to take part in a duel. (See the chapter on the Cilley-Graves confrontation.)

Brooks considered his other options. He later said he "speculated somewhat as to whether I should employ a horsewhip or a cowhide; but knowing that the Senator was my superior in strength, it occurred to me that he might wrest it from my hand."

So Brooks decided to confront Sumner in the Capitol Building, and insist they step outside to the Capitol grounds to have it out. Then he changed his mind, and instead loitered on the Capitol grounds, hoping to encounter Sumner leaving the building. Losing patience, the mercurial Carolinian then determined on a direct attack in the Senate.

THE CANING HEARD ROUND THE COUNTRY

Late in the day on May 22, Brooks, flanked by Keitt and Edmundson, entered the Senate chamber. Sumner was at his heavy desk, its legs bolted to the floor, sending out copies of his speech. He was attaching the "franking" marks that let a congressman send out correspondence for free. At that late hour, most lawmakers and spectators had left, and Brooks and his two House companions waited impatiently for the stragglers to go.

One of those remaining was a young woman. Brooks asked a congressional secretary to tell her to leave. The male secretary was reluctant, jesting that the lady was "very pretty." Brooks answered, "Yes, she is pretty, but I wish she would go."

Finally, all the spectators departed. Only Sumner and some other congressmen and political officials remained.

Brooks, limping from his old dueling wound, walked up to the front of the senator's desk.

He grasped an eleven-and-a-half-ounce walking stick, hollow-bodied but of hard latex, with a gold knob on its end.

Sumner was nearsighted, and too vain to wear glasses. He looked up and eyed the blurry figure before him.

"Mr. Sumner," Brooks began in a low voice, "I have read your speech twice over carefully. It is a libel on South Carolina, and Mr. Butler, who is a relative of mine."

As Sumner rose, Brooks suddenly struck. He smashed the cane onto the top of Sumner's head. The first blow was so crushing that Sumner momentarily lost his eyesight.

Standing over the senator, Brooks raised and brought down his cane half a dozen times. His weapon cut into Sumner's face and scalp.

The senator tried to get up, but his big legs got stuck under the bolted-down desk. Brooks reared above him, smashing away.

Brooks may have intended at first to merely humiliate Sumner, perhaps with a few blows, and then pulling his nose or ears. But his blood was up.

Sumner, stunned, unable to see or fight back, tried to take cover under the desk. Brooks continued his thrashing. Then, with a mighty effort, Sumner rose up—and tore the desk from its hinges.

But Brooks kept attacking, even as his stick splintered and broke. He gripped the fractured part that remained, and struck again, and again. He grabbed Sumner by his jacket lapel to steady him for more lashings. He later recalled that "every lick went where I intended."

Sumner cried out in agony: "Oh Lord, oh!" He staggered down the Senate's aisle. Brooks followed right behind, smashing away. The cane's gold head popped off from the pummeling and rolled along the floor.

Several men, including a New York reporter, moved in to stop the carnage.

But Keitt and Edmundson blocked their way. Keitt, pistol gleaming on his hip, waved his own cane at the would-be peacemakers, screaming: "Goddamn! Leave them alone!"

Meantime some other onlookers called out: "Go, Brooks, go!", according to author Stephen Puleo.

Sumner futilely held up his arms to try to ward off the blows. His large physique smashed into another desk, knocking it from its bolts too.

Sen. John Jordan Crittenden of Kentucky, known in Congress as a compromiser, moved toward the stricken Sumner. Crittenden shouted out: "Don't kill him!"

But Keitt blocked Crittenden's way. Then Georgia senator Robert Toombs warned Keitt not to attack Crittenden. Toombs kept mum on the caning itself, and in fact favored it.

In an adjoining room, Stephen Douglas realized what was happening. He thought of taking action, then stayed put. He later claimed any intervention, due to the unfriendly relationship he had with Sumner, might have been misconstrued as support for Brooks.

Two stunned New Yorkers, Rep. Ambrose Murray, and Edwin Morgan, the chairman of the Republican National Committee, were nearby. Sumner toppled next to them, crashing onto an overturned desk, with Morgan breaking his fall.

Murray rushed over to Brooks and grabbed his arm. Crittenden took the remnants of the walking stick from him. Several men pulled the sweating, red-faced congressman away.

In sixty seconds that seemed an eternity, Brooks had delivered thirty blows.

He uttered: "I did not intend to kill him, but I did intend to whip him."

With Keitt and Edmundson, he limped steadily away from the scene, stepping over the blood-spattered floor. He stopped at an anteroom, where a man treated a cut over Brooks's right eye from the backswing of the lashings.

Sumner lay sprawled out, legs in the aisle, his shirt and tweed coat soaked through with blood. Morgan cradled his ravaged head.

A Senate page and the sergeant-at-arms, along with Morgan and Murray, helped Sumner to a side room. There a physician stitched his gashes. The senator suffered from neural damage, deep head wounds down to the skull, a concussion, blood loss, and welts on the arms and shoulders. Still, he gamely told New York senator William Seward he hoped the beating would aid the cause of abolition.

As he left the Senate chambers, helped by friends, Sumner staggered by Sen. John Slidell of Louisiana, a strong backer of Kansas-Nebraska, and a future Confederate ambassador. Slidell coldly recalled feeling "no particular emotion" about his fellow legislator.

House Speaker Banks and Sen. Henry Wilson took Sumner in a carriage to his lodging at 3rd Street N.W., a few blocks from the Capitol Building, and near the site of the future Union Army Pension Building.

Massachusetts senator Charles Sumner was the recipient of the bloodiest assault in the Capitol Building by another member of Congress.

He was stricken but unbowed, telling Wilson, a political ally: "When I recover I will meet them again, and put it to them again." He then lapsed into sleep, after muttering, "I could not believe that a thing like this was possible."

DIVIDED RESPONSES

The reaction in the South and North to the congressional caning mirrored the nation's yawning divide.

Brooks was lauded as a hero in much of the South. Virginia's influential *Richmond Enquirer* hailed the attack as "good in conception, better in execution, and best of all in consequences." It opined, "The vulgar Abolitionists in the Senate are getting above themselves. . . . They must be lashed into submission." It suggested caning Sumner "every morning." Brooks's hometown newspaper stated simply: "Hit him again." Washington was then a mostly Southern town and, at a rally, a banner backing the violence was unfurled, reading: "Sumner and Brooks: Let Them Bleed." The lawmaker received hundreds of gift canes. Southern congressmen scooped up the fragments of the broken stick from the Senate floor and attached them to necklaces that they wore like holy relics. Braxton Bragg, then a colonel in Louisiana's militia, and later the head of the Confederate Army of the Tennessee, stated: "You can reach the sensibilities of such dogs only through . . . a big stick." Some in the Border-South states, though put off by Sumner's rhetoric, objected to the savagery of Brooks's means.

In the North, Sumner was hailed as a figure of defiance, according to Puleo. Massive, boisterous rallies were held in his honor from Boston and Providence to Cleveland and Detroit. The senator had sought to reach a wide audience with his speech, and after his caning a million copies of "The Crime Against Kansas" were printed.

Sumner, like Brooks, was deluged with hundreds of letters of support, the largest number from Illinois, the home of future President Lincoln. One missive reflected on a prior war while foreseeing a future one: "the blood boils in my veins . . . of the cowardly brutal assault . . . by the fiend from South Carolina . . . no other provocation was needed . . . in shouldering the musket and fighting the battles of the revolution over again." Another letter—from Kenosha, Wisconsin—stated prophetically the "nation is on the brink of civil war."

Henry Wadsworth Longfellow wrote the attack had "torn the mask off the faces of traitors." He also thought of the American Revolution while looking ahead to civil strife. In a patriotic plea he'd soon compose

"Paul Revere's Ride," popularly referred to as 'The Midnight Ride of Paul Revere.' His fellow New England scribe, Ralph Waldo Emerson, presaged Lincoln's remark about a "House divided cannot stand." Wrote Emerson: "I do not see how a barbarous community and a civilized community can constitute one state. I think we must get rid of slavery, or we must get rid of freedom."

An uneasy feeling grew in the North that the South, by pushing to make new territories slave states, even those north of the Mason-Dixon Line, and by mauling a Massachusetts senator, was trying to impose its own system on the entire nation.

James Watson Webb, the editor of the *New York Courier and Enquirer*, was no stranger to duels and street fights, having precipitated the Cilley-Graves duel. (See the chapter on that bloody encounter.) Yet even he condemned the attack, writing that "the persuasive arguments of the bludgeon, the bowie knife, and the revolver" might now "refute and silence any member" of Congress. In response, Brooks fired off an angry letter to Webb, suggesting a duel, but Webb demurred.

Indeed, in the wake of the caning Brooks was more belligerent than ever, to those who condemned his act. He sent letters requesting duels to Senator Wilson and Rep. Anson Burlingame of Massachusetts. Wilson agreed to a street fight, which Brooks declined. Burlingame, who'd called Brooks the "vilest sort of coward," agreed to a duel, but on his own, unusual terms. Given prohibitions on duels in many US states, Burlington called for a gunfight on the Canadian side of Niagara Falls. The face-off would be with rifles, a weapon at which Burlingame excelled. Brooks, a decided underdog in such a confrontation, backed off. He claimed traveling through hostile Northern states to such a faraway destination was too risky.

ACTIONS IN COURT AND CONGRESS

Brooks was arrested for the Sumner assault. He posted bail of $500 (about $15,000 in 2020 dollars). A city court convicted him, but only fined him $300, with no jail time.

A House committee investigated the attack. Defending himself before the House, Brooks argued he had deliberately avoiding killing

Sumner, explaining that "it was expressly to avoid taking life that I used an ordinary cane." The House censured him. It also voted to expel him, 121–95, short of the required two-thirds margin.

In response, Brooks resigned his seat, dramatically walking out of the House two months after the caning. He then ran for the vacant post, with approving voters putting him back in. The House also censured Keitt, who also resigned and easily won office again. Edmundson escaped censure by the full House.

Sumner tried to return to the Senate, but for a long time was too weak physically and mentally. He recuperated at the Maryland home of Francis Preston Blair, formerly President Andrew Jackson's chief advisor, and later a counselor to President Lincoln. The stricken senator also took two restorative trips to Europe. There he allowed a French doctor, without using anesthesia, to burn the flesh above and along his spinal column in a bootless attempt to repair nerve damage. Still, Sumner built ties with many statesmen and cultural figures overseas, including Harriet Ward Beecher Stowe, author of *Uncle Tom's Cabin*.

Despite his absence from Congress, Massachusetts re-elected him. His empty chair in the Senate was a potent reminder of the attack. It took Sumner three years before fully resuming his duties. He was unrepentant, telling Congress: "When crime and criminals are thrust before us, they are to be met by all the energies that God has given us by argument, scorn, sarcasm and denunciation."

Brooks met a horrible fate. He surprised his admirers by flipping his views and calling for the admission of Kansas to the Union even under a free-soil constitution. Perhaps he felt guilty. He fell ill, suffering terribly from croup, a severe respiratory disease. He died in 1857, at age thirty-seven, after trying "to tear his own throat open to get breath." His relative Senator Butler died of edema the same year.

In retrospect, the Civil War was presaged by the caning of Senator Sumner by Congressman Brooks. Violence and spite rendered impossible civilized discourse and compromise at the Capitol.

Chapter Eleven

Gangsta Rip Raps and Misfiring Marines: Washington's Bloodiest Riot in 130 Years

Just north of the Capitol Building at the former Baltimore and Ohio Depot; Old City Hall, 4th and E Streets, N.W.; and Mt. Vernon Square, 7th Street and K Street, N.W.

Washington City mayor William Magruder had reason for worry on June 1, 1857. The local elections scheduled that day threatened to be raucous. In fact, the city teetered on chaos from two rival blocs. One was made up of native-born Americans, largely of English ancestry, who backed the Know-Nothing Party, the anti-Catholic, anti-immigrant group. The second consisted of immigrants of German and Irish-Catholic background.

Magruder, physically imposing, a doctor by training, thought back to his own election the previous year, when local Know-Nothings had threatened to "crop his ears." He also recalled the wild mayoral election the prior autumn in Baltimore, less than forty miles to the northeast, when Charm City elected a Know-Nothing mayor, Thomas Swann.

In Baltimore's electoral contests, violent gangs of Know-Nothings such as the Plug Uglies, as well as rival Irish-Catholic thugs, had attacked polling places and fire stations. Over twenty people had been killed. The nativist Swann had largely won as a result.

Washington's mayor had good reason to fear trouble, and trouble came.

Panic at the Polls

That election day, Know-Nothings in Baltimore hired fifteen to twenty Plug Uglies and sent them on the railway down to Washington. The mission of the gangbangers was to attack immigrant voters and their sympathizers, sow havoc throughout the city, and thus ensure the election of Know-Nothing candidates.

Early in the morning, the Plug Uglies arrived at the old Baltimore and Ohio (B&O) Depot, Washington's main train station just north of the Capitol Building. Soon the Plug Uglies, along with an allied local gang the Rip Raps, were assaulting voters and others they deemed foreign-looking, near polling places in three of the city's seven wards. (The Gangs of DC surely had colorful names.)

One wave of assault was at Pennsylvania Avenue and 11th Street, a little more than a mile from the Capitol. Beatings were administered; gunshots rang out.

The largest batch of rioters swarmed into Ward 4, to a voting place across from the Northern Liberties Market. The roofed, bustling Market was a center of Know-Nothing sentiment. It sat next to Mt. Vernon Square, just south of today's Convention Center, where the Apple Store is located inside the former Carnegie Library.

An angry throng gathered, up to a thousand in number. Its minions glared and shouted at the Irishmen, Germans, and others waiting to vote. Many among the nativists grasped weapons. Their vast, if ramshackle, arsenal included crowbars, pistols, stones and brickbats, Bowie knives, and dagger-like dirks.

The Plug Uglies were from laboring districts in Baltimore, and many of the Irish were from similar haunts. In fact, just east of the Market was the aptly named neighborhood of Swamppoodle. Long before the construction of Union Station and the Route 395 exit, it was a marshy, disease- and crime-ridden place of tenements and shacks, peopled by "shanty Irish."

In Baltimore, Washington, and other cities, the Irish and their rival "Yankees" of Anglo-Saxon descent often vied for the same jobs and turf. It was as if they had brought their centuries-old animosities from the Old

Sod to the New. The same competition went for the Irish and African Americans.

Outside the Market's polling place, it was 11:00 a.m. For several hours, the anger of the Plug Uglies and the Rip Raps had been building. Then their leaders cried out: "Wade in, natives, wade in!" They rushed to attack.

The city's police did little to stop them. In 1857, for a city of about fifty-seven thousand, the municipal force had just seventeen officers, plus thirty Auxiliary Guardsmen for night patrols. Just one magistrate for every twelve hundred residents.

At the Marketplace poll, the rioters made short work of the cops. Most of the officers fled their posts. They left the voters waiting outside helpless and exposed. Given free rein, the gangsters punched, knifed, and stomped their way through the stunned mass of immigrants.

About two dozen people were injured; one Irishman's face was reduced to a scarlet pulp. The vandals also turned their rage on the buildings in the neighborhood, smashing up walls and windows.

MARCHING TO THE RESCUE

At the Old City Hall and federal courthouse on Judiciary Square, just six blocks from the melee, the city fathers worriedly received reports on the violence.

Washington's federal district attorney, Philip Barton Key II, the son of Francis Scott Key, thought back to the city's first ethnic riot of 1835.

A widower, the younger Key was a wealthy and handsome man with an eye for the ladies. Twenty-two years prior, his father, as district attorney, had suppressed the "Snow Riot" of Irish workmen against black businessmen and clergy. In 1835, the disorder had also overwhelmed the city's small police force. Francis Scott Key had responded by calling in armed federal help. (See the chapter on the Snow riot.) Philip Barton Key II figured the same solution could apply this time.

At City Hall, on learning of the Market fracas, Mayor Magruder was also determined to restore order. He ordered the voting near the Market suspended. And he contacted President James Buchanan at the White House. The mayor asked the president for special aid. Buchanan, a political ally of Magruder's, and a foe of the Know-Nothings, assented.

The president got in touch with Navy Secretary Isaac Toucey, a former senator from Connecticut. Toucey sent out orders to the US Marine Barracks.

At the command of Maj. Henry B. Tyler, 115 Marines marched out of their quarters with bayonets fixed. Tyler had split the mostly raw recruits into two companies commanded by officers.

One of the Marines in charge was Lt. Charles A. Henderson. He was a son of the legendary Marine Corps commander, seventy-four-year-old Brig. Gen. Archibald Henderson, then in his record thirty-seventh year of leading the Corps. (Henderson Hall in Arlington, Virginia, where Navy cryptanalysts broke Imperial Japan's navy codes in the Second World War, is named for him.) General Henderson, dressed in civilian clothes, accompanied the formation.

The Marines strode past the Capitol Building. Along their route, they passed by backers of the Plug Uglies, who rushed up to them cursing and spitting. Still, as they marched on, their presence quelled the smaller disturbances downtown. They strode on to City Hall.

There Mayor Magruder instructed the Marines under Major Tyler to head to Mt. Vernon Square. Magruder went with them. Along with the coming face-off, the mayor and the major had much on their minds. Some of the Plug Uglies had threatened their families and their homes, including the Marines Commandant's House. They had their family members sent to safe havens and took steps to protect the properties.

CONFRONTATION AND CHAOS

When the leathernecks arrived at the Market, they found the rioters waiting for them, and ready. The Plug Uglies and their allies had gotten hold of a cannon. The brass six-pounder, stolen and transported from near the Navy Yard, was mounted on a swivel. Some of the rioters had pushed it into position. The artillery piece was crammed with powder, rocks, and cannon shot. The mob swiveled the gun toward the approaching Marines.

A large crowd of spectators, government workers, and people from the neighborhood watched from the street and from the windows of nearby buildings. They were transfixed, wondering what would happen next.

The Marines marched up toward the big gun. They paused. They knew it could blow a big hole in their formation, killing many.

Suddenly appearing next to the cannon was an older, but trim and vigorous man, in civilian garb, and brandishing not a weapon, but an umbrella.

It was Archibald Henderson, the Marine commandant! Mayor Magruder was next to him.

The general pressed his body up against the muzzle of the cannon. Waving his umbrella, he looked over the rioters, and commanded them to leave the area.

Henderson sternly told the Plug Uglies: "Men, you had better think twice before you fire this piece at the Marines."

In an act of unimaginable bravery, during the Election Day turmoil of 1857, Marine Corps commandant Archibald Henderson placed his body on the muzzle of a cannon, daring the rioters who'd stolen it to fire away.

He was daring them to blow him up, gambling they'd back down, fearing his soldiers would slaughter them in return. The rioters hesitated.

Suddenly, a gang member raced over to Henderson, and pointed a pistol square in his face. He fired the gun.

For a moment, a cloud of gunpowder obscured the scene.

Then the smoke cleared.

Henderson was unhurt! Either the gun had misfired, or the bullet had missed.

A Marine shot the attacker in the arm. Henderson grabbed the wounded assailant and pushed him to Mayor Magruder for safekeeping. The other Know-Nothings backed off. It seemed the worst might be over.

The Marine officers continued to slow-march their men toward the large mass of rioters near the Market. The latter retreated. The bystanders continued to watch the spectacle.

According to the *Evening Star* newspaper, the Plug Uglies fired off pistol shots as they retreated. Their bullets and brickbats injured some of the Marines. One of them took a gaping bullet wound in the face. The rookie Marines were nervous, unsure. They had trained for battle, not crowd control.

What happened next is still debated. Several residents testified, at a community meeting the following night, that Magruder ordered the

After seemingly quelling the violence at the city's Mt. Vernon Square, US Marines fired wildly into lawbreakers and spectators alike, killing innocent bystanders.

Marines to fire. A military investigation concluded that neither General Henderson, Major Tyler, nor any other officer gave a command to shoot back.

It seems likely one of the young soldiers lost his cool or his temper when his fellow Marines were injured. He aimed his rifle and fired back. This set off a fusillade of fire from the two Marine companies. Some of the Plug Uglies fired their pistols in return.

The rioters fled the field. The terrified spectators fled to their homes and offices.

Then a horrible aftermath became clear.

Eight to ten people lay dead or fatally wounded, and twenty to thirty others were wounded.

The marksmanship of the Marines, and perhaps, the rioters, had been awful. None of those killed or wounded were Plug Uglies. All were spectators.

According to the history blog the *Streets of Washington*, the fatalities included: "Francis M. Deems, a clerk in the General Land Office, [who] was viewing the riots from a second story window . . . Archibald Dalrymple, a brakeman from the Washington Branch Railroad; constable D. H. Alston; Ramy Neal, an African American waiter at Walker & Schadd's restaurant; and Christian Lindig, sixteen-year-old German immigrant."

The rioters hightailed it back to the train depot. Mayor Magruder and President Buchanan received reports that more Plug Uglies were heading down from Baltimore by train. In response, the secretary of war rushed cavalry from Fort McHenry, about which District Attorney Key's father had penned "The Star-Spangled Banner." The horse soldiers rushed over to the B&O Depot. Within eyesight of the Congress, American troops rushed over toward the urban rioters.

The military arrested some of them. District Attorney Key would put some of them on trial. The other Plug Uglies coming from Baltimore turned around and went back to Charm City.

The Election Day riot of 1857, the deadliest in the city's history until the race riots of 1919, and the Martin Luther King riots of 1968, was over.

CHAPTER TWELVE

The Spies Among Us: The Cunning Confederates of the Old Capitol Jail

1 First Street N.E., front steps of the Supreme Court Building

THE SITE OF TODAY'S SUPREME COURT BUILDING WAS LONG ASSOCIATED with the South.

After the marauding British burned down the Capitol Building, and most of the rest of official Washington during the War of 1812, many congressmen urged moving the capital. The original, temporary federal capitals of Philadelphia and New York beckoned. They were cosmopolitan cities, while the District was a small, ruined town strewn out along a swamp.

THE SALON OF THE SOUTHLAND

To entice the federal government to stay, Washington's business community pitched in to build a long, squat residence, in time known as the Old Brick Capitol. It replaced a hotel that had been operated there by a William Tunnicliff. (Tunnicliff's Tavern at the city's Eastern Market recalls that lodging.) In the brick structure, Congress met in temporary sessions until 1819, when it moved back into the rebuilt Capitol Building.

The Old Brick Capitol was turned into a private school, then a boardinghouse. Some referred to it as the Old Capitol Boarding House. It was a convenient lodging for legislators right across the street from their work. And in an era when most congressional leaders, and presidents, were Southerners—Henry Clay, John C. Calhoun, James Monroe,

Andrew Jackson—it became the lodging of choice for quite a few from that region.

For many years before the Civil War, the boardinghouse was run by a woman, Mrs. H. V. Hill. Her hostelry became a social network. Residing there for a long time was Calhoun, the most prominent advocate of secession, and the nullification of federal laws by the states. In fact, Calhoun died there, in 1850, as the Union already seemed on the edge of imploding, before Clay's legislative Compromise of that year. On his deathbed, Calhoun foresaw ruin, crying out, "The South, the poor South!" Ruinous war would come, eleven years later.

A FEMME FATALE

A young helper for Mrs. Hill was her niece, Rose O'Neal, of Port Tobacco, Maryland. Although witty, and a dark-haired beauty, she may have been psychologically scarred by a tragedy of the Southland and its peculiar institution. Her father was murdered by one of his slaves. Rose would become ferociously pro-South in her views.

Calhoun in fact became her friend and mentor, schooling her in the politics of Southern rights. The young lady became an object of attention of other congressmen, in particular Tennessee representative Cave Johnson. He began courting Rose when she was just sixteen. Johnson was heading places, in time becoming the postmaster general for President James Polk. But the vivacious Rose found him dour and ended the courtship.

When she was eighteen, "Wild Rose," as she'd become known, settled down, for a while. In 1835, she married a Virginian, Robert Greenhow. They had four daughters together, including one nicknamed "Little Rose." Greenhow was a cultured man who introduced the intellectually curious Rose to many subjects, and to many dignitaries in town. Mr. Greenhow had studied medicine and law and was a linguist and historian. The State Department hired him as a translator and an expert on the Southwest, conquered during the Mexican-American War. In fact, in 1850 Greenhow died from a fall, while in the newly American city of San Francisco. Wild Rose sued for damages and won the case. She acquired a fine townhome on 16th Street, three blocks north of the White House.

Like Dolley Madison before her, she became a grand dame of the town's high society.

By the late 1850s, a special friend was the president, James Buchanan, formerly a Pennsylvania senator, and an ex-chairman of the House Judiciary Committee. A bachelor, he'd often visit Rose at her home. The presidential carriage was spotted at late hours outside the place. William E. Doster, later a Union general and provost marshal, the Army's top lawyer, recalled: "There was much gossip at this time arising from the intimacy between Mrs. Greenhow and the President."

A JAIL HOUSE FOR A WARTIME CAPITAL

When the great conflict erupted in 1861, most of the Southern legislators at the boardinghouse went back to their respective states, and to the Confederacy. Due to war-time casualties, almost every large building in Washington was turned into a hospital, including the Patent Office off 7th Street. Walt Whitman labored there as a male nurse. The Old Capitol Boarding House, perhaps due to its links to the South, was transformed into the Old Capitol Prison.

The bleak, three-story pile of bricks became a holding pen for many sorts of people, including: rebel spies; actual or suspected Southern sympathizers; slaves escaped to Union lines, the so-called "contrabands"; captured Confederate soldiers; Union officers charged with various offenses; mariners caught trying to run the Union navy blockade; and common criminals.

Eventually the African Americans, about five hundred in number, were moved down 1st Street to the Carroll Row boardinghouses, part of the same wartime complex, and formerly a residence for Northern congressmen. It was also called Duff Green's Row, after Duff Green, the pro-Southern journalist and industrialist who'd owned the property. (See the chapter on Lincoln's lodging.)

Some prisoners were consigned to individual cells on the Prison's first floor. The cells were dark, cramped, and infested with lice. Most inmates were kept on the more tolerable second floor, where Congress had met, in one of five large open spaces marked off by partitions.

Presiding over the sprawling set of buildings was the warden, Col. William Patrick Wood. Careless in appearance except for a trim

mustache, he was just five-feet, six-inches, yet stocky, and able and energetic. Wood had gotten the job of prison superintendent, and the title and
pay of a Union officer, through connections with the highest of places. In
1858, in a case before the Supreme Court, a twenty-eight-year-old Wood
had been technical advisor to a noted attorney. This was future secretary
of war Edwin Stanton, who won a patent case regarding the mechanical
reaper, over the reaper's famed inventor, Cyrus McCormick. In Stanton's
stable of attorneys was a man specializing in the new technologies of the
North—railroads, reapers, and iron bridges—one Abraham Lincoln, later
Stanton's boss in the Civil War.

Warden Wood worked in a street-level office at the Prison's southwest corner. During his tenure, thirty thousand denizens shuffled
through the jail, from the war's first summer in 1861 to two months after
its conclusion in 1865.

Col. W. P. Wood, as he was called, was thought to run a tight but fair
ship. He ensured prisoners got three meals a day, of beans, rice, and salted
pork. While over 10 percent of the Southerners in Union prisons died
during the war, only a few hundred perished at the Old Capitol Prison.
And Wood ordered solidly made coffins for those who did pass away.

He allowed inmates to receive mail, but only after letters were
checked for treasonous or military-related content. In fact, Wood infiltrated and took over much of the Confederacy's mail system running
from Richmond to its sympathizers in Washington. Appreciating Wood's
many skills, Lincoln also made him the first chief of the Secret Service.

Though raised a Catholic, Wood had been a fervent adherent of the
Know-Nothing Party. In him, its fierce anti-Catholicism had bled into
ardent atheism. As such, he relished debating any Southern preachers
in his jail. He was also known to punch contraband blacks whom he
deemed insolent. But he also got many contrabands, many of whom were
penniless, paid work as laborers for the Union army.

Undercover Activities

After the outbreak of war, Rose Greenhow, then forty-three years old,
continued her role as society queen. At the Capitol Building, she'd visit
friends and acquaintances who were congressmen or staff members, and

chat with them on the preparations, financing, and strategies for the upcoming military campaigns.

Another favorite haunt was the Washington Monument, then an ugly granite stub, its construction suspended by the war. But it remained a popular gathering place for city residents as well as tourists, and the countless Union officers and administrators passing through town. Rose would hobnob with them too. And perhaps end her busy day of conversing in Lafayette Square. There a steady stream of soldiers, agency officials, contractors, favor seekers, and well-wishers queued up to meet President Lincoln, Vice President Hannibal Hamlin of Maine, or Secretary of War Simon Cameron of Pennsylvania. Rose already knew some of the visitors, who were pleased to meet the lively, rich, and well-connected widow.

Finally, Rose Greenhow would end her busy day by walking or riding back to her townhouse.

Where she'd do something unusual.

She'd carefully arrange the shutters on her windows that faced the street. And, after going inside, she'd meticulously arrange the blinds of the windows, and place candles at spots along the windowsills.

At length, a man passing by her house would furtively examine the windows—and the messages she'd encoded with them! For the man was a Confederate agent, and "Rebel" Rose Greenhow was a Confederate spy. She passed on the cache of information she'd gleaned from her countless contacts through a secret language. In fact, Rose was the key operative of the main Confederate spy ring in Washington, run by her handler, Capt. Thomas Jordan, of Luray, Virginia.

Along with chitchat, Wild Rose obtained some of her info through romantic liaisons. One was with Sen. Henry Wilson, the chairman of the Senate Committee on Military Affairs. Wilson had, with Stanton, made Wood the Prison's warden. One of Wilson's love letters to Rose, penned on Senate stationery, read: "You well know that I love you and will sacrifice anything. Tonight, whatever the cost, I will see you, and then I will tell you again and again that I love you."

Rose's biggest intelligence scoop involved the war's first big battle: Manassas, also called Bull Run, a Virginia railroad junction thirty-two miles west of the capital. Rose obtained the size and composition of the Union force marching on Manassas, as well as its route and date of attack. Confederate commander Pierre Gustave Toutant-Beauregard, duly warned, crushed the attack—with the help of an up-and-coming officer, one "Stonewall" Jackson.

Among the throngs of Union supporters who rode out to the battle that day, expecting to cheer on a Northern victory, was Senator Wilson. He lost his carriage and picnic basket in the panicky retreat back to town. Afterwards, Rose got congratulatory messages from Beauregard and Confederate president Jefferson Davis. Massachusetts senator Charles Sumner would later admit: "Mrs. Greenhow is worth any six of Jeff Davis' best regiments."

But Rose met her match with the Union's counterintelligence chief, Allan Pinkerton. Pinkerton had been a noted private eye in Illinois, where he rolled up train robbers who'd vexed railroad executives such as George McClellan, the future head of the Union army. In wartime, Pinkerton found a weakness in Rose the spy: her inability to hold her tongue. By speaking openly of her affection for the Southern cause, she fell under suspicion.

Pinkerton and his squad staked out her townhouse. One rainy night, he climbed on the shoulders of one of his men and peered in through Rose's second-floor window. He spied a Union army visitor giving Rose a map of the fortifications for Washington. Pinkerton also spotted them entering a boudoir and holding hands on exiting. Later, after his men found scraps of coded messages in her fireplace, Pinkerton placed Rose under house arrest. Her home became known as "Camp Greenhow." But Rose kept sending out intel buried in the undergarments of her maids, in the hair curls of fellow spy Betty Duvall, and with eight-year-old daughter "Little Rose." Finally, Pinkerton had had enough, and he clamped Rebel Rose in the Old Capitol Prison, in a cell that had been the very place where Senator Calhoun had breathed his last, and where Rose had cared for him!

It can be hard for a spy to cease her errant ways. Rose kept signaling from her window—at the prison. A prison photo of her and her daughter, Little Rose, shows a boarded-up window behind them, nailed shut by guards because she had been sending messages to Confederate operatives in the street below, right across from the Capitol Building.

Shown with her daughter at the Old Capitol Prison, master spy Rose Greenhow transmitted coded intel on the Union military to her Confederate handlers, before taking her wiles across the sea.

In the Victorian era, it was thought unseemly to keep a woman in jail, even one who was a dangerous spy. In spring 1862, Rebel Rose was released, and sent over the Confederate lines.

In summer 1863, Jefferson Davis decided to make use of his valuable intelligence asset. He sent Rose off to the kingdoms of Europe, as a spy and as a kind of ambassadress at large for the South. Many blue bloods in Old Europe sympathized with her region's aristocratic ways and contributed money to her cause.

She visited the French court of Emperor Charles-Louis Napoleon Bonaparte, the nephew of Napoleon Bonaparte. She dazzled the court of England's Queen Victoria. Most impressed was the Second Earl of Granville, like Rose a widow. They soon married. Rose also earned considerable royalties with the publication of a book. Its title was telling: *My Imprisonment and the First Year of Abolition Rule in Washington.*

In summer 1863 she sailed back to America, her destination North Carolina, with a fortune in her possession. Much of it, a heavy load of gold coins, she kept on her person, in a bag chained to her neck. Her intent: give it to the Confederate treasury. But alas, her ship tried to alight near Fort Fisher, treacherous for ships, and ran aground. To avoid capture, and imprisonment again, she risked rowing ashore in high water. But rough waves overturned her boat. Weighed down by the load of bullion, she was carried down to the ocean floor.

Soon after, a rebel sentry patrolling the beach found the hoard of British gold sovereigns and rejoiced at the riches found. Then he learned that the South's most famous and effective spy had been lost at sea. He turned the money over to the Confederate cause. Rose got a heroine's funeral in Wilmington, North Carolina. And if you visit her grave on her birthday, you may find a bouquet of roses on her tomb.

KISSING COUSINS

The Prison was also the holding place for a daring Confederate raider and spy. This was Walter "Wat" Bowie, of the family that founded the nearby town of Bowie, Maryland. Wat Bowie had an aunt, Mary Bowie Tyler, who was married to a noted Georgetown physician, Dr. Grafton Tyler.

The Tyler clan was even more prominent than the Bowies. John Tyler of Virginia, for instance, had been a congressman, senator, president pro tempore of the Senate, vice president—and president. He was also the only ex–US President, when the Civil War came, to be a congressman in the Confederate States Congress.

Grafton, Mary, and Wat were staunch supporters of the Confederacy. Wat Bowie was tall, with piercing eyes and a drooping mustache, the son of a lawyer and plantation owner from Prince George's County, a hotbed of secessionist sentiment. Indeed, in the election of 1860, the county had tallied exactly one vote for Abe Lincoln.

Twenty-three years old when the war erupted, Wat operated as a spy for the Confederate Secret Service in the capital city region. As an expert of disguise and adept with horse and gun, he made bold escapes. One time, Union troops surrounded him at the plantation home of a relative. Cornered, Bowie put on the red calico dress and handkerchief of a house slave and blackened his face with soot. He blithely walked past the gulled Northern soldiers, and swiftly escaped by horse. (Such use of "blackface" would likely be frowned upon today.)

Grafton and Mary Tyler feared for their relation, when Union forces captured Wat Bowie in October 1862. He was thrown into the Old Capitol Prison. A date was set for hanging the notorious spy.

Mrs. Tyler declared she would bid a final, tearful farewell to her nephew. In mid-November, just before Wat's scheduled walk to the gallows, she arranged to meet with him in his prison cell.

As Union guards watched, Mary Tyler entered her son's holding place. Aunt and nephew moved to embrace for the last time. Mrs. Tyler kissed her nephew on the cheeks and then, to the guards' shock, she began kissing him on the mouth. And not just a peck on the lips. But a full-throated kiss. The guards turned away in disgust.

Finally, Mrs. Tyler finished up. The shaken guards led her away.

When he was sure the watchers were watching no more, Wat Tyler reached inside his mouth. He took out a small, sealed parchment that his cunning aunt had transferred to him with the smooch. He carefully unwrapped the brief missive. Its words were to this effect: 'My dear boy. Take hope. You will soon escape. We have bribed the guards!'

The rest of the plan was this. At 7:00 p.m. that very night, a black servant was to bring food to his cell. The door to it would be unlocked. The light to the corridor outside would be extinguished, and a ladder left in the hall. The bribed guards would look the other way.

Things went as expected, mostly. At the appointed time, Wat slipped out of his cell, grabbed the ladder, and got up to the roof of the prison. Ignoring a rainstorm, he crept over to a drainpipe leading to the street. In the gloom he waited, soaked to the skin, and nervously listened for the tread of the sentry making his rounds outside the ground floor of the jail.

Wat heard the guard approach, pass by the drainpipe, and walk into the distance, the sound of his steps slowly fading. Seizing his chance, he shimmied down the pipe. But in the dark and the wet his grip gave way. He came crashing down, twisting his ankle in the fall. The sentry heard the crash, and retraced his steps.

Wat thought fast, very fast. He stayed on the ground, and complained of the pain, pretending to have tripped while walking on the sidewalk. He both accosted and pleaded with the guard, begging him to help him up as he loudly cursed the rain, the dark sidewalk, the slippery street, the city, everything! The sentry helped Wat to his feet, then helped him walk, limping, all the way to the end of his patrol, to safety at the other side of the prison.

Bidding the guard adieu, Wat found confederates waiting for him with fresh horses. He made his escape to Virginia, according to the book *Scouts and Spies of the Civil War.*

It was the prison escape that was sealed with a kiss.

Both the Tyler and Greenhow tales have moments of levity, but a story relating to another prison is uniformly grim.

THE DOOMED DOCTOR OF DEATH

The Union soldiers climbed high up in the trees for a choice view of the big event. They had small sympathy for the man in question, on that grim morning of November 10, 1865. But they were startled, and sickened, at what they saw. For the thing didn't go as planned.

Fate plays tricks, and none more so than for Dr. Hartmann Heinrich Wirz, or Henry Wirz. Like thousands from the German-speaking lands of Europe, he came to America after Europe's failed democratic revolutions of 1848. They've been dubbed the "48ers." Indeed, some wound up in California's gold mines the following year as "49ers." Dr. Wirz, like the other immigrants, came seeking freedom, opportunity, and adventure. His lot was to settle in the antebellum American South. After his arrival in 1849, he worked as a manager in industry and on plantations.

As a physician, he was, as a believer in homeopathy, something of a quack. But physicians were in short supply, especially during war. When the war came, the South prized his knowledge of medicine, and of Europe. Jefferson Davis made him his go-between to the Confederate envoy to France, former representative and senator John Slidell of Louisiana, and to the envoy to Britain, James Murray Mason, also an ex-congressman and senator.

In spring 1864, Wirz was made the administrator of a place in Georgia that required an incalculable amount of medical care for tens of thousands of sick and wounded soldiers, most of them lacking medicine and sufficient food and decent shelter. Because the forty-one-year-old Dr. Wirz, by a stroke of ill fortune, had become the commandant of the infamous Andersonville Prison. The largest, and deadliest, of the Confederate prisoner of war (POW) camps.

The slave-constructed place was called Camp Sumter in the South, after the bombardment and capture of Fort Sumter, South Carolina, that had ignited the war. Of the forty-five thousand Union soldiers kept in its jammed, open-air stockades, 29 percent perished. (About 24 percent died at the grim POW camp for Confederate prisoners in Elmira, New York.)

Inmates fell in such numbers at Andersonville that bodies were left lying on the ground in the deep Southern heat. When the corpses were buried, along with kitchen wastes, they were placed in all-too-shallow graves. A Confederate physician who inspected the camp, and contracted influenza there, noted: "The action of the sun upon this putrefying mass of excrements and fragments of bread and meat and bones excited most rapid fermentation and developed a horrible stench."

A CLAN OF INCOMPETENTS

Many were responsible for the dire circumstances: for instance, the Winder family, maybe the most criminally negligent family of soldiers in American history. Gen. William H. Winder, a bungling political appointee, had been in overall command at the 1814 Battle of Bladensburg, the debacle that led to the British burning of the Capitol. General Winder foolishly decided to fight a pitched battle against the highly skilled Royal Marines, instead of hit-and-run tactics for which the American militias were better suited. He also failed to position the American array so they could support themselves with interlocking lines of fire. Moreover, he assumed victory, and thus did not produce a fallback plan, a plan of retreat, so that when defeat came the retreat turned into a rout.

The inept general's relations and descendants were much involved with Andersonville. One, Capt. Richard B. Winder, sited its kitchen on a river upstream of the prison. This ensured the water passing by the encampment would be foul and disease-ridden. The inmates washed in and drank from the stream. Captain Winder would admit his error with the kitchen's location and write of his failed efforts to obtain lumber to provide coffins for the prison dead. Another relative, Capt. W. Sidney Winder, selected the overall location of the camp. The site itself had a stream which, filled with the human waste of countless prisoners, turned into a maggot-ridden sludge.

Capt. Richard B. Winder wrote a superior: "Immediate arrangements should be made in which the prisoners may be sheltered from the rains and protected from the heat of the sun. Buildings should be commenced as soon as practicable. . . . Without this they will die off by hundreds and will be a dead loss to us in the way of [prisoner] exchange." Along with physical woes, thousands of the men were afflicted by severe depression.

The worst of the Winders may have been the general's son, John Henry Winder, himself a general, for the Confederacy. (Richard B. Winder was his nephew, and W. Sidney Winder a cousin.) John Henry Winder seems to have been, unlike his father, a skilled soldier. However, he was a terrible administrator. A decorated soldier of the Mexican-American War, he'd been a failed plantation owner. He was fired from a teaching position at West Point. By 1864, he was the head of the Confederate Bureau of Prison Camps. After a stint at running Andersonville, he handed the job over to Wirz.

Dr. Wirz didn't have ultimate authority over the camp. The man who did was Gen. John Henry Winder, as chief of all the camps. It's said he stated of Andersonville: "I am killing off more Yankees than twenty regiments in Lee's army."

At the war's conclusion, General Winder might have expected to face the hangman as a war criminal. But in February 1865, two months before Appomattox, he died of a heart attack.

CONDITIONS OF CRISIS

At Andersonville, an overlapping chain of command undercut attempts that Dr. Wirz might have made to improve conditions. He was the commandant of the prison, but another officer was the overall head of the camp. Wirz did not have authority over the quartermaster, responsible for provisions, nor over the camp hospital, responsible for the sick.

Wartime shortages were his greatest headache. Medicine was scarce, and the Union navy blockade made it scarcer. For shelter, inmates scrounged bits of wood and clothing from dead prisoners to construct shebangs, or rude huts. Confederate soldiers, not Union POWs, had priority for foodstuffs, and the filthy drinking water triggered epidemics of intestinal woes.

Shortages were worsened by a huge influx of new captives. In late 1863, the Union military suspended the exchange of prisoners between North and South. The goal was to deny manpower to the outnumbered Confederacy. The food supply worsened further when Union general William Tecumseh Sherman marched through Georgia in autumn 1864. His quick-moving troops lived off the land, taking food for themselves. They also wrecked infrastructure, ripping out the railway tracks that supplied the prison. Some of Sherman's troops themselves became POWs— they swelled the already overcrowded camp. In fact, the conditions at the camp reached their lowest point during this time. The situation markedly improved when the number of prisoners fell sharply, after exchanges with the North started up again.

Commandant Wirz wrote a Confederate officer in charge of providing food and implements: "The bread which is issued to prisoners is of such an inferior quality, consisting fully of one-sixth of husk, that it is almost unfit for use and increases dysentery and other bowel complaints. . . . Rations of rice, beans, vinegar, and molasses cannot be issued to prisoners for want of buckets." Some prisoners, wasting away, resembled the skeletal figures of Second World War concentration camps.

Still, there were reports the orchards near Andersonville abounded with fruit. And the camp was near forests from which firewood and materials for building better lodgings could have been taken.

Wirz's angry, moody personality seemed to fracture during his time as commandant. He brooded over his situation, instead of focusing on bettering the plight of the prisoners. He seemed to think he could control the inmates, not through normal discipline, but through threats and bouts of rage. On one occasion he ordered a guard to shoot a prisoner and, after the sentry shot the man to death, claimed his order was only meant as a threat. Other times he was seen striking or beating prisoners.

An Angry Capital and a War Crimes Court

The war's aftermath might have led to, in Lincoln's grand phrase, "malice toward none, with charity for all." But on the night of April 14, 1865, Lincoln was assassinated at Ford's Theatre one mile from the Capitol by actor John Wilkes Booth. The Union, already dismayed at the war's vast death toll, was apoplectic over the murder.

That ire almost hit the inmates of the Old Capitol Prison. On that terrible night, mobs fell upon Confederate soldiers who hailed from the Washington region. Still garbed in their tattered gray uniforms, some happened to be trudging through town back to their homes after their armies' surrender. Enraged mobs savagely beat some of them.

Washingtonians knew that many Confederate officers, about eight hundred in all, were interned at the Prison. Responding to the attack on the president, about two thousand furious citizens gathered outside. They called for burning the place to the ground and incinerating its prisoners. Quartermaster Gen. Montgomery Meigs, the builder of the newly completed Capitol dome, had reason to be angry himself, as his son had been killed in a skirmish with rebels. However, General Meigs ordered in troops and extra guards to prevent a holocaust.

Junius Brutus Booth Jr., the brother of Lincoln's killer, was briefly interrogated at the Prison, and found innocent of any connection to the crime. The owner of Ford's Theatre, John T. Ford, and his brothers, were detained there for up to thirty-nine days, before they were released as well.

Given the public mood, it seemed a sacrificial lamb might be offered.

Congress authorized a tribunal, the Special Military Commission, a predecessor of one that in 1942 would try German secret agents in Washington. (See the chapter on the Nazi saboteurs.) The Commission's sessions took place at the old Court of Claims in the Capitol Building.

Its chairman was Gen. Lew Wallace of Indiana. He was under a cloud for alleged tardiness at the bloody 1862 Battle of Shiloh. He would partly dispel that cloud in 1880, by authoring a spectacularly successful novel—*Ben-Hur*.

At first, the tribunal indicted Dr. Wirz, as well as the former president of the Confederacy—and former superintendent of the Capitol—Jefferson Davis. It also indicted the former head of the Confederate Army of Northern Virginia, Robert E. Lee. It was alleged the Andersonville commandant "had conspired with" Davis and Lee to murder prisoners. However, the charge was without foundation. It was changed to a vague statement that Wirz "has conspired with others. . . ." The indictments against the former high-ranking Confederates were dropped.

Dr. Wirz was kept in a cell at the Old Capitol Prison. He would spend about two months there. There were only a few war crimes trials in 1865, no other ones in DC, and none nearly as notable.

The tribunal met from August 21 to October 18, 1865. Its panel consisted of seven Union generals and two colonels. It included Brig. Gen. Edward S. Bragg, a cousin of Confederate general Braxton Bragg, and later a congressman from Wisconsin. The officers gathered about a table in the middle of a high-ceilinged space. Wirz, suffering from assorted ailments, lay listening on an adjacent divan. The trial took testimony from 160 witnesses, most of them Andersonville POWs, as well as Confederate soldiers. The Congressional Record devoted over eight hundred pages to the court transcript.

Secretary of War Stanton opened the proceedings by reading the charges. The tribunal alleged Wirz had acted "maliciously, traitorously, and in violation of the laws of war, to impair and injure the health and to destroy the lives—by subjecting to torture and great suffering; by confining in unhealthy and unwholesome quarters; by exposing to the inclemency of winter and to the dews and burning sun of summer; by compelling the use of impure water; and by furnishing insufficient and unwholesome food—of large numbers of Federal prisoners. . . ."

The Commission accused Wirz of thirteen separate murders. He was charged with ordering guards to fire muskets at prisoners; beating prisoners; clamping prisoners in stockades; setting bloodhounds on escaped prisoners; and hitting or shooting prisoners with revolvers. Wirz pleaded not guilty to all counts.

The chief prosecuting attorney was the Army's judge advocate general, Joseph Holt of Kentucky. Holt and his team had considerable powers. They could and did reject witnesses that Wirz's defense team wished to bring forward. The prosecution disallowed as a defense the overcrowding that stemmed from the suspension of prisoner exchanges.

The tribunal relied much on hearsay or indirect evidence and did not identify by name any of the men whose deaths Wirz allegedly caused.

One witness was Union soldier Boston Corbett, who testified prisoners were shot for merely approaching the "deadline" near the prison wall. (Inmates were forbidden on pain of death from coming within nineteen feet of the barrier.) After his release from Andersonville, Corbett had joined the Union force that hunted down Lincoln assassin John Wilkes Booth. In fact, it was probably Corbett who fired the fatal bullet into Booth. Yet Corbett may have been a less than reliable witness. He suffered from mercury poisoning and, as a mentally unstable man, had mutilated his private parts.

After the trial, it was revealed a prosecution witness who called himself Felix de la Baume had lied about his identity. He claimed to be a Frenchman descended from Lafayette, when in fact he was a Prussian named Felix Oesser, and a deserter from the Union army. He had obtained a job with the Interior Department, possibly in exchange for his testimony.

Nonetheless, the tribunal convicted Wirz on almost all of the murder counts. It declared that "the Court do sentence him, the said Henry Wirz, to be hanged by the neck until dead." Judge advocate Holt wrote President Johnson, regarding Andersonville's operations, that "a system for the murder of men more revolting in its details could not have been planned."

Some historians believe Wirz should have received a prison term, not a sentence of execution. Some authors believe the same about Mary Surratt, the Maryland woman who had run a downtown DC boardinghouse where the Booth conspirators met. The extent of her knowledge of Booth's murder plans remains unclear. Surratt was also detained at the Capitol Prison and tried before a tribunal. She was the only American woman of the nineteenth century to suffer the death penalty.

From his cell, Wirz wrote the following to President Johnson: "The pangs of death are short, and therefore I humbly pray that you will pass on your sentence without delay. Give me death or liberty. The one I do not fear; the other I crave." Johnson set the date of execution.

On the morning of November 10, Wirz was marched out to the yard of the Old Capitol Prison, to the wooden platform of the gallows With the Union troopers climbing high in the trees to get a better look.

Wirz told the hangman: "I know what orders are . . . and I am being hanged for obeying them."

The hangman tied and adjusted the noose. The trap door opened. Dr. Wirz dropped from the platform.

But something went wrong. For when Wirz plunged down from the gallows, his neck didn't snap. Instead, he dangled for minutes in agony, the rope burning his skin, and slowly choked to death.

To the horror of the Federal soldiers watching in the trees above.

The old lodging, and prison, of the South, had witnessed its grisliest death.

This remarkable photo shows the scaffold from which Dr. Henry Wirz, the commandant of the Confederacy's notorious Andersonville prisoner-of-war camp, was hanged. The nearby Capitol Building, and Union troops watching from the trees, can be discerned.

THE CONFEDERATE WHO HELPED WIN THE
SECOND WORLD WAR

Probably the most famous soldier detained at the Old Capitol Prison was the "Gray Ghost," Col. John Singleton Mosby of Virginia. For much of the war, Mosby was a pain in the rear of Union forces seeking to occupy and pacify nearby northern Virginia. Mosby and his "raiders," a battalion of swift cavalrymen, were feared for their lightning, guerrilla-war attacks on Federal depots, trains, and encampments.

Mosby's most famous exploit took place near the Fairfax County, Virginia courthouse, just twenty miles from Washington, at the expense of hapless Union army brigadier general Edwin Stoughton. In spring 1863, the thirty-three-year-old Mosby and a picked force slipped through Union lines and entered a private home where Stoughton had set up headquarters. They literally caught the general snoozing, in his bed clothes.

Rousting Stoughton from his dreams, perhaps with a slap to the derriere, Mosby demanded:

"Have you heard of Mosby, General?!"

A startled Stoughton answered: "Yes! Have you got the rascal?"

"No," came the retort. "I am Mosby. He has got you!"

The Gray Ghost and his men made off with Stoughton, thirty other prisoners—and fifty-eight horses.

When he learned of the embarrassing seizure, President Lincoln was typically laconic, and wry. He commented that, "I did not so much mind the loss of a brigadier general, for I could make another in five minutes; but those horses cost $125 apiece!"

During a rare miscue, Mosby was himself captured, by Union horsemen as he waited to board a train. He was kept for ten days at the Old Capitol Prison. Then he was traded for Union soldiers as part of an exchange of prisoners. (Colonel Wood, the Prison warden, personally ran some of the exchanges, taking hundreds of Confederate prisoners to Richmond and North Carolina, and taking back Union prisoners in turn. Along the way, Wood bought the favor of uncooperative rebel officials with gifts of whiskey and morphine.)

As he was taken to Southern lines, Mosby kept careful note of a nearby buildup of Northern ships and troops, preparations for what

The feared "Gray Ghost of the Confederacy," Col. John Mosby, became an unlikely campaign advisor for former Union army chief Ulysses S. Grant, and an equally unlikely federal envoy to Hong Kong.

became the Second Battle of Manassas, or Bull Run. On arriving in Richmond, he shared what he learned with Robert E. Lee, who won a smashing victory in that 1862 encounter.

An opponent of slavery, and even an opponent at first of secession, Mosby fought to prevent the "invasion" of his "homeland" of Virginia, as he saw it. After Lee's surrender, he swiftly reconciled with the Union. Noting this, and admiring his martial skills, in 1865 Union army chief

Ulysses S. Grant arranged a pardon for the former rebel. When Grant entered politics, he made Mosby a campaign counselor, to the ire of many Southerners. In 1879, Grant's presidential successor, Rutherford B. Hayes, made Mosby, of all things, the US envoy to Hong Kong. The ex-Confederate horse soldier who'd haunted the backroads of the Blue Ridge found himself a federal diplomat in the Far East.

Later in life, from 1886 to 1901, he lived in California, where he worked as a railroad attorney for Leland Stanford, the founder of Stanford University and the head of Southern Pacific. There Mosby befriended the young son of a wealthy family, a boy who was descended from a Confederate colonel. He was a precocious lad, who loved hearing Mosby's tales of derring-do from the War Between the States. The old man and the youth would walk and ride with each other replaying old battles, with Mosby playing himself and the youth playing General Lee.

The boy would revel in the elderly man's accounts of moving fast and hitting the enemy hard where and when he least expects it.

The youth took the lessons to heart and grew up to be a soldier himself. He graduated from West Point. He fought with Gen. John "Black Jack" Pershing, in the campaign against the Mexican bandit Pancho Villa. In that fight he'd drive about Mexico in an automobile, in the first US military campaign to deploy motorized vehicles. He'd drape killed enemies over the hood of his car.

In the First World War, he founded a tank school, and led one of the first tank brigades.

In the Second World War, he married motorized warfare with

The conqueror of huge swaths of North Africa, France, and Germany in the Second World War, George S. Patton was mentored in the art of hard-hitting military tactics as a young boy, remarkably, by former Confederate raider Mosby.

the lightning tactics of Mosby, and Sherman, and Stonewall. And with his mighty Third Army of tanks and close-support fighters conquered great chunks of North Africa, then Sicily, then France, and finally Nazi Germany.

For the young boy Mosby had mentored, in the art of swift, sudden attack, was none other than General George S. Patton.

Now that's national reconciliation, across two centuries. And on a transcontinental scale.

Chapter Thirteen

Railways and Ripoffs: A Vast Infrastructure Project Corrupts Congress

The House and Senate chambers

Rep. Oakes Ames was handing out bribes like candy in the winter of 1867-1868. The Massachusetts Republican plied his trade outside the Capitol Building, near Lafayette Square, in dining salons, and in the Senate and House corridors. The payoffs to congressmen took the form not of cash, but of sharply discounted stocks with extremely high dividends.

If a legislator didn't want his good name attached to the securities, Ames held it for him in a trust. If an interested congressman was short of cash, Ames would accept as payment a pledge of future dividends. Ames knew the stocks were guaranteed to rise, for he and his business partners had the government underwrite and bankroll the companies issuing the stock.

The wealthy, sixty-three-year-old Ames was eager to assure legislative support for the firms, which were overseen by congressional committees, indeed by the very congressmen to whom he dispensed the favors. He stated, with bald-faced honesty: "I have used this [bribe] where it will produce most good for us."

A Cross-Continental Vision

The start of one of the worst financial scandals in America's history dated back to 1862. With the Southern states out of the Union due to the Civil

War, Congress authorized a project long cherished by Northern industry: construction of a transcontinental railway stretching from the Midwest to California.

Two companies would build the iron road: the Central Pacific, eastward, from Sacramento, California, and the Union Pacific, westward, from Council Bluffs, Iowa. In 1869, construction gangs from both firms famously met up at Promontory Summit, Utah. There the heads of the railroads hammered in a golden spike to complete the binding of East and West.

The Central Pacific was managed by California magnates such as Collis Huntington and Leland Stanford. They managed to pull off the feat, with the great aid of industrious Chinese coolies. Yet Union Pacific faced an even tougher challenge. It had to lay over sixteen hundred miles of track across an expanse of prairie and mountains mostly bereft of settlers. At enormous expense, it had to haul into this wilderness the mountain of materials required for its wood and metal trail. Further, its engineers and laborers were subject to attacks by Native American tribes who prized the land as their own.

In 1862, Congress and the Lincoln Administration passed the Pacific Railroad Act. It made a vast land grant of sixty-four hundred acres per mile, for the land on either side of the tracks. It arranged to finance the project with massive amounts of federal bonds. However, the Act also placed a floor on the price of stock a participating company could offer. This limited profits and the ability to raise funds. Few corporations or shareholders would invest in an enterprise with so many risks, and so little prospect of making money.

GREASING THE SKIDS
Enter an exceedingly colorful, able, and corrupt figure, Thomas Clark Durant. Born in 1820 in Massachusetts, Durant bootlegged illicit Southern cotton during the war. A physician and entrepreneur, he established Iowa's Mississippi and Missouri (M&M) Railroad, to forge a railway across the Hawkeye State.

In 1856, M&M built the first bridge across the Mississippi River. However, when a steamboat crashed into the span, the boat's owners sued to have the bridge taken down. Durant retained a meticulous railroad attorney—one Abraham Lincoln—to argue the case for retaining the bridge. Lincoln won. The case was appealed, and years later the Supreme Court upheld the ruling, when Lincoln was president.

By 1862 Durant was head of Union Pacific. With the transcontinental railroad stalled, and shunned by investors, Durant and seven partners, including the aptly named George Francis Train, quietly bought out a Pennsylvania investment firm. They retitled it after a prestigious French railroad bank with an evocative name, Crédit Mobilier.

Durant made Crédit Mobilier the general contractor for the railroad's construction. A shell company, its owners and shareholders were the same people running Union Pacific. They paid themselves to build the railway by funneling the construction funds through Crédit Mobilier. Footing the bill was the taxpayer.

A disgusted Charles Francis Adams, son of John Quincy Adams, and former ambassador to Britain during the Civil War, wrote that "in Washington, they vote the subsidies . . . upon the Plains they expend them, and in Crédit Mobilier they divided them."

Durant, Representative Ames, and others pushed Congress in 1864 to pass legislation to greatly expand government and taxpayer support for the two railroad companies. Ames served on the committee authorizing the law. Durant hired a highly paid lobbyist to distribute a fortune in railroad bonds to influential Washingtonians. The Congress, preoccupied by the Civil War, paid little heed to the influence peddling.

The rail project got thirty-year government loans, of $16,000 to $48,000 for each mile of track. The total loan guarantee was valued at more than $60 million (roughly $1.2 billion in 2020 dollars, conservatively estimated). Significantly, Ames inserted a provision to the Act permitting the railroad to issue its own bonds "dollar for dollar" to those of the Treasury. The land grant stood at twenty million acres, including the swath of land on each side of the tracks. The rail firm also got mineral rights. And Congress boosted the outright funding for the project. Meanwhile Durant had Crédit Mobilier covered by the new limited liability laws. This meant wary investors might only lose their investment, and not their personal liberty with a stint in debtor's prison.

Early in 1865, Ames got the verbal backing of a former congressman and ex-railroad lawyer, now the chief executive. "Ames, you take hold of this," President Lincoln said to him. "The road must be built, and you are the man to do it. . . . By building the Union Pacific, you will be the remembered man of your generation."

Crédit Mobilier took full advantage of the lavish support. Its accountants padded expenses even as they stiffed contract laborers. Because the company was paid by the mile of track, it ordered puzzled engineers to lay tracks that ran in circular loops back to their starting points, profitable rails to nowhere. The tracks were often poorly constructed, as the company built them with cheap materials, and pocketed the difference between billing and cost. For each dollar in construction expenses, Crédit Mobilier took in about a dollar. The chaotic, crooked construction, spiced by Indian raids, and by brawls between former slaves and ex-Confederates who made up part of the work force, would be colorfully depicted in the 1990s TV series, *Hell on Wheels*.

KING OF THE ROADS

Oakes Ames had a background befitting such a "Big Dig." He was a wealthy head of the Ames & Sons shovel company, in business since the American Revolution. In fact, his nickname was the "King of Spades." In addition to Union Pacific, he invested heavily to start up Central Pacific.

His firm had supplied much of the digging equipment for the California Gold Rush of 1849 and would provide much of the equipment for the Panama Canal, as well as the entrenching tools for US soldiers during the two world wars. Ames is a major garden tool company today.

Oakes Ames's business relationship with Durant soured. In 1866, in a battle for control of his railroad, Durant was temporarily sidelined, and Oakes Ames's brother, Oliver Ames, became Union Pacific's president. The rewards for those taking charge were considerable. The relative value of Crédit Mobilier stock rose from five cents in 1866 to over three dollars in 1868, with annual dividends topping out at 805 percent, according to *The Encyclopedia Americana*. The government poured $94 million into the railway's construction, with the bank taking in $44 million of that in profits ($1.9 billion and $0.9 billion in 2020 dollars, respectively).

To further bolster congressional support for Crédit Mobilier, Ames went on his "bribery tour" of the District and its federal legislators. He sold hundreds of shares of stock at "par," at a sharp discount to their actual premiums. He cajoled his fellow lawmakers to get in on "the diamond mine." Quite a few, swooning at the stratospheric dividend rates, needed little persuasion. Yet sternly honest Gideon Welles, the secretary of the navy, wrote of Ames: "This man, worth millions, takes the position of Representative—seeks and gets it—for the purpose of promoting his private interest."

MEDIA REVELATIONS

But the high-rolling congressman faltered after a dispute with Delaware businessman H. S. McComb. He argued Ames owed him 375 shares in stock. He didn't get them, and eventually went public about the railroad swindle.

In September 1872, as President Grant's re-election campaign heated up, the *New York Sun* newspaper published McComb's charges. The full-page exposés were politically slanted, and contained some false accusations, but they captured the scandal's gist. The "King of Spades" was rebranded the "King of Frauds."

The anti-Grant newspaper revealed that members of Congress and the administration had pocketed stocks and dividend payments from Ames. They included some very big names: Grant's sitting vice president, Schuyler Colfax of Indiana; Massachusetts senator Henry Wilson, running as Grant's vice-presidential nominee that year; Ohio representative and future president James Garfield; and the Speaker of the House, Maine representative James Gillespie Blaine. All the legislators involved were on committees that either funded or oversaw the railroad. As Ames was later quoted: "We want more friends in this Congress," to persuade members "that we should not be interfered with."

President Grant was not a participant; the scheme had been put together years before he was elected. However, his administration, already rocked by scandal, was tarred by association with the many fellow Republicans who were implicated.

No proof was found that Speaker Blaine accepted Ames's solicitations. However, Blaine's hopes for the presidency were damaged four

This cartoon has Uncle Sam urging politicians—attired in Japanese kimonos, and enmired in the Crédit Mobilier scandal—to commit ritual suicide.

years later when he was accused of taking $64,000 in bond payments from Union Pacific.

COMMITTEES, HEARINGS, COVERUPS

The Republican-controlled House and Senate found themselves in an awkward spot. Almost all of the accused were in their party. Republicans didn't want to be seen as covering up the affair, but they also didn't want to hurt the re-election chances of Grant or their own congressmen.

So the Congress investigated, after a fashion. It set up investigative committees, several in the House and one in the Senate. But it clamped on a time limit for the inquiries. Further, the hearings were closed, for a while. After public protest, the transcripts were made public. A House committee headed by Republican Rep. Luke Potter Poland of Vermont met in December 1872. A second House committee, chaired by Rep. Jeremiah Wilson of Indiana, met when Congress reassembled in the new year.

Ames himself testified, in rambling and contradictory statements. He insisted he had done nothing wrong. And in fact, some of his colleagues were glad the cross-country railroad had been completed, by hook, or by crook. Moreover, Ames was irate at his apparent role of fall guy for the many lawmakers who'd taken part in, and profited from, his scheme. To strike back, he produced his "little black book," a ledger of the names of congressmen who'd bought or received stocks, with the dollar amounts listed. Still, Ames stated: "There were so many who talked to me about getting an interest in" Crédit Mobilier that "I cannot recollect all the names."

A major casualty of the inquiries was Vice President Colfax. He'd played ball with Ames in Congress as chair of the House Post Office Committee. Ames testified Colfax had bought stock from him with dividends. Colfax replied he never got dividends from Ames. But the House sergeant-at-arms produced evidence he had, according to an official Senate history. Then Colfax insisted Ames had signed the dividend check in question. But the House Committee turned up a deposit slip from Colfax's bank and in Colfax's handwriting. Then Colfax asserted he had gotten most of the money from a campaign donor. But the Committee produced indications the donor had bribed Colfax to obtain a Post Office contract.

Once considered the favorite to be the next president, Colfax left office in March 1873 in disgrace.

In testifying before the House, Representative Garfield issued a blanket denial. He swore he had "never owned, received, or agreed to take any stock of the Crédit Mobilier or of the Union Pacific Railroad, nor any dividends or profits arising from either of them." But he later admitted Ames's pestering had worn him down, and he'd obtained ten shares, about $1,000 worth, roughly $20,000 worth in 2020 dollars.

Garfield informed Congress that Ames told him "if I was not able to pay for it, he would hold it for me 'til I could pay, or until some of the dividends were payable." The future president also asserted rather dubiously he thought Crédit Mobilier was a construction firm for homes, not railroads, according to the book *Congress and the King of Frauds.*

The partisan legislature focused much of its ire, and punishment, on the lone Democrat fingered, Rep. James Brooks of New York. Brooks was not a villain from central casting. His family had freed their slaves before Emancipation. In New York, he ran against the Democrats' corrupt

Tammany Hall political machine. However, Brooks had a clear conflict of interest. While serving in Congress, he had also worked as Union Pacific's director of government affairs. In that role, it was illegal for him to buy the firm's stock. So, after dickering with Durant, it was arranged for his son-in-law to purchase upwards of $15,000 in stocks and bonds, which were discounted more than 65 percent. Brooks also got $9,000 in dividends. The House formally censured him.

The House also censured Ames, who gained another new nickname, "Hoax Oakes" Ames. He left Congress at the end of its session. Disgraced, he suffered a stroke. He died two months after departing the Capitol. Brooks died two months after leaving Congress as well.

SENATE OVERSIGHTS

The Senate's Committee of Investigation assembled in February 1873 and met for just three weeks. It was chaired by the usually upright Republican Sen. Lot Myrick Morrill of Maine. He was the namesake of fellow New Englander Justin Smith Morrill. Under his Morrill Act, Sen. Justin Morrill of Vermont sponsored legislation that over time set up a great many land-grant agricultural and technical colleges, from Penn State University to Texas A&M. Another Committee member was Democrat Sen. John P. Stockton of New Jersey. He was the son of Sen. Robert F. Stockton, who'd captained the ill-fated Navy warship the USS *Princeton*. In 1844, the secretary of state, the secretary of the navy, and four others were killed when one of the new ship's giant cannons exploded off of Mt. Vernon. Despite the gross negligence involved, Congress and the John Tyler Administration declined to seriously investigate the matter.

In his testimony before the Committee, Senator Wilson stretched credulity. He claimed he had known nothing about Ames or Crédit Mobilier. Wilson denied he'd bought stock, then admitted he had, he said, with money of his wife who, having died three years before, was unavailable for comment. Wilson said he then sold the shares back to Ames.

A motion to impeach Wilson failed along party lines. Some thought the Senate whitewashed the matter. It wasn't the first time Wilson had fallen under a cloud. Years before, he allegedly had an affair with Rose Greenhow, later the Confederate spy extraordinaire.

Wilson went on to be Grant's vice president, taking the place of the disgraced Colfax. However, during the 1872 campaign, Wilson undertook a ten-thousand-mile speaking tour, aimed in part to overcome the railroad allegations. The strenuous schedule undermined his health. He died in late 1875, leaving Grant without a vice president for his final year in office.

The Committee also found out that Sen. James Harlan of Iowa had taken $10,000, not from Ames, but from Durant, as a campaign donation. Like Wilson, however, Harlan avoided censure, in part because he was leaving office in March 1873.

Sen. Henry Laurens Dawes of Massachusetts came under fire. He was the cousin twice removed of William Dawes, famous with Paul Revere for warning the militia at Lexington and Concord during the American Revolution. He had bought $1,000 worth of stock, got cold feet, returned it, but kept a modest amount of dividends. He also pushed through a bill shielding Union Pacific from judicial review.

New Hampshire senator James Patterson, like Garfield, was caught denying buying stock from Ames, then admitting it before Congress. He said he gave Ames $7,000 to invest in Crédit Mobilier and Union Pacific but asserted he didn't own any stock in the companies. His story blew up when Ames produced the signed receipt proving Patterson had bought Crédit Mobilier shares. The Committee concluded the greatly discounted stock was in effect a bribe. However, Congress did not punish Patterson.

Cleared of illicit connections to the railway was powerful New York senator Roscoe Conkling. However, Conkling would later have a scandalous affair with Kate Chase, the wife of Rhode Island senator William Sprague IV, and daughter of Lincoln Treasury secretary Samuel Chase. Conkling would also benefit politically from a kickback operation at the US Customs House in New York City. (See the chapter on the Garfield assassination.) Also cleared was former Sen. James A. Bayard Jr., of Delaware, who had left the Senate three years before the scandal broke. Bayard was the son of Sen. James A. Bayard Sr., the pivotal congressman in the Electoral College deadlock over the 1800 presidential election. (See the chapter on the wild election of 1800.)

REVERBERATIONS AND REWARDS

The hearings, too quickly, wrapped up. Calls for an audit of Crédit Mobilier went unheeded. Many observers suspected then, and historians suspect today, that quite a few of the accused got away with taking bribes, and that up to a dozen or more other congressmen were involved, but never exposed. In the end, no one in Congress served any prison time.

Still the scandal had a big impact politically. The country was already souring on Washington City due to the Grant scandals. Then came a severe recession, the Panic of 1873. Firms like Crédit Mobilier helped trigger it through overinvestment in the railroads, the nation's largest industry. In the midterm elections of 1874, the Democrats picked up nine Senate seats, and a stunning ninety-four seats in the House. The party gained control of a house of Congress for the first time since the

Despite being financially drained, and its reputation besmirched by the scandal egged on by Rep. Oakes Ames, the Union Pacific railroad firm built a Wyoming memorial to Ames and his brother.

Civil War. (The House of Representatives had further fueled voter rage by giving itself a retroactive pay hike, at a time when people's livelihoods were stricken.) Crédit Mobilier was also a factor in blocking President Grant's nomination in 1880 for a third term. Tarred by the scandal, the Republican nominee that year, Garfield, barely eked out a victory.

The federal government sued Union Pacific for pilfering public monies. However, the Supreme Court declared a federal lawsuit against the firm had to wait all the way until 1895. In 1876, Durant, under pressure, quit the railroad firm. Taking it over was another "robber baron," Jay Gould, who, with the aid of a crooked Grant associate, had in 1868 reaped huge profits in an illicit attempt to corner the gold market.

Astonishingly, Union Pacific, while still stung from its association with Crédit Mobilier, built a sixty-foot granite monument in Wyoming to honor the Ames brothers. Its designer was renowned architect Henry Hobson Richardson, builder of the Henry Adams and John Hay mansions in Lafayette Square. The maker of its simple carvings of Oakes and Oliver Ames was Augustus Saint-Gaudens, creator of the *Grief* funereal statue for Henry Adams, a noted critic of the Gilded Age that Ames typified. Attending the 1882 dedication was President Hayes, who had been declared the winner of the 1876 election through a suspect political deal. Union Pacific declared bankruptcy after the Panic of 1893, another deep recession sparked largely by overinvestment in the iron horse. The company reorganized and is today a large and profitable concern.

With the exception of the mortgage collapse of 2007-2008, which Congress triggered in part through lavish support for subprime loans, rarely have the House and Senate been tarred by such financial malfeasance.

CHAPTER FOURTEEN

To a Horrible End: An Assassination and Its Aftermath

Garfield statue, Maryland Avenue and 1st Street, S.W.

BELOW THE SOUTHWEST CORNER OF THE CAPITOL BUILDING IS A meticulously preserved bronze statue of a relatively little-known president. One might wonder why James Abram Garfield gets a place of honor there, next to the legislature and just south of the grand Ulysses S. Grant Memorial. Garfield is one of those obscure, bearded presidents who served in the latter half of the nineteenth century, between Abraham Lincoln and Theodore Roosevelt. He was in office for only five months and had no significant accomplishments.

One reason Garfield is honored is he was a war hero. In fact, at the 1862 Civil War Battle of Shiloh, he helped save Grant's bacon. Grant, and his lieutenant, William Sherman, had nearly been pushed into the Tennessee River on the first day of fighting, before reinforcements, including Garfield's, arrived to push back the Confederates. The next year, General Garfield helped save the Union's bacon, at the Battle of Chickamauga, perhaps the war's bloodiest after Gettysburg, after rebel forces had again carried the start of the fight.

Another reason is that Garfield was a classic Horatio Alger story: born in a log cabin yet rising to the highest office in the land. In fact, his presidential campaign biography was authored by none other than the actual Horatio Alger.

PRELUDE TO TRAGEDY

But there's an even more significant reason why the Ohioan stands in that distinctive place. To learn why, you might follow the line of the statue out toward the National Mall and take a trip to his time in office. To the grandly turreted Baltimore and Potomac train station, which stood, on July 2, 1881, just six blocks to the west, on the corner of 6th Street and B Street, as Constitution Avenue was then called . . .

. . . Looking forward to a respite from the brutal heat of the Washington summer, Garfield was riding by carriage to the depot that morning with his secretary of state and political ally, James G. Blaine. The two

Though pleasing to the eye, the old Baltimore and Potomac railway depot on the National Mall caused deaths from trains hitting pedestrians and was the scene of the assassination of President Garfield.

top-ranking officials traveled, as was customary, without guards. Much of Garfield's Cabinet, and two of his sons, would be traveling with him to New England. They were already at the station.

Despite the beauty of its Gothic Revival design, the forty-nine-year-old president loathed the station, built in 1874. Every year, its trains ran over pedestrians and smashed into carriages. The smoke of its coal- and wood-burning engines and the din of its clanking wheels marred the grand public park Pierre L'Enfant had envisioned. Garfield wanted the station removed. (And over time it was, replaced by the out-of-the-way Union Station in 1907.)

As their horse and carriage pulled up to the depot, DC policeman Patrick Kearney met the two dignitaries. The cop told the president his train would depart in ten minutes. Garfield got out of the carriage, and Blaine went with him, as he "did not think it was proper for a president to go entirely unattended."

Inside the crowded station, a lean, politically obsessed man in a clean shirt and tattered suit had been pacing worriedly back and forth between the waiting rooms for ladies and gentlemen. It had been a busy day thus far for the thirty-nine-year-old Charles Julius Guiteau of Illinois.

That fine-weather morning, as had been his wont for months, he'd sat in Lafayette Square outside the White House. He knew from the newspapers when and from where the president was leaving town. For weeks, he'd been preparing

By firing his ivory-handled, .44-caliber British Bulldog revolver. Sometimes shooting at targets on the banks of the Potomac.

Destitute, he'd stayed at various lodgings in town for short periods, then skipped out on the bills. In fact, the innkeeper of his latest lodging had taken out an ad demanding payment. So, he'd escaped to the lobby of the prestigious Riggs Hotel and, after obtaining hotel stationery, had written out several unusual letters.

One was addressed to the White House. It read: "The President's tragic death . . . will unite the Republican party and save the Republic. Life is a fleeting dream, and it matters little when one goes. I presume the President was a Christian and that he will be happier in Paradise than here."

Another was addressed to General Sherman, then the commander of the Army:

"I have just shot the President. I shot him several times, as I wished him to go as easily as possible. His death was a political necessity . . . I am going to the jail. Please order out your troops and take possession of the jail at once.—Charles Guiteau."

AN OFFICE SEEKER MAKES HIS ROUNDS

Guiteau had been an attorney but spent much of his time as a bill collector, often stealing the money he collected. For years he was a member of the Oneida Community, a utopian endeavor that mixed socialism and Christianity. He wrote rapturously of its leader, John Humphrey Noyes, before suing him in court, and then plagiarizing his works for a book of his own. He married, then supported his wife's divorce case by openly sleeping with a prostitute. His family members considered Guiteau insane and tried to put him into an asylum.

In the 1880 presidential campaign, Garfield, a Republican, very narrowly defeated the Democratic candidate, fellow Union army war hero Winfield Scott Hancock. Guiteau had played a very minor role in favor of the winner. He wrote and distributed a few hundred copies of a speech, "Garfield vs. Hancock." One time he'd started to speak about it at a Republican function, before getting cold feet. Yet he was convinced his effort was the critical reason for Garfield's win. He thought he should receive a high-ranking federal position as a result. In New York, he met vice president–elect Chester Alan Arthur over ten times, badgering him unsuccessfully for a top job.

On the day after the president's inauguration on March 4, 1881, Guiteau traveled down to Washington. He joined the thousands of people applying for jobs with the new administration. He haunted the White House and, next door, the old State, War, and Navy Department Building. He tried wangling interviews with the new president and with Secretary of State Blaine. His aim was to get an appointment as minister to Austria, then the controlling half of the Austrian-Hungarian Empire, even though he didn't know German, and had no diplomatic background.

Blaine dismissed one of Guiteau's job letters as having "unparalleled audacity and impudence."

Denied the Austrian post, Guiteau pushed for the job of envoy to France, though he didn't know French. He wrote: "I think I prefer Paris to Vienna." An exasperated Blaine informed him: "Never speak to me again of the Paris consulship as long as you live!"

One day at the White House, Guiteau entered the office of the president's trusted chief of staff, young Joseph Stanley Brown. There Guiteau happened to meet Garfield himself. He slipped into the president's hands his campaign speech, with the words "Paris Consulship" scrawled on it. The president did not respond, though he wrote of the "Spartan band of disciplined office hunters" who "drew paper on me as highway men draw pistols." Guiteau even had a chance encounter with First Lady Lucretia Rudolph Garfield, and gave her his business card. Brown noticed Guiteau, who seemed to appear out of nowhere, at least a dozen times in and around the White House. Security was looser in the Executive Mansion back then.

Blaine's rejection infuriated Guiteau. He wrote Garfield, urging him to dismiss his secretary of state. Otherwise, he warned, "you and the Republican party will come to grief."

Customary Corruption

His rancor merged with a political donnybrook. President Garfield, usually a reformist, clashed with the powerful leader of New York's Republican Party, Roscoe Conkling. Senator Conkling, who had backed the scandal-tinged Ulysses S. Grant for a third-term as president in 1880, headed the stand-pat "Stalwarts" faction of the party. Garfield backed the "Half-Breeds" faction, which favored a civil service overhaul.

Garfield himself wasn't always scandal-free. As a congressman heading investigations into the 1867 "Black Friday" attempt to corner the gold market, he had gone easy on the perpetrators, in part because they were members of his own party. Further, in an even bigger scandal—the 1869 Crédit Mobilier payoffs to congressmen, relating to the construction of the transcontinental railway—Representative Garfield had himself accepted some shares in the railroad's stocks. (See the chapter on Crédit Mobilier.)

During his presidency, a big bone of contention was the patronage afforded by the US Customs House in lower Manhattan. It collected the federal tariffs on foreign goods entering America's busiest port. The employees there were required to kick back a percentage of their salary to New York's Republicans. Their head, the collector of the Port of New York, had been a Conkling protégé, one Chester Arthur. To unify his divided party at the 1880 convention, Garfield had made Arthur his running mate and, through his victory, vice president.

After his inauguration, Garfield, to Conkling's fury, had appointed a Half Breed to clean up the Customs House. Conkling and the other Republican senator from New York pressured the president to reconsider, by resigning from the Senate, but to no avail.

After Blaine refused to consider him for a diplomatic post, Guiteau came under the delusion he was divinely ordained to unify the Republican Party, and the nation, by killing Garfield. And thus make Arthur, a Stalwart, president. The logic of lunatics can be hard to grasp.

THE STALKING OF THE PRESIDENT

Guiteau considered different means of murdering Garfield. At first, he thought a simple knife might do. But he concluded the vigorous ex-soldier, in confronting Guiteau and a stiletto, "would have crushed the life out of me with a single blow of his fist." He also pondered using TNT. But he deemed an anarchist-style bombing "too Russian, too barbarous. No! I wanted it done in an American manner," he wrote. He was also concerned for his own safety: "I was afraid to handle the stuff." He noted that "in my inexperience it might explode in my hands . . . tear me to pieces," according to *Smithsonian*.

One time he'd gotten close to Garfield with a loaded gun but backed off because the president's sons were with him, and he didn't want to upset them. Another time he followed Garfield on an earlier trip to the Baltimore and Potomac depot, but decided against shooting him because his ailing wife Lucretia was there. "No!" Guiteau recalled. "The country must wait a while . . . because if I shoot that man at this time before his wife, it will kill her." He was a finicky and rather reflective assassin.

On July 1, the night before the deed, Guiteau was in Lafayette Square when he spotted the president leave the White House and stroll through the park, then head over to the home of Blaine one block away. Guiteau waited outside and, when Garfield and Blaine walked out together, the stalker readied his revolver. But Blaine and pedestrians kept blocking Guiteau's line of sight, spoiling the chance for a clear shot.

These abortive attempts drove Guiteau close to despair. "Well, you are no good," he told himself. "Your President comes right to you to be shot, and you let your heart get in the road of your head and your hand."

On July 2, Guiteau rode to the train station with a female acquaintance. As he bid the woman farewell, he said: "You told me one day . . . to go do something that would make me famous. Just keep that in your mind till you see it accomplished." His long hunt was coming to an end.

At the depot, Guiteau gave his letters intended for Garfield and Sherman to a young man running a newspaper stand. He knew the fellow would later alert the authorities about the missives. To make sure he looked his best, Guiteau got a shoeshine.

He also arranged for his getaway carriage. Outside, at B and 6th, he asked a hack driver how much it cost to ride to Congressional Cemetery, two miles to the southeast. The graveyard was next to the City Jail where he expected to be detained. Guiteau agreed to the $2 fare and asked the driver to wait for him.

The assassin went inside and entered a waiting room. For one last time, he took the .44-caliber revolver from his pocket, removed the paper sleeve protecting it from the sweat of his hands, and made sure the mechanisms worked.

At 9:30 a.m., Guiteau was standing outside the ladies waiting room when President Garfield, with Blaine alongside him, came striding into the station, and walked right by.

Silently addressing himself, Guiteau thought: "Immortality will shortly be yours." Looking at Garfield, he silently breathed: "This is the hour of your doom!"

The *chargé d'affaires* for the Venezuelan embassy, Simon Camacho, happened to be standing nearby. He got a direct look at Guiteau.

"His eye was steady," recalled Camacho, and it "presented the appearance of a man . . . determined upon a desperate deed, and meant to do it calmly. . . ."

Guiteau, hand on the gun, extended his right arm toward the president. From three feet away, he pulled the trigger.

A bullet shot through Garfield's right arm and smashed into the toolbox of a startled glassmaker.

The president twisted around, and called out:

"My God! What is this?!"

According to Camacho, Guiteau then lost his composure. He hurriedly fired off his second shot.

Still, this bullet hit home. It struck Garfield in the right side of his lower back. His knees buckled and, vomiting, he sank to the floor of the station, his hands breaking the fall. A stain of blood spread through his shirt.

A stark rendering of Garfield's assassination at the hands of the crazed office seeker Charles Guiteau. The assassin was tried for murder after the president's physicians botched Garfield's care.

A stunned Blaine stood alongside him, then shouted out to close the exits. Policeman Kearney hurried into the station.

In the busy depot, there was stunned silence. Then cries of "Catch him!" Then fury, as people rushed toward Guiteau, with the goal of beating him bloody.

"Lynch him!" cried a group of black workmen. They had a special animus, perhaps, as Garfield was a backer of civil rights.

Guiteau, the color drained from his face, wheeled around, and made a run for the B Street exit. But Camacho rushed over to block his way.

The assassin reversed course and dashed toward the 6th Street exit. But a ticket agent reached out and grabbed him by the neck. Then Kearney raced over and caught him in a bearhug.

Terrified of being torn to pieces, Guiteau pleaded with Kearney to take him into custody. The cop hauled him outside the station and to a nearby police station. Just in time, for enraged citizens swirled about the depot, shouting for his death.

In a ride to the City Jail, Guiteau's nerves settled down. He told a detective that Vice President Arthur was his friend, and the gumshoe could be made chief of police.

He exulted: "I am a Stalwart of the Stalwarts! I did it, and I want to be arrested! Arthur is President now!"

First, Do Much Harm

As the president lay on the station floor, a crowd of the curious gathered about him. His young sons Harry and Jim screamed at people to give their father breathing room. Within minutes of the attack, the District's chief medical officer, Dr. Smith Townsend, arrived. After pushing his way through the crowd, he examined the president as his bloodied back lay on the dirty floor. With unwashed hands, the physician inserted a finger into the wound, feeling for the bullet, but was unable to find the slug.

Garfield was placed on a hay-and-horsehair mattress and carried up to an empty room on the station's second floor. Soon, ten physicians who had rushed over on hearing the news were attending to him. Each one examined the president's wound with unwashed hands, probing the bloody cavity with his fingers.

The president slipped in and out of consciousness. When awake, the old soldier was calm, with his wife Lucretia a major concern. She was still recovering from a serious bout with malaria. Given her frail health, he feared news of his shooting might kill her. He had a friend, Almon Rockwell, compose a telegram that broke the news to the first lady: "The President wishes me to say to you from him that he has been seriously hurt—how seriously he cannot yet say. He is himself and hopes that you will come to him soon. . . ."

Although the groundbreaking work of Joseph Lister and Ignaz Semmelweis on antiseptics was by then widely practiced in Europe, it was still mostly ignored in America. Many US doctors also dismissed Louis Pasteur's related research on bacteria. (Robert Koch's discovery of viruses lay in the future.) A skeptical physician had stated three years prior: "To successfully practice Mr. Lister's Antiseptic Method, it is necessary that we should believe . . . the atmosphere to be loaded with germs."

Still, one attending medico had doubts about the rough handling of Garfield. This was Dr. Charles Burleigh Purvis. The first African-American surgeon in the Union army, he was then head of the anatomy department of Howard University's medical school. But his concerns were dismissed.

One of the Cabinet members on hand was Garfield's secretary of war, Robert Todd Lincoln, President Lincoln's surviving child. Lincoln thought back to sixteen years before, and his horrifying death watch over his stricken father, just seven blocks away at the Petersen House across from Ford's Theatre.

"How many hours of sorrow I have passed in this town?" sighed Lincoln. Incredibly, he would also be present at the 1901 assassination of President William McKinley in Buffalo, New York. When McKinley's successor, Theodore Roosevelt, invited Lincoln to an official function, he demurred, believing three presidential killings enough for any man.

At the depot, Lincoln made a fateful, and fatal, decision, one that President Garfield would later heartily endorse. He sent his carriage for Dr. D. Willard Bliss, a well-known doctor whom Garfield had known since childhood. When he arrived, the arrogant, hidebound Bliss seized control over Garfield's care. He would not relinquish it for the next eleven weeks.

Like the other doctors, Bliss manually inspected Garfield's wound. His prognosis was grim. He said the president "will not probably live three hours," perhaps not even a half hour more.

In 1881, hospitals were crowded and unhealthy places. When people got sick, they were usually cared for in their homes. At Garfield's insistence, measures were taken to bring him back to the White House. The president was placed into a horse-drawn ambulance, whose driver maneuvered it slowly along the streets' uneven bricks. So slowly that a procession of concerned citizens and police were able to accompany the carriage. Whenever a pothole was encountered, they lifted the carriage wheels over it.

One of the tragedies of the president's slaying was the large family he left behind, including daughter Mollie, pictured with her father.

At the Executive Mansion, Garfield was taken to a room on the second floor of the northeast corner, across from the Treasury Building and the old Freedmen's Bank for former slaves. The president was conscious, and resolute. He used a naval analogy to console his son Jim: "The upper story is alright. It is only the hull that is damaged."

Downtown, thousands of Washingtonians wandered the streets in a daze, unable to comprehend what had happened.

At the jail, the police who had taken Guiteau into custody realized, to their chagrin, they had neglected some elementary policing. When they emptied Guiteau's pockets, they discovered his revolver, tucked away and with cartridges still in it.

Guiteau was placed in Cell Two, in Murderers' Row on the top floor of the prison's south side. To prevent escape, his cell was sealed with a five-lock tumbler. It was impossible for anyone to crack. Except for escape artist Harry Houdini, who would unlock it in a demonstration years later.

The prisoner crowed about his deed, and his certainty that Arthur would soon release him. One guard, named William Mason, got fed up, and decided to assassinate the assassin. He fired a gun at Guiteau as he stood at his cell window. The bullet just missed and smashed into a wall. Mason would spend eight years in jail for the assault. Copies of his bullet were made, and souvenir hunters snapped them up.

IGNORANCE IS BLISS
At the White House, Dr. Bliss turned optimistic. He contacted various physicians: "Dear Doctor: At the request of the President, I write to advise you that his symptoms are at present so favorable, as to render unnecessary any further consultations. . . ."

Bliss barred doctors from offering advice contrary to his own. He also forbade other physicians from treating the president, other than two trusted colleagues: Dr. David Hayes Agnew, the professor of surgery at the University of Pennsylvania, and Dr. Frank Hamilton, a surgeon at a New York medical college. The prohibition applied even to two doctors close to the Garfield family: Dr. Silas Boynton, the president's cousin, and a female doctor, Susan Edson, Lucretia Garfield's personal physician. Bliss forbade the pair from performing anything other than nursing duties.

At least one physician objected strongly to Bliss's medical quarantine: the president's personal physician, Dr. Jedediah Baxter. When he tried to see Garfield, Bliss blocked him, and exploded: "I know your game. You wish to sneak up here and take this case out of my hands!" Baxter retorted, "That is a lie!", and stormed out. Later, Lucretia Garfield would openly deny Bliss's claim that she had approved his taking over the case.

Dr. Bliss had a checkered career in medicine. He'd promoted a South American herb as a cure-all for cancer. He'd been kicked out of the D.C. Medical Society for advocating homeopathy, the largely discredited notion of treating toxic reactions with tiny doses of the toxin. On the other hand, he'd been a respected Civil War surgeon at the busy Armory Square Hospital, on the National Mall site of today's Air and Space Museum. After rejoining the Society, Bliss was fearful of another rejection by the medical establishment. He grew to distrust any novel medical therapy, such as Lister's use of antiseptics.

Bliss deemed it critical the president maintain his strength. He put a man with a gunshot wound in his abdomen on a heavy diet. The president was fed eggs, steak, bacon, milk, and lamb chops. Bliss also plied him with champagne, brandy, and morphine. Garfield "was nauseated with heavy food," commented his cousin. The presidential patient threw up constantly.

The White House was not an ideal place to treat an ill person. It had undergone no major renovation since its reconstruction after the War of 1812. Rats scurried through the basement kitchen, leaving their droppings near the food preparations. The water was barely potable, as the plumbing was falling apart. The Tidal Basin down the hill was still marshy, sending off swarms of mosquitoes. Four of Garfield's White House staff came down with malaria, and the first lady had nearly died from it. Bliss and the other doctors, believing the disease stemmed from the bad odors of the nearby swamp, plied Garfield with quinine as a preventative.

The insects thrived in the bogs and the summer heat. Indeed, the high temperatures were a potential killer for Garfield. He lay, never getting up once, in a stuffy room on the opposite side of the mansion from the region's prevailing breeze.

Artificially cooled air was then unknown. But Navy engineers, aided by explorer John Wesley Powell, devised a brilliant innovation. One that took advantage of the early days of electricity, albeit in a rather Rube Goldberg way.

In the room next to the president's, they placed big chunks of ice in two metal containers. They rigged up a thirty-six-inch electrical fan that blew over the ice. The cooled air was forced into tin pipes leading to Garfield's chamber. The temperature there dropped dramatically, to below 60 degrees Fahrenheit, alleviating the confined patient's suffering. The tin pipes made a terrible racket, so the technicians muffled them with canvas. It was the first air conditioner.

PATIENT PROPAGANDA

As he controlled access to the president, Bliss tightly managed the flow of information about his patient. He issued regular medical bulletins that newspapers and telegraph companies placed outside their offices in large-script posters.

The bulletins were uniformly positive. Knowing Garfield read the newspapers every morning, Bliss reasoned the president's mental state might worsen if he saw bad news about himself. "If the slightest unfavorable symptom was mentioned," said Bliss, "it was instantly telegraphed all over the country, and appeared in every newspaper." In a talk with a *New York Times* reporter, he termed Garfield's injury "a happy wound," stating, "we have very little to fear."

For several weeks, Garfield did seem to stabilize. And his family took heart from the hundreds of Washingtonians who camped out on the White House lawn, praying and pulling for him, anxious for any news on his status. But on July 22, the president took a sudden swerve to the worse. His temperature rose to 104 degrees. Abscesses filled with pus, a sign of infection, erupted throughout his body. He couldn't hold down food and lost his appetite entirely. Also, the president had constant, excruciating pain, from his testicles down to his feet.

Bliss, Hamilton, and Agnew responded by draining the pus, with unclean instruments. They judged their work a success. The president, proclaimed Bliss, "discharged several ounces of healthy pus." In addition, they probed Garfield's body, in the same unsterilized, intrusive way. During the procedures, they teased out bits of bone and muscle. Medical historians surmise one of the procedures punctured Garfield's bladder.

In these examinations, the physicians searched for the bullet on the assumption it lay on the right side of Garfield's body, where the slug had entered. Their probing dug out a long, infected channel in his back. But in fact, the bullet had veered in the opposite direction to his *left* side. It was buried, harmlessly it seems, in a layer of tissue near the pancreas.

FROM TELEPHONY TO TREATMENT

As Garfield's status veered to critical, Bliss finally reached out beyond his own small team. He called on the greatest engineer of the day: Alexander Graham Bell, the inventor of the telephone and, later, a prototype wireless phone. Bell had a downtown laboratory on Connecticut Avenue, and later another one on Georgetown's aptly named Volta Place. He often visited the Patent Office to defend the rights to his inventions.

The Scottish-born Bell, then thirty-four years old, had closely followed Garfield's illness. He was horrified at the doctors' crude methods of probing for the bullet. Bell knew his invention of the "induction balance," which cancelled out interference on phone wires, could also detect the presence of metal. He figured it could find the lead bullet buried in Garfield's back. Fighting off crippling headaches, he worked furiously to improve the device. It could detect a piece of metal buried at least three inches below the skin. It functioned like a crude X-ray, an invention fourteen years in the future.

With Bliss's permission, Bell made two visits to the White House, on July 26 and August 1. On both occasions, he and his assistant hauled in the complex device and its tangle of wires. Bell and the doctors gathered around the president; Garfield turned on his side, and had his bedclothes hitched up above his waist.

After an initial technical glitch, resulting from the worried haste in which Bell had labored, the induction balance worked. However, there were three major flaws in Bell's examinations.

The first was Bliss insisted that he, not Bell, search for the bullet. Bell, the only person experienced with the machine's use, stood nearby,

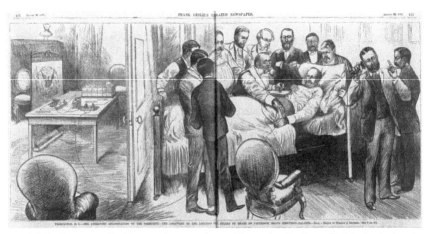

Garfield's doctors called in peerless engineer Alexander Graham Bell to try to locate the assassin's bullet buried in the president's back.

and listened with a telephone receiver for the tell-tale buzzing sound that indicated the presence of metal. As Bliss ran the device up and down along the president's spine, Bell heard a faint noise, but nothing like the definitive sound he had heard in his lab. He reluctantly concluded, and Bliss announced with great fanfare, that they had identified the bullet's proximate location. Dr. Bliss issued a bulletin his team was "now unanimously agreed that the location of the ball has been ascertained with reasonable certainty, and that it lies . . . about five inches below and to the *right* of the navel. [*italics mine*]"

Thus the second flaw. Incredibly, Bliss insisted on maneuvering the flat, wooden device only on the right side of Garfield's body, where he was convinced the bullet was located. He could easily have examined the left side too. But he refused to.

To his horror, Bell realized the third flaw when returning to his lab after the second procedure. Garfield had been lying on a horsehair mattress—which had been placed atop a steel mattress. The metal could very well have interfered with the induction balance.

Bell sought a third visit to detect the bullet. But by then Garfield's condition had turned dire, the pus and the infections spreading throughout his body. And Bell faced a crisis of his own. He rushed up to Boston to be with his ailing and pregnant wife Mable. Soon after his arrival, she gave birth to a son, who died soon after. Crushed by his own tragedy, the great scientist was knocked out of the picture.

FINAL JOURNEY, AND FINAL INTRUSION

The president expressed a wish, perhaps a death wish—though couched as a desperate bid to regain his health—to visit the shore. To go to the northern New Jersey town of Elberon, where Lucretia Garfield had rebounded from her malaria. Bliss was reluctant, but at this point was himself glum about saving his patient. Perhaps the ocean air and its change of scenery might help. Yet astonishingly, Bliss continued to put out blissful bulletins on the president. He reported: "no abscess, no pus. . . . The trouble . . . is going away." By then reporters, and the president's men, no longer believed him.

Meanwhile, remarkable preparations were made for Garfield's trip. The ceiling of his train compartment was lowered to afford better air circulation. Gauze was wrapped around the outside of his car to keep out soot from the locomotive's smokestack. In the District, new tracks were laid to spare the president from going past the depot where he was shot. Along the route to northern New Jersey, engineers cleared rolling stock from the tracks to make way for the president. At Elberon, workmen laid down new tracks to let the train proceed almost to the door of Garfield's lodging, a twenty-two-room house that a wealthy admirer had lent him.

The home overlooking the Atlantic was, alas, too steep for the train's engine to climb. But, in a heartening scene, hundreds of sturdy locals pitched in to push the president's car up the hill to his abode. Getting his wish, President Garfield was propped up at a window overlooking the ocean.

On September 19, at 10:00 p.m., with his friend Almon Rockwell at his side, Garfield called out that he had a terrible pain in the chest. Bliss told Lucretia Garfield the end was near. This time, he put out no optimistic bulletin. At 10:35, Garfield's faint heartbeat faded to naught. His two hundredth, and final, day as president was over.

Garfield's body was returned to Washington by the same train that brought him to New Jersey. He lay in state at the Capitol Building, where over seventy thousand citizens paid their respects. But not before an autopsy was performed at the cottage where he died. Performing the incisions was Dr. Daniel S. Lamb, of the Army Medical Museum, now the National Museum of Health and Medicine.

A hospital administrator and pharmacist during the Civil War, Dr. Lamb would perform an autopsy in 1890 on slain congressman William Taulbee. (See the chapter on the Taulbee-Kincaid clash.) At his procedure were Bliss, Hamilton, Agnew, and three other doctors, including Dr. George F. Shrady Sr., who would fail to successfully treat former President Grant during his fatal bout with cancer. (Shrady's son would sculpt the Grant memorial next to the Garfield statue.)

Dr. Lamb made a long vertical cut along Garfield's spine, and a long horizontal cut. He found much evidence of infection: abscesses in the head, back, kidney, and liver. The examiners saw evidence of pneumonia in both the lungs. They found the immediate cause of death was a hemorrhage to the artery of the spleen.

Lamb searched in vain for the bullet on the right side of the corpse. Then, to his and the others' shock, he found it—on the left side, next to the pancreas.

Dr. Agnew commented: "Gentlemen . . . we made a mistake."

A Circus Trial

The president's death meant Guiteau's trial could go ahead, with a charge of murder. The proceedings were held a short walk from the Capitol at the old Supreme Court of the District of Columbia, now the US District Court for DC at Pennsylvania Avenue and 3rd Street, N.W.

As in any highly publicized murder case, and given the public's wrath toward Guiteau, it was hard to find an unbiased jury. In the end, twelve not as angry men were selected from 175 potential jurors. Among the courtroom spectators was Frederick Douglass, who had campaigned for Garfield.

Presiding over the trial, which started on November 14, was Judge Walter Cox. The lead prosecutor was Garfield's former attorney general, and now President Arthur's attorney general, Wayne MacVeagh. Another prosecution lawyer was Elihu Root, a future senator who'd be the secretary of war during the Spanish-American War for President McKinley, and then secretary of state for President Theodore Roosevelt.

In counterpoint to the high-powered prosecution, the chief attorney for the defense resigned after a week. His place was taken by George Scoville, the husband of Guiteau's sister Frances. Scoville was a patent attorney with scant experience in criminal law.

He was also hamstrung by his brother-in-law's courtroom antics, according to Candice Millard's *Destiny of the Republic*. Guiteau loudly interrupted the judge and witnesses, while gleefully shaking the hands of spectators. When the judge forbade the defendant from making a public statement, he simply handed copies of it to the reporters in the court, who duly published it. Guiteau savagely attacked his in-law, telling Scoville, "You are a jackass on the question of cross-examination." Judge Cox, hoping to avoid grounds for a retrial or appeal, declined to gag Guiteau or order him out of the court.

On learning a goodwill fund had been set up for Garfield's widow, Guiteau demanded the same. "The rich men of New York gave Mrs. Garfield $200,000," he proclaimed in one court session. "It was a splendid thing. . . . Now I want them to give me some money."

For a New York newspaper, the assassin composed an autobiography, in which he announced his intent to run for president in 1884. He also offered himself up for marriage. He sought "an elegant Christian lady of wealth, under 30," from "a first-class family."

Guiteau entered a plea of not guilty. Due, he stated, to "Insanity, in that it was God's act and not mine. The Divine pressure on me to remove the president was so enormous that it removed my free agency. . . ."

One semi-rational point Guiteau brought up was that Garfield's doctors were his true killers. "General Garfield died from malpractice," he stated. "According to his own physicians, he was not fatally shot. The doctors who mistreated him ought to bear the odium of his death, and not his assailant."

Guiteau was fortunate to make it through the trial. After one session, when guards took him by carriage back to the City Jail, an irate farmer rode up and fired off a pistol at the killer. The bullet missed, barely, leaving a hole in the terrified prisoner's jacket.

A darkly comic cartoon of the "disappointed office seeker," assassin Charles Guiteau.

As Guiteau admitted to shooting Garfield, and witnesses had seen him do it, the trial hinged on whether he was sane. The testimony included thirty-six experts in psychiatry. About two-thirds who took the stand backed the prosecution's case. Dr. John Purdue Gray of the New York Lunatic Asylum told the court: "A man may become profoundly depraved, and degraded by mental habits, and yet not be insane. It is only depravity." Also testifying were senators, Secretary Blaine, and President Arthur, via written statement.

One of the prosecution's lawyers was District Attorney George Corkhill. He was known for exposing crooked politicians benefitting from the federally subsidized Pony Express mail service. Corkhill had contempt for Guiteau's claims of lunacy, stating: "There's nothing of the mad about Guiteau: he's a cool, calculating blackguard, a polished ruffian. Finally, he got tired of the monotony of deadbeating. He wanted excitement of some other kind . . . and he got it."

For its part, the defense noted a history of mental illness in Guiteau's family. If the defendant were a petty criminal, and not a presidential assassin, it was argued, many asylums would have classified him as insane. Indeed, just one year later, Maj. Henry Rathbone—who had lapsed into insanity after being wounded during the assassination of President Lincoln—murdered his wife. Authorities consigned Rathbone to an asylum.

The trial concluded on January 26, 1882. The jury reached its verdict within an hour. Foreman John Hamlin declared to the court: "Guilty as indicted."

The courtroom, reflecting the public mood, exploded in applause. Guiteau exploded in anger.

"My blood be on the head of the jury!" he shouted. "God will avenge this outrage!"

After his date of execution was set, Guiteau made a late appeal for clemency from President Arthur. He wrote: "I made you . . . the least you can do is to let me go." He added, "But I appreciate your delicate position." Arthur met with several psychiatrists about Guiteau's mental state. But he and his attorney general rejected intervention, and the Supreme Court declined to hear an appeal.

Frances Scoville made desperate attempts to save her brother's life. She wrote Lucretia Garfield, pleading: "In Heaven . . . we are known. The sainted Garfield knows now that [Guiteau] 'had to do it,' . . . if [Garfield] could speak, he would say, 'Forgive that deluded man . . . safely keep him from doing any more harm but forgive.'" Lucretia did not reply. So Frances traveled to the former first lady's home in Cleveland, and called on the widow. Lucretia refused to see her.

Day of Doom

On Death Row, Guiteau befriended a minister, and asked warden John Crocker for a special favor. That he let Guiteau read from the scaffold a prayer of his own composition. At the conclusion of which, he'd be hanged. The warden agreed to the theatrical demise.

The execution was the hottest ticket in town. For the 250 slots available, twenty thousand people applied.

Workmen built a gallows in a courtyard at the northeast part of the jail. The windows of the prison blocks overlooking the yard were covered up with thick drapery.

At noon on June 30, 1882, three days shy of the one-year anniversary of the shooting, Guiteau met his end. Grinning, he danced over to the scaffold. He waved at the onlookers. He shook the hand of the hangman.

On the platform, he read out his written prayer: "I am going to the Lordy, I am so glad . . . Glory hallelujah! . . . I am going to the Lordy!" He finished, and dropped the prayer, his signal to the hangman.

His body dropped, and his neck cleanly broke. As with the District's first hanging, of James McGirk in 1802, spectators took bits of the hangman's noose, prizing them as souvenirs.

POSTMORTEMS

Dr. Lamb also performed the autopsy on Guiteau. His brain was sliced up, and shipped to psychiatrists nationwide, who examined the remains for indications of a warped mind. Nothing out of the ordinary was noted. However, the postmortem found Guiteau had suffered from an unusual malady that might have contributed to psycho-sexual problems. He'd been afflicted with phimosis, an inability to remove the foreskin from one's penis.

Guiteau's left hand, left foot, and some of his bones were sent to the Army Medical Museum, where they remain in a drawer. Next to a drawer containing the spine of Garfield, and the spine of John Wilkes Booth. Parts of two presidential assassins and one assassinated president have lain in close proximity for a century and a half.

After Garfield's murder, presidents remained without formal protection. The Secret Service would not take charge of guarding the chief executive until Theodore Roosevelt, after the assassination of William McKinley.

As for the unfortunately named Dr. Bliss, he was unrepentant. He claimed Garfield had died, not from infection, but from a broken back. He brazenly demanded Congress pay him $25,000 for medical services. Congress, irate, offered about a quarter of that. And after the Garfield case, Bliss's medical services were in little demand.

CHAPTER FIFTEEN

Stain on the Steps: A Reporter Shoots an Ex-Congressman at the Capitol

House of Representatives, second-floor stairway landing

WASHINGTON CORRESPONDENT CHARLES KINCAID HAD FINALLY HAD it, up to his ears, so to speak, that February 28th of 1890. For several years, William Preston Taulbee, a lobbyist and former Kentucky congressman, had bullied, browbeaten, and outright beaten him.

UNFAIR ADVANTAGE

That very morning, on the House side of the Capitol, the athletic, six-foot, two-inch Taulbee had run into Kincaid. The reporter, who was waiting in a hall for a meeting, tried to avoid a confrontation.

"I have no time to talk with you," he told his hulking tormentor. "I don't want any trouble with you." He continued meekly: "I am a small man and unarmed."

The ex-lawmaker sneered: "You had better be armed or go and arm yourself."

The strapping Taulbee caught ahold of Kincaid. It was an unequal match. The journalist was hardly over five feet, was sickly from bouts with typhoid, and suffered from nervous indigestion and eye disease. The lobbyist pulled his ear, grabbed his collar, and tossed him about. House doormen pulled the men apart.

The thirty-eight-year-old Taulbee, a Kentucky Democrat, often tormented the thirty-four-year-old Kincaid. In their chance encounters, he was known to stomp on Kincaid's feet or throw him into a railing. He stalked him at the Capitol, telling him one time: "I ought to cut your throat." Kincaid, a former city judge and like Taulbee an attorney, was humiliated. He feared for his life.

That morning, the journalist fled the Capitol Building, and went to his residence in town. With Taulbee's threats ringing in his ears, he decided on a preemptive strike.

A SCANDALOUS COMEDOWN

It had all started in December 1887, when Taulbee was a second-term congressman. Kincaid published in the *Louisville Times* an exposé. Taulbee, who was the married father of five sons, was having a sordid affair with a Miss Laura L. Dodge. The article's headline blared: "Kentucky's Silver-Tongued Taulbee Caught in Flagrante, or Thereabouts, with Brown-Haired Miss Dodge."

Dodge worked at the Patent Office Building, today's National Portrait Gallery. It seems the lovers cavorted before lunch amidst the rows of patent files. Taulbee and his mistress, according to Kincaid, engaged in "sweet communion for half an hour."

After brief coverage, the *Washington Post* and other local papers buried the story. However, the *Louisville Times* and other Kentucky sheets gave it major play. Kincaid even looked up Miss Dodge and interviewed her, at her parents' house on Capitol Hill. He described her as "a little beauty, bright as sunshine and saucy as a bowl of jelly. She is petite of figure, but plump as a partridge. . . ."

The publicity about the affair wrecked the reputation of Taulbee. He was an ordained Methodist church minister as well as a politician and was branded a hypocrite. He and his wife, wed for over fifteen years, temporarily parted. His promising career as the "Mountain Orator" of Congress ended. He bowed out of a bid for a third term.

FROM CONGRESSMAN TO CAJOLER

However, after jumping from his lover's cot, he landed squarely on his feet. He became a noted example of what has been called "Washington's revolving door," moving nimbly from legislator to lawyer-lobbyist.

In so doing he quintupled his salary. He became a happy component of the Gilded Age, where wealthy corporations and their hired hands on the Hill openly bought and sold legislation and at times lawmakers.

As his work was at Capitol Hill, where he peddled influence, Taulbee often ran into Kincaid, whose work as a Hill reporter placed him in the same halls. This gave Taulbee opportunities for revenge. He took to pulling on Kincaid's nose, crushing his toes, bullying and threatening and fill-

After his extramarital affair was exposed, former Kentucky representative William Taulbee mercilessly bullied investigative reporter Charles Kincaid.

ing the little man with dread about the next encounter with his far larger antagonist.

Then came the collar-pulling incident, and Kincaid's flight from Congress to his home. At 1:30 that afternoon, he returned to the House side of the Capitol.

SAVAGERY AMIDST THE STAIRS

After the morning confrontation, Taulbee sensed trouble. He asked the House's doorman, a friend of his named Samuel, to walk with him down a stairway in the House.

They were on its second-floor landing.

Suddenly Kincaid came into view. He had a pistol with him.

Accounts differ on what happened next.

According to Taulbee's supporters, Kincaid was walking down the stairway behind Taulbee. He pointed his gun at the lobbyist and cried out: "Can you see me now?!"

The former legislator turned toward him. A frightened Samuel fled.

According to Kincaid's side of the story, Taulbee acted first. When he spotted Kincaid, he moved toward him, raising his left arm threateningly.

Kincaid told him, "You're going to kill me. Stand back!"
Kincaid pulled out his gun.

Taulbee kept moving toward him, according to Kincaid. Taulbee told him: "I'll show you!"

Kincaid took some steps backward. Taulbee got to within about three feet of him.

The reporter pointed the gun at Taulbee, and fired a single shot. The bullet entered the man's skull just below his left eye.

He staggered, took a few steps, then fell, blood pouring out from his head onto the marbled floor.

A policeman quickly arrived on the scene. He asked Kincaid: "Who is responsible for this?"

The reporter responded: "I did it."

The police arrested Kincaid.

Taulbee was taken to the city's Providence Hospital.

Remarkably, despite a bullet in his skull, he got noticeably better for over a week. He was able to speak. According to his brother, he was able to recall the confrontation with Kincaid leading up to the shooting.

However, his condition suddenly worsened, as swelling caused by the slug pushed his brain against his skull. He died on March 11, twelve days after the shooting.

JUDGE, JURY, JOURNALIST

Kincaid's trial was delayed for a long time due to sessions of Congress. Many of the would-be witnesses for both men labored on the Hill and were preoccupied with their work. Meanwhile Kincaid was released on his own recognizance, due to ill health, and recuperated in Kentucky. Finally, he was put on trial for murder in Washington, on March 23, 1891, over a year after Taulbee's death.

The prosecution argued the killing was an open-and-shut case. But its lead lawyer, US Attorney Charles Cole, was a novice with high-profile controversies. In fact, President Benjamin Harrison had just appointed him to his job.

In contrast, Kincaid had a strong defense team, headed by Indiana senator Daniel Voorhees, and by Ohio representative Charles Grosvenor. The defense stressed the many times Taulbee had badgered and threatened Kincaid. It had many persuasive witnesses, including eight congressmen, current or retired, who testified on the reporter's behalf. One recalled Taulbee stating that Kincaid "ought to be killed. By God, I'll kill him."

The trial took two weeks, the jury deliberation just several hours. The jurors acquitted Kincaid, concluding he had truly acted in self-defense.

Most of the politicians and the press agreed, though Taulbee's family thought the trial a travesty of justice. Today, some of his descendants still feel the same. His great-granddaughter commented that "his murderer got away with murder. And five boys were left without a father. A wife was left without a husband to support her."

After he was cleared, Kincaid had a distinguished career, working as a journalist, a US diplomat, and a Kentucky railway administrator. But his health was ever frail; he died in 1901 at age fifty-one.

As for the woman in the affair, Laura Dodge kept her eye on successful men. She married a manager at the vast Pension Bureau complex north of the Capitol, and when he died in 1927, she wed a prominent lawyer.

To this day, a stain mars the marble floor where Taulbee's blood was spilled.

The killing remains the only time a violent incident in the halls of the House or Senate caused the death of a current or former member of Congress.

CHAPTER SIXTEEN

Coxey's Ragtime Ragtags: An Uproarious March Presages Large-Scale Protests

Southern and eastern edge of the Capitol Building, New Jersey Avenue, S.W. and S.E.

ON MAY DAY, 1894, THE ONE HUNDRED OR SO THREADBARE MARCHERS were near the very end of their exhausting, thirty-seven-day trek. Around 1:00 p.m., they paused outside Brock's Hotel on New Jersey Avenue and B Street, S.W., today's Independence Avenue. To their left was the looming hulk of the Capitol Building. All around them were the thousands of the curious, who'd come to see the spectacle of Coxey's highly publicized "Army."

Its "petition in boots" called for unprecedented federal action to tackle the nationwide depression, and long-term joblessness, which had ensued from the financial Panic of 1893. The long march had begun in late March, at Massillon, Ohio. It wended 350 miles through Pennsylvania and across the Allegheny Mountains into Maryland, then on to Washington City.

A COLORFUL CAST

In front, following a flying squad of mounted police, was the flag bearer holding Old Glory: Jasper Johnson, an African-American man from West Virginia. Barking at his feet was a bulldog tagged "Bunker Hill."

Close behind was one of the pageant's leaders: its controversial "Marshal," Carl Browne. He mimicked the image of William "Buffalo

Bill" Cody, whose wildly popular Wild West revue had started up the previous year. The forty-six-year-old Browne was a big, straggly-bearded California activist, born on the Fourth of July during the Golden State's Gold Rush. Perched on a thickly maned Percheron stallion named Courier, he sported a greasy, fringed buckskin shirt with silver-dollar buttons. His cowboy hat was slung at an insouciant angle. Though the former jail bird was loud and domineering, he was also a romantic. He garlanded his neck with an amber string of beads from his late wife.

Behind Browne, in contrast, was the march's founder and co-commander: "General" Jacob E. Coxey. A bespectacled, gentle-mannered man of forty, Coxey wore the broad necktie and tailored suit of a wealthy businessman. He rolled along in a fine, dark-colored carriage, accompanied by his second wife Henrietta, and their two-month-old son. (In a

Coxey's army of the unemployed on the march, with Coxey and wife, his daughter Mamie, and co-leader Carl Browne on the left.

hint he had a wild side, his first wife had divorced him for gambling on the horses he bred.)

The infant's actual, legal name was Legal Tender. A nod to his dad's stubborn demand for a cheaper, silver-based currency to replace the gold standard, and ease the repayment of debts and perhaps aid the creation of jobs.

Between Coxey and Browne was the "Goddess of Peace," Mamie Coxey, draped by a light-colored riding cloak, and riding resplendent on her father's crème-white Arabian thoroughbred. Mamie was the general's daughter from his first marriage. She was a self-possessed seventeen-year-old whose locks were crowned with a cap inscribed "Free."

From his mount, Carl Browne gazed at her wide-eyed; he'd remark she had "starlit eyes and iridescent golden hair, loosely flowing in the wind." Perhaps noticing his love interest was Mamie's brother Jesse Coxey, a year older than she.

In contrast to Mamie was Annie LaPorte Diggs. Riding in an open carriage with her husband and two children, she was a primly dressed advocate of temperance, that is, laying off the booze. Diggs was an ardent reformer in other ways: a suffragette and lecturer at a free-thinking Unitarian church in Lawrence, Kansas, formerly a center of abolition. The lady backed the new, populist People's Party, and its support of workmen's unions. Like Coxey, it also called for an inflated, silver-backed currency.

Behind General Coxey, and standing out with a long white beard and stove-pipe hat, was a man named after another long-distance traveler: Christopher Columbus Jones. The small-statured yet fierce-eyed fellow, made bigger by the silken top hat, was seated in a hansom. He led a contingent of half a hundred marchers from Philadelphia. Those from the City of Brotherly Love, fittingly, had their own Goddess of Peace, a plump lady rider, in a red, white, and blue dress.

The procession was spiced with a marching band of a half a dozen players that featured a trumpeter and flutist. A drummer knocked out percussive beats for the marchers' stride; a bit further back wailed a Scottish bagpiper. The ensemble's signature song was the popular "Marching Through Georgia," about General Sherman's Civil War storming of the Peach State. The tune played counterpoint to Sam Coxey's usual uniform, a composite of blue and gray that symbolized postwar reunion.

The circus-like novelty of the event was enhanced by "Oklahoma Sam," a trick-riding cowboy who rode his horse backwards. Display wagons showed off Browne's slogan-filled writings and amateurish artwork. A few men zipped along on a newly popular contraption, the bicycle.

Despite its equestrian leaders, most of the Army's "soldiers" were too poor to afford horse and buggy. Most, jobless and without savings, walked. Many tramped along in shoes that were falling apart. Some in the "Commonweal" carried long wooden staves with banners imprinted with a Christian, yet anti-plutocrat, slogan: "Peace on earth; good will to men; but death to interest on bonds." They'd signed up for the trek frustrated from being out of work, or simply from a sense of adventure and camaraderie.

Poison Pens

Bringing up the rear were dozens of somewhat better-dressed men that the marchers disdained: newspaper reporters. There was in fact one journalist for every three men in Coxey's Army. The march was one of the first "media events." It fed the insatiable appetite for stories demanded by the cheap, mass-circulation newspapers of the day. With the reporters were telegraph operators, who provided instant communication of the reportage from wired offices along the route.

The men from the press returned the marchers' disdain. Most journalists were skeptical of Coxey and his outlandish crew. For weeks their columns had lampooned them. Along the trail, Browne had blown his stack over this. Referring to Argus, the prying, multiple-eyed figure of Greek mythology, he'd screamed at the scribblers: "You're nothing but a bunch of Argus-eyed demons of Hell!" Although the procession, even at the time of Jim Crow, was racially integrated, Browne consigned the scribblers to a 'segregated section' at the 'back of the march.'

It was a coincidence the marchers paused at Brock's Hotel, a decade thence linked to one journalist who'd become sympathetic to the Army. Ray Stannard Baker of Michigan had covered the event since its Ohio start. Years later he'd join the famous "muckraking" writers, including Ida Tarbell and Lincoln Stephens, who exposed scandalous defects in the new industrial economy. Which led President Theodore Roosevelt to push through the pure food and drug laws of 1906.

But Roosevelt felt some of those crusaders went too far—when they attacked his allies in the US Senate. In spring 1906, with the likes of Baker in mind, Roosevelt delivered memorable remarks at the Brock's Hotel site, while laying the cornerstone of today's Longworth House Office Building. Quoting *Pilgrim's Progress*, he sneered at those "who could look no way but downward with the *muck-rake* in his hands; who ... continued to rake to himself the filth on the floor." Thus did the word muckraker, a negative term as TR saw it, enter the public lexicon as a word for a constructive, if strident, critic.

Mixed in with the procession were others who observed the marchers as keenly as the reporters. These were Secret Service agents. Their Treasury Department bosses had them infiltrate the ranks to glean intelligence on any violent radicals on hand.

THE GREAT DEPRESSION OF THE "GAY NINETIES"

At that time, law enforcement all over the country was watchful. The economic plunge paralleled rising militancy in the nascent labor movement.

The previous year, 1893, Wall Street had panicked. In the aftermath of its financial crash the nation's largest industry, the railroads, underwent two hundred bankruptcies, including the downfall of Union Pacific. Those failures in turn smashed the related industries of steel and investment banking. Six hundred banks closed their doors. (Railway overbuilding and associated scandals had also fed the Panic of 1873. See the chapter on the Crédit Mobilier scandal.)

The United States entered its steepest depression up until that time. Between 15 and 20 percent of Americans lost their jobs. For the first time, lengthy bread lines formed in the world's richest country.

There was then no federal "safety net." Local and state charities and workhouses were pressed to the limit. Many people became rootless and wandered about the country. Police in Chicago patrolled train depots to keep out-of-state vagrants from entering town.

With profits imploding, the heads of corporations laid off workers, or cut their wages to match the declining prices of goods. Laborers struck back in sometimes bloody actions. Back in 1892, at Andrew Carnegie's Homestead Steel Works in Pittsburgh, deadly gun battles had erupted between strikers and company guards. Cities around the country, including the capital, feared turmoil on their own turf.

A Protest in Boots

In northern Ohio in 1893, Jacob Coxey ruminated on the economic distress. Yet he seemed an unlikely choice to lead a movement against corporate America. Born in a log cabin, he had "pulled himself up by his bootstraps." The father of six children, he made a small fortune supplying raw materials such as scrap iron and silica to the railroad and steel industries. He made another pile by raising thoroughbred horses.

But like others in the Populist movement, Coxey was convinced the federal government's adherence to a strictly gold-backed currency tied its hands. He called for a "Good Roads Bill," a massive half-a-billion-dollar federal highway building program. Paid for by floating a giant bond issue with zero interest rates, so that no bank could make a profit on the bonds.

His notion got little interest until, at an 1893 Chicago convention on silver currency, he met Browne. It was instant chemistry: Browne the aggressive, energetic marketing man, and Coxey the quiet thinker, with enough money to bankroll both.

They dreamed up a combined protest march and publicity stunt: a lengthy march of the jobless to the capital, to plead for Coxey's highway and bond plan.

Coxey's Army started out on an Easter Sunday. The choice of a religious holiday was no accident, for both men were highly religious, though in an eccentric way. Browne was a believer in reincarnation, and felt the soul of his late wife had entered his own. He also thought—and this was anathema to Christians and laughable to reporters—that Jesus Christ had been reincarnated, in a pool of souls, and had entered his soul and Coxey's. He averred that Coxey was the "Cerebrum of Christ," and that he was the "Cerebellum." For good measure, Browne thought he and Coxey also shared the soul of Andrew Jackson, who as president had been the populist foe of big bankers.

Unconventional indeed, as the march also featured Dr. James "Cyclone" Kirkland, a physician and practitioner of astrology. Each evening, the Cyclone forecast the next day's events. "Dark clouds are tumbling," he'd inveigh. "The blood of Mars is dripping. . . . Is it a misguided hand? We shall see."

Coxey came to share Browne's beliefs on reincarnation. His notion of interest-free bonds to finance the new roads, he said, had come to him in a vision-like dream on New Year's Eve.

For their march, Browne and Coxey enforced a kind of discipline that anticipated the out-of-work Bonus Army marchers of the Great Depression. (See the chapter on the Bonus Army.) The men strode daily from late morning to middle afternoon. In the night-time encampments, alcohol was forbidden. Only "respectable women" were allowed to visit. Religious hymns were sung. And Coxey and Browne delivered jeremiads denouncing their era's "1 percent" as well as the Washington elite.

"Congress takes two years to vote on anything," Coxey would say. "Twenty-millions of people are hungry and cannot wait two years to eat." Browne's rhetoric was harsher: "The infernal bloodsucking bank system will be overthrown, for the writing is on the wall."

Getting over the Appalachian Mountains in early spring meant persevering through wet and cold. But the locals were generally friendly and supplied the Army with simple fare. Yet the march had its low points. Near Frostburg, Maryland, while Coxey was away from his Army, an angry dispute broke out. The quarrel involved Browne and a handsome, anonymous young man who rode a horse with a bright-red saddle. Browne had used him to ride herd over the marchers and, with his gift for publicity, had nicknamed him "the Great Unknown." The reporters covering the march had speculated endlessly on his identity.

However, the Great Unknown was upset over doing much of the work while Browne mouthed speeches. The Unknown branded his rival as a "leather-coated polecat," and a "fat-faced fake." He himself would be unmasked as A. P. B. Bozarro, aka Wizardo Supremo. In his other life, he'd sold patent medicines, of the type the pure drug laws would regulate.

Yet the Great Unknown was far more popular than the sharp-edged Browne. In a vote, the marchers opted 158 to 4 in his favor. Even Jesse Coxey took his side. Alarmed, Browne telegraphed Coxey's dad, who raced back by carriage to the Army. General Coxey intervened on the side of his co-leader. He cashiered the Unknown, aka Bozarro, aka Wizardo.

After a frigid, hungry crossing of the Allegheny Mountains, Coxey gave his men a break. He rented out two barges at Cumberland, Maryland, and they floated most of the final 135 miles to Washington, down along the Chesapeake and Ohio (C&O) Canal. Bringing up the rear on the waterway were the reporters, consigned by Browne like second-class citizens to their own boat. One reporter avenged the slight with an article that pegged the water-borne nomads as "ragged forms swarming like rats over every foot of the craft." A *Washington Post* cover story would chide their arrival in the capital as the "Climax of Folly."

A TRIUMPHANT ENTRANCE

On B Street next to the Capitol, Browne called the march to a halt, and got off his stallion. Nearby, Coxey kissed his wife, and got out of his coach. Under a tree, he and Browne held a tête-à-tête, watched over by unfriendly police and thousands of cheering spectators. They had come far, and were just one hundred yards from their goal, the Capitol's steps. Yet the police seemed to form an obstacle far greater than the Appalachians.

The day had started out so well. After breaking camp at the Brightwood Riding Park close to the city's Rock Creek, the Army had marched along 14th Street into downtown. They had been joined by around four hundred local jobless men, assembled by a District welcoming committee.

When the walkers turned onto Pennsylvania Avenue, they spied to their right the large form of the Treasury Building. There, the federal government had placed armed soldiers. The accountants within had been given guns in case of trouble.

In the White House next door, President Grover Cleveland affected business-as-usual with a Cabinet meeting. However, his aides updated him on the progress of the march.

On the tree-bracketed Avenue, Coxey's minions were received like conquering heroes of ancient Rome. "The crowd," noted the *Post*, "swelled to a size such is seldom seen outside of a Presidential inauguration." Washingtonians lined the broad street, applauding, and calling out, "Coxey! Coxey!"

Occasionally Coxey bowed to the many thousands of onlookers. Some supported his goals. Many others simply wished to participate in what had become a grand public festival. They rushed into the street up to the marchers and the horses. The usual spearhead of four mounted police swelled to a squad of twenty-five, with the equestrians clearing a path forward.

Outside the National Hotel on 6th Street, later the site of the Newseum, Mrs. Coxey had her husband stop their carriage. She went inside the Hotel and handed over their infant son to a nurse for safekeeping. At the Avenue's terminus, at the Peace Memorial on the Capitol's northwest corner, crowds were so thick that men climbed up into trees and atop lamp posts to steal a look. Then the Army strode past the greenhouse of the Botanical Gardens then at the foot of the Capitol, and by the grounds landscaped by Frederick Law Olmsted, of Central Park fame, and then along B Street up steep Capitol Hill.

READYING FOR A RIOT

Coxey had previously obtained a parade permit from the city commissioners, who made up Washington's government before today's mayor and city council. However, according to the Capitol Grounds Act, a display of political symbols at the Capitol was illegal.

The five House and ten Senate members of the Populist Party deemed the Act a violation of the First Amendment. Further, they wished, as a courtesy, to let Coxey offer his ideas for a Good Roads bill. As Populist senator William V. Allen of Nebraska told the Senate: "Are American citizens coming here for a lawful purpose to be met at the confines of the capital of their nation by a hired soldiery . . . and kept out of the city and beaten into submission if they persist in coming?" Still, most of Congress disdained a welcome mat.

Moreover, the municipal police had decided on extraordinary measures to thwart the "invading Army." For years the police force had been small and behind the times. A new chief, William G. Moore, had been appointed to change that. During the Civil War, he'd been the adjutant general of volunteers. After the Lincoln assassination, he was personal secretary to President Andrew Johnson. As police chief, he directed vice squads to root out opium dens and to crack down on prostitution. In the year before the march, Moore's men had made a remarkable twenty-seven thousand arrests. He was a formidable opponent for Coxey and Browne.

He also reflected the ethnic attitudes of the time. Before the demonstration, according to Carlos Schwantes's book, *Coxey's Army*, Moore told reporters: "There is a colored population numbered 85,000 in this city, fully half of whom are unemployed and many of whom are vicious. We could not . . . afford to permit any demonstration which would arouse them. Hence the thoroughness of our preparations."

To block off Coxey, Browne, and the rest, Moore assembled a phalanx of 191 police, and arrayed them in a crescent southeast of the East Portico. Hundreds more cops stood in reserve, with many inside the Capitol Building itself. The police chief also arranged to have sixteen hundred city militia nearby. Congress made its own preparations. Its sergeant-at-arms placed guards outside the metal safe holding the money to pay the legislators' salary.

PANDEMONIUM AT THE PORTICO

Below the lines of blue-clad police, the marchers waited. Like San Francisco of old, B Street then had cable cars, and the clang of trolley wheels against metal rails mixed with the loud chatter of the spectators. Coxey and Browne finished their short strategy session. Browne uttered a few tart words to a policeman close by.

Suddenly, the two leaders plunged into the crowd. The pair leapt over a retaining wall and ran toward the Capitol Building. A horde of spectators, a "rushing, scrambling mob," followed "at their heels." Christopher Columbus Jones also darted into the throng.

The hulking Browne, holding a "Peace on earth" banner as he raced along, made it to the southeast side of the plaza fronting the steps. He was a big target, however, and cops on horses, galloping through the shrubbery, zeroed in. One cop ordered: "You can't enter here with that flag!"

Two policemen on horseback grabbed him by the collar. Cops smacked him in the head with billy clubs and tore his shirt. They ripped off his amber necklace, the beads honoring his late wife falling to the ground. Ray Baker, the sympathetic reporter, picked up the beads, and later returned them to Browne.

Two cops arrested Browne and dragged him away. Lawmen also detained Chris Columbus Jones. They pulled his stovepipe hat down over his face. Both he and Browne were taken to the police court. At the White House, President Cleveland got a police telegram that Browne had "received a clubbing."

The law officers, shaken by the mass of people, some of whom may have attacked the mounted police, treated onlookers roughly. "Police cavalry with horses rearing and plunging," reported the *Washington Post*, "charged upon the crowd to keep them back. Clubs were freely used, and several of the spectators must have gone away with crushed hats or sore heads ... men and women were knocked down and trampled in the mad rush."

Flagbearer Jasper Johnson was also hurt in the melee. Shrubs and bushes about the Capitol's entrance were flattened by hoof and heel.

Coxey, blending into the crowd, had better luck than Browne. He pushed through a thicket of bystanders and sidestepped many of the cops. He made it to the middle of the Portico and rushed up the Capitol steps. Above him, hundreds were watching. Below, some fifteen thousand spectators spilled over and out of the plaza. Near him was an iconic statue of George Washington portrayed as a Greek god.

It was the chance of a lifetime for a public speaker.

But it was not to be.

A police sergeant came up to him.

Coxey told the cop: "I wish to make an address to the American people."

"Well," said the sergeant, "you can't make it here."

"Then, I want to enter a protest against this perversion of the Constitution."

A police captain and a lieutenant took Coxey off the steps. Foiled from giving his prepared remarks, he handed them off to a reporter.

The frustrated officers, their way blocked by the crowd, cleared a way forward with their clubs. They led Coxey back to his carriage, which had been moved to near the new Library of Congress building. He was let free pending a court appearance.

As his carriage rolled back to B Street, the crowd cheered, "Coxey! Coxey!" He was again, for a moment, a conquering hero. He took comfort his marchers had emerged from the mayhem mostly unscathed. Only Browne and Jasper had been injured, and not seriously.

Coxey also earned the sympathy of Rep. Tom Johnson, from Cleveland, Ohio. On the House floor the next day he stated that "unoffending citizens were cruelly beaten . . . the dignity of this House has been violated." But Johnson's views were the minority.

Sad Aftermath

Over the next few weeks, a city court tried Coxey, Browne, and Chris Columbus Jones. They were convicted of breaking the law against taking political banners onto the Capitol grounds. The judge sentenced them to twenty days in a workhouse. Coxey and Browne were also fined $5—for trespassing on the grass.

Coxey went back to Ohio, and Browne to California. The latter, to Coxey's distress, wed Mamie Coxey in 1895. They had a son together, and later separated. Browne, a life-long dreamer, would attempt, some years after the Wright Brothers, to build his own flying machine. Coxey, like Browne, would join the Socialist Party. He'd also become the "Harold Stassen" of early twentieth-century politics: forever running for Congress, and even the presidency, and forever losing.

As for the foot soldiers of Coxey's Army, they camped out at a smelly, disease-ridden place a mile south of the Capitol. The spot, at M and 1st Streets, S.W., was on an abandoned garbage dump near the stagnant, fly-ridden James Canal. They soon moved to a more bucolic setting in Bladensburg, Maryland. But in August, state officials arrested 102 of the "hoboes." They were released, then pushed out of the region.

During the William McKinley Administration that followed, the economy recovered. It was fueled by new inventions like the telephone, car, and lightbulb—and the discovery of gold in Alaska. This reinforced President McKinley's gold-only currency views and undercut "silver bugs" like the Populists.

Long-Term Impacts

Though the march failed to attain its goals, the long-run influence of activists like Coxey was marked. The Populist Party and its platform morphed into the Progressive movement. In the early twentieth century, it won reforms of the pharmaceutical and meat-packing industries, as well as child labor laws, popular referenda, and other measures. It in turn laid the groundwork for President Franklin Roosevelt's New Deal programs, during the longer and more severe 1930s depression. These included public works programs such as the Public Works Administration which, by building roads and highways throughout the nation, with money borrowed through deficit spending, essentially followed Coxey's outline.

And, exactly fifty years after Coxey was barred from giving his talk on the Capitol steps, he gave it. With the approval of Roosevelt allies—House Speaker Sam Rayburn of Texas and Vice President Henry Wallace of Iowa—a very elderly Coxey spoke from the East Portico. It was on May 1, 1944, when armies other than Coxey's were marching on assorted continents during the Second World War. Due to conscription and wartime production, there were jobs for all.

Coxey, then ninety years old, hearty and in firm voice, gave the short oration he had once intended. Surrounded by curious spectators, including sailors and soldiers, and recalling his own Army's long trek, he stated:

"We have come here through toil and weary marches, through storms and tempests, over mountains, and amid the trials of poverty and distress, to lay our grievances at the doors of our National Legislature, and ask them in the name of Him whose banners we bear, in the name of Him who plead for the poor and the oppressed, that they should heed the voice of despair and distress that is now coming up from every section of our country, that they should consider the conditions of the starving unemployed of our land, and enact such laws as will give them employment, bring happier conditions to the people, and the smile of contentment to our citizens."

Coxey died, at age ninety-seven, in 1953, the year of the inauguration of President Dwight Eisenhower, who would create the Interstate Highway System, Coxey's "Good Roads Bill" writ large.

The head of Coxey's Army was ahead of his time and, perhaps, somewhat out of his mind, but his impact was lasting. His was the first of political parades that led to ones as disparate as the Bonus Army, the Ku Klux Klan, the Vietnam War protests, the suffragettes, the Tea Party, the Million Man March, and MLK's march on Washington.

CHAPTER SEVENTEEN

Tortured Artist: The Tragic
End of an Intrepid Sculptor

The Ulysses S. Grant Memorial trio of statues, below the west grounds of the Capitol Building

WHILE THE LINCOLN MEMORIAL ACROSS THE NATIONAL MALL IS FAR better known, the Ulysses S. Grant Memorial at the foot of the Capitol Building may be an even more skillful work of sculpture. It exceeds the esteemed Vietnam and Korean Veterans Memorials in evoking the glory and the horrors of war. And its creator paid the grimmest price to conjure up his masterwork.

Henry Merwin Shrady seemed fated for his task, but also under-qualified.

A VALIANT LAST BATTLE

His father, Dr. George Frederick Shrady Sr., had been a physician for the retired President Grant, the former commanding general of the Union army. This was during Grant's gravest personal crisis, greater than the challenge of his Civil War campaigns against Confederate general Robert Edward Lee.

It was at the end of Grant's life. In 1884, when biting into a peach, he felt pain in his throat. He did nothing about it, for too long. When he finally got a medical examination, he asked, "Is it cancer?" The doctor's silence told him it was fatal.

Along with his health crisis, the famed former soldier faced a financial disaster. Due to his son U. S. Grant Jr.'s association with a swindler, and his own ineptitude with finance, Grant was bankrupt. On his death, his family would face abject poverty.

Grant had about eight months to live. Under great time pressure, and in great pain, he got to work researching, writing, and, when he no longer had the strength, dictating. As his *Personal Memoirs* neared completion, Grant, ever clueless about money, prepared to sign a paltry contract with a publisher. Luckily, a friend, Mark Twain himself, then working on his own literary effort, *Huckleberry Finn*, tore up the contract and obtained a much better book deal.

Grant's doctors, including the elder Shrady, could do nothing to stay the cancer. They did relieve the patient's suffering though, usually through solutions of chloroform and of cocaine.

The general finished the book manuscript just before expiring in July 1885 at age sixty-three. It was a sensational bestseller and put his family in clover. It is considered a classic of clear, to-the-point prose.

Preparations for a Masterpiece

Equestrian statues are difficult to design. A sculptor has to balance as much as five tons of bronze atop the four thin legs of the horse. But Henry Shrady created two masterworks in that style.

His first was a grand, if somewhat unsung, statue of George Washington, near the Williamsburg Bridge in Brooklyn. Shrady rejected the notion of depicting Washington in retreat across New York's East River, after losing the nearby American Revolution Battle of Brooklyn Heights. Instead, he rendered the general at his iconic winter encampment of Valley Forge. But his Washington is less heroic than stolid, wrapped in winter cloth, the head of his mount determinedly bowed against the wind and cold.

The sculptor's approach is similar with Grant. The general is revealed, true to life, in a plain soldier's uniform, his unadorned hat pushed down on his head, his countenance calm, reflective, determined. So he was in battle, often silent, watchful, but a commanding figure when the moment came to order and to act. The contrast with Grant's predecessor as overall Union commander, Winfield Scott, "Old Fuss and Feathers," a man of spit and polish, however capable, was marked.

When Shrady fashioned Grant's equestrian image, he drew on his father's notes on the condition of the cancer sufferer in his final days, as well as on the death mask retained by the Smithsonian Institute.

Indeed, to research his subject Shrady immersed himself in Grant's life and wartime service. To get the details of his statuary right, he pored over Civil War emblems, epaulets, and swords. He convinced Army officers at West Point to let him observe maneuvers of infantry and cavalry, to master how men and horses moved about on actual terrain. To better acquaint himself with the military generally, he served in the National Guard for four years.

Shrady's early artistic and anatomical training aided him in his depictions. As a young man in New York City, he'd visit the Bronx Zoo and study animal physiques. Later he dissected horses. He borrowed a live one from the New York Police Department for further examination.

And his Grant monument is overwhelmingly equestrian. In the middle of the trio of statues, the general sits atop his thoroughbred Cincinnati. On either side, cavalrymen and artillerymen pulled by horses frantically race toward, or away from, battle. It can be hard to tell if they're attacking or retreating, which adds to a sense of drama and unease.

Selecting a Sculptor

Shrady almost didn't get, and maybe shouldn't have gotten, the commission for the Grant memorial. His portfolio at the time was thin, namely the Washington statue, and not much else of note. A chief rival for the job was Charles Henry Niehaus, who argued, correctly, he had greater experience, and arguably more expertise. His works included statues of Presidents Lincoln and Garfield for other cities, and later the statue, recently removed, of Confederate general Nathan Bedford Forrest in Memphis. (Yes, that's the soldier for whom Forrest Gump was named.)

For years, sculptor Henry Shrady studied horse anatomy and military processions to prepare for his masterwork, the Ulysses S. Grant Memorial.

The competition came near the turn of the twentieth century, after veterans from Grant's old Army of the Tennessee petitioned Congress for a homage to their hero. It was with those soldiers that "U.S." Grant had earned his nickname by bringing about the "Unconditional Surrender" of Fort Donelson, Tennessee, in 1862.

In 1901, Congress established its commission to select a sculptor. On its board were two great artists, renowned for military-related themes. One was Daniel Chester French, later the creator of Lincoln's noble figure at his Memorial. French would craft a statesman pensive, seated on his throne-like chair with its fasces bundle of ancient Roman sticks signifying the power and peril of authority and Union. The other was Augustus Saint-Gaudens, the New York–bred creator of the Robert Gould Shaw Memorial honoring the Massachusetts 54th Regiment, featured in the movie *Glory*. The commission chose as sculptor the talented yet less proven Shrady, then just thirty-one years old. Its selection paid off, barely.

Fortunately, Shrady had the help of a terrific designer, Edward Pearce Casey. A mining engineer as well as an architect, Casey had completed the incomparable Thomas Jefferson Building of the Library of Congress. He'd come on board after his father, Army Corps of Engineers general Thomas Lincoln Casey, in charge of the project, passed away. As a teenager, the younger Casey followed how his father decisively managed the completion—after a century of changes, debates, and delays—of the Washington Monument.

The Agony of War

With Casey taking care of the overall layout, Shrady labored on the figures themselves. Surpassing even his Ulysses S. Grant statue are his twin groups of figures flanking the general. To Grant's left and rear, three horses rear and strain uncontrollably to haul a cannon and caisson. One of the bridles has broken; the rider, nearly thrown, lurches backward while grasping a flag. The statue's base tilts upward in front of the horses, making their forward progress seem more strained. In the caisson, two soldiers sit with shoulders hunched; they seem stunned, and grimly consigned to their fate.

The depiction is so dark that Shrady may been affected—along with the Civil War, America's costliest—by the First World War. Its blood-bath, which darkened the outlook of many artists, raged as he worked on the statues.

Even grimmer, to Grant's right and rear, is the depiction of five charging cavalrymen. Shrady's realistic portrayal of them is astonishing. The bronzed clogs of mud kicked up by the horses convey a dizzying sense of movement in static art. An officer raises his sword, and a trumpeter presses a bugle to his lips, but their intent is undercut by the rider in front. He's fallen into the morass of mud, his horse crashing on top of him. His right arm hangs hopelessly around his mount's neck, his face looks out forlornly from the tumble.

All this reflects, along with the carnage of Grant's battles, at Shiloh and Cold Harbor and many more, the collapse of the artist's own life in his final years of labor.

A PERSONAL CATASTROPHE

The Grant Memorial Commission had grown impatient at Shrady's painstaking approach. By 1920, he'd labored on the project for eighteen years. The artist was fifteen years behind the original, scheduled date of completion. He'd blown through ten deadlines. The project budget, at first $10,000, had soared to $250,000.

Commission members and Congress wanted the complex of statues completed by the one hundredth anniversary of Grant's birth, April 27, 1922. The Army Corps of Engineers threatened to cancel Shrady's contract if he didn't come through.

"I was a boy when I won the competition," he admitted, "and never realized the great task before me."

Meanwhile Shrady had taken on at least one project too many, namely, the statue of Grant's nemesis, Robert E. Lee, at Charlottesville, Virginia. (That was the statue at the center of the 2017 melee between protestors and counter-protestors, including skinheads and Antifa, over its proposed removal.)

To meet his deadline, Shrady worked even harder. But the strain was too much. He was hospitalized for nervous exhaustion. Aides had to complete the finishing touches of the statues.

His health broken by long years of labor, artist Shrady crafted this astonishing self-portrait—of a doomed soldier trampled by his own horse.

On Grant's centennial, Vice President Calvin Coolidge, General of the Armies John Pershing, Chief Justice William Howard Taft, and other notables assembled at the memorial. They greeted a military parade of ten thousand, including aged veterans of the Civil War, North and South, who strode down Pennsylvania Avenue from the White House. The statues were unveiled as one hundred carrier pigeons, airborne military messengers, were loosed into the sky. They were freed by Grant's granddaughter, Princess Julia Dent Grant Cantacuzène, wife of an aristocratic Russian general.

Tragically, missing in action amid all the celebrations was Shrady. He'd died two weeks before, at age fifty, broken by his labors.

Yet he attained immortality of a sort, in the image of that unfortunate horseman being trampled to death. For the cavalryman constitutes the most remarkable of artist's signatures. His face is that of the sculptor himself—Henry Shrady.

He crafted the self-portrait while conjuring up the masterpiece that cost him his life.

CHAPTER EIGHTEEN

Professor Death: The Madman Who Bombed the Senate

Senate wing, the old telegraph office

ERIC MUENTER WAS DEPRESSED, BLOODIED, AND ANXIOUS, JUST TWO days after Independence Day, 1915, as he sat in his Long Island jail cell.

It had been an event-filled week. It would be eventful again.

MANSIONS AND MUNITIONS

Muenter was a thin, sallow-faced man of forty-four years. On July 3, he'd called on one of America's wealthiest men, J. P. Morgan Jr., the son of banking mogul J. P. Morgan, and himself a noted financier. When the butler answered the door to the Glen Cove mansion, Muenter demanded to see the master of the house.

To back up his request, he brandished two loaded revolvers.

On entering, Muenter detained several of the rich man's children. Whether he intended kidnapping or murder was unclear.

Then the butler, a man named Physick, did a cunning thing. He walked Muenter to the home's library. Physick then went racing down the hall shouting, to warn Morgan Jr., his wife Jessie, and a breakfast guest, the British ambassador, Sir Cecil Spring Rice.

The Morgans fled upstairs. Muenter burst from the library, corralled Morgan's young children, and went up the staircase.

The intruder approached the stoutly built banker.

Muenter shouted: "Now, Mr. Morgan, I have you!"

Morgan, weighing in at 220 pounds, made a bull rush at his foe.

Muenter fired his gun twice, striking Morgan in the thigh and groin, before Morgan collapsed on top of him. As Muenter pushed the wounded man off him, Morgan managed to snatch away one revolver, and his wife the other. The stalwart Physick then smacked Muenter in the head with a big lump of coal, knocking him out. The police arrived and carted him off to the local precinct.

In his second-floor cell, Professor Muenter felt the ache from his bandaged head.

And the shock of his plan gone awry.

Just hours before the attack on Morgan, he'd had a success. After arriving on the midnight train from Washington, DC, he'd hurried to a New York City wharf. There Muenter slipped aboard the SS *Minnehaha*, a munitions ship bound for Britain, then fighting Germany during the First World War. He placed a "cigarette bomb"—a thin, timed incendiary device—in the ship's hold, and crept off the ship. Days later, when the vessel was steaming in the Atlantic, the bomb caught fire, causing some modest damage.

But in the police station's jail, Muenter felt the sting, the shame, the horror of having been photographed. His arrest was making headlines around the world. And the cops were uncovering his secret life, and the terrible crime he'd committed almost a decade before.

A Senate Spectacular

All this angst after another success, that he'd pulled off just hours before planting the bomb on the ship.

It had been so easy. The Capitol Building was nearly deserted late that Friday afternoon, July 2, the start of the Fourth of July weekend. Congress was out of session. Security was light. Tourists were allowed to freely enter the place.

Muenter had slipped into the Senate entrance, from the steps on its northeast side. Inside, he found the legislative chamber securely locked. So, he placed his package of three sticks of TNT with a slow-burning fuse in the nearby Reception Room, under the telephone switchboard, next door to the Senate office of the vice president, Indiana's Thomas Marshall.

The interloper spent the next seven or so hours walking around downtown, mailing off letters, then pacing anxiously outside the Capitol. At 11:43 p.m., Muenter saw the Senate lit up by a bright flash. Satisfied, he strode to Union Station, and boarded a midnight train to New York's Grand Central.

His bomb had wrecked the telephone exchange, shattering windows, knocking pieces of plaster from the ceiling. A lone sentinel, policeman Frank Jones, was shaken from his chair, gripped by fear the Capitol's iron rotunda was about to collapse.

It was the first successful bombing of the Capitol Building.

As Muenter intended, no one was hurt. His action was only supposed to send a message. A written message, composed by the bomber, was

In the midst of World War I, German sympathizer Eric Muenter planted a bomb that destroyed a Senate reception room, before heading to New York to shoot financier J. P. Morgan Jr.

sent to newspapers such as the *Washington Star* under the pseudonym R. Pearce. In it, the writer expressed hope the blast might "make enough noise to be heard above the voices that clamor for war and blood-money. This explosion is an exclamation point in my appeal for peace."

ASSUMING AN IDENTITY

In his Long Island jail, Muenter was an emotional mess. His placement of the ship bomb and his bombing of the Senate had been flawless. But his confrontation with Morgan had been a debacle. And the press and authorities were piecing together his alter ego.

Nine years before, in 1906, he'd been a respected scholar. Originally from Germany, and adept with languages, Muenter was working as a professor of German at Harvard University. He was married, and his wife Leona was pregnant.

Around this time, however, he became fascinated with crime, particularly capital crimes. He haunted the private library of a fellow Harvard professor, and his collection of books on forensic science and related topics such as poisons.

Also around this time, his pregnant wife took sick. Muenter, normally reserved, became very solicitous toward his spouse. Charmingly so, thought observers. He insisted he make the meals for his indisposed wife. Each day, he fed her a broth he swore would help her condition.

As the close ministrations of her husband continued, Leona's condition worsened. In April 1906, she died, ten days after giving birth to a baby girl.

Muenter quickly made arrangements for an undertaker to prepare his wife for burial. He swiftly arranged to take her remains to her family's hometown of Chicago, and he traveled there himself.

That might have been that, except the local undertaker had determined, before the body of Mrs. Leona Muenter was taken away, to remove some of her body organs.

During subsequent tests, a Harvard professor detected massive amounts of arsenic. Mrs. Muenter had been poisoned to death. By her solicitous spouse.

Alarmed, the Cambridge police informed the Chicago police. But Muenter had disappeared. The authorities searched for the murderer in vain. Weeks later, the in-laws received a crazed letter from him, in which he threatened to destroy both Chicago and Cambridge.

Muenter fled to Mexico, and then to the western reaches of the United States. He assumed a new identity, calling himself Frank Holt. He married again, to another woman, with a first name similar to that of his murdered spouse. Leone Sensabaugh, of Dallas, Texas, afforded him the perfect cover, being the daughter of an upright Methodist minister.

Fluent in multiple languages, he was again hired as a teacher. He obtained work at Vanderbilt, and in time pursued a doctorate at Cornell University in upstate New York. He had a scary moment there, when a former Harvard colleague recognized him but decided not to inform authorities.

A Secret Agent

Whether he was Frank Holt, or Eric Muenter, he was always loyal to his country of birth. When the Great War broke out in 1914, he was adamantly pro-German. He raged that the United States, though officially neutral, helped Germany's enemies by granting Britain and France millions in loans to purchase a great deal of munitions. He knew many of the loans came from the Morgan bank.

Early in 1915, it seems he drifted into Germany's secret, US-based network of spies and saboteurs. It targeted companies and factories making or transporting munitions to the Western Allies. This network, in 1916, would blow up the vast Black Tom munition dock close to Jersey City, opposite lower Manhattan. The massive blast killed seven; shrapnel hurled across the harbor damaged the torch of the Statue of Liberty. The network also placed dozens of incendiary devices aboard ships bound for ports like Le Havre, France. It even ladled Maryland horses, slated for shipment to the French army, with anthrax.

In this context Muenter, as he sat brooding in his cell, felt he'd been right in putting the incendiary bomb in the hold of the munitions ship. Right in placing a bomb in the legislative house of the country aiding the enemies of his native land. And right in shooting the financier of those very same foes.

But his actions had exposed his other life: the inexecrable, cold-blooded murder of his pregnant wife, followed by his secret life on the lam.

Weary, his head throbbing, Muenter likely thought of the loathing he would face for the remainder of his life, from the public, and from his ex-colleagues and in-laws and friends. To the prideful fanatic, the shame may have been unbearable.

A FINAL EXIT

So, in his cell, on the day after Independence Day, he picked up a pencil eraser. He bent back the wrapping and cut into his wrists with the metal.

A guard rushed into his cell and stopped him before he could do himself much harm.

The following day, July 6, 1915, the guard in his second-floor cell left without locking the door behind him. Muenter seized his chance.

He rushed outside and hurled himself head-first into the rock-solid inner court twenty feet below.

The fatal impact smashed in his skull so badly the fractures looked like bullet holes.

In fact, the police at first thought he'd been shot. But an autopsy indicated otherwise, though some still maintain Muenter didn't kill himself, but was thrown to his death. For years, conspiracy theories would swirl that somehow German agents were involved.

Whatever the case, the life of the mad bomber of the Senate—one of the most villainous figures to haunt the Capitol—came to its bloody end.

Chapter Nineteen

Beauties and the Beasts:
Chaos and Class at the Suffrage March

West along Pennsylvania Avenue from the Capitol Building

The trouble started quick, just blocks into the parade of over five thousand meticulously attired women. Louts came pouring out of the Pennsylvania Avenue saloons, the city's "bowery," and took liberties with the ladies. They uttered vile slang from the barnyard and the gutter. They poked and grabbed and pushed. Hooligans tried climbing onto the floats of the procession.

Big Parade, Bigger Audience

"Many of the women were in tears under the jibes of the crowd," reported a local newspaper.

"I never knew men could be such fiends," said a participant.

The cretins even disturbed the presidential reviewing stand. Shocked by the potty mouths, President William Howard Taft's wife and his daughter Helen hurried away.

Yet more threatening than the drunks were the sober. The Avenue overflowed with a swirling horde of sightseers. Downtown was jammed by visitors and residents alike, on hand for the parade, and for President-Elect Wilson's inaugural the following day.

In fact, when Woodrow Wilson arrived at a deserted Union Station, an aide wondered, "Where are all the people?"

"At the suffrage parade," a policeman told him.

This photograph outside the Willard Hotel on the west end of Pennsylvania Avenue reveals the swirling mass of spectators that nearly wrecked the Capitol's first large suffragette march.

The massive crowd was watching or, as it turned out, taking part in, the novel spectacle of the suffragette march. March 3, 1913 saw the first very large demonstration, and accompanying audience, in the city's history.

Many of the two-hundred-fifty-thousand-plus onlookers climbed over the ropes strung along the sidewalks in a feeble attempt to keep order. Masses of people filled the Avenue, blocking or surrounding the marchers and their floats, musical bands, and state and workplace organizations.

Amid the teeming throngs, the females and spectators alike were pushed, pulled, knocked to the ground, even trampled. Men screamed, women fainted.

One of the most terrified was Helen Keller, then thirty-two, the deaf-and-blind author and lecturer. She could not see nor hear, but only sense, the rumbling chaos around her. Nervous exhaustion overwhelmed Keller; she cancelled a scheduled speech.

At first, the authorities made things even worse. The police on foot were vastly undermanned; a suffragette leader said they just melted into the crowd. Later about fifteen mounted policemen, and other cops in a squad of cars, pushed into the crowds to try clearing out a path along Pennsylvania Avenue.

Police on horses, led by a Sgt. Michael Ready, swung their batons with abandon. Horrified pedestrians scrambled out of their way. Over a hundred people were injured in the melee, and some cops too, both uniformed and in plainclothes. Several had their police badges ripped from them.

Drivers of horse-drawn and motorized ambulances took hours pushing through the crowds to reach the stricken. Some spectators, fearful of being run down, punched and pummeled the drivers and medical personnel undertaking the rescues.

KNIGHTS IN SHINING ARMOR

Yet while some men that day were craven, many others were chivalrous.

Students from the Maryland Agricultural College, today's University of Maryland, rushed in to protect the ladies. So did troopers from the Pennsylvania and Massachusetts National Guards.

US Marines and Army soldiers volunteered to form a wedge to help the cops clear a path ahead. African-American drivers jumped off the horses hauling the floats to join the other guardians. Baton-wielding Boy Scouts pushed back waves of onlookers! The event's herald—the adept equestrian Inez Milholland—reared her charger at the onlookers, forcing some back.

One "member of the 'petticoat cavalry'," noted the *Washington Post*, "struck a man a stinging blow across the face with her riding crop in reply to a scurrilous remark."

At length, the vanguard was able to push out a narrow passage for the women to walk down the fifteen blocks of the Avenue. The hundreds of thousands along the boulevard cheered. But when the suffragettes turned down 15th Street, toward their grand pageant outside the Treasury Building, disaster nearly struck again. The immense crowds overwhelmed the rope lines there. The throngs swelled toward the Treasury grounds, threatening to stomp marchers and the pageant's performers alike.

Fortunately, the cavalry came to the rescue, literally. An event leader had contacted her brother-in-law, Secretary of War Henry Lewis Stimson. He sent out an alert to US Army horsemen at Fort Meyer, in nearby Arlington, Virginia. Two swift columns of horse soldiers galloped over to Treasury. They charged the crowd, and it fell back in wild disarray. Then the cavalrymen, like knights of yore, escorted the ladies to the end of their trek.

The heroes helping the heroines prevented stampedes that might have killed dozens.

A PAGEANT OF BEAUTEOUS IDEALS

The chaos and oafish acts formed a stunning contrast to the classy event itself.

Outside the Treasury, dramatist Helen MacKaye produced a visually stunning pageant of feminine and republican virtue.

MacKaye's choreographed star was "Columbia," the female embodiment of America. She was played by Mademoiselle Hedwig Reicher,

A vast, out-of-control crowd threatened an alluring display of feminine virtues, before the US cavalry, literally, came to the rescue of the suffragette rally.

robed in red, white, and blue, and grasping an American eagle scepter. Columbia waited until musicians positioned along the walking route relayed trumpet blasts to sound the tableau's start. An orchestra played the "The Star-Spangled Banner," and Columbia descended the broad steps leading from the Treasury's tall exterior columns.

Then Charity made her benevolent entrance, as rose petals were scattered in her path. After her came Liberty, to the sounds of the triumphant march from the opera *Aida*. Actresses representing other feminine virtues appeared: Justice, Hope, and Peace. All were garbed in flowing robes of crimson and purple. The Virtues danced and pranced to orchestral sounds.

Along with their skill, the performers were picked for their beauty. "The prettiest of the younger suffragists were cast for the parts," noted a newspaper. Organizers wanted to undercut a stereotype that suffragettes were unattractive and mean.

A WELL-ORGANIZED PROCESSION

Womanly ideals were underscored at the march's launching point, below Capitol Hill at the Peace Monument. This memorial's statues, fittingly, were and are the robed female figures of Grief, Victory, History, and Peace. There the parade was led by Milholland, draped in broadcloth and a bright cloak with a gold Maltese cross, and poised atop a magnificent

The brilliant visuals of the suffrage event included angelic-looking ladies on horseback.

white steed. Milholland struck a figure out of the Arthurian legends, or the pre-Raphaelite paintings popular a generation before. (In her own life, she advocated free love and open marriages.)

The parade's grand marshal was Jane Walker Burleson, a "handsome" Army officer's wife. From Philadelphia, she brought with her a replica of the Liberty Bell. Adding classical imagery were women driving gold-colored chariots. Burleson sent out these heralds with instructions for event officers positioned throughout downtown.

Behind the leaders came the five-thousand-plus marchers. They were split into groups aimed at quelling skeptics of suffrage, while demonstrating the achievements of women worldwide.

The initial procession had floats from countries that already had the vote. The ladies on these platforms, many from the city's embassies, wore traditional, peasant costumes, of such Northern European lands as Belgium, Denmark, and Sweden.

Then came the many delegations from the United States. They were grouped by state, with the largest in number, some five hundred women, from New York. Other important contingents were from western states where women had gained the suffrage.

They were followed by a college section of one thousand women, outfitted in their commencement gowns, mortar boards on their heads. Next came a large group organized by occupation. First the more traditional, with farm girls in gingham dresses, then ending with "professional women," doctors and pharmacists prominent among them.

One marcher, Jeannette Rankin, would four years later become the first woman elected to Congress. After a long interval, she was elected again in 1941. In fact, on the day after the Pearl Harbor attack, December 8, 1941, she'd cast the sole dissenting No vote on the declaration of war against Japan. Police protected her until she could safely leave the Capitol Building.

Some of the displays were moralistic, reflecting the movements for urban reform and child labor laws that many women championed. A Labor float had actors representing "women and children bending over sewing machines, dirty and disheveled, in squalid quarters."

A parade that so adeptly promoted itself naturally had a float for journalists and illustrators. On its platform, women represented authors, cartoonists, and readers "as molders of public opinion." Its banner read: "An Enlightened Press Is Making an Enlightened People."

Bringing up the rear were females in the newfangled contraption of the automobile. Supportive male members of Congress joined the procession too. The media was entranced by the assemblage, judging from such headlines as: "Women's Beauty, Grace, And Art Bewilder The Capital: Miles of Fluttering Femininity Present Entrancing Suffrage Appeal."

A PRINCESS OF PUBLICITY

The organizer of the march was the National American Woman Suffrage Association, or NAWSA. Its aim: energize the faltering movement to gain the female vote in all the forty-eight states. The brains behind the parade was a planner and marketeer of some genius, Alice Paul of New Jersey.

Twenty-nine years old with a haunted expression, Paul was a Quaker. In fact, she was descended from William Penn. She was a veteran of the more activist suffragette movement in Britain, where violence marked some rallies. The heads of NAWSA, Anna Howard Shaw, of Massachusetts, and Carrie Chapman Catt, of Ripon, Wisconsin, favored a methodical process of gaining state approvals. Paul, in contrast, wanted quick passage of a constitutional amendment that applied to every state. She figured the publicity from a march would build support for that approach.

She and her colleague, Lucy Burns of New York, took over the event planning in December 1912.

Alice Paul, a young woman of striking aspect, skillfully organized the Washington voting march.

Their office had an initial budget of $10. A year later it stood at $25,000.

In just weeks, Paul brought in over 125 volunteers. In just two months, she negotiated the event's permits and arranged for its alluring pageantry.

Alice Paul ran into obstacles. She found it difficult to persuade the chief of the Metropolitan Police, Richard H. Sylvester Jr., to permit a march on Pennsylvania Avenue. Sylvester warned her of the low-class saloons on the congressional side of the Avenue, in the "Murder Bay" neighborhood. He recommended holding the event along 16th Street, in the district north of the White House, and on the day after the inaugural. But Paul fought for, and got, a grander venue, and on the day before the inauguration when more people were in town.

In a time of segregation, in the South, and much of the North, race was an issue. Paul waffled on allowing black women's groups to march. Members of the predominately black Howard University, and local civil rights leader Mary Church Terrell, urged they be allowed to march with everyone else. A compromise was reached when a Quaker-led men's group walked as a "buffer" between white women's college groups and those from Howard.

Other African-American ladies marched with their state organizations. However, the head of the Illinois delegation refused to let black suffragette and integrationist Ida B. Wells-Barnett, from Chicago by way of Mississippi, into her group. Years before, Ida Wells, a precursor to Rosa Parks, had been thrown off a Memphis train for trying to integrate it. Midway through the suffragette march, after wiping away tears from her ill treatment, she joined up with the Illinois group.

INDIGNANT REACTIONS

The evening after the march, the suffragettes gathered at Continental Hall, on 15th Street down from the White House. (It was later expanded into today's Constitutional Hall complex.) Given the disaster that had been barely averted, the gathering was stormy. The *Washington Post* noted it turned "into an indignation meeting."

Paul cleverly took advantage of the angst to fundraise off it, taking in enough donations to pay for the march. More dramatically, she and other leaders pressured Congress to hold hearings.

The Senate's Committee on the District of Columbia assembled to listen to over one hundred witnesses, including Paul, police chief Sylvester, and former and future Secretary of War Stimson.

Witnesses and congressmen berated the police for not clearing Pennsylvania Avenue ahead of time, and for lax crowd control. One testified that "only Divine Providence prevented a catastrophe which might have placed many a home in Washington in mourning."

Sylvester's seeming failure was odd given his otherwise sterling career. During his seventeen-year tenure as chief, he put in place such reforms as a fingerprint office and a separate jail for women and children, who previously and dangerously had been incarcerated with men. For a decade he headed the International Association of Chiefs of Police. He even invented the "third degree," the process of questioning, sometimes harshly, detainees.

Paul failed to attain her immediate goal of the vote. The suffragettes met with President Wilson after his inaugural. However, he was cool to Paul's amendment, and more sympathetic to Shaw and Catt's state-by-state approach. In fact, the suffragettes soon split over these differences, with Paul in 1915 founding the National Women's Party. Its headquarters is today at the old Albert Gallatin house burned by the British in 1814.

New York State's approval of suffrage in 1917 helped change the president's mind. So did a very controversial action, and the reaction to it, led by Paul and Burns. In 1917 and 1918, after the United States had entered the First World War, they led demonstrations for the vote outside the White House gates. Women protestors known as "Silent Sentinels" held up provocative signs such as: "President Wilson Is Deceiving the World When He Appears as the Prophet of Democracy." Many, including the president, deemed these actions unpatriotic during wartime. Police arrested twenty-eight of the women; some were consigned to the dank Occoquan prison in Lorton, Virginia. There prisoners were beaten or force-fed during hunger strikes.

Nationwide negative publicity about that helped pushed lawmakers in the direction of the suffragettes. In spring 1919, the House and Senate passed the Nineteenth Amendment. In August 1920, with the approval of three-quarters of the states, it became the law of the land.

The raucous parade below the Capitol seven years before helped spark its passage.

COUNTERCURRENTS

Though it seems strange today, some women reformers opposed suffrage. The National Association Opposed to Women Suffrage, with national headquarters in DC, was founded the same year as the suffrage march. Led by women, it presaged the traditionalist arguments against the proposed Equal Rights Amendment in the late twentieth century. One of its circulars read: "the great advance of women in the last century—moral, intellectual and economic—has been made without the vote; which goes to prove that it is not needed for their further advancement along the same lines."

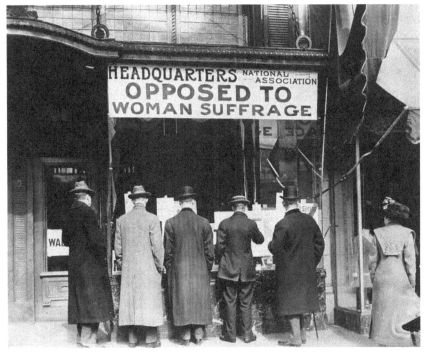

Some women were opposed to ladies' suffrage, and even set up a national headquarters in the capital for that purpose.

Muckraking journalist Ida Tarbell, no stay-at-home, called for women to take on their "true role as wives, mothers, and homemakers." Still other anti-suffragettes opposed the vote for fear it would lead to suffrage for black women like Ida Wells.

Philanthropist Emily Bissell of Delaware worried that political fights might undermine women's vast involvement in charitable work. Along those lines, Bissell founded the March of Dimes, to raise funds for fighting tuberculosis, a prime killer of children in the early twentieth century.

Washingtonians watching the suffrage parade, whatever their views on voting, witnessed the largest demonstration in the city's history up to that time.

CHAPTER TWENTY

Undercover at the Capitol: A Spirited Agent Flouts the Laws of Congress

Cannon House Office Building, Independence Avenue and 1st Street, S.E.

HE HAD MAD SKILLS FOR UNDERCOVER WORK.

George was a veteran, having served in the First World War with one of the first US tank units. In fact, he would set up America's Irish War Veterans Association.

A KEEPER OF CONFIDENCES

He could keep a secret. He worked discreetly in the shadows. Like any valuable agent, he built contacts and maintained relationships with men privy to confidential information. He made the acquaintance of dozens of congressmen and senators, and scores of their staffers. They were aware his work was technically illegal, yet deemed it necessary, as a means of protecting the nation's liberties.

One congressman even procured a room, in the basement of the Old House Office Building, today's Cannon House Office Building, to store his dangerous materials. He may have given George the key to it with some trepidation. He knew the substances, if ignited a certain way, could set off a firestorm.

George had begun to ply his quiet craft after a surreptitious meeting at the Varnum Hotel, a block from the House offices. At that site Thomas Jefferson—the devisor of the Jefferson Cipher, which for 160 years encrypted messages for the military and diplomatic corps—had lodged before his inauguration as commander-in-chief. In the hotel's sumptuous lobby, two congressmen had recruited George to set up his secret operations.

He cultivated contacts with criminals, and their transportation networks, in Maryland and Virginia. His most daring exploits happened out of town, in Philadelphia, Newark, and New York City. Most outrageous were his excursions by train up to Manhattan. At Seventh Avenue and 34th Street, he'd warily enter his supply depot. He'd fill two large suitcases with the illicit matter. Then he'd step down a corridor watched over by security men, and step lightly into Pennsylvania Station, noting if he was being followed. After the train trip back to Union Station, he'd hail a taxi, and gingerly load his volatile cargo in the trunk. Then to the House offices, to stow his contraband in the basement hideaway.

Like many soldiers of the Great War, George found himself out of work after the armistice. Hyperinflation succeeded the wartime boom, when price controls were lifted, and was followed in turn by recession, with the jarring lurch from making arms to producing civilian goods.

Now twenty-eight years old, George was married, with a family to support. When the legislators enticed him with work that paid five times more than his prewar job with the railroads, he accepted.

Thus did George Lyons Cassiday become, during Prohibition, the bootlegger to Congress. With a liquor storeroom in the House basement. With an itinerary of train trips to Manhattan and other towns to procure illicit hooch. With contacts among the motorized suppliers who trucked the banned beverages into Maryland, Washington, and Virginia, from as far away as Canada and the Deep South.

Bootlegging Around Congress

Growing up in West Virginia, Cassiday was raised by a mother with membership in the Women's Christian Temperance Union, a leading pro-Prohibition group. However, by the time his troop ship steamed back from fighting in Europe, he'd changed his views. In a straw poll, George voted with his fellow thirsty soldiers, twenty-two hundred to ninety-eight, against Prohibition. French wine and Belgian beer will do that to you.

Back in Washington, he was out of work. The nationwide "dry laws" had begun on January 17, 1920, under Congress's Volstead Act, which put into effect the Eighteenth Amendment to the Constitution.

But it was the start of the Roaring Twenties. To the soundtrack of Dixieland jazz, people wanted an escape from the troubles of the war and the postwar period.

George Cassiday later recounted that "a friend of mine told me, that liquor was bringing better prices than anywhere else in Washington, and that a living could be made."

He started out small. He agreed to supply the two congressmen he'd met in the Varnum Hotel. He thought this odd, as the lawmakers voted with "dry" districts in the South. No matter. He bootlegged liquor into the House building and other locales by hiding bottles in his coat. The lax security of the time aided him. To stop theft, guards checked people leaving the place, yet rarely those entering.

In 1922, however, he was detained and indicted as part of a sting operation, when a Volstead Act agent, pretending to be a congressman's relative, got Cassiday to deliver alcohol to him at an apartment. Luckily for George, the incident never made it to trial.

Wary of further arrests, he determined to only supply hooch to congressmen he met personally, usually in their offices. A legislator who liked his product would recommend his services to another representative, and then another. Like any talented entrepreneur, Cassiday built up his business through word of mouth and by keenly attending to his customers' needs. His most popular products were Scotch, rye whiskey, and bourbon. Congressmen usually bought a case at a time.

The ex-soldier employed clever tactics in making his "House calls." Typically, he entered at night through the side entrances. During the day, he'd wait until the end of office hours, when the doorways would crowd with departing workers, letting him mix in, and avoid the attention of the two policemen stationed outside every exit.

It was cumbersome lugging the stuff into the House quarters. But one day, a congressman from the Midwest told him: "George, did it ever occur to you it would be easier to bring supplies into the building in larger lots, and distribute them from a base of operations from the inside?"

Basement Boozers

Soon he had set up a storeroom in the very basement of the building. A congressman gave him a key to it.

As Cassiday's reputation spread, legislators put more trust in him. Instead of placing orders, some would simply give him the keys to their workspaces and desks. He'd slip bottles into their filing cabinets.

He delivered between twenty to twenty-five packages a day, according to Garrett Peck, the author of *Prohibition in Washington, D.C.: How Dry We Weren't*. His largest deliveries were stuffed inside two big pieces of luggage, each with fifteen to twenty bottles of booze.

Cassiday's work could be nerve-racking. "Frequently I would have a close shave," he recalled, "when a member might receive an expected call from a dry constituent or from some member of his family, who disapproved drinking." One time a thief broke into his storeroom and stole $600 worth of 90 proof.

When Congress was in session, and holding important votes or nominations, his work got hectic. "I used to attend the caucuses in the House when the members were selecting candidates for Speaker," Cassiday wrote in a front-page *exposé* for the *Washington Post* in October 1930. "It always meant a busy night. . . ."

When business was brisk, liquor was scarce. So he'd turn his basement sanctum into a distillery, and water down the supply. The storeroom had a bathroom with hot running water, and a big table on which to set down bottles and jugs. After bolting the door, and pulling down the blinds to the corridor window, Cassiday got to work.

"Using one gallon of pure rye whiskey as a base, adding one gallon of pure grain alcohol and one gallon of hot water from the spigot, and then adding a little bouquet coloring," he explained, "it was possible to turn out 12 quarts of about 90 to 96 proof that was entirely satisfactory."

Despite the temptations all around him, and his Irish heritage, Cassiday never drank the profits. He eschewed the hard stuff entirely and stuck to hops. (The author had an Irish grandmother who bootlegged whiskey in Manhattan, for making tasty Manhattans, so he's allowed a jibe at that Celtic tradition.) "He loved his beer," recalled his son Frederick Cassiday.

The Capitol complex became a home away from home for Cassiday. "It was not long before I had the run of the Senate and House Office Buildings," he stated, "and was spending more time there than most of the Reps." Clerks and tippling congressmen formed with Cassiday an informal "Bar Flies Association." In the House building, they'd hold parties and singing sessions. "From 1920 to 1925 were the good old days for me," he recalled fondly.

The fun extended from potables to poker. In some congressional offices, card games laced with liquor featured six congressmen at a time seated in upholstered swivel chairs arrayed around a fine mahogany table with a green felt top.

Sometimes voters visiting from the home districts would drop in on the fun. Constituents "often relied on their senator or representative to help them out when they were attending conventions or stopping off to see the sights in Washington," wrote Cassiday. "Some of them got a real thrill out of having a drink right under the shadow of the Capitol dome."

Cassiday never disclosed how much money he took in, stating simply that "I never made more than a good living to support myself and my family." Still, as pay for bootleggers, such as a rum runner driving a truck, was nearly 900 percent more than a federal worker, he must have done fine.

WIDESPREAD FLOUTING OF THE LAW

In 1925, Cassiday's high times at the House were suddenly suspended. One day, he was entering the congressional offices, when a policeman checked his briefcase, and found liquor bottles inside. He arrested Cassiday who, according to House Sergeant-at-Arms Joseph Rodgers, was wearing a light-green felt hat. He was tried in court, to much publicity, as the "Man in the Green Hat." The nickname stuck. (In 2012, DC's first micro distillery dubbed its inaugural beverage Green Hat Gin.)

After Cassiday's conviction, he spent a few weeks in jail. His arrest and imprisonment got lots of attention in Congress. In fact, the House passed a rule specifically banning Cassiday from its Office Building.

The master bootlegger was unfazed. He nimbly moved all his operations over to the Senate side of the aisle.

George Cassiday, the bootlegger to Congress, set up a liquor shop in the basement of the House, during the Prohibition that Congress itself had passed into law.

Highballing It to the Other Side of the Hill

Cassiday learned the atmosphere there was more highfalutin than in the House. "I found the senators more cautious and a shrewder class of people," he recalled. "Most of the senators would order their liquor through their secretaries. . . .

"When a young girl or a committee clerk receiving a salary of $150 or $200 a month ordered a case of stuff that sold . . . from $100 to $160 . . . you could be pretty sure you were dealing with a go-between."

One senator employed coded language and a unique hiding place to conduct his transactions with the Man in the Green Hat. In his private office, the lawmaker kept liquor at the top of a bookcase containing bound volumes of the Congressional Record. When his stash was nearly empty, the senator asked Cassiday, his "librarian," to get him some new "reading material."

"I'd slip a couples of volumes off the shelf" and "put in the supplies," Cassiday wrote, "and put the Congressional Record back in place." He didn't have a storeroom at the Senate Office Building, the SOB, but he used its stationery room as a base of operations.

Cassiday was struck by the hypocrisy of the legislators. He stated: "I have sat in the gallery and heard one of my customers deliver a rattling good prohibition speech . . . I have heard members of the House and Senate making strong arguments on the floor that prohibition was being well enforced, when I knew good stuff was being regularly delivered at their own offices. . . .

"I would say that if the entire membership would vote today as they drink," he wrote in 1930, "you could get the required two-thirds majority in the House and Senate" for repeal. "Four out of five senators and congressmen," he continued, "consume liquor either at their homes or their offices. . . ."

Another brush with the law came on Halloween, 1929, when police nabbed him going into the SOB with a bottle of booze cloaked by newsprint. The cops also found liquor in his auto and in his house. Cassiday was indicted but freed on bail and his trial postponed. He went back to his Senate labors. However, pressure mounted when the vice president himself, Charles Curtis of very dry Kansas, heard complaints Cassiday was taking advantage of Senate facilities.

Liquored Up Legislators

During the decade of the Untouchables, Cassiday wasn't the only one busted for trading in illicit spirits. In the 1920s, authorities nabbed three congressmen for violating Prohibition.

Rep. Alfred Michaelson of Illinois was arrested for going through customs, after a trip to Panama and Cuba, with bottles of rum and crème de menthe, among other potables, all stashed in six trunks. At the trial, his brother-in-law swore the liquor was for him. The congressman was acquitted. The self-incriminating relative was arrested and fined.

Rep. Edward Everett Denison, also of Illinois, Al Capone's turf, was arrested after Prohibition agents at DC's Union Station noted his suitcase was leaking alcohol. Denison was convicted for illegal possession and lost his bid for re-election.

Rep. John Wesley Langley of bourbon-loving Kentucky was Congress's most notorious offender. He was convicted of pressuring Prohibition officers to wink at his removal of fourteen hundred cases of whiskey from a Kentucky distillery, according to author J. Anne Funderburg. However, the voters in his district overwhelmingly re-elected him. Moreover, when Langley was sent to jail, his wife won election to his House seat. Her husband defended himself in a book, *They Tried to Crucify Me.*

The Feds never busted a senator for violating the Volstead Act. Cassiday attributed this to the small, one-room offices of representatives, as opposed to the two- or-three-room Senate offices. Senators had more space to hide their illegal substances. Members of the upper chamber also have greater prestige and clout, affording them more protection from the law.

In addition to several representatives, authorities targeted some civilian bootleggers operating remarkably close to Congress itself. A 1932 map from the pro-sobriety group The Crusaders marked the location of hundreds of speakeasies that authorities raided. One takedown occurred outside the main Prohibition lobbying organization, the wonderfully named Anti-Saloon League, a half-block from the Capitol Building on Pennsylvania Avenue N.W. Two raids occurred on speakeasies just one block west of the Capitol, on Maryland Avenue S.W. A ramshackle home across from the House offices themselves hosted three stills for making brandy!

In fact, for all his influential clients, Cassiday was but a small component of a vast illegal liquor trade in Washington. The town hosted an estimated two thousand speakeasies, serviced by five thousand bootleggers.

THE END OF AN ERA

On October 21, 1929, as the stock market crash began to hush the Roaring Twenties, Cassiday's decade-long career came to an end. Partly because he broke his rule on selling only to lawmakers he met personally.

He was lured from his home, on 303 17th Street S.E., to the SOB after getting a letter purporting to be from the relative of a congressman. Two policemen from the city's "flying squad," or vice squad, tailed him. Police sergeant George Little collared him and a helper outside the Senate offices as they carried bottles of Scotch inside.

Cassiday plaintively told the cops, "You got me right this time." The police returned to his house and confiscated 266 quarts of liquor there. They also took his "little black book" of high-level contacts.

A trial, and much publicity, ensued. Cassiday argued the arresting police didn't have a search warrant. The judge at the city's high court wasn't swayed. In July 1930, he socked the Man in the Green Hat with an eighteen-month sentence. His undercover career was over.

But his prison time was hardly dispiriting. Cassiday's son later recalled his father would go to the jail every morning, sign himself in, and then, at the end of the day, sign himself out. He spent the nights in the comfort of his home.

Lenient treatment. But the man, after all, had high-balling friends in very high places.

CHAPTER TWENTY-ONE

Boys in the Hood: A Mammoth Countermarch to the Roaring Twenties

North side of the Capitol Building along Northwest Drive; Maryland Avenue S.W.; and west on Pennsylvania Avenue N.W.

WASHINGTON HAD HOSTED POLITICAL RALLIES BEFORE. THE HUMON-gous women's suffrage march event. "Coxey's Army," a far smaller parade aimed at highlighting widespread joblessness.

DC'S LARGEST DEMONSTRATION TO DATE
In terms of size, at least, the event of Saturday, August 8, 1925 fell into the former category. An array of scrubbed, carefully dressed men, women, and children stacked up for twelve blocks, from their start at the Capitol's Peace Memorial. On a stiflingly hot summer afternoon, they queued up and down Maryland Avenue, past the long-gone slave pen on Independence Avenue. They spilled four blocks deep onto adjacent streets. Wiping away sweat, some massed on Northwest Drive and along East Capitol Street, out to near Lincoln Park, with its centennial statue of the Great Emancipator, and later the black civil rights advocate Mary McLeod Bethune.

Though the public associated the thirty-five thousand or more marchers with the South, most attendees were from New York, New Jersey, and Pennsylvania, and many were from the Midwest. The organizers, to speed the flow of activists into town, had reserved some eighteen railroad trains. Participants poured in from Union Station. Others arrived not by train, but via Model T Fords, and the novel pleasure of spontaneous, long-distance travel.

The *Washington Post* lauded it all as "one of the greatest demonstrations this city has ever known."

Indeed, many in the District were thrilled about it. City residents by the tens of thousands, and hordes of the group's members in civilian garb, lined up that hot afternoon all along Pennsylvania Avenue. A cable was strung along the thoroughfare to separate the milling masses of onlookers from the march.

The event strained the city's businesses. Hotels were all booked up; restaurants could barely keep up with the crush. Cigar stores sold out their inventory of stogies and chewing tobacco. One Jewish entrepreneur at the city's commercial center, 7th Street, put up a big welcome sign.

Still, other Jews in downtown were wary. And many blacks took pause. They recalled the blood-soaked riot just six years before, which started when enraged whites had attacked black pedestrians. And they had an instinctive dread of worse outrages committed decades before. Gospel-church ministers urged their flocks to avoid the march. The police department looked into reports, proven false, that blacks had been buying up second-hand guns to protect themselves.

At 3:00 p.m., at the height and heat of the day, the leaders of the group were ready to start the procession. A man named D. C. Stephenson was chief of the national organization, and L. A. Mueller led the Washington chapter. They were resplendent, if sweaty, in their satiny raiment, which hung colorfully from their heads to their feet. The city's acting chief of police, to keep order, walked right behind them.

Most of the marchers wore similar, if less expensive, clothes of cotton. Their nightshirts had a distinctive, slanted white cross, on a red background, with a figurative drop of blood stitched in the middle. Most kept their distinctive headgear off, which were slung about their necks. The city had made this a precondition for holding the event.

Some of the striders, veterans of the Great War, wore khaki, and Army helmets, and puttees about their lower legs. And "Sam Browne" belts, with straps attached military-style to their necks. One large group, in a patriotic touch, waved several hundred American flags.

SYMBOLS OF HOSTILITY

To the cheers of watching Washingtonians, the demonstrators strode down America's Avenue. They ambled in undulating rows of fourteen people deep, with eighteen to twenty-two people to a row. At times, they strode with arms folded before their chests; other times they locked arms shoulder-to-shoulder. The phalanxes of walkers were interspersed with marching bands. Local members had actually asked the Community Center band, an African-American ensemble, to participate. The band's leader vetoed the notion.

For much of the route, they passed by symbols of things they disdained. Portions of old Chinatown poked through 7th Street: The organization called for barring Asian immigration, as well as Italian and Polish newcomers. The Avenue there was noted for its German restaurants. The group had taken some of its inspiration from First World War watch groups that harassed German Americans for suspected disloyalty.

At 14th and Pennsylvania Avenue, they passed "Newspaper Row," where many periodicals had their national offices. Including the *New York World*, which had exposed a lovers' scandal between the group's two leading marketeers. And the *Baltimore Sun*, known for the cynical, critical H. L. Mencken, who merrily mocked the group in his essays.

Newspaper Row was nicknamed Rum Row, due to reporters' predilection for drink. It was sited in "Murder Bay," aka "Hooker's Alley," the town's Red-Light stretch. Its taverns were often packed with Irish-Catholics. It had places of commercial intercourse filled with fallen women. The marchers, who saw themselves as upholding all-American values, had a special dislike for such venues.

Still, they did pass by a few more favored sites. At 3rd Street, the group walked past the national headquarters of the main Prohibition lobby, and a political ally, the Anti-Saloon League. Just off 7th Street, at Pennsylvania and Indiana Avenues, they took comfort in the strange, fish-and-ibis form of the Temperance Statue, erected four decades before by a fellow foe of drink. And not far away was their group's national headquarters, at 17th and I Streets, a fortress-like structure but two blocks from the White House.

However, their starting point, the Peace Memorial, had been an odd choice. The first version of their group had roiled the South's Reconstruction, after the Civil War, through lynchings and through paramilitary attacks on freed blacks and Yankee troops. Yet the Peace Memorial is a homage, along with war's end, to the Union navy. It's flanked by the Ulysses S. Grant Memorial to the Union army commander, and by Frederick Law Olmsted's brick Grotto, designed by the renowned landscape architect and supply commissioner for the Northern forces.

A SECOND ITERATION

Yet this was a very different Ku Klux Klan from that of the 1860s. Due to deft organization, and by marketing itself as a mainstream group, the KKK of the 1920s had grown to enormous size.

Klan Version 2.0 was started up in 1915 by William Joseph Simmons, of Alabama. Simmons founded the new organization at a meeting on Georgia's Stone Mountain, later the site of enormous, sculpted figures of Confederate icons. He was inspired by bestselling author Thomas Dixon's *The Clansman*, a homage to the first KKK. For his rallies, Simmons borrowed Dixon's stunning image of a burning cross. Another influence was movie director David Wark (D. W.) Griffith's *Birth of a Nation*. At the White House, President Woodrow Wilson had a featured showing of that blockbuster, a technically advanced silent film, which also lionized the first KKK.

Simmons pitched his Klan as a fraternal organization, of patriotic, middle-class folk. Exploiting a postwar crime wave, it styled itself as an upholder of law and order. At the same time, it engaged in violence and intimidation. For instance, it targeted blacks having relations with white women, women having relations out of marriage, and bootleggers violating Prohibition. In 1921, the Rules Committee of the House of Representatives called Simmons to testify. He falsely stated that many "alleged outrages have been attributed to the Klan, but none of these were against Roman Catholics, Jews, and negroes per se. . . ."

In the United States, the First World War and its aftermath were marked by fear and turmoil. 1917 saw the bloody Bolshevik Revolution in Russia, and the spread of extremist ideas worldwide. 1919 witnessed

The founder of the Ku Klux Klan's second iteration, William Joseph Simmons, appeared before Congress to sidestep accusations of violence and intimidation on the part of his organization.

the "Red Summer" of foreign anarchist bombings in America, including a blast at Attorney General A. Mitchell Palmer's home near Dupont Circle. This led to nationwide "Palmer raids" against suspected radicals.

During the war, some five hundred thousand blacks moved to Northern and border states to work in war-related industries, while a third of a million others served in the military. This fueled backlash. In 1919, nationwide riots broke out in which bands of whites attacked blacks.

In 1920, the Nineteenth Amendment granted women in every state the right to vote. Suffrage, and the wartime movement of many women into the workforce, sparked other concerns. The traditional family, in a Jazz Age of higher hemlines and looser morals, seemed under siege.

Further, the war's end promised the renewal of large-scale immigration of Catholics and Jews from Eastern and Southern Europe, which awakened concern the arrivals would push aside America's dominant culture of Anglo-Saxon Protestantism.

The KKK tapped into all these sentiments, particularly the anti-Catholic dread, in a sort of twentieth-century revival of the nineteenth-century Know-Nothing Party.

The New Klan's expansion by the early 1920s was astonishing. Estimates wildly vary, due to incomplete records, but its paid membership ranged from two to five million. Politically, at its peak, it influenced the election from both political parties of sixteen senators, and ten governors. In 1924, during the Democratic Party convention in New York, about half the delegates at the so-called "Klan Bake" were sympathizers. They blocked the nomination of New York's Irish-Catholic governor, Al Smith, by decrying his opposition to Prohibition as well as chiding his faith.

The Klan soared to prominence after hiring two marketing gurus, and out-of-wedlock lovers, Mary Elizabeth Tyler and Edward Young Clarke, both of Atlanta. They were exemplars of modern advertising, birthed in the First World War's propaganda campaigns and the postwar boom in consumerism. Tyler and Clarke founded the Klan's aptly named Propagation Department to promote the notion of "One-Hundred Percent American." They sent hundreds of salesmen about the country as recruiters. Each hawker kept 24 percent of each new membership fee and each purchase of the hooded uniform. Tyler and Clarke got 15 percent. It was a kind of pyramid scheme for a group with triangular headgear.

In 1922, Simmons was pushed out the door by a new Klan leader, Hiram Wesley Evans, a former dentist from Texas by way of Alabama. Evans made the New Klan more conformist than criminal, more professional than blue-collar. His group took after fast-growing civic bodies like the Shriners and the Knights of Columbus. Downplaying the Klan's vigilantism, in which he had himself engaged, Simmons set up women's and children's chapters. He promoted charities, July 4th celebrations, and even KKK softball teams. (Though Jackie Robinson need not apply.) Evans also expanded the group's Southern base into the Midwest and Northeast. To boost its political heft, he moved the headquarters from Atlanta to Washington. From the capital, he organized its 1925 parade.

The Klan reached its height of influence in the 1920s under the tutelage of Hiram Wesley Evans, pictured here in KKK regalia at one of its large Pennsylvania Avenue parades.

FIGHTS OVER FREE SPEECH AND SCIENCE IN THE SCHOOLS

Concerned Washingtonians wanted the city to ban the Klan procession. Thomas L. Avaunt, a former KKK official then heading a Christian organization promoting tolerance, handed out flyers that urged residents to "Arise and Stop this Farce."

Yet others wanted the "Invisible Empire" to be seen. Stated an upstate New York newspaper: "Ku-Kluxism is least harmful and menacing when the sun shines on it. Only in the dark can it make trouble . . . we say let them parade."

Still others viewed the event as an amusing summertime diversion. A Baltimore editor wryly wrote: "Washington languishes, a fit place for hookworm and sleeping sickness. Into that depressing solemnity comes the Ku Klux Klan to kick up a few didoes [*sic*]. Deprive it of its fiery cross? Gosh, no!"

The city commissioners who then ran Washington had to approve a parade permit. They came down on the side of free speech and assembly, however controversial the group. The officials stated they "could not discriminate between applicants for the right to use the streets for parading. . . ."

At the end of Pennsylvania Avenue on 15th Street, the marchers reached the stretch run of their event. They turned sharply to the left, with the White House on their right. Many weren't fond of its occupant, Calvin Coolidge of Vermont. He adhered to an America not of a particular ethnicity, but of an ideal, one that applied to and uplifted all people. In his addresses, Coolidge, as his predecessor Warren Harding had done, denounced the Klan. "This isn't fraternity," he described it, "this is conspiracy." The previous year, the president had given a welcoming talk to a major Catholic organization in town. He declined the Klan's invite to address its Washington rally.

Fresh in the minds of many marchers was the end, just two weeks before, of a sensational court case. This was the Scopes "Monkey Trial" in Dayton, Tennessee. It was, among other things, a publicity stunt by local businessmen. Drawing worldwide press attention, a court put on trial science instructor John Scopes, for teaching evolution in violation of state law. Scopes was convicted and received a modest fine.

Admired by the New Klan, which backed the Tennessee law as upholding religious values, was William Jennings Bryan. He'd been an advisor to the prosecution, as dramatically depicted in the classic film *Inherit the Wind*. In the wake of World War I's carnage, he expressed fear, rather eloquently stated, that a loss of traditional values could open a whirlwind of anything-goes. After a career as a Nebraska congressman, presidential candidate, and secretary of state, Bryan had died five days after the trial's conclusion. During the weekend of the parade, many marchers placed flowers atop his fresh grave at Arlington National Cemetery.

A THUNDEROUS AND FIERY CLIMAX

Down the steep 15th Street hill went the parade. On its right was the Treasury Department, and on its steps were Marines, with bayonets affixed. The Coolidge Administration claimed such soldiers were stationed at important buildings for any public event. In fact, the military was on alert. Yet the marchers weren't intimidated: By the thousands they flocked to the Treasury steps, as the Marines looked on. The Klanners admired the new statue of Alexander Hamilton, the Founding Father from the British Caribbean whose High Federalist backers were wary of French and Irish-Catholic immigration.

Given the blazing temperatures, organizers had ambulances on hand, for victims of heat stroke. They had blundered by holding the event in August, when Washington weather is predictably tropical. Starting it in the mid-afternoon was another mistake. In the Tidewater South, August temperatures typically peak in the late afternoon, with the high heat lasting beyond dusk. Quite a few collapsed from exhaustion or dehydration from the four hours of marching.

The weather errors culminated at the rally's finish, near the Washington Monument.

The Monument had been the scene of a fracas back in 1854, by members of the Know-Nothing Party. At the time, it was managing construction of the Monument, and had run out of funds. It announced, to aid the construction, it would accept stones from donors throughout the world. But to the horror of the anti-Catholic group, it received a block of marble from the Pope, Pius IX. The angry nativists didn't take the insult lying down. One night, a group of them waylaid the site's watchman, hauled the stone to the nearby Potomac, and tossed it in the river.

In 1925, above the Monument that sultry evening, storm clouds gathered, as they often do in Washington at the end of a hot, humid day.

The crowd braved the threat of downpours by gathering about the Sylvan Theater bandstand. As the skies rumbled, Mueller, the local Klan leader, told his listeners not to fret. "I have faith enough in the Lord that He is with every Klansman," he consoled. "We have never had a drop of rain in Washington when we got on our knees."

Yet the Lord who, according to some depictions—by the Italian-Catholic Michelangelo, for instance, resembles an elderly Jewish prophet—responded with wrath. The heavens opened up, and torrential rains sent the white-robed figures scurrying for shelter.

On the night after the march, after drying out, thousands of Klan motorists jammed the new Francis Scott Key Bridge, crossing from Georgetown to Arlington's old Horse Show Grounds. Traffic cops said the then-sleepy town hadn't seen that many cars since the 1921 dedication of the Tomb of the Unknown Soldier at Arlington National Cemetery. The destination was a follow-on rally, of seventy-five thousand Klan men, women, and kids. Mueller, Evans, and the other leaders lit up an eighty-foot cross. Not by torch, but by electricity, as lightbulbs, not fire, provided the illumination in the age of Edison and Westinghouse.

The Klan's 1925 march in Washington was the city's largest demonstration until the mass assemblies of years later, for very different aims: Marian Anderson's 1939 concert at the Lincoln Memorial, for instance. It was a protest of sorts about the black operettist being barred, under the era's segregation laws, from performing at Constitutional Hall. And the Reverend Martin Luther King Jr.'s 1963 March on Washington, which drew half a million persons to the same locale for a related cause.

The KKK procession proved a last hurrah of sorts. Klan membership fell off due to internal scandals, due to the adoption of immigration restrictions, and due to the 1920s boom, as folks turned more to making money than to spite. And when the Great Depression struck, its appeal collapsed, as economic survival overwhelmed all other concerns.

CHAPTER TWENTY-TWO

MacArthur, Eisenhower, and Patton vs. the War Veterans: Tear Gas and Tanks at Capitol Hill

East Portico of Capitol Hill; and 3rd Street and Pennsylvania Avenue, N.W.

SOME THOUGHT IT WAS CONGRESS'S MOST PERILOUS MOMENT SINCE the start of the Civil War. In April 1861, with fears of a Confederate assault on the capital, the new Lincoln Administration had rushed thousands of federal troops into the House and Senate chambers. The troops bivouacked there until the threat of attack waned.

STANDOFF AT THE CAPITOL STEPS

On June 17, 1932, thousands of veteran soldiers gathered on the east promenade of the Capitol Building. They were focused on the legislators inside, who were voting on a bill they had traveled many hundreds of miles to support. The government feared that, if the men were denied their demands, they might storm the building.

The protestors, some eight thousand in number, were part of the "Bonus Army," a host of First World War veterans. During the low point of the Great Depression, and practically penniless, they had journeyed to the capital from throughout the country by foot, train, and car. To demand the immediate payment of their war pensions.

Under a 1927 federal law, these men of the "Bonus Expeditionary Force," or B.E.F., could take out loans against their future bonuses. However, they couldn't receive their full payments until 1945. So, with most out of work and out of savings, they wanted the money right away, for themselves, and for the 4.7 million other Americans who'd served in the Great War.

On June 14, 1932, the House had debated the bonus bill, sponsored by Rep. Wright Patman of Texas, then at the start of his forty-eight years in the House. Speaking for the measure, Rep. Edward Eslick of Tennessee intoned: "Uncle Sam, the richest

Thousands of Bonus Army veterans from the First World War gathered in 1932 on the lawn of the Capitol Building, during the Great Depression, to pressure Congress.

government in the world, gave [each veteran] . . . an IOU 'that I will pay you twenty-seven years after the armistice'. . . . But I want to divert you from the sordid. . . ."

At that moment, Eslick keeled over, from a heart attack. As his wife looked on, the physician of the House failed to revive him. On June 15, five thousand Bonus Army veterans stood along city streets to watch a hearse transport his coffin to Union Station, and from there to burial in his home state.

That same day, the House voted to approve payment of the pensions, by 211 to 176.

The Senate was much more reluctant about the precedent of granting funds under pressure. In the days before massive deficits, it was also worried about the bill's cost. On June 17, it debated the measure into the evening.

The huge crowd of veterans, law enforcement officers, and the curious waited anxiously on the grounds outside. Some ex-soldiers satirized

George M. Cohan's song from the First World War, "Over There," and its lyrics, "The Yanks are coming". They sang out: "The Yanks are starving, the Yanks are starving. . . ."

The police grew more anxious. They had already raised the old drawbridge into town from Anacostia, to prevent ten thousand more veterans camped out there from crowding into Capitol Hill.

Senator Thomas Pryor Gore of Oklahoma got a sudden shock, as his driver took to him to the Capitol for the vote. A protestor hurled a stone his way, and it smashed through the car window. It landed next to his startled grandson, future novelist Gore Vidal. The perceptive lad recalled seeing "shabby-looking men holding up signs and shouting at occasional cars," the protestors resembling "white skeletons like those disjointed cardboard ones displayed at Halloween."

The head of the Bonus Army was Walter W. Waters. From Oregon, and in his early thirties, he'd been a sergeant and a medic in the war. Dressed in quasi-military attire, he was lean, excitable, unpredictable. Many of the veterans wondered how he would react to the vote. At 9:30 p.m., Senate aides called him into the legislative chamber.

Soon, he came outside with news of the outcome. He announced to the veterans the Senate had voted the bill down.

There was silence among the multitude. And fear at what might happen next.

Then Hearst reporter Elsie Robinson, standing next to Waters, whispered a suggestion. He thought a moment, then pronounced: "Sing *America!*"

The veterans broke into, "God bless America, land that I love. . . ."

The tension was broken. The crowd broke up, and most of the men headed back to their makeshift lodgings about the capital city. To discourage any from staying, according to *American Heritage* magazine, "the Capitol police turned on the lawn sprinklers."

A Nationwide Encampment in Washington

Starting in late May, some twenty-five thousand veterans, wives, and children had gathered in the capital to pressure Congress for the bonus. Quite a few were African American, integrated into the novel army.

Out-of-work farmers, miners, factory hands, clerks, and mechanics from every region in the United States had thrown up twenty-seven makeshift camps around town.

The ex-soldiers followed a rough form of military discipline. They elected their own officers, and Waters forbade them to drink, beg, or spread communist propaganda. He and his aides verified the men were actual veterans by examining their discharge papers.

Among the largest sites was a tent city in Hillcrest, on privately donated land in northeast DC overlooking the Anacostia River. Another sizeable camp was on 12th Street, near today's Museum of American History. The biggest encampment was two miles from the Capitol, across the drawbridge on the eastern side of the Anacostia River mudflats.

In its jammed thirty acres, as many as fifteen thousand veterans and their families pitched tents and patched together huts. The *Washington Star* reported their rude building materials consisted of: "egg crates . . . paper boxes . . . rusty bed springs . . . O.D. blankets . . . newspapers . . . junked automobiles . . . wall-paper . . . corrugated iron . . . rusty frames of beds . . . tin cans . . . straw . . . parts of baby carriages . . . auto seats." The teeming shantytown had aspects of civilization. Waters and his veterans built a theater stage, published a newspaper, held baseball games, and set up a barbershop.

Just down the hill from the Capitol was a smaller encampment. It was formed from the shells of brick buildings slated for final demolition, at Pennsylvania Avenue and 3rd Street, N.W., just three blocks from Congress. On the Avenue's south side were the remnants of old Murder Bay, the city's "entertainment district." The buildings included a warehouse, an outdated armory, a cheap restaurant, a worn-out hotel, and an undertaker's shop. Among its shattered walls over two thousand men and family members had bedded down in tents and lean-tos.

The place would be the flashpoint of the Capitol's next, and climactic, drama.

HARD TIMES, AND FOOD FOR THE POOR
In summer 1932, the Great Depression was nearing its abyss. A quarter of all Americans were out of work. Thousands of banks were shutting

down. Women sold companionship for "a dime a dance." With local charities and assistance depleted, over a million people wandered around the country, searching for sustenance and work.

The response to severe downturns today is massive economic incentives, which might include more government spending, slashed taxes, interest-rate cuts, and suspension of some business regulations. However, in the 1930s the response worldwide imposed hurdles to employment and business growth: hikes in tariffs, spending cuts, tax increases, protecting the value of the currency, keeping interest rates stable, and greater regulation of business and agriculture. The global economy would stagger for a decade.

Trying to handle the mass of indigent people in the already economically depressed city of Washington was the lanky, forty-nine-year-old chief of the Metropolitan Police, Pelham Glassford. The pipe-smoking top cop had been the youngest American general of the First World

Metropolitan Police head Pelham Glassford was the man in the middle with the Bonus Army, attempting to provision it while under coming orders to oust it from town.

War. As Glassford rode his blue-tinted police motorbike about the Bonus Army camps, he grew more sympathetic to the former soldiers' plight. They were "just middle-aged men out of work," he stated.

As they arrived in droves, Glassford secured them food and volunteer doctors. Acting as a treasurer for the Bonus Army, he held fundraisers for it at wrestling matches and at a house of burlesque. He persuaded the National Guard to donate tents and portable kitchens. President Herbert Hoover, though staunchly opposed to a bonus payment, quietly arranged to provide the veterans with victuals, tents, and medical assistance.

Glassford befriended heiress Evalyn Walsh McLean, possessor of the Hope diamond, and spouse to the *Washington Post's* owner. One night at a diner, he and McLean placed a take-out order for the Bonus Army: for one thousand packs of cigarettes, one thousand sandwiches, and an ocean of coffee, according to *Smithsonian*. Mostly from his own wallet, Glassford would procure the Bonus Army $2,000 worth of food.

Many city residents and officials disagreed with the chief's approach. They fretted the impoverished men would overstay their welcome and swamp the town's overburdened soup kitchens and relief agencies. Glassford himself worried about a diversion of food from such charities. Meantime the Hoover Administration, and the three city commissioners running the District, disliked the veterans' pressuring of Congress, and their occupation of the Treasury-owned property below the Capitol.

This was reflected in a meeting Glassford had with the city commissioner in charge of police affairs. He was retired major general Herbert B. Crosby, the Army's former chief of cavalry. Glassford asked Crosby for extra bedding and food for the veterans. Instead, Crosby suggested Glassford use force to evict them.

"Is that an order?" queried Glassford.

"Oh no, it's merely a suggestion," replied the former general. "I don't need to remind you that in the Army a suggestion is as good as an order, do I?"

A LIVELY PARADE AND A DEATH MARCH

Some in government worried that events in Germany over the prior two years—where bloody street fighting between fascists and communists led to Hitler's taking power—might repeat themselves in America. The Hoover Administration was getting misleading Army intelligence reports that radical leftists, seeking to overthrow the government, made up much of the Bonus Army. Glassford himself had his police agency compile five thousand files on radicals in the District. He also had his men infiltrate meetings of Communist Party members.

There was a smaller, Red encampment, off 14th Street S.W., just east of the Bureau of Engraving and Printing. When a left-wing group, the Workers' Ex-Servicemen's League (WESL), nicknamed the Weasels, announced a parade for July 8, Glassford persuaded Waters to preempt it with a Bonus Army demonstration.

His event turned into a mammoth affair. Tens of thousands of Washingtonians lined Pennsylvania Avenue to watch about six thousand veterans march to the Peace Monument. Waters's men threatened to stone the Reds' rally. Irate that the Bonus Army had stolen their thunder, the radicals cancelled their own march.

After June's Senate vote, Waters had pledged to send the Bonus Army home. Then he backtracked, and many of his men stayed well into July. On July 7, Congress appropriated $100,000 for train tickets to give the veterans free rides out of town. But there were few takers.

Hoover and city officials were aware that summer is high season for public disturbances. There were memories of DC's bloody, July 1919 race riot, which was largely begun by servicemen. Yet Waters now promised to stay in Washington "until 1945 if necessary to get our bonus."

At the same time, food at the camps grew scarce, and sanitation began breaking down. The Spanish influenza had devastated Washington, and the world, in 1918, and another epidemic seemed possible. Waters told Evalyn McLean: "I'm desperate. Unless these men are fed, I can't say what won't happen."

Some of his men took part, starting on July 12, in a three-day "Death March," organized by a radical splinter group from Los Angeles. Faced with a ban on sleeping at the Capitol grounds, hundreds of demonstrators responded with a continuous slow-walk. Pedestrians at the Hill heard the clatter of their canteens. Some in the group damaged the cars of congressmen. The latter, to evade the rowdies, took to entering and leaving their workplace by the tunnels under the Capitol Building.

On July 14, the French Revolution's Bastille Day, Vice President Charles Curtis demanded US Marines keep the marchers away from the Capitol. However, when sixty Marines trooped over, the veterans met the servicemen with cheers, not jeers. Glassford got the Navy Yard commandant to intervene. He ordered the leathernecks, some of whom were sympathetic to the ex-soldiers, to return to Barracks Row.

July 16 was the final day of the congressional session. Fifteen thousand Bonus Army members were gathered on Congressional Plaza just east of the Capitol Building. On the spur of the moment, the mercurial Waters, at the head of a small group, tried rushing into the Capitol. He was detained, then released, by Glassford. Once again, for an instant, "It looked like the start of a riot ahead," noted a reporter.

Then, in a weird repeat of the Senate vote's resolution, a nurse shouted to the crowd: "Let's all sing 'America'!" The veterans did. Then they added a sarcastic: "My Bonus Lies Over the Ocean." Waters and a bunch of the veterans were permitted to sit in protest in the middle of the Capitol steps. After a while, they dispersed.

A Push to Evict

In Lafayette Square that same day, things got tense. A force of four hundred police broke up a group of dozens of radicals as they approached the White House. President Hoover decided against a planned visit to Congress and declined to meet with veterans at his residence. Fifty members of the Bonus Army marched toward the Executive Mansion, but under orders from Hoover, police closed Pennsylvania Avenue and broke up that group as well.

With support from the city commissioners and the military, the president decided he'd had enough. He would force the Bonus Army out of town.

When Waters was informed of the government's intent, he offered no opposition. He distributed a flyer urging his men to take the free train rides home. Thousands of the veterans, wearying of the camp conditions, began to leave Washington. But about twelve thousand remained about the city, and some others continued to filter in.

On July 26, Waters met with the secretary of war, Patrick J. Hurley, and Gen. Douglas MacArthur, then US Army chief of staff, and the recipient of seven Silver Stars during the First World War.

The face-to-face was icy. "You and your bonus army have no business in Washington," Waters said Hurley told him, as MacArthur paced about the meeting room. "We will not co-operate in any way with your remaining here. At the first sign of disorder or bloodshed in the B.E.F.," Hurley continued, "we have plenty of troops to put you out." Secretary Hurley, who saw the Bonus Army as an "invasion," would take on an important diplomatic role in the Second World War. As Franklin Roosevelt's emissary to China, he had the arduous task of trying to forge an alliance against the Japanese army between Nationalist Chinese strongman Chiang Kai-Shek and Communist Party dictator Mao Zedong.

The following day, July 27, the city commissioners summoned Waters to their office. They refused to meet the Bonus Army chief in person, so he sat in an anteroom. Glassford served as an odd intermediary, shuttling between the officials and Waters. "It isn't every ex-sergeant," Waters later crowed, "that can have an ex-general for messenger boy!"

With some back-and-forth confusion, the commissioners, Glassford, and Waters hashed out a plan. The initial focus would be on the partially demolished buildings at the foot of the Capitol. The federal government had ordered the veterans out of the Treasury-owned property multiple times, to no avail.

The eighteen hundred veterans and their five hundred family members at 3rd and Pennsylvania would start to vacate the buildings the following morning, on Thursday, July 28. By Monday, August 1, according to the scheme, the Bonus Army would depart from all their downtown encampments.

The commissioners instructed Glassford's police to direct the evacuation. As backup, however, the Hoover Administration assembled a military force near the White House.

Early in the morning of July 28, hundreds of US Army soldiers gathered on the lawn of the Ellipse, the park below the South Lawn of the White House. Leading the force, remarkably, were three officers who would have very prominent roles in the Second World War: General MacArthur, who had de facto command, and who later would lead the US Army in the Pacific; his aide, and liaison to the commissioners, Maj. Dwight David Eisenhower, later the Supreme Allied Commander in Europe; and Maj. George S. Patton, later famous for his Third Army's race across France and Germany.

On the Ellipse, MacArthur assembled three hundred infantry, two hundred cavalry, and six French Renault tanks. He had more than twenty-five hundred men in reserve.

Further, the War Department stationed several hundred soldiers at the Munitions Building, a big block of Army offices then located on the National Mall a few blocks south and west of the White House. Incredibly, the role of the troops there was to prevent any attempt by insurrectionists to mount an assault on the Executive Mansion.

FRACAS AT THE FOOT OF THE CAPITOL

That morning, tensions were again boiling over. Near the White House, nightstick-wielding cops broke up a rally by several hundred communist sympathizers.

At 9:45 a.m., at the Treasury-owned structure at 3rd and Pennsylvania, Waters was ready to start moving the veterans

Army Chief of Staff Douglas MacArthur, a leading commander of both world wars, led the troops that evicted the Bonus Army from its encampments on Capitol Hill and Anacostia.

out. Treasury Department agents, backed by Glassford and one hundred police, arrived to enforce the departure. The cops set up a rope line around the condemned buildings. Thousands of veterans and other onlookers were gathering to watch events unfold.

To Waters's shock, a police aide handed him a Treasury order to empty the building—by 10:00 a.m. Instead of four days, he had just two hours. Waters announced the directive to the men and told them: "You're double-crossed." He and the occupants took a poll; about seventy veterans decided to stay.

After the police had cordoned off the area, however, and the cops and Treasury agents began to clear the dwellings, most of the occupants decided they'd been defeated.

Veterans and some family members, taking their belongings, left some of the ramshackle dwellings. Waters, undecided between cooperating with the authorities or standing with the radicals, took off downtown. He would be incommunicado for hours.

Then, around noon, things got ugly. Several dozen from the militant WESL group pushed up against the ropes. Some men were carrying an American flag and tried to re-enter the properties; the police stopped them. Some began heaving brickbats at the cops.

One missile hit a policeman in the face, badly injuring him. "Give the cops hell!" a man shouted. Some rushed in on the police, some with boards or iron bars, and the cops struck back with nightsticks.

At the foot of the Capitol Building, a brawl erupted that led to the deaths of two Bonus Army members, as well as severe injuries to policemen.

Glassford jumped into the fray to restore order. "Be peaceful, men! Be calm!" he shouted. "Let's not throw any more bricks." The chief was himself floored by a stone, and had his chief's badge ripped from him, according to a *Time* magazine report. Five police were injured, one with a fractured skull.

"Come on, boys," Glassford cried gamely, from atop a mound of bricks. "Let's call an armistice for lunch." His words had the desired intent. The riot ground to a halt, for a while. The evacuation continued.

At 1:45 p.m., however, a fight broke out among Bonus Army members on the second story of a building. Police officers went over to break things up and were themselves caught in the fray. "Let's get 'em," cried one of the brawlers.

Officer George W. Shinault, under assault from several men, fired his revolver—and killed thirty-eight-year-old William Hushka. Another policeman fatally shot a California man. Three policemen were severely hurt.

Once again, Glassford intervened. "Stop that shooting!" he shouted. He urged both sides to cease, and once again the violence ended. Waters would later plead: "The men got out of control. There's nothing I can do."

Meanwhile news of the tumult got back to the White House. The city commissioners formally asked Hoover to send in the military. They endorsed a statement that read: "A serious riot occurred. . . . This area contains thousands of brickbats and these were used by the rioters in their attack upon the police. . . . [It is] impossible to maintain law & order. . . . The presence of Federal troops will result in far less . . . bloodshed."

President Hoover gave his assent. Secretary of War Hurley informed MacArthur: "You will have United States troops proceed immediately to the scene of the disorder . . . clear it without delay. . . ." He added, "Any women and children should be accorded every consideration and kindness."

Glassford learned of the directive, and raced his motorcycle to the Ellipse, as Patton was readying the horse soldiers. Around 2:00 p.m., Glassford asked MacArthur to grant him more time to evacuate the Bonus Army. The general gave him two more hours.

The US Army vs. the Army Veterans

At 4:00 p.m., MacArthur moved his troops out of the Ellipse, and up Pennsylvania Avenue toward the encampment.

The veterans, and the public, learned of the decision to deploy the military from the newspapers' early-afternoon editions. Spectators along the Avenue awaited a spectacle. There was an almost carnival atmosphere that summer afternoon, as vendors sold hot dogs and cold drinks. Some in the Bonus Army took up their own viewing spots, in the windows of the building shells.

Down the "Nation's Avenue" came the two hundred cavalry with sabers raised, their carbines glinting. They were led by Patton, who had earlier performed a reconnaissance.

The horse soldiers were assigned the north end of the boulevard, near the spectators. On the south side came the three hundred infantrymen, with rifles loaded, gas masks and bayonets affixed. They approached the building remnants. The tanks rumbled behind the foot and horse soldiers.

Recalled a city resident: "We thought it was a parade because of all the horses." The mood began to shift as police roughly pushed out a path for the troops along the Avenue.

Then, to the shock of the onlookers and veterans, the soldiers attacked.

The infantry lobbed dozens of tear gas grenades into the buildings. A few veterans may have lobbed some of the grenades back. Spectators screamed, some waving their fists at the military. Lean-tos were crushed under tank treads. Watching nearby was a nattily dressed senator, Hiram Bingham of Connecticut, who looked down to see a tear gas canister smoking by his shiny shoes.

The cavalry troops, yelling, with swords brandished, pushed and poked veterans and civilians off the Avenue, and up to C Street near Judiciary Square.

Patton would recall: "Bricks flew, sabers rose and fell with a comforting smack, and the mob ran," according to authors Paul Dickson and Thomas B. Allen. Major Patton was no ally of those encamped. He'd state: "When a mob starts to move keep it on the run. . . . Use the bayonet to encourage its retreat."

One of the people forced out by Patton's horsemen was a veteran named Joe Angelo. In a First World War battle, he saved a wounded Patton's life by dragging him into a foxhole.

The wives of veterans, their throats gagging from the gas, grabbed children and personal items, and fled. Some set sheds on fire. Soldiers lit fires to other structures and ordered civilians to "get the hell out of the way!" Many ran away across the National Mall.

By around 8:00 p.m., the Army had cleared everyone out. Near the other end of the Mall, soldiers also demolished the communist camp.

END GAME ON THE ANACOSTIA

With their first mission accomplished, the troops strode and rode up Capitol Hill, and closed down smaller encampments near the Capitol Building. Then MacArthur's columns headed to the drawbridge leading to the Anacostia Flats, and the main Bonus Army camp.

President Hoover, twice, sent couriers to MacArthur directing him to not approach the Anacostia site that evening. But the headstrong general ignored the directives. He was eager to complete the evictions if it took all night. He marched his troops to the bridge. He prepared to destroy the shack city.

Waters had retreated to the Anacostia encampment. Around 9:00 p.m., he admitted defeat. A subordinate of his, waving a white shirt of surrender, met MacArthur. He pleaded for time to let the remaining residents grab their belongings. MacArthur gave them until 10:00 p.m.

In the gloom, the men, women, and children of the Bonus Army left behind their sheds and lean-tos. They headed up a rise, the site of the camp's theater, which overlooked the temporary city.

The vanguard of the troops marched behind a city fire truck, whose headlights lit the camp up in an eerie glow. An artillery searchlight also pierced the night. The soldiers, the cavalry behind them, marched through the doomed settlement. They set fire to the hovels and huts and threw tear gas canisters. Two thousand tear gas bombs were dispensed that day and night.

The smoke and the gas in the light of a crescent moon, recalled an Army captain, "was like riding through the steam of a tea kettle." In nearby neighborhoods, residents ran out from their dwellings, coughing from the tear gas that wafted through their windows, according to writer Kendall D. Gott.

The temporary city's former residents watched the conflagration from the knoll. Then they tramped out into the darkness.

Eisenhower later recalled: "the whole scene was pitiful. The veterans were ragged, ill-fed, and felt themselves badly abused. To suddenly see the whole encampment going up in flames just added to the pity."

In the White House, Hoover witnessed the glow from the fires to the east. Later he stated: "A challenge to the authority of the United States Government has been met, swiftly and firmly. . . . Government cannot be coerced by mob rule."

At an early-morning press conference, MacArthur opined the Bonus Army "had come to the conclusion that they were going to take over the government in an arbitrary way or by indirect means."

With the Capitol Building as backdrop, soldiers set fire to the main Bonus Army camp on the Anacostia River flats, sending thousands of veterans and family members fleeing into Maryland.

Later, Eisenhower said of MacArthur: "I told that dumb son-of-a-bitch not to go" with the troops. "It was no place for the Chief of Staff." Still, Eisenhower authored the Army's report on the Bonus Army that found no fault with MacArthur's actions.

The medical and arrest tally from that day: two dead veterans and fifty-five wounded, the wounded policemen, and 135 arrests.

Blocked from entering Virginia, the retreating Bonus Army turned toward the Maryland border five miles away. That state had set up trucks to send the vagrants out of state. Many went on to Pennsylvania and bedded down for a short time at an abandoned tract, once known as the Ideal Amusement Park. It was located near Johnstown, Pennsylvania, whose 1889 flood wrote another grim chapter in history. Soon forced out of their latest, tumbledown camp, most went back to their home states, or drifted back into the ranks of the rootless unemployed.

A Hoover Administration official summed up the Bonus Army saga: "There is no glory in this terrible episode—no hero."

CHAPTER TWENTY-THREE

Bittersweet Bowers: The Real Story Behind *Saving Private Ryan*

Northeast lawn of the Capitol grounds, across 1st Street N.E. from the Supreme Court Building

MOST PEOPLE PASSING BY THIS SPOT FAIL TO NOTE ITS SIGNIFICANCE. They're going to or from the Supreme Court and the Senate side of the Capitol, across a seemingly insignificant lawn with a scattering of five low-slung trees. Almost no one sees the small memorial plaque in the grass.

However, most have seen the movie *Saving Private Ryan*. With its Matt Damon character, the sole surviving member of four brothers in the Second World War US military, who is rescued by the Tom Hanks character. Viewers may think the film was based on real-life Ryan brothers.

FACT INSPIRES FICTION

That Steven Spielberg movie was inspired, in fact, by an actual band of brothers named Sullivan from the very military-sounding town of Waterloo, in Iowa. They served together in the US Navy during that war.

The plaque notes their names: George, age twenty-seven at his death; Francis, twenty-six; Joseph, twenty-four; Madison, twenty-three; and Albert, twenty. All in their twenties, in the fullness of life.

In November 1942, during savage battles for control of the Southwest Pacific island of Guadalcanal, a Japanese submarine torpedoed the USS *Juneau*, a thinly hulled cruiser on which all five Sullivans served. The ship sunk, killing 687 officers and crew, including all five brothers.

There's a scene in *Saving Private Ryan* in which Mrs. Ryan, the mother of the Ryan brood, is at her wood-frame house in Iowa farm country. It's a lovely and lonely setting out of a Norman Rockwell painting. The woman spots rumbling toward her home a car with an Army star painted on it. The matronly lady realizes there's only one reason the military might send a vehicle all the way out to her rural enclave. As an Army officer and a priest bear the grimmest of tidings up to her porch, she collapses to the floorboards in sorrow.

The scene captures how Mrs. Alleta Sullivan must have felt on January 12, 1943, when two Navy officers and a physician visited her and her husband in their home.

"I have some news for you about your boys," stated a lieutenant commander.

"Which one?" asked Tom Sullivan grimly, steeling himself.

"I'm sorry," answered the officer. "All five."

The Navy and the government tried to console the bereaved parents. President Franklin Roosevelt wrote Alleta Sullivan a letter of appreciation. First Lady Eleanor Roosevelt, and Vice President Henry Wallace, met with both parents. (In *Saving Private Ryan*, Army Chief of Staff George Marshall recites an actual letter of President Lincoln's to a mother who lost at least three of her sons in the Civil War.)

Mrs. Sullivan had already been selected, as the mother of five servicemen, to christen a Navy tugboat. In April 1943, after the deaths of their sons were confirmed, the Sullivan parents agreed to christen the destroyer the USS *Sullivan*. They went on to take part in many wartime fundraisers and bond drives. In 1944, 20th Century-Fox made a movie about their sons, *The Fighting Sullivans*.

FAMILY AND NAVY TRIBULATIONS

The Sullivans seemed an ideal, if star-crossed, family. To bolster the war effort, the parents and brothers were portrayed as models of upright, hard-working folk. The truth was different, according to author Bruce Kuklick. The father was an abusive alcoholic. And his sons were what a postwar generation might have called juvenile delinquents. They picked fights in the poor neighborhood of their town. They joined a motorcycle gang, the Harley Club, and sported gang regalia that aped fascist uniforms. They pilfered their drunken dad's liquor. Their mother understandably suffered from depression. The film, and the newspaper and magazine articles written about the brothers, were sanitized. Still, they were brave young men who had given their lives for their country.

The Navy had reason to feel especially remorseful about the parents' great loss. For a bureaucratic foul-up had resulted in the death of at least one, and perhaps two, of the Sullivan brothers.

After the torpedo struck the *Juneau*, probably near its ammunition hold, the ship exploded, and quickly sank. Some four hundred of its sailors perished from the blast. However, over one hundred were thrown into the ocean. Many were badly wounded; all began a desperate fight to survive.

The ship was part of a fleet battered in the fighting near Guadalcanal. The seas there were infested with Japanese submarines. The US fleet commander, Capt. Gilbert Hoover, decided against mounting a rescue operation for the *Juneau*'s survivors. Instead, he returned his ships to base. An Army Air Force bomber spotted the survivors in the sea, and after landing relayed the sighting. However, its report got lost in the mass of information about the chaotic battles in the region. Ranking officers didn't learn about it for several critical days.

By the time a rescue was attempted, only twenty or so sailors were still alive. The rest had suffered horrible fates. They died of exposure from sun and sea, from their wounds, or from sharks.

Albert Sullivan lived through the wreck but drowned the day after the sinking. His brother George endured for four or five days. He fell into a delirium from hypernatremia, a buildup of sodium from dehydration. According to a witness, gunner's mate Allen Heyn, George was on a life raft during this time. Then one evening, George said "he would go for a swim, he stripped off his clothes, a shark was seen near him, and he was never seen again."

When the commander of the military region, Admiral William "Bull" Halsey, found out about Captain Hoover's decision to leave *Juneau*'s men behind in the ocean, he court-martialed him. The resulting tribunal, however, sided with Hoover. The judges determined it was too risky to mount a search with damaged ships in waters swarming with enemy subs.

Congress in 1952 honored Alleta Sullivan, mother of the five Sullivan brothers slain when a Japanese submarine sank their Navy ship in 1942, by planting five memorial trees on the Capitol lawn.

PLANTINGS FOR THE FALLEN BRETHREN

In 1952, in a lasting tribute to the Sullivan brothers, a senator and a congressman from Iowa stood, along with mother Alleta and others, on the Capitol's northeast lawn. During a ceremony, five crabapple trees were planted in the ground, one for each of the brothers. Ironically, the trees are native to Japan, the nation the brothers fought.

When they bloom, the trees exhibit a red hue, evocative of sacrifice and blood. Moreover, crabapples have a very sour taste.

They suggest the indescribable sadness of Mrs. Sullivan when she received the news about her sons.

CHAPTER TWENTY-FOUR

Enemy Combatants and the Supremes:
The Nazi Plot to Blow Up America

West steps of the Supreme Court Building, 1 First Street N.E.

IT WAS ODD BEHAVIOR FOR A SABOTEUR DURING HIS FIRST DAY IN THE enemy capital. George Dasch entered the Olmstead Grill on 13th and G Street, four blocks from the White House, and got stinking drunk.

Long before studying bomb-making at a Nazi training camp outside Berlin, the gaunt, thirty-nine-year-old Dasch had become a naturalized citizen of the United States. He had a stint in the peacetime US Army, and worked in civilian life as a waiter. At the Olmstead Grill, on that Thursday, June 18, 1942, he struck up a conversation about restaurants with a waiter. During the schnapps-fueled chat, Dasch told the man the outlines of his secret mission of mayhem. The waiter dismissed it as fantasy.

A WILD NIGHT IN THE HAMPTONS

Six days prior, late in the evening of Friday, June 12, German submarine U-202 had pulled up near East Hampton, on the southern coast of Long Island, New York. Dasch, the high-strung leader of four saboteurs, all clad in German military uniforms, climbed with his men into an inflatable raft, and amidst a thick fog paddled ashore. On the beach, they changed into civilian clothes, and hurriedly buried four waterproofed boxes of dynamite, incendiaries, primers, and detonators. Dasch carried a suitcase of $50,000 in US dollars, and much more cash hidden elsewhere, to bankroll bombings.

Then, as Dasch stood on a dune, twenty-one-year-old Coast Guard Seaman Second Class John Cullen, his flashlight twinkling, came along on his night patrol. Dasch rushed over to Cullen and told him he and the other men were lost fishermen without IDs. Cullen was suspicious.

Another saboteur, Ernest Burger, not seeing Cullen in the gloom, walked up toward Dasch, and asked him a question in German. "Shut up you fool!" Dasch retorted, and Burger hurried away.

Dasch grabbed the startled Cullen. He told him: "I wouldn't want to kill you. Forget about this." He pushed $260 in cash at him, stating: "Take this and have a good time. Forget what you've seen here."

He took Cullen's flashlight and shone it on his face, strangely saying, "Do you know me?!" It was as if Dasch was giving away his identity. Indeed, the Coast Guardsman noted a prominent silver streak of gray in the stranger's slicked-back hair.

Cullen took off, expecting a bullet in his back at any moment. He hurried to the Coast Guard station nearby. He told his colleagues what had happened.

Though dubious of the outlandish tale, the Coast Guardsmen picked up weapons and went with Cullen back to the landing spot. In the mist, they eyed the blinking light of a U-boat pulling away from a sandbar. Alarmed, they saw footprints leading them to the buried explosives. They also found German uniforms, cigarettes, clothing—and a bottle of schnapps. Later that morning, they alerted the FBI's office in New York City.

Meanwhile the four saboteurs hiked to a depot and took the 6:57 a.m. Long Island Railroad commuter train into Manhattan. There they got hotel rooms.

All the members of the sabotage team had worked in America before returning to Germany after the war's outbreak. Along with Dasch, they were: Burger, thirty-six, a former member of Hitler's Brown Shirts; Heinrich Harm Heinck, thirty-five; and Richard Quirin, thirty-four. The latter two had worked in the United States as machinists and while in America had joined the pro-Nazi, German-American Bund.

On June 17, another submarine, U-201, pulled up off the coast of Florida, eighteen miles south of Jacksonville. It landed four more saboteurs, all of whom had also lived in America, before loyally returning to the wartime "Fatherland."

That group's leader was Edward Kerling, thirty-two. He'd worked in America as a butler and, after returning to Germany, had a position in top Nazi Josef Goebbels's Ministry of Propaganda and Public Enlightenment. The other three were: Herbert Hans Haupt, twenty-two, who'd worked in Chicago in an optician's office; Hermann Otto Neubauer, thirty-two, a veteran of the Russian front who in America had been a cook and a Bund member; and Werner Thiel, thirty-five, an itinerant laborer and Bund member in America, and a factory worker in Germany.

On the Florida shore, the foursome buried their bombs without being discovered. They intended to later retrieve the explosives—from far away. For they immediately got on trains that took Haupt and Neubauer to Chicago, and Kerling and Thiel to Cincinnati and then to New York.

A Saboteur's Subterfuge

That same night, in Manhattan, Dasch and Burger intimated over dinner that they were both opposed to Hitler and to their mission. At their hotel room, next to an open, upper-floor window, Dasch made sure Burger was on his side. He threatened to kill Burger, if he didn't join him. Dasch told him that "only one of us will walk out that door—the other will fly out this window!" Burger threw in his lot with Dasch.

Dasch had determined to sabotage the sabotage. But first, to calm his nerves and to renew an old love of cards, he binged on pinochle, a game invented in Germany and then popular with Americans of German descent. At a waiter's club he played the pastime, and drank and ate, for two-and-a-half days straight.

He told Burger to keep the others on ice, while he traveled to Washington to tell top FBI officials of the plot. He'd already called the Bureau's headquarters in Manhattan with an odd message: that a U-boat had landed, that he had vital information, and that "I'll be in Washington within the week to deliver it personally to J. Edgar Hoover." The agent he reached figured it was a crank call. But his office got the Coast Guard call about the submarine, so its agents reasoned the caller might be legit.

On June 19, Dasch took a train to DC. He booked Room 351 at the plush Mayflower Hotel, five blocks from the White House. (And one block from a Russian spy nest at the Soviets' Pullman House embassy.) He was lucky to get a room, given the scarcity of lodging from the war's massive influx of military personnel into town.

Then he got drunk and loose-lipped at the Olmstead Grill. Late the following morning, he called FBI headquarters. The monstrous-looking J. Edgar Hoover Building on 9th Street was still thirty-three years in the future. The Bureau was then on the second floor of the Justice Department on 10th Street and Independence Avenue.

Dasch demanded to speak to Hoover, but twenty-eight-year-old Duane L. Traynor, whose beat was counter-sabotage, took the call. Dasch told him: "I'm the man who called your New York office." Traynor believed Dasch's tale enough to send a car to the Mayflower to pick him up. When they met, Traynor noticed the streak of silver hair that the Coast Guardsman had described.

To allay remaining doubts, Dasch took his carrying case and dumped over $80,000 worth of cash on the desk of a counterintelligence agent. Further, Dasch unveiled a handkerchief with the names of his contacts and mail drops inscribed in invisible ink. Bureau chemists were able to display the names by suffusing the cloth with ammonia fumes.

Now convinced, the FBI supplied Dasch with multiple stenographers over multiple days to take down his story. After confession sessions, the Bureau let their prized stool pigeon stay overnight at the Mayflower. During the day, Hoover's G-men cased his hotel room, and found souvenirs he'd taken from the U-boat. Dasch offered up the possible whereabouts of the other saboteurs. He saw himself as a hero for having blown the whistle, and expected the Americans to recognize him as such.

A PROGRAM OF TERROR, AND BLUNDERS

Dasch had quite the tale. After war broke out in Europe, he and the other seven had headed back to Germany. All knew English to some extent, and some had labored in American industries the Nazis hoped to attack. They became targets of recruitment for the Abwehr, the German military intelligence agency seeking to plant spies and saboteurs abroad.

They underwent a brief period of intense training in a spy school outside Berlin. There they learned about different types of explosives, and detonators such as ampoules of acid, blasting caps, and a fountain pen that concealed a delayed charge. They were taken to factories and shipyards throughout Germany to identify the weak points of such installations.

The planned new sabotage was codenamed Operation Pastorius, after Francis Daniel Pastorius, the eighteenth-century German immigrant who founded Germantown, Pennsylvania. (During the Second World War, the Germantown statue of Pastorius, an abolitionist and democratically inclined man, was covered over, due to fears it might inspire Nazi sympathies.)

Operation Pastorius was ambitious. The sabotage list contained premier industrial and infrastructure projects: Niagara Falls hydroelectric plants; a key part of the Chesapeake and Ohio Railroad; New York City's Hell Gate Bridge; the New York City water supply; aluminum factories vital to making long-range aircraft; and canal locks in Cincinnati and St. Louis critical to the Ohio-Mississippi "river highway." The operatives were also told to leave bombs in the locker rooms of train stations and in Jewish-owned stores like Macy's. They were instructed to explode the ordinance during off hours to avoid casualties, the intent being more to spread fear and terror, not stoke anger and revulsion.

Yet the plan had major defects. Notably, the saboteurs. Burger, for instance, had wildly mixed views of the Nazis. Stocky and aggressive, he'd taken part in Hitler's failed 1923 "beer hall" coup. But he'd run afoul of the Gestapo, who so mistreated his wife she miscarried their child.

Espionage and paramilitary operations take courage and expertise. Yet none of the eight, except for Neubauer, had combat experience. None had espionage experience, and all had trained for less than a month before being sent back to America.

The saboteurs bungled even before they left Europe. One got drunk in a Paris bar and bragged about his secret mission. During the railway trip that took Dasch's team to their U-boat, Dasch left secret papers about the mission on the train. And Dasch's English spelling was so bad that any American reading his script would peg him for a foreigner.

Once in America, the would-be bombers hardly acted like seasoned spies. In Chicago, Haupt bought a car and proposed marriage to his old girlfriend. Astonishingly, he visited his draft board, and he spilled the details of the plot to his parents. A lonely Neubauer spent much of his time in movie houses and told distant acquaintances about his submarine. Kerling took out time to see his mistress.

A competent spy handler might have discharged the lot of them from such a challenging mission. But Hitler thought it essential to blunt America's growing "arsenal of democracy." He envisioned waves of sabotage teams to follow the first two squads.

Armed with Dasch's intel, FBI chief Hoover launched his agency into its largest manhunt to date. Burger, Dasch's accomplice, led G-men to Heinck and Quirin. Also in New York City, FBI agents followed Kerling, who met with one of the contacts betrayed by the invisible ink. Kerling led the agents to Thiel, and they arrested both. In Chicago, FBI

FBI mugshots of the saboteurs sent by Nazi Germany in 1942 to blow up US power plants and factories. One of the enemy agents, George Dasch, upper left, provided details of the plot to the FBI.

men collared Haupt, and used him to lure in Neubauer. Within two weeks of the first landing, all eight were in custody.

Hoover duly informed President Franklin D. Roosevelt, and the press, of the arrests. The FBI director gave all the credit to his agency, while leaving out Dasch and Cullen's key roles. The Coast Guard struck back by leaking to the newspapers its participation. Dasch was enraged when the government clamped him in the City Jail with the other plotters. "I had all reason to believe," he wrote, "I would be greeted with open arms, befriended as an ally."

THE CHIEF EXECUTIVE'S COMMISSION

The president's instinctive reaction to the saboteurs was severe, and it set in motion the judicial action that followed. FDR told his attorney general the saboteurs are "guilty of high treason. This being wartime, it is my inclination to try them by court martial . . . it seems to me that the death penalty is almost obligatory. . . . This is an absolute parallel to Major Andre in the [American] Revolution and of Nathan Hale [British and American spies who were hanged] . . . I want one thing clearly understood. . . . I won't hand them over to any United States marshal armed with a writ of habeas corpus. Understand?"

Roosevelt was referring to the Anglo-American legal doctrine that authorities must "have a body" of evidence to try or imprison someone. On July 2, the president issued Proclamation No. 2561, that the saboteurs "be subject to the law of war and to the jurisdiction of military tribunals."

FDR's attitude reflected that of the public. It was traumatized by the sneak attack on Pearl Harbor less than six months before and shaken again by Hitler's U-boat campaign against US merchant vessels. By June 1942, enemy subs were in the midst of a seven-month rampage off the Atlantic seaboard and the Gulf of Mexico. They sank 233 cargo ships and tankers, killing five thousand sailors and members of the Merchant Marine. Further, the "Duquesne spy ring" was still fresh in mind. A year before, the FBI, with the aid of double-agent William Sebold, had exposed the main Nazi spy network in America. Hoover's men bagged thirty-three operatives seeking intel on US maritime and commercial targets.

The resultant caution verged at times toward paranoia. Worried that disloyal Americans might obtain sensitive information from military officers, the Justice Department ordered the dismissal of barbers and waiters of Japanese, German, or Italian ancestry. It thought persons in jobs where they chatted with clients posed a special security risk. The FBI had earlier arrested fourteen hundred German Americans suspected of loyalty to Berlin. Against Hoover's wishes, the Roosevelt Administration was interning one hundred twenty thousand Americans of Japanese descent. Neither the public, nor officialdom, was in a forgiving mood.

To try the accused saboteurs, the War Department, for the first time in seventy-seven years, set up a military tribunal. Unlike civilian courts, a tribunal or commission consists of military officers, not a judge and jury of one's peers. Prosecuting attorneys face fewer legal hurdles and penalties are usually more severe. For instance, the tribunal could impose the death penalty by a majority, not unanimous, vote.

The Justice Department and White House fretted a civilian court, if it focused on the hard-to-read intent of some of the saboteurs, might impose light prison terms. They were also concerned a civilian process might reveal details on U.S counterintelligence.

The last such tribunals had been in the Civil War. In 1865 a military commission in the Capitol Building tried and sentenced to death for war crimes Dr. Henry Wirz, the Confederate commandant of the prisoner-of-war camp Andersonville. (See the chapter on the Confederate prison.)

ORGANIZING A SPECIAL COURT

On July 8, the military commission started up in a large meeting room on the fifth floor of the Justice Department building. (The building was part of the 1930s Federal Triangle renovation project that replaced the old "entertainment district.") President Roosevelt appointed seven generals to its panel. It was led by the tough two-star general Frank R. McCoy. He was a veteran of the Rough Riders of the 1898 Spanish-American War. Its leader, Theodore Roosevelt, had termed him the "best soldier I ever laid eyes on." McCoy and his fellow generals sat at the head of the room, and the accused saboteurs, all of whom pleaded not guilty, sat diagonally across from them.

Security was airtight. Blackout curtains were placed on the windows of the improvised court. Before each session, soldiers with Tommy guns put the eight prisoners at the City Jail into armored cars; they were whisked through backstreets to Justice. At the prison, an armed detachment of thirty-four officers and enlisted men kept an around-the-clock watch.

Leading the prosecution was the attorney general, Francis Beverley Biddle. Six-foot-two, dapper in a white suit, Biddle was American royalty, descended from a family of noted Philadelphians, one of whom, Nicholas Biddle, had taken on President Andrew Jackson in the 1830s brawl over the Bank of the United States. Biddle was a biographer of civil libertarian Justice Oliver Wendell Holmes, and some viewed him as soft on crime. But on the sabotage matter he shared FDR's no-nonsense views.

Aiding the attorney general was the Army's judge advocate general, or chief military lawyer: Gen. Myron C. Cramer. His short, bespectacled appearance belied a sharply sarcastic approach to legal disputes.

Newspaper and radio interest in the case was immense, but mostly stifled. Secretary of War Henry Lewis Stimson wanted to shut the press out entirely. (He was the same Stimson who three decades before had sent the cavalry to the rescue of the suffragette marchers.) On the other side of the media dispute was former CBS radioman Elmer Davis, the chief of the Office of War Information. This was the agency for dissemination of vetted articles and newsreels. The war secretary ignored Biddle's requests he meet with Davis and permitted just one photo op of the courtroom. Journalists marooned outside scrambled to identify witnesses who entered the proceedings. (Stimson's concerns may have been justified, but not for the obvious reason. During the war, Soviet spies penetrated the Office of War Information.)

The public found other ways to fill its ferocious appetite for stories about espionage. Books about spies and saboteurs flew up the bestseller lists. And that April, 350 US representatives, and most senators, attended the Washington premier of the Alfred Hitchcock thriller *Saboteur*.

POINTS AND COUNTERPOINTS

The defense had a thankless, seemingly hopeless task, yet also a skilled advocate at its head. The president also appointed the defense team, led by Lt. Col. Kenneth Royall, a six-foot-five-inch, Harvard-trained attorney from North Carolina. He'd studied law under Supreme Court justice Felix Frankfurter. He was later secretary of the army under President Truman.

Royall figured his defense was doomed; he likened it to the legal railroading of African Americans in his native, segregated South. But he hoped, by presenting a compelling defense, to spare some of the defendants from execution.

During the four-week trial, Royall argued the accused should not be viewed as soldiers, as they did not carry weapons nor, after landing, handle any bombs. He noted they had not committed, and claimed they did not intend to commit, any violent acts. Royall's team pointed out Dasch had let Coast Guardsman Cullen go, which led to the alerting of the Coast Guard and FBI.

Another line of defense was the prisoners had simply used the mission to get to the United States, not wage war on it. Advocate General Cramer poured scorn on this, wondering sardonically if the aim of the eight was to "fraudulently obtain from the . . . German government the sum of $180,000 . . . eight boxes of explosives, and a free trip across the Atlantic in a submarine."

General McCoy rejected Royall's plea that executing the prisoners would encourage the Germans to kill American prisoners of war. Cramer and Biddle argued the death penalty would deter further attempts at sabotage. Royall tried getting the court to throw out the prisoners' confessions but was rebuffed by McCoy.

A LAST-MINUTE APPEAL

With the commission's verdict a *fait accompli*, Royall put a gambit in play. He arranged to meet with Supreme Court Justice Owen Roberts at his Pennsylvania farm. Also on hand was Justice Hugo Black, who after a stint with the Ku Klux Klan had changed his views and become a civil libertarian. Some of the justices had qualms about military tribunals, and the suspension of *habeas corpus* in such cases.

Roberts and Black contacted the other justices, who were out of session and scattered around the country. The Supremes, including Chief Justice Harland Fiske Stone of New Hampshire, agreed to take the remarkable step of short-circuiting the Court of Appeals, and meeting about the case in extraordinary session during their summer recess. Stone went along as he had his own doubts about granting too many wartime powers to the president. The White House and Biddle acquiesced to the quick review of the commission's constitutionality.

The interest of the media and the public in the Supreme Court action was marked. On July 29, the day the three-day process began, lines of the curious snaked around the massive, ancient-Greek-style temple of the Supreme Court Building, built in 1935. Those in the queue braved Washington's summer heat for a chance to be one of the three hundred daily spectators.

Press photographers took special heed of the white-suited Biddle, and of Royall and Hoover. The FBI director strode up the broad, marble steps of the building, immaculate in a summer suit and snap-brim hat. His attire was identical to his constant companion, assistant director Clyde Tolson. Twelve of Hoover's G-men combed the judicial chamber for bombs.

Longtime FBI chief J. Edgar Hoover, pictured in his office two years before launching a massive manhunt that apprehended, with a big assist from the Coast Guard, the German saboteurs.

As the black-robed Supremes convened in their marble-pillared chamber, Royall again had his work cut out for him, because the justices, like almost every American, were outraged by the sabotage plot. Chief Justice Stone privately noted that "from time out of mind, it is within the power of the commander in chief to hang a spy." Justice Frankfurter, who was Jewish, saw the war against Nazis as a battle for civilization itself. He was also a friend of FDR, who'd appointed him, and was a close friend of Stimson's. Several months later, Frankfurter would write a fictional dialogue in which he addressed the defendants this way: "You damned scoundrels have a helluvacheek to ask for a writ. . . . You are just low-down, ordinary, enemy spies who . . . could immediately have been shot by the military."

Justice Frank Murphy, along with his Court job, was serving in the US military, as a lieutenant colonel for Army Chief of Staff George Marshall. Murphy recused himself and listened to the legal dueling from behind the courtroom's red-tinted drapes.

The Court review hinged on a Civil War case, one involving a Confederate activist from Indiana named Lambdin Milligan. In 1864, he was charged with opposing the wartime draft and trying to incite a rebellion in Indiana. A military court tried and sentenced him to death. His case was sent to the president for review. However, in 1865, Lincoln was assassinated before he could look it over. In 1866, after the war's end, the Supreme Court agreed to give Milligan's lawyers a writ of *habeas corpus*. (One of the attorneys was Union war hero and future president James Garfield.)

In its *Ex parte Milligan* decision, the Court ruled his conviction was unconstitutional. Its reasoning was Milligan, who operated far from the front lines, should have been tried before a civilian court. On that legal precedent rested the slight hopes of the defense attorneys and their clients that the tribunal would be judged unlawful.

Before the Court, Royall thus argued the accused had not operated within a theater of war. "No location was ever selected for" their explosives, stated the chief defender, as they hadn't dug their dynamite up. "There was no specific plan." He also averred the men were "unarmed."

Justice Robert Jackson shot back that dynamite was surely an armament.

Some of Royall's points seemed a stretch. He claimed U-boats, though weapons of war, were only used in this case for transportation, not attacks. (Those in the courtroom were unaware that U-202 had torpedoed the American passenger ship *City of Birmingham* on July 1, killing nine.)

From the bench, Frankfurter queried: "Suppose an enemy should place a chemical in the Glenn Martin [aircraft] plant so that whole plant explodes.

"Would you say that soldier was engaged in a military operation?"

"No, I would not say so," replied Royall.

The courtroom erupted in derisive laughter.

In Royall's view, each prisoner was akin to an angry man who buys a gun with the idea of murdering someone, but who never puts that idea into action. In such cases, where no actual crime is committed, the criminal penalties are light.

He also placed the case in the context of a war that pitted a democracy against a tyranny. "We want to win this war," he told the Court, "but we don't want to win it by throwing away everything we are fighting for." Biddle countered that a commander-in-chief could wage war in ways Congress hasn't strictly defined.

On July 31, the Court issued its ruling, named *Ex Parte Quirin* after defendant Richard Quirin.

It unanimously decided against applying *habeas corpus*. It found the prisoners were "held in lawful custody" and that the military commission had been "lawfully constituted."

Chief Justice Stone stated: "Those who during time of war pass surreptitiously from enemy territory into our own . . . for the commission of hostile acts involving destruction of life or property, have the status of unlawful combatants punishable as such by military commission."

Still, some justices worried about undermining *Ex Parte Milligan*. Others thought any case involving capital punishment mandated a normal and methodical, not a quick and extraordinary, review. In fact, their opinions so varied they were unable, as customary, to issue concurring decisions as part of their ruling. Michael Dobbs, author of the book *Saboteurs*, noted that, "The Justices had agreed on a verdict without agreeing on the reasons for the verdict."

They wouldn't publish their opinions until that autumn. In 1953, Frankfurter would have regrets about his *Quirin* decision during the Supreme Court review of the conviction and death penalty for atomic-bomb spies Julius and Ethel Rosenberg. Justice William O. Douglas, who grew to have his own doubts, would famously say: "In the Supreme Court, cases are decided 90 percent on emotion, only 10 percent on the law."

The *Quirin* precedent would have much bearing sixty years later, when the federal government decided how to handle accused terrorists linked to the September 11 attacks. And whether those detainees should be tried before civilian courts, or before tribunals at the US military base in Cuba's Guantanamo Bay.

On August 4, four days after the Court's decision, the military commission, its status validated, called its month-long session to an end.

Its seven generals voted unanimously to convict all eight defendants. They also sentenced all eight prisoners to death.

CAPITOL PUNISHMENT

The case went to the commander-in-chief for final review. FDR took the commission's 2,967-page report to "Shangri-la," as Camp David was then dubbed. With the German military piling up victories abroad, he mulled the case over. He now knew what Hoover hadn't told him at first: that Dasch and Burger had played important roles in exposing Operation Pastorius.

The president commuted the death sentence of Dasch to thirty years in hard labor, and Burger to life. He retained the death sentences for the other six.

At the City Jail, Gen. Albert Cox, the District's provost marshal, informed each prisoner of his sentence. Dasch was irate at the news, while Burger was nonplussed, and kept reading a magazine. Most of the condemned, expecting the worst, took the news with relative equanimity.

The officials in charge of Death Row were more concerned. In 1925, the city had changed its method of execution from the gallows to the electric chair. The prison had put twenty-four people to death by that means. But it had never executed six people on the same day. There was fear "Old Sparky," as the device was called, might blow out its fuses. On the day of reckoning, the prison lights were turned off to conserve electricity.

For one last time, media and public attention peaked. One day, four servicemen passing by the prison asked to serve as a firing squad; that privilege was denied. Reporters loitered outside the jailhouse to scoop up scraps of information. They learned less than long-term inmates, who heard officials had placed an order for a bag of salt with the prison kitchen. They knew a saline solution was applied to the legs and shaved heads of the condemned to aid the conduction of electricity.

In their final letters, Quirin, Kerling, and Neubauer declared their loyalty to Germany and to the Nazis. Quirin also accused Dasch and Burger of betrayal.

The prisoners wrote out a document thanking their legal team: "Before all we want to state that defense counsel . . . has represented our case . . . unbiased, better than we could expect and probably risking the indignation of public opinion."

Before high noon on August 6, on a rain-swept morning, guards walked the six condemned men down a long corridor to Old Sparky. Two guards carried a stretcher in case one of the doomed fainted along the way.

The six were electrocuted in alphabetical order. Two thousand volts were applied to each man. Herbert Haupt went first, at 12:01 p.m. Werner Thiel was last, expiring at 1:04 p.m. The mouths of the deceased were left contorted in final agony.

It was the end of the largest execution in DC history, and the finale to the last large-scale effort of Hitler to plant saboteurs in America.

CHAPTER TWENTY-FIVE

An Author's Bloom: An Offshoot of Sadness and Memory

Chestnut sapling at the southwest lawn of the Capitol Building

IT'S THE MOST UNIMPRESSIVE OF TRIBUTES, AT FIRST GLANCE. It's dwarfed by the 288-foot-tall Capitol, a mountain of marble and sandstone.

A HUMBLE SPROUT

It's fragile: It often has a short protective fence around it. It's just a few feet high, and just inches wide, and came from something very small: a sapling of a tree that was rotting out, then knocked down by a storm.

Someday, in a century or more, the chestnut shoot may grow up to be a mighty ornament, seventy feet tall, symbolic of lasting beauty. It may rival in size some of the other trees—forty-two hundred of them—on the lawns landscaped 150 years ago by the great Frederick Law Olmsted.

And be a bookend of sorts, to the memorial crabapple trees on the opposite, northeast side of the Capitol Building. (See the chapter on the Sullivan Brothers.) They both mark, and honor, heroes and heroines of the same era.

The horse chestnut tree from which the sapling was taken once gave inspiration and hope to a young lady far, far away. In spring 1944, she wrote of it that, "April is glorious. . . . Our chestnut tree is in leaf, and here and there you can already see a few small blossoms."

Exodus and Trickery

She was born in 1929, a bad year for countless millions as the Great Depression began, especially bad for her Jewish family in Germany, as the economic collapse aided Hitler's rise. Her worried father Otto brought her, sister Margo, and their mother Edith to the Netherlands, a nation with a long tradition of tolerance. Otto was industrious, and in the Dutch capital of Amsterdam he set up two food extract companies.

However, in spring 1940 the German army invaded their adopted country. By summer 1942, the Nazis were rounding up Jews and other "undesirables" for shipment to slave labor factories and concentration camps. To be consigned to such places was usually a death sentence. Inmates were worked to death slowly or killed quickly by bullet or poison gas. Of Holland's one hundred forty thousand Jews in 1940, only about twenty-five thousand would live until 1945.

Facing such a prospect, Otto put together a creative plan of survival. His family would "disappear," after apparently having fled to another country. His Opekta company had a spice warehouse that overlooked one of Amsterdam's characteristic city canals. Above its ground-floor office were the upper floors of an attic. In July 1942, he and his family took up residence there, in the *Achterhuis* (attic house). He had a workman from his company install a bookcase that cloaked the doorway to the stories above.

On the day they moved from their old apartment to their new abode, the family members put on many layers of apparel. As his perceptive younger daughter, thirteen-year-old Annelies Marie, or Anne, later described it: "No Jew in our situation would dare leave the house with a suitcase full of clothes. . . . The four of us were wrapped in so many layers of clothes it looked as if we were going off to spend the night in a refrigerator . . . I was wearing two undershirts, three pairs of underpants, a dress, and over that a skirt, a jacket, a raincoat. . . ."

To fool the Gestapo, the family left their old apartment a mess, as if they had fled in haste. Otto left behind a note suggesting they had made off for neutral Switzerland.

The four settled into rooms on the three stacks of floors up high. The space contained several small bedrooms and living rooms, a washroom and toilet, a kitchen and dining room, and a loft. Otto's household was soon joined by another family of three, including a sixteen-year-old boy named Peter, and by a dentist friend of Otto's family.

Otto's sixteen-year-old Margo was placid and affable, and got along well with the others. Anne, however, was distant and critical; she resented it when the others moved in.

The eight people in close quarters were careful to converse quietly, as a furniture maker and another firm occupied the buildings on either side. Exercise outdoors was impossible; even glancing out a window was risky. Still, they tried to maintain some normality. Anne posted photographs of movie starlets on a wall, and her father inscribed on wallpaper the growth spurts of her and her sister.

Four loyal company employees were privy to Otto's secret. They and several of their relatives kept the eight attic dwellers supplied with food and drink and with news from the outside world.

A MEANS TO MEMORIALIZE THE TIMES

For her thirteenth birthday, June 12, 1942, Otto gave Anne a gift of a blank autograph book. She turned it into a diary. In it, she penned "letters" to her cheerful, imaginary friend Kitty.

She was observant and analytical, solid traits for a budding scribe. She was aware of her talent, noting: "I'm so grateful to God for having given me this gift, which I can use to develop myself and to express all that's inside me!" The diary proved a release for someone in a self-imposed prison. "When I write I can shake off all my cares. My sorrow disappears, my spirits are revived!"

For two years, she wrote about their lives in a bubble, while reflecting on the war raging outside. When the diary filled up, she continued to describe her experience in notebooks.

On the radio, she heard the exiled Dutch government in Britain urge people to document their time under Nazi rule. So, when she was fifteen, Anne rewrote her original entries as a thirteen-year-old into a projected book, *Het Achterhuis* (*The Hidden Attic House*). She also penned thirty-four short stories.

In her adopted Dutch language, sprinkled with German and English, Anne wrote of the oppressive acts taken against Jews and her affection for the helpers who sustained those in hiding. She described the impact of a nearby bombing raid, during which the "houses trembled like a wisp of grass in the wind."

In stylish handwriting, Anne outlined a young woman's coming of age in claustrophobic space. She had a brief, tentative romance with the teenaged boy Peter. But the hiding place was hardly a spot for youthful love, and her affection cooled.

After a dark winter of food shortages and little fresh air, she'd gaze through a loft window at a chestnut tree. It bloomed with pinkish petals in the yard below. It was a symbol of freedom denied, and hope for better times. For her, or for any prisoner in any time or place. Broken down into separate lines, her observation of it is evocative:

Nearly every morning I go to the [top] attic
To blow the stuffy air out of my lungs,
From my favorite spot on the floor
I look up at the blue sky and the bare chestnut tree,
On whose branches little raindrops shine, appearing like silver,
And at the seagulls and other birds as they glide on the wind . . .
As long as this exists and I may live to see it,
This sunshine, the cloudless skies,
While this lasts, I cannot be unhappy.

In early August 1944, American and British armies were liberating France. Anne and her fellow residents eagerly followed their progress, hopeful they would soon be free.

ARRESTS AND ANNIHILATIONS
Yet the attic dwellers' cocoon of safety ended on August 4, 1944. German police led by a Nazi SS officer stormed into their refuge, arresting everyone. As the constables rummaged through their rooms, Anne's precious writings were scattered on the floor. Later, two of the helpers retrieved them for safekeeping.

The eight hideaways were detained, interrogated, and imprisoned at a forced-labor camp. Otto and his family were shipped to the infamous Auschwitz concentration camp, where he was separated from the women. Captives under fifteen were immediately killed; Anne was three months past her fifteenth birthday.

At Auschwitz, her mother Edith died of starvation—after giving up her meager food rations for Anne and Margot. In October, the Germans moved the sisters to another notorious camp, Bergen-Belsen. Food and medicine were scant; epidemics raged through the barracks.

Anne was afflicted by scabies, a severe irritation from the mites burrowing into her skin. Still, she managed to secure additional food rations for her sister and friends. Even so, she was convinced her father had died, and told friends she no longer wanted to live. Anne and Margot became delirious and feeble. They both perished, probably in February 1945, probably from typhus. Their young bodies were tossed into a mass grave.

A Book and a Symbol for All Time

Otto survived Auschwitz. At the war's conclusion he returned to the Opekta warehouse. His old helpers gave him Anne's diary and other writings. He was gripped by Anne's powers of description and depth of feeling. He had the diary published.

In 1947, it came out in book form in Holland, and was soon a success throughout much of Europe. In 1952, it was published in America as *Anne Frank: The Diary of a Young Girl*. A bestseller, the book was adapted into a popular play and an affective movie.

The diary remains the best-known book about the Holocaust, from the view of a perceptive youth who personalized the murder of millions. The hiding place of the attic residents was transformed in 1960 into the Anne Frank House museum. Over a million people visit it annually.

Over the years, concerns grew over the white horse chestnut tree outside, which Anne had evoked so eloquently. Over 150 years old, it was infiltrated by fungi and eaten up by moth caterpillars. In 2010, wind gusts battered it to the ground.

But the Dutch took unique action to ensure the tree would live on, along with the legacy of the doomed diarist. The Anne Frank House sent

On the grounds of the Capitol, a sapling taken from a chestnut tree that Anne Frank gazed upon from her World War II attic hideaway. It memorializes the most famous victim, and chronicler, of, the Jewish Holocaust.

saplings of the fallen chestnut to schools, parks, and museums around the world. Over time, each sample will grow into the majestic flowering tree that Anne looked upon for inspiration.

Among the recipients was the US Congress. On April 30, 2014, the House and Senate leadership attended a ceremony for Anne Frank in Statuary Hall. That day, representatives planted the three-foot sapling in a place of honor, near the west front of the Capitol Building.

As the tree grows, it refreshes the memory of the young lady, and her enduring wish to be free.

Chapter Twenty-Six

Shooting Gallery: Radicals Ravage the House of Representatives

Floor and gallery of the House of Representatives

THE FOUR PERSONS PAUSED AT THE EAST STEPS OF THE CAPITOL BUILD-
ing. The three men among them were hesitant. One of them remarked
they were behind schedule, and it might be wise to hold off until another
day.

But their slim, smartly attired leader, a former beauty pageant queen,
reacted with bitterness.

"*Yo soy solo,*" she complained in her native Spanish. "I've been left all
alone."

Shamed, the men agreed to follow Lolita Lebrón into the House of
Representatives, on that cloudy afternoon of March 1, 1954.

The building then had no metal detectors. The security guards
simply asked them if they had cameras, which were not allowed. They
replied they did not. They were not checked for weapons. They were
waved inside.

Thirty-four-year-old Lolita Lebrón entered the Capitol, accompanied by Rafael Cancel Miranda, Andres Figueroa Cordero, and Irving
Flores Rodríguez. They walked up stairs to the Ladies' Gallery, as the
second-floor visitors balcony was called. They sat down next to some
Maryland sixth graders.

The quartet anxiously peered down into the well of Congress, which
was in session. The House was debating a bill to reauthorize entry into

the United States of Mexican migrant workers. Some 240 Congressmen milled about, waiting to vote.

At 2:30 p.m., the four visitors took out three German Lugers and one rapid-fire pistol.

They quickly recited The Lord's Prayer.

They pointed their weapons and began firing.

CAPITOL CARNAGE

Paul Kanjorski, a sixteen-year-old page, and later a congressman from Pennsylvania, thought at first the thudding sounds were firecrackers. Then, he recalled, "I felt the spray of marble" bits unloosed by the bullets.

Members of Congress were stunned as slugs crashed into desks and the floor, and into marble columns.

Above, Lebrón unfurled a Puerto Rican flag.

Her shrill voice could be heard screaming:

"*Viva Puerto Rico Libre!*" "Long live a free Puerto Rico!"

The Speaker of the House, Joe Martin of Massachusetts, added a tragicomic touch to the terror. At the Speaker's rostrum, as the bullets flew, he took a moment to gavel the session to a stop.

"The House stands recessed," Speaker Martin intoned. Then he ducked behind a column.

The attackers fired off sixteen shots. Lebrón aimed her gun at the ceiling, her henchmen at the representatives below.

Cordero's pistol jammed. Miranda fired most of the bullets at the lawmakers, Rodríguez a few.

Five representatives were wounded.

After the initial shock, onlookers and lawmakers charged the assailants.

Frank Wise, a middle-aged spectator from Takoma Park, Maryland, seized Cordero's weapon. Rep. James Van Zandt of Pennsylvania, after diving into a cloak room, ran upstairs to the Gallery. An ex-Navy captain, Van Zandt confronted Miranda, and wrestled his gun away. Next, he kicked Rodríguez in the rear as another man took away his pistol. In the bedlam, Rodríguez fled to a stairwell. Someone else grabbed Lebrón's flag, as she shouted, "Give it back!"

On the House floor, after the gunfire ceased, interns and representatives looked over the injured congressmen.

Maryland's George Hyde Fallon and Alabama's Kenneth A. Roberts were lightly injured. But Tennessee's Clifford Davis had a leg wound, Iowa's Ben F. Jensen had a bullet in the back, and Michigan's Alvin Bentley had turned ashen from a bullet to the chest.

Interns scrambled for stretchers. They carried those stricken to waiting ambulances. All the congressmen would recover. (Bentley would later set up a fund for impoverished Latin Americans.)

On the Capitol steps, chaos reigned. Police blocked the exits. Ambulances and reporters rushed toward the entrances. Rep. Barratt O'Hara of Illinois, unaware of the attack, and late for a meeting, hurriedly parked his car near a doorway. He was nearly shot by a policeman who mistook him for an attacker.

Adding to the confusion was the escape of Rodríguez. Police put out an all-points bulletin. Across the city, lawmen put up roadblocks. They

Guard Congress After Gunfire

4 Puerto Ricans Held in $100,000 Each

Bentley, Gravely Hurt, Given 50-50 Chance

20 Bullets Spray House, Wounding Five Members

McLeod Loses Personnel Power

Dulles Curbs Authority of His Controversial Aide

In 1954, four Puerto Rican extremists led by Lolita Lebrón entered the visitors' gallery of the House, and rained gunfire on the legislators in session below, wounding five congressmen.

combed through cavernous Union Station, searching. Finally, Rodríguez was found waiting for a bus, and arrested.

Seething Separatists

The attack echoed the attempted assassination of President Harry Truman four years before, at the Blair-Lee House in Lafayette Square. In 1950, two gunmen, Gregorio Torresola and Oscar Collazo, had hoped to win independence for the island of Puerto Rico—by murdering the US president.

Puerto Rico, an American territory since the Spanish-American War of 1898, had an elected legislature and governor that handled many domestic matters. The United States controlled its foreign policy. In 1952, Puerto Ricans had voted by margins of 95 percent for statehood or Commonwealth status with its neighbor to the north.

The Capitol Building attackers hoped to reignite the stalled independence movement by shooting up Congress. In a missive written before the assault, and found in her purse, Lebrón condemned the United States for "betraying the sacred principles of mankind in their continuous subjugation of my country."

She and her band were linked to a violent uprising which wracked Puerto Rico that year. Later in 1954, twenty-eight were killed and forty-nine wounded during insurgent attacks on police stations and government offices in San Juan, Ponce, Jayuya, and other Puerto Rican towns. The United States called in troops and planes to help put down the revolt.

Lebrón had grown up in the Puerto Rican town of Lares and gloried in its past. In 1868, it had revolted against Spanish control of the island. As a teenager, Lebrón, an intense, striking brunette, won a beauty contest. Then she married, had a child, divorced, and had another child with a different man.

Like many in her impoverished island, she moved to New York City, with its large Puerto Rican population. While working as a seamstress making uniforms for the American military, she became active with pro-independence groups. Lebrón corresponded with Pedro Campos, the head of Puerto Rico's Nationalist Party. She and Campos agreed on a scheme whereby she would lead an attack on several symbols of US power. Later Lebrón determined that an attack on a single target, Congress, was more feasible.

On that fateful March day in 1954, she and her clutch of radicals had gathered in New York's Grand Central Station, then taken a train to Union Station. On the short walk to the Capitol, they'd gotten lost, before a passerby pointed them in the right direction.

PARDONS, PRISONS, AND A HOMECOMING

The foursome was tried in federal court that June, and in an appeals court in July. The judge, Lawrence Walsh, meted out sentences ranging from seventy-six to eighty-five years. (Walsh would be, in the late 1980s, the independent prosecutor of Reagan Administration officials enmeshed in the Iran-Contra scandal.) He reserved the stiffest penalty for Miranda, the main shooter. Because Lebrón had fired her gun at the ceiling—she stated she wanted to make a statement, and not harm anyone—a jury acquitted her of intent to kill.

Miranda was incarcerated at Alcatraz, Rodríguez at Fort Leavenworth, and Cordero in a Georgia prison. Lolita Lebrón was consigned to a women's penitentiary in West Virginia. There she became a devoutly mystical, and political, Christian. She claimed to have visions of Jesus in which the Galilean was trampled by a horse. She interpreted the rampaging animal as a symbol of earthly tyranny.

In 1978, President Jimmy Carter pardoned Cordero, who was sick from cancer. In 1979, Carter pardoned his three accomplices, including Lebrón, as well as Oscar Collazo, a survivor of the attack on Truman. On their return to Puerto Rico, all five were met by thousands of cheering aficionados at San Juan's airport.

Some attributed the pardons to presidential politics, that Carter, facing a re-election battle in 1980, was appealing to Latino voters. More likely, the inmates' release was part of a deal with Cuban despot Fidel Castro. After the Puerto Ricans were let go, Castro freed CIA agents whom his regime had arrested and jailed.

Castro welcomed Lebrón and Cordero to Cuba for a visit. Lebrón remarked: "I love and admire Fidel. He's the only person who, as a head of state, stood up to the greatest imperial power."

Lolita Lebrón lived until 2010, dying at age eighty-nine. She survived past September 11, after which a wall of security fell upon the Capitol. Indeed, the elderly Lolita Lebrón condemned the 2001 terror attacks, but remained mostly unrepentant about her assault on Congress. On its fiftieth anniversary in 2004, she marked an occasion to "celebrate" the event.

She was the leader of the only mass shooting in Congress's 230-year history.

CHAPTER TWENTY-SEVEN

The Life and Death of the Great American Neighborhood: Building a Brutal Boulevard

"Brutalist Boulevard," starting at 3rd Street S.W., extending to L'Enfant Plaza S.W.

IN 1971, THE ARCHITECT OF THE CAPITOL WAS WORRIED ABOUT THE start of construction of the headquarters of the Department of Health, Education, and Welfare, or HEW. The agency is now known as Health and Human Services (HHS), and its headquarters the Hubert Horatio Humphrey Building, after the late senator and vice president from Minnesota. It's the department that handles Medicare, Medicaid, and Social Security, as well as assorted welfare programs.

AN UNWELCOME INTRUSION

The Architect of the Capitol, or AOC—an abbreviation also for a more famous, more contemporary public official—was apprehensive because the construction site was on Independence Avenue and 2nd Street, S.W., just two blocks from the Capitol Building. And even without looking at its blueprints, it was easy for observers to guess what style its designer, the Hungarian-born, German-bred Marcel Lajos Breuer, had up his easel. The resulting structure would despoil the view of the Rayburn House Office Building across from the Capitol and tar the beauty of the Capitol itself.

The AOC was well aware of his esteemed predecessors, and Washington's grand building tradition. There was the original architect of the

Capitol Building, Benjamin Latrobe, the "father of American architecture," selected by the "godfather of American architecture," Thomas Jefferson; Charles Bulfinch, the Bostonian who rebuilt the ruined Capitol with a low yet stately dome after the War of 1812; Thomas Walter and Gen. Montgomery Meigs and their host of sweaty laborers, who placed the great cast-iron dome atop the Capitol's current iteration; the wonderful Beaux-Arts concoctions of turn-of-the-twentieth century DC, which yielded Daniel Burnham's imposing Union Station depot, and the stately Carnegie Library to the north and the west of the Capitol; and the many classically inspired creations, from the Lincoln Memorial to John Russell Pope's National Archives.

But things were changing, just several blocks away. A harbinger of it was the monstrous IBM research institute that Breuer created in France the decade before. It resembled an alien invader, with its endless arrays of rectangular windows in concrete frames, supported by cruciform, crucifix-like pilons stabbing the earth.

The AOC recommended the HEW chockablock be set back from 2nd Street. And it was, by just forty-five yards, which was enough to do the trick. Visitors approaching or leaving the Capitol from anywhere but 2nd Street never see it.

DC's "Brutalist Boulevard" begins just blocks from the Capitol with the Department of Health, Education, and Welfare (HEW) headquarters, now known as the Hubert H. Humphrey Health and Human Services (HHS) Building.

Out of sight, out of mind.

What materialized there was another example of a then-established genre of architecture, with the very descriptive name—Brutalism.

But it was just the start of what emerged as the city's "Brutalist Boulevard." Reaching from HEW/HHS and continuing to the monolithic Lyndon Baines Johnson Department of Education building, finished in 1961, and staffed first by HEW. Over to the Orville and Wilbur Wright Federal Aviation Administration (FAA) buildings, with their endless rows of identical rectangular windows. The FAA opened on November 22, 1963, the day of John F. Kennedy's assassination.

Those inert stylings were but preparation for L'Enfant Plaza, which from the late 1960s has occupied 9th Street to 12th Street, S.W. It includes Breuer's other inhuman creation, the Housing and Urban Development (HUD) building.

With several structures on the lists of the world's ugliest edifices, Brutalist Boulevard may be the most heinous stretch of real estate on the planet.

The Birth of the Brutal

Breuer's beasts, and the others near them, came out of a design movement in Europe that quickly went awry, then spread like a coronavirus all over the world.

Starting in the early 1920s, Marcel Breuer cut his teeth at the Bauhaus, the Building House, or School, in Weimar, capital of Germany's doomed postwar republic. The Bauhaus was a hugely influential center of radical ideas on architecture and interior design. The theorists there rebelled at the prevailing classical, Renaissance, and Beaux-Arts styles. They saw these as part of the hidebound culture that had brought on the disaster of the Great War. In contrast, their work paralleled the wild abstract art of the post-Impressionists. The architects among them would employ novel techniques in steelmaking, plate glass, and poured concrete to fashion structures taller and weirder looking than any ever before.

At the Bauhaus, Breuer was mentored by architects, such as Walter Gropius and Ludwig Mies van der Rohe, who'd become the leaders of the "International Style." Van der Rohe, whose name means Lousy, had adopted the Dutch "van" to sound more aristocratic. Gropius kept his name, but throughout his career kept illustrators at his side, as he couldn't draw. Their genre produced the rectangular, glass-and-steel skyscrapers now ubiquitous in downtowns.

The Bauhaus hosted another seminal figure, the father of Brutalism: a French-speaking Swiss named Charles-Édouard Jeanneret. He took on the name Le Corbusier, roughly, the Crow.

Le Corbusier was a syndicalist, a revolutionary who believed in workers' violent takeover of industry. He diagrammed out an architectural utopia termed the Ville Radieuse, the Radiant City. Under his scheme, the downtowns of cities such as Paris, with their reputedly outdated classicism, would be bulldozed and replaced with identical, vertiginous towers, buffered by wide public spaces, and serviced by vast highways radiating outward. "The result of repetition," Le Corbusier insisted, "is ... the perfect form."

Years after he cooperated with fascist, Vichy France, he effused over one of his own Brutalist creations: "It is an architectural symphony. . . [it] flashes and develops under the light in a way which is unimaginable and unforgettable. . . . Adorable. . . . In all the centuries no one has seen that."

Le Corbusier's Radiant City became the template decades later for claustrophobic, crime-ridden housing projects in America. Such as the Pruitt-Igoe Apartments of St. Louis, constructed in the mid-1950s, and literally blown up as a monumental failure by 1976. Or the Cabrini-Green Homes in Chicago, built in the 1950s and 1960s, and toppled by the wrecking ball by 2011.

By the way, if you ever create an architectural style, don't call it Brutalist. Modern, Postmodern, Abstract—anything but Brutalist!

BITES OF THE BIG APPLE

The men of the Bauhaus were chased out of Germany by the Nazis, who fancied themselves upholders of classical art and science—as well as Nordic pagan mysticism—even as they wrecked the culture of Dürer, Goethe, Humboldt, and Beethoven.

Fittingly, the architecture of the National Socialists, as in the Aviation Ministry in Berlin, and Mussolini's Fascists, as in Milan's Justice Palace, was Brutal-like: sullen, conformist, oppressive.

In 1937, Breuer followed Gropius to America, where the latter headed up Harvard University's Graduate School of Design. Many commissions followed. When he or Gropius followed the lead of another innovative architect, Frank Lloyd Wright, and worked on private dwellings that conformed to the landscape around them, the result was eye-catching, and limited in scale. But when they took on large commercial or public constructions, the result was often, well, brutal.

The defining example for Breuer involved Manhattan's Grand Central Station, finished by 1913 in grand Beaux-Arts style. By the mid-20th century, its owner, Pennsylvania Railroad, was bleeding money, due to competition from the car-centric suburbs and the jet plane. Breuer was brought in to design a skyscraper replacement. His blueprint was the ultimate expression of the modernists' wish to crush classical design. Breuer would have set a ninety-story building on top of the Station.

His wasn't the only gargantuan design competing in that space. Leading International Stylist Ieoh Ming (I. M.) Pei, later famous in DC, and developer William Zeckendorf Sr., later the force behind L'Enfant Plaza, proposed to replace the Station with the world's largest building: a 108-story hyperboloid, a structure wide at the top and bottom, but tapered thin in the middle.

Fortunately, the widow of a very wealthy and influential Massachusetts politician intervened. Jacqueline Kennedy Onassis, and a host of outraged New Yorkers, would block "Breuer's beast."

The former first lady asked: "Is it not cruel to let our city die by degrees . . . until there will be nothing left of all her history and beauty . . . this is the time to take a stand, to reverse the tide, so that we won't all end up in a uniform world of steel and glass boxes." She also led a fight that blocked the demolition of much of Lafayette Square next to the White House.

Developers did in fact put up a skyscraper, but behind Grand Central. It was the Pan Am building, now the MetLife building. The architect of that fifty-nine-story hexagon, and exemplar of the International Style, was Breuer's mentor: Walter Gropius.

THE SAVAGING OF SOUTHWEST

Despite his Grand Central defeat, Breuer staged so-called triumphs at IBM and the Campus Center at the University of Massachusetts at Amherst. And despite the revulsion his visions triggered among some, he was picked to design the HUD building at L'Enfant Plaza.

The Plaza was the culmination of a half-century effort to transform Southwest Washington.

"Urban renewal" and "slum clearance" had begun as far back as the Woodrow Wilson Administration. First Lady Edith Wilson took special interest in clearing out the ramshackle alley dwellings, largely populated by poor blacks, southeast of Capitol Hill. (That her husband was an ardent segregationist may have colored her views.)

During the Great Depression, thousands of new federal employees flocked to DC to administer FDR's New Deal. In 1937, Congress passed the Housing Act, which supplied federal funds for public housing projects to replace slums. During the Second World War, the number of federal workers exploded, causing an extreme scarcity of work and residential space. This ignited a huge demand for more office buildings and for middle-class housing in Washington.

The laboring district of Southwest, just on the other side of the National Mall from the main federal offices, was a tempting target for absorption.

Southwest DC was then a neighborhood of African Americans, Jews, Italians, and Irish and other "white ethnics." The area was shopworn, but vibrant. Perhaps the greatest American male singer before Sinatra, Al Jolson, the son of a cantor, grew up there. Also hailing from Southwest was another soulful vocalist: Marvin Gaye. Like other local musicians, they soaked up the blues and jazz funneling into the capital city from the South, as well as the vaudeville and big band sounds flowing down from the northern cities.

In 1945, Congress approved the District of Columbia Redevelopment Act. It created a Redevelopment Land Agency to eliminate the "causes of blight." In 1949, Congress passed the American Housing Act. It offered funds to cities to demolish lower-income districts, and sell the properties to developers or provide the land to public housing agencies. Southwest came under the crosshairs.

One local business, Berman's department store, at 712 4th Street S.W., refused to kneel. Its owner resisted the taking of his property through eminent domain, that is, the assertion of a government's authority to seize private property for the "public good." Berman challenged the Redevelopment Act before the DC Circuit Court. The plaintiff argued it was unconstitutional to seize the store for the benefit of a developer.

But Judge E. Barrett Prettyman, after whom the sterile-looking federal courthouse just northwest of the Capitol is named, ruled in favor of the Act. On appeal, the US Supreme Court in 1954 upheld the lower court's decision. Justice William O. Douglas stated "plans for redevelopment would suffer greatly" if the decision were reversed. (It's odd that Douglas in that same year led a movement to stop the transformation of Georgetown's C&O canal walking paths into a highway.) Also in 1954, the Court was outlawing school segregation in its *Brown v. Board of Education* case—even as it was greenlighting the destruction of a local neighborhood of ethnic minorities.

With the resistance of Berman and others swept aside, the wrecking balls moved in. In 1955 and 1956, the urban "renewal" forced out twenty-five thousand people, including over four thousand African-American families, and many Italians and Irish. Some two thousand businesses were displaced. When it was over, just 1 percent of Southwest's structures were left.

Author James Baldwin termed the episode a "Negro Removal Program." Many of the whites moved to the suburbs, and many of the blacks moved to Anacostia in Southeast DC and Northeast DC, where public housing awaited.

Southwest's destruction was also hastened by the Interstate Highway System, begun under the Eisenhower Administration in 1956. Back in 1919, young Lt. Col. Dwight Eisenhower had traveled coast to coast in a crawling caravan of motorized vehicles, as part of an Army experiment to examine how the nation's then-primitive road network could support the movement of troops. Eisenhower was more impressed, in 1945 as Supreme Allied Commander during the Second World War, with Germany's high-speed autobahns. As president, he determined to replicate them in America.

In DC, these "uber-bahns," with nine-tenths of the cost picked up by the federal taxpayer, took the form of the Southwest-Southeast Freeway. (Also called Route 695, it's an extension of Interstate 395.) After crossing from northern Virginia over the 14th Street Bridge, the Freeway cut a swath of destruction through the heart of old Southwest. Its remnants were split off from downtown, left withering and clinging to a decaying riverfront. The historic Maine Avenue Fish Market became a cul-de-sac in the shadow of a highway overpass. For over fifty years, the area was a magnet for winos and prostitutes, until its recent revival with the Washington Nationals baseball stadium. Now it's a trendy place for "young professionals," the lively, prior neighborhood consigned to history's dustbin.

UNPLEASING PLAZA

With the construction of the Southwest-Southeast Freeway, DC planners focused on the remnants of the old neighborhood to the roadway's north, near the National Mall. More than a dozen years of wrangling and redesigns ensued. President John Kennedy signed off on the look of the buildings. Construction of L'Enfant Plaza finally began in 1962 and took a decade to complete.

The overall project architect was I. M. Pei, Gropius's student at Harvard. The developer was Zeckendorf, the investor who'd tried squashing Grand Central Station with Pei's geometric slab. Then one of the country's richest men, Zeckendorf would go bankrupt in 1965 after developing Century City in Los Angeles. Another major investor was the Rockefeller family, which was also a prime mover behind the Brutalist Albany Plaza in New York State's capital.

Not surprisingly, L'Enfant Plaza emerged as the high point of Brutalism. A set piece is Breuer's Robert C. Weaver Housing and Urban

The Brutalist Housing and Urban Development (HUD) building has been described as "among the most reviled in all of Washington," and even the world.

Development (HUD) building. At the ceremony opening it, Weaver, then the HUD secretary, termed it "urban and urbane," while President Johnson called it "bold and beautiful." The *Washington Post* hailed the "brooding, strangely graceful concrete honeycomb."

The building is set on weird concrete pilons that look like the bicuspids of a tyrannosaur. The "honeycomb" is nine stories of massive concrete blocks, thirty-two blocks to a floor, which dwarf the windows they encase. Outside, a bleak stone piazza offers no seating and no shelter, freezing in winter, and baking during Washington's unforgiving summers.

Opinions of it changed over time. Shaun Donovan, HUD secretary in the Obama Administration, said the edifice is "among the most reviled in all of Washington—and with good reason." Jack Kemp, HUD secretary in the George H. W. Bush Administration, mocked it as "10 floors of basement."

Along with its ugliness, critics attacked the HUD building for looking too much like Breuer's other creations. His response: "I can't design a whole new system every Monday morning." Surprisingly, HUD is on the

National Register of Historic Places, perhaps because it's been around for over fifty years, the minimum time to qualify.

Bisecting the Plaza is 10th Street, the "Road to Nowhere." Mostly devoid of traffic, it drops down to an ugly urban park, mostly stone, little green, that replaced some of the neighborhood cleared out in the 1950s. It's named after Benjamin Banneker, the noted black astronomer who surveyed the District's boundaries. It's a dishonor to one of the District's founding figures.

The Plaza is capped at its north end by its most brutal construction of all, the James V. Forrestal Building. It was originally slated for military personnel who worked in the "tempos"—the temporary buildings built on the Mall during the world wars. The new Department of Energy staffed it in 1977.

The epitome of the Brutalist style at L'Enfant Plaza is the James V. Forrestal Building housing the Department of Energy.

The building consists of the familiar concrete window blocks. Its massive form seems ready to crush through its thin pediments to smash down upon the streetscape. One critic likened it to an "elephant tottering on the legs of a giraffe."

From street level, one can glimpse, barely, a bit of James Renwick's Romanesque masterpiece, the Smithsonian Castle, on the National Mall side of Independence Avenue. In fact, Plaza designer Pei tried to prevent construction of the Forrestal Building, because it seals the Plaza off, like a tombstone's slab, from the Mall and the city's core.

Given the terrible luck associated with the name Forrestal, the developers might have heeded Pei's advice. James Forrestal, the first secretary of defense, committed suicide in 1949 by jumping out of a window at the National Naval Medical Center, in Bethesda, Maryland. In 1967, the aircraft carrier the USS *Forrestal*, named for him, suffered a fire that killed 134 sailors and aviators. Moreover, James Forrestal had been the owner of Georgetown's ill-starred Prospect House. During the War of 1812, its builder, Revolutionary War hero Gen. James Lingan, was lynched by a pro-war mob.

I. M. Pei would atone somewhat for his sin by designing the National Gallery of Art's East Wing, finished in 1978. It is Modernist, but with aplomb. On the outside, it takes the form of a giant letter H, and its open-ended interiors shout creativity and broadmindedness. It contrasts nicely with the austere classicism of John Russell Pope's West Wing, the storehouse of Old Masters paintings.

From his grave atop Arlington National Cemetery, the spirit of Pierre L'Enfant must look down beneficently at the city he envisioned, except when his gaze turns to the brutal Plaza bearing his name.

Chapter Twenty-Eight

Botched Coverup: Senate Revelations Lead to a President's Exit

The Senate and House hearing rooms

IN THE FIRST HALF OF 1973, SCANDALOUS REVELATIONS AND HIGH-PRO-file congressional hearings battered the administration of President and former congressman Richard Nixon, only months after a landslide re-election win. Still, it seemed Nixon himself might survive his second term.

A Crime in the Shadows

The nation had been stunned to learn top advisors to the president had authorized, and covered up, the sordid Watergate affair. That was the break-in, on June 17, 1972, of the headquarters of the Democratic Party at the Watergate complex. (It's a hodgepodge of offices and residences next to the Kennedy Center, on the Potomac River at the edge of Georgetown.) A goal of the caper was to wiretap the phones and photograph the documents of opposition-party officials.

The five men caught during the break-in included James McCord, an employee of the president's campaign organization, the Committee to Re-Elect the President (abbreviated as CRP or, perhaps fittingly, CREEP). McCord, the ex–head of building security at CIA headquarters in Langley, Virginia, presumably knew a lot about illegal entries.

The other four operatives in the "black bag" job had in the 1960s taken part in CIA-backed plots to overthrow or kill Cuban dictator Fidel

Castro. The scheme was financed via a "slush fund" of cash siphoned off from Nixon campaign donations.

An FBI investigation soon turned up ties between the felons and E. Howard Hunt, another former CIA official and campaign employee. Indeed, it was the fifty-three-year-old Hunt who'd planned and managed the operation, along with an ex–FBI agent, and CREEP's top lawyer, forty-two-year-old G. Gordon Liddy. Before joining CREEP, Liddy had been an aide to Nixon's domestic policy advisor, John Ehrlichman.

The FBI tied Hunt and Liddy to the White House. Later it would be found officials there had arranged for hundreds of thousands of dollars in "hush money," also taken from campaign funds, to buy the silence of the burglars.

FIGURES OUT OF A JAMES BOND NOVEL

Both Hunt and Liddy had colorful pasts. Hunt had worked for the CIA and its predecessor agency for a quarter-century and had directed covert-operation offices in Western Europe and Latin America. In Mexico, he'd supervised CIA policy analyst, and future conservative publisher, William F. Buckley Jr. Hunt had been an organizer of the 1962 Bay of Pigs invasion, the doomed, CIA-funded attempt of Cuban émigrés to depose Castro. A prolific author, McCord would write over seventy books; he'd ghostwritten for CIA director Allen Dulles. In fact, in 1964 Dulles stationed McCord in Spain, during the height of the James Bond movie craze, with the aim of writing a fictional, American equivalent of 007.

His partner in crime, Liddy, also seemed a character from pulp fiction. An officer of artillery in the Korean War, he became the youngest manager ever of the FBI's DC headquarters. However, he turned heads when he ran an FBI background check on his future wife, and future grandmother of twelve. In one of his weird presages of Watergate, Liddy was mistakenly arrested during an authorized break-in, before he was let go, after intervention by Clarence Kelley, then a police chief, and later an FBI director during the Watergate scandals.

On leaving the Bureau, Liddy worked as a high-profile lawyer. Archibald Cox, the future Watergate special prosecutor, approved Liddy's application to plead cases before the US Supreme Court. Liddy became a prosecutor himself in New York State, where he busted LSD advocate Timothy Leary and the future heads of the rock band Steely Dan on drug charges. However, he once got into hot water himself for firing a pistol at the ceiling of a courtroom.

In 1968, the tumultuous year of Nixon's election, Liddy lost a House race to Hamilton Fish IV, the great-grandson of President's Grant's secretary of state. Fish would serve thirteen terms in the House and serve on the House Judiciary Committee that investigated Watergate.

In his tell-all bestseller *Will*, Liddy disclosed his unique method of convincing undercover colleagues he'd never give in to torture. Without complaint, he'd hold his palm above a lit cigarette lighter until his flesh crackled and burned.

INVESTIGATIONS AND RESIGNATIONS

After the Watergate break-in, the US District Court for the District of Columbia assembled a grand jury. In September 1972, it indicted the five burglars, plus Hunt and Liddy, who were dubbed the Watergate Seven.

The judge presiding over the court near the Capitol was sixty-eight-year-old John Sirica, a pugnacious former boxer. Nixon's former boss, President Dwight Eisenhower, had appointed "Maximum John," known for handing out stiff prison terms. In the grand-jury proceedings, Sirica smelled a rat, figuring higher-ranking White House officials were behind the break-in. Along with the prosecution lawyers, he began grilling the defendants.

On January 30, 1973, all seven were convicted of burglary, wiretapping, and conspiracy. Sirica handed the convicts provisional terms of up to forty years in jail, as incentive to turn state's evidence. In late March, McCord cracked. He attested to a Watergate coverup that extended to the White House counsel, John Wesley Dean III, as well as to Nixon's former attorney general and former campaign director, John N. Mitchell.

The plot thickened. In February 1973, the Senate Judiciary Committee held confirmation hearings for acting FBI director L. Patrick Gray. After longtime FBI director J. Edgar Hoover had died in May 1972, Nixon had chosen Gray as his replacement. The hearings revealed

Gray and Dean had hidden or destroyed Watergate-related cash and documents that Hunt had kept in a White House safe. Gray had been told the materials related to national security. Further, Gray testified he thought Dean had lied during the Bureau's investigation of the break-in.

Behind the scenes, an angry Ehrlichman told Dean he wished Gray was left to "twist, slowly, slowly in the wind." The domestic policy chief was unaware that Dean, even while continuing to help direct the coverup, had begun secretly cooperating with federal prosecutors. Under fire, Gray resigned as acting FBI director on April 27.

On April 30, the scandal exploded on the front pages, as a knot of high-level Nixon aides were forced to resign: Ehrlichman; the crew-cut chief of staff, H. R. Haldeman; and the attorney general who'd replaced Mitchell, Richard Kleindienst. On the same day Nixon, while continuing to deny knowledge of the affair, fired Dean.

On May 24, the Senate started up its own formal investigation through the Senate Select Committee on Presidential Campaign Activities, popularly known as the Senate Watergate Committee. Its chairman was Democrat Sen. Sam Ervin of North Carolina. Born in 1898, Ervin was a self-described "country lawyer" allergic to abuse and overreach by the federal government. Other Committee members included the ranking Republican, Howard Baker of Tennessee, and Lowell Weicker of Connecticut. It was arranged to televise the hearings live, gavel-to-gavel.

On May 25, the new attorney general, Elliot Richardson of Massachusetts, chose a Watergate special prosecutor: the sixty-one-year-old Archibald Cox, the former Harvard legal expert. Nixon privately seethed over the appointment, as the liberal Cox didn't hide his political leanings, and had been the solicitor general, and effective litigator, for Nixon's onetime arch political rival, President Kennedy.

In late June, Dean gave testimony before Ervin's Committee. Dean knew the process well: During the preceding Johnson Administration, he'd been chief counsel for the Republicans on the House Judiciary Committee. He spoke to a huge national audience; the televised proceedings were more popular than the daytime soap operas. Dean became the first former or present White House aide to implicate Nixon in the coverup. Dean also admitted he directed the payment of hush money for the burglars. Nixon, and his press secretary, Ron Ziegler, strongly denied Dean's allegations.

Plumbers and Dirty Tricks

The Watergate saga evolved from the over-the-top politics of the Vietnam War era, and the large-scale, sometimes violent, demonstrations against it. In the late 1960s and early 1970s, Hoover's FBI had continued its COINTELPRO program of wiretapping and harassing protestors and suspected radicals, including members of the extremist Weather Underground group. (See the chapter on the Capitol Building bombings.)

In 1971-72, CREEP took a page out of the Hoover playbook. The re-election committee began conducting "dirty tricks" and covert operations against the president's political foes. In mid-1971, for instance, Nixon's head of public liaison, Charles "Chuck" Colson, directed Hunt to spy on Sen. Ted Kennedy. This led to an unsuccessful effort to collect dirt on Kennedy's alleged extramarital affairs, as well as on Kennedy's 1969 Chappaquiddick Island scandal. (In the latter incident, which deep-sixed a potential 1972 presidential bid, the senator had driven a car off a bridge, resulting in the drowning death of his female passenger.)

In early 1972, then–Attorney General Mitchell hosted a dirty-tricks planning session at his office. Attending were Liddy, Dean, and CREEP's deputy head, Jeb Stuart Magruder, named by his Civil War buff dad after the Confederate cavalry commander, J. E. B. Stuart. (The Magruder name has long been prominent in the DC area, and includes War of 1812 Clerk of the House Patrick Magruder, and William Magruder, a physician during the cholera epidemic of 1832 and mayor during the Know-Nothing riot of 1857.)

At the secret powwow, Liddy asked Mitchell for a million dollars, to mount a major effort of sabotage against the president's political adversaries. Liddy envisioned such outlandish capers as entrapping top Democrats with prostitutes and kidnapping radical leaders. For these endeavors he chose a Jason Bourne–like codename: Operation Gemstone.

Mitchell was taken aback by the size and outrageous character of these schemes. If he had fired Liddy, and forbade Gemstone, Watergate would have never happened. Instead, he temporized. Several months later, Mitchell approved $250,000 for a scaled-down operation.

A dry run of sorts for Watergate took place in 1971. The trigger was the publication of "The Pentagon Papers." These were seven thousand pages of top-secret Defense Department, CIA, and State Department documents and analyses on the Vietnam War. They were leaked to the press by MIT foreign affairs specialist Daniel Ellsberg. The forty-year-old Ellsberg, a former Marine Corps officer and then an antiwar activist, had worked on the materials while an analyst at the RAND Corporation think tank.

The Pentagon Papers detailed deceit and bungling in the US involvement in Indochina, from the end of the Second World War through the Kennedy and Lyndon Johnson Administrations that preceded the Nixon presidency. In June, the *New York Times* and the *Washington Post* started publishing the documents, accompanied by articles critical of the Nixon Administration's own war effort.

Nixon might conceivably have used the Pentagon Papers against his political foes, by contrasting Johnson's approach with his own Vietnam strategy—of US troop withdrawals, "Vietnamization" of the war by bolstering South Vietnam's military, and severe aerial bombing campaigns—dubbed "peace with honor." (Johnson had followed an approach of "gradual escalation," of steadily increasing troop deployments, peaking with five hundred thousand US soldiers in Vietnam, that seemingly telegraphed America's war strategy to the North Vietnamese military, coupled with self-imposed limits on bombing or invading Communist "sanctuaries" in the adjoining countries of Laos and Cambodia.) Although Nixon's strategy was controversial, it wasn't failing militarily, and it had significant public support.

Instead, Nixon and his aides played hardball with leakers of sensitive data like Ellsberg. The president was angry at the newspapers, political foes of his, that had published the Papers. He also feared their revelations would undermine his Vietnam policies. His Justice Department briefly blocked their further publication, until the Supreme Court ruled in favor of the media outlets. The Justice Department also indicted Ellsberg for theft of government property. (His trial would last into 1973, until the charges were dismissed due to Watergate.)

More significantly, Nixon's men set up a secret "Plumbers" unit to plug or discourage further leaks of sensitive information. This undercover team broke into the office of Ellsberg's psychologist, to try to find embarrassing information on the famous leaker, and then leak it themselves. However, the Plumbers discovered nothing damaging in Ellsberg's files.

Most significantly, the break-in team included Hunt, Liddy, and two of the Cuba-related burglars who would take part in Operation Gemstone, and its prime covert op, the Watergate burglary.

A Tragicomic Caper

The Watergate break-in, actually break-ins, were Keystone Cop, or Keystone Criminal, in their execution. In May 1972, the Plumbers unit broke into and wiretapped the Democratic Party headquarters. However, some of the wiretaps proved defective, and the lock specialist may have brought along ineffective keys. The famous, follow-on break-in happened early in the morning of June 17. Liddy and Hunt managed, or mismanaged it, from a room at the nearby Watergate Hotel.

A main screw-up this time would be the team's spotter, who'd taken a room across the street at the old Howard Johnson Motor Lodge. The lookout had a CIA-issue radio with which to contact the burglars in case of trouble.

The Watergate's twenty-four-year-old night watchman, Frank Wills, discovered that a door to a stairwell had been taped, but thought nothing of it, and removed the tape. In a later check of the stairway, however, he discovered that tape had been put back on the locks, evidently to aid a getaway for a robbery. Wills's search by flashlight could be seen through the Watergate's windows from the Howard Johnson. Yet the spotter didn't notice—as he was watching television. In the meantime, Wills contacted the DC police.

A car pulled in front of the complex. Out came three plainclothes cops, in peculiar apparel, according to the *Washington Post*. The police on the graveyard shift often went after drug dealers, and so they were outfitted in hippie regalia. They entered the Watergate. The spotter, finally alert, saw them, and radioed one of the Plumbers—but he had switched off his walkie-talkie! The cops detained and handcuffed the burglars.

When news of the break-in broke, the White House began immediately to lie, or "stonewall," to use one of the phrases the scandal made famous. Press Secretary Ziegler dismissed the matter as "a third-rate burglary attempt." Which it was, among other things.

The leak-obsessed administration was soon hit by leaks of information from high-level government sources. Within days of the break-in, two reporters for the *Washington Post*—thirty-nine-year-old Bob Woodward of Illinois, a former Navy officer, and forty-year-old Carl Bernstein, from Washington, DC—were drawing on insider information to piece together much of the actual story. Woodward nicknamed a key source, "Deep Throat," after a porn movie star. The journalist and Deep Throat would secretly meet in an Arlington, Virginia, parking garage. (Decades later, the source revealed himself as Mark Felt, then the associate director of the FBI, and the former manager of the COINTELPRO program.) The reporters' revelations led to headline stories about the scandal by October 1972. However, the exposés did not affect the outcome of the November 1972 election.

AN UNNECESSARY CRIME?

Oddly enough, Nixon hardly needed to eavesdrop on his political opponents to win office again. The election contest took place after a string of administration initiatives where he'd stolen the thunder of his political rivals and soared in the public opinion polls.

At the dawn of the environmental movement in 1970, Nixon established the federal Environmental Protection Agency. The following year, he'd intervened heavily in a slowing economy hit by inflation, by temporarily freezing wages and prices. Fortunately for Nixon, the American economy temporarily improved for the election.

In February 1972 Nixon, long a fierce critic of communism, traveled to Beijing for the first US summit with Communist China, beginning a de facto alliance. Three months later, he traveled to Moscow to sign with the Soviet Union a major weapons limitation attempt, the Anti-Ballistic Missile (ABM) Treaty. The phrase "like Nixon going to China" became a catchphrase for a leader who goes against the grain of his beliefs to pull off a triumph.

In Indochina, he steadily pulled out troops from Vietnam, while employing US airpower to beat back North Vietnam's 1972 "Year of the Rat" offensive. Meanwhile the Democrats picked as their presidential nominee an ardent antiwar figure, South Dakota senator George McGovern. Further, the Democrats' presidential ticket imploded when McGovern chose as his vice-presidential pick Missouri senator Thomas Eagleton. He bowed out of the race after revelations he'd undergone shock treatments for depression. Nixon engineered a forty-nine-state Electoral College blowout.

Watergate was thus unnecessary, if inevitable, given the president's instincts to dissimulate.

RECORDING REVELATIONS

In summer 1973, even after his top advisors had resigned, it seemed Nixon—if he could make it through the congressional Watergate hearings—might serve out his presidency.

His support among Republicans on Capitol Hill was still strong. Most of the public, though it deemed his behavior unpresidential, did not favor impeachment.

Then came the Butterfield bombshell.

Forty-six-year-old Alexander Butterfield, head of the Federal Aviation Administration (FAA), had been the top aide to Haldeman, the ousted chief of staff. On Monday, July 16, Butterfield testified before the Senate Watergate Committee to Tennessee senator Fred Thompson, later a well-known actor in fictional movie thrillers.

The Woodward/Bernstein stories as well as some of Nixon's statements on Watergate seemed to have contained verbatim reconstructions of White House conversations. This led some to wonder, including Dean in his testimony, whether the president had a tape-recording system.

The Tennessee senator inquired:

"Mr. Butterfield, were you aware of the existence of any listening devices in the Oval Office of the president?"

To a rapt Committee and millions of viewers, Butterfield replied:

"I was wondering if someone would ask that. . . . Everything was taped as long as the president was in attendance. There was not so much as a hint that something should not be taped."

Among the senators prominent at the Watergate hearings were, left to right, Tennessee's Fred Thompson and Howard Baker, and North Carolina's Sam Ervin. Thompson's questioning of former Nixon aide Alexander Butterfield revealed the existence of a White House recording system that led to the president's resignation.

Butterfield revealed how, at Haldeman's direction, and under Nixon's orders, he had instructed Secret Service agents to install hidden microphones throughout the president's workspace. In spring 1971, they placed the devices in the Oval Office, the Cabinet room, the Lincoln Sitting Room, and Nixon's private office. Almost every presidential conversation since, Butterfield noted, had been recorded. (Some in the Senate had first learned of the recording system a few days before, during preliminary questioning of Butterfield by Committee staff under the supervision of Chief Counsel Samuel Dash.)

The nation drew in its collective breath. For months, in the words of Senator Baker, many had wondered, "What did the president know, and when did he know it?" More specifically, was he lying, or were Dean and others lying about him?

Now all the president had to do to show his innocence was release the tapes.

But Nixon refused, citing "executive privilege." He argued that Congress had no power to compel confidential information from another branch of government.

But few believed the stated rationale of a man increasingly referred to as "Tricky Dick." Overnight, Nixon's political support crashed.

More to the point, both the Senate Watergate Committee and Special Prosecutor Cox issued subpoenas for the tapes. Nixon and his White House legal team fought the subpoenas. A "constitutional crisis" between the Executive Branch, the legislature, and the judiciary ensued.

A WEEKEND MASSACRE

The battle over the tapes moved to a stunning culmination. First, Nixon tried a compromise of sorts. He offered to hand over, not the tapes, but written transcripts of them. Their faithfulness to the recordings would be verified by seventy-one-year-old, conservative Democrat Sen. John C. Stennis of Mississippi. But Cox turned down the deal.

Then Nixon made a wild gamble for public support. On October 20, 1973, he ordered his new attorney general, Elliot Richardson, to dismiss Cox.

But Richardson refused, and resigned instead. His abrupt departure was shocking, as the former war hero had been Nixon's secretary of defense, as well as his secretary of health, education, and welfare.

Nixon then ordered his deputy attorney general, William Ruckelshaus, to fire Cox. But Ruckelshaus refused and resigned as well! Like Richardson, he believed such a firing would interfere with a lawful investigation.

The task of axing Cox next fell to the number three official at Justice, the solicitor general, one Robert Bork. In a face-to-face meeting, Bork informed Nixon he would not resign if ordered to fire Cox. Bork then dismissed Cox, the end point of the so-called Saturday Night Massacre. (In 1987, President Reagan's nomination of Bork for the Supreme Court was "borked," or shot down, by Democratic senators such as Kennedy, and future president Joseph Robinette Biden Jr. of Delaware, partly as payback for the Cox dismissal.)

The administration underscored the firing with actions at the workplaces where the investigators had labored. On orders of the White House chief of staff, Alexander Haig, who'd replaced Haldeman, FBI agents sealed off Cox's offices. They also forbade employees from taking with them any public or private documents. Further, agents blocked off the offices of Richardson and Ruckelshaus. As Judge Sirica watched the carnage on television, he wondered if America verged on becoming a banana republic.

The general public was enraged. The White House mail room was swamped with over four hundred thousand telegrams, most condemning the actions. Comedians such as Rich Little and David Frye had a field day doing Nixon impersonations and mocking the president's credibility.

The Speaker of the House, Democrat Carl Albert of Oklahoma, began transferring resolutions on impeachment to the House Judiciary Committee. Cox himself stated: "Whether we shall continue to be a Government of laws and not of men is now for Congress and ultimately the American people" to decide.

However, Bork proved no patsy. To replace Cox, he soon appointed a former head of the American Bar Association, sixty-eight-year-old Leon Jaworski of Texas. And for his investigations, Jaworski was granted more authority and leeway than Cox.

The Autumn of His Discontent

That fall proved one of the most trying for any president in American history. Even as the drama over the special prosecutor approached, Nixon and his secretary of state, Henry Kissinger, had to handle a major foreign crisis: the October War, with Israel fighting off large-scale invasions by Egypt and Syria. As the United States, Israel's ally, and the Soviet Union, backing the Arab states, faced off in a confrontation of nuclear powers, the administration scrambled to ship massive amounts of military supplies to Israel, which ended up winning the conflict.

Incredibly, in the same month Nixon was blindsided by another big-league scandal, separate from Watergate. On October 10 came the resignation of his vice president, Spiro Theodore Agnew, the former Maryland governor and Baltimore County executive. Federal investigators in the Bay State found Agnew had taken kickbacks from government contractors, both as a Maryland official and as vice president.

Nixon chose as Agnew's successor the House minority leader, Republican Gerald Rudolph Ford of Michigan. Some figured the president chose Ford to buttress his support in Congress in the event of impeachment.

Watergate ground on. Before Judge Sirica, John Dean pleaded guilty to obstruction of justice, while continuing to cooperate with prosecutors. In mid-November, an increasingly embattled president declared at a convention of newspaper editors: "I am not a crook." Then days before Thanksgiving, Nixon suffered another major embarrassment when his White House lawyer announced a key Watergate tape contained a gap of eighteen-and-a-half minutes. The recording was of a June 20, 1972 conversation between Nixon and Haldeman about the Watergate break-in. The White House claimed the tape had been mistakenly erased by Nixon's longtime personal secretary, fifty-five-year-old Rose Mary Woods.

A farcical scene played out when Woods demonstrated to reporters in her White House office how she had supposedly performed the erasure. With press cameras clicking, she contorted and stretched out her body, with a foot on a pedal and a hand on the machine's Erase button. Moreover, Woods said she had only erased five minutes of the recording, not eighteen-plus minutes. Some blamed Nixon's known ineptitude with mechanical devices for the erasures. Chief of Staff Haig blamed it on a "sinister force." (Two decades later, experts found that up to nine separate attempts had been made to delete segments of the tape.)

EDITS AND EXPLETIVES

Paralyzed by the scandals, Congress and the president accomplished little on other pressing business through the winter and spring of 1974. Sirica and Jaworski, from the courtroom and the special prosecutor's office, insisted Nixon deliver the tapes, even as they prosecuted those involved in Watergate-related crimes.

In February and March, Sirica's grand jury named the president as an unindicted co-conspirator, while indicting Mitchell, Haldeman, Ehrlichman, Colson, and three others, on obstruction of justice, conspiracy, and perjury. (Colson would later found Prison Fellowship International.)

In April, the House Judiciary Committee, led by sixty-three-year-old Rep. Peter Rodino of New Jersey, issued a subpoena for forty-two tapes. Soon Judge Sirica, on the request of Special Prosecutor Jaworski, subpoenaed another sixty-four tapes, for evidence in the trials of Nixon's aides.

In late April 1974, the White House buckled before the pressure. It released transcripts of the tapes, about twelve hundred pages worth. The documents were edited, replacing vulgar language with the term "expletive deleted." The contents were damning for Nixon's aides, if not quite Nixon himself. However, his coarse and prejudiced patter and cynical approach dismayed the electorate. The Senate minority leader, Republican Hugh Scott of Pennsylvania, deemed the transcripts "disgusting, shabby, and immoral." Nixon's standing fell further still.

In early May the House Judiciary Committee, unappeased by the transcripts, started up impeachment proceedings.

ARTICLES OF IMPEACHMENT AND SMOKING GUNS

As the capital entered summer, Congress began looking ahead to the autumn mid-term elections. Republican leaders worried about a potential Democratic landslide made greater if a crippled Nixon clung to office.

With the president at odds with the Senate, the House, the Sirica court, and the special prosecutor, one other institution had the means to break the deadlock. In late May, Jaworski asked the Supreme Court to rule on the president's claim of executive privilege over the tapes. The High Court agreed, acting to hear the case in a special summer session, and without first going through the normal channel of the US Court of Appeals. Its extraordinary action recalled the Court's expedited 1942 review of the Nazi saboteur case. (See the chapter on Hitler's secret agents.)

On July 24, the Supremes ruled eight to zero the president could not deny the special prosecutor the sixty-four subpoenaed tapes. (Nixon's recent Court appointee, Chief Justice William Rehnquist, recused himself from the decision.) A few diehard Nixon backers suggested the president burn the tapes. But Nixon, bowing to the Court, turned them over to Jaworski.

The recordings proved fatal to his presidency. They showed Nixon was aware of his re-election committee's role in the break-in at least as soon as the burglars' arrests. And that he had actively taken part in the coverup from the start, including encouraging the payment of hush money. A taped conversation from March 21, 1973 revealed Dean telling Nixon that "Bob [Haldeman] is involved . . . John [Ehrlichman] is involved . . . I am involved . . . Mitchell is involved. . . . And that's an obstruction of justice."

The public and congressional pressure for Nixon to quit became overwhelming. People were enraged the nation had been deadlocked for two years over blatant deceit.

In votes taking place July 27 to July 30, the House Judiciary Committee recommended the full House impeach Nixon on three articles: obstruction of justice, abuse of power, and contempt of Congress. Fully ten Republicans on the Committee who had previously opposed impeachment now declared themselves for it.

One tape, released on August 5, proved a coup de grâce. Recorded on June 23, 1972, less than a week after the break-in, it revealed Nixon agreeing with Haldeman to tell the CIA to get the FBI to stop its investigation of Watergate.

On the night of August 7, a delegation of leading Republicans, including Scott, Baker, Barry Goldwater of Arizona, and the House minority leader, Republican John Jacob Rhodes Jr. of Arizona, met with Nixon in the Executive Mansion. They informed him the House would vote to impeach, and the Senate to convict and remove him from office.

On the evening of August 8, Nixon, in a televised address from the Oval Office, announced he would resign the following day. On August 9, from the White House South Lawn, he boarded the Marine One helicopter, and was whisked away to retirement.

One of the great political scandals was over, one in which congressional hearings played a critical role.

CHAPTER TWENTY-NINE

Femmes Fatales: The Women Terrorists Who Bombed the Senate

Senate's ground-floor hallway; Senate's second floor corridor

THE RECORDED MESSAGE CAME INTO THE SENATE'S SWITCHBOARD ON November 7, 1983, at 10:48 p.m. A voice informed the operator:

"Listen carefully, I'm only going to tell you this one time. There is a bomb in the Capitol Building. It will go off in five minutes. Evacuate the building." The phone line went dead.

About the same time, the news desk of the *Washington Post* received a similar message.

At 10:58 p.m., the bomb went off in a hall on the second floor of the Senate side. It blew up ten yards from the Senate chamber, and near the office of the Senate minority leader, Democrat Robert Carlyle Byrd of West Virginia.

The explosion sent a "shower of splintered wood, plaster and brick flying across the hall, shattering the windows of the Republican cloakroom," reported *Congressional Quarterly*. "The doors to Byrd's office were blown off their hinges, nearby windows were blown out, and surrounding walls were pockmarked with fist-sized holes."

Chandeliers shattered. The hands on a grandfather clock that had kept time for 124 years stopped. Daniel Webster's face was blown off a venerable portrait of the nineteenth-century senator. (Aides painstakingly collected its fragments from trash bins, and the image was reconstructed.) Pedestrians outside the Capitol heard a noise like a sonic boom.

A 1983 bombing by an extremist group caused much damage near the office of the Senate minority leader.

Detonated late at night, when the Capitol was mostly empty, the bomb caused no casualties. But it might have.

"It was indeed fortunate," reacted the Senate majority leader, Republican Howard Baker of Tennessee, that "the Senate was not in session ... as had been announced. Had we been in session at 11 o'clock, undoubtedly there would have been grave injury and perhaps loss of life."

The bomb blew up near the Mansfield Room, named for a former Senate majority leader, Mike Mansfield of Montana. A reception had taken pace there not long before the explosion.

On the morning after, a group that claimed to be the "Armed Resistance Unit" sent a "Communique" to National Public Radio. It read: "*Tonight we bombed the U.S. Capitol....* We attacked the U.S. government to retaliate against imperialist aggression that has sent the Marines, the CIA, and the Army to invade sovereign nations, to trample and lay waste the lives and rights of the peoples of Grenada, Lebanon, El Salvador, and Nicaragua. . . ."

The message echoed the events of the time. In October 1983, President Reagan sent US troops into the Caribbean island of Grenada, to oust its Cuban-backed government. Two days before that invasion, the terrorist group Hezbollah, with support from the Islamic Republic of Iran, blew up a US Marines base in Beirut, Lebanon, killing 241 Americans. During this period, the administration was supporting guerillas fighting the socialist Sandinista government of Nicaragua.

The Communique added: "We purposely aimed our attack at the institutions of imperialist rule rather than at individual members of the ruling class and government. We did not choose to kill any of them at this time. But their lives are not sacred, and their hands are stained with the blood of millions."

Despite the threat, both houses convened the next day. "The Senate will not be deterred from its business," said a defiant Baker, adding he and his colleagues would meet "in the rubble" if need be.

In the bombing's aftermath, the Capitol's security was tightened. All entering the building were ushered through metal detectors; before, only visitors to the second-floor galleries were checked for weapons (a response to the armed assault on the House in 1954 by Puerto Rican nationalists; see the chapter on that attack). The number of ways to enter the Capitol was cut by half; more security guards were hired. Over time, public parking on the east side of the Capitol was banned. Tourists were blocked from the corridors near the Senate and House chambers.

Still, lawmakers tried to maintain some liberty in the face of demands for more safety. "I think a free society such as ours owes a degree of access of the public to the public buildings," said Democrat House majority leader, Rep. Jim Wright of Texas. "This is not our building. It's the building of the people of the United States."

A Bevy of Bombings

The Senate bombing was accompanied by three attacks on Washington military installations in 1983 and 1984. The most significant took place on April 20, 1984, one mile from the Capitol Building, at the Washington Navy Yard on 11th and M Street S.E.

At 1:50 a.m., a powerful bomb went off near the first-floor dining room of the Officers Club. The blast wrecked the first floor and damaged all three floors of the concrete and brick building. It threw glass shards from smashed windows fifty yards down the street. Due to the late hour, no one was injured.

On this occasion, the calls came minutes after the bombing. An unidentified woman phoned United Press International and the *Washington Post*. She played a recording that denounced American policies in Central America and a US Navy exercise in the Caribbean, while demanding independence for Puerto Rico.

The prior August, a bomb was set off, minutes after a warning, outside the Navy Yard's computer installation. In that pre–September 11 era, anyone could enter the Navy Yard at any hour.

The pattern had been set at the first, and least damaging, of the four bombings. That was on April 26, 1983, at Fort McNair in far southwest Washington. Formerly an arsenal, it is the site of the National War College, a military university for ranking US officers and allied foreign personnel.

The blast occurred at the front entrance of the College at 10:00 p.m. The five- to ten-pound timed device shattered windows but caused no injuries. It happened a few minutes after a caller reached the Pentagon switchboard and played three prerecorded messages that warned of an imminent bombing.

In 1984 and 1985, the organization responsible also staged bombings in New York City. They included an early-morning blast in a bathroom of the Patrolmen's Benevolent Association. Just after the detonation, equivalent to ten pounds of dynamite, a woman called news outlets to play a recorded message which stated the attack was revenge for two New Yorkers recently killed through violent police misconduct. The messages stated the Association "promotes racist murder and killer cops. The 10,000 racists are not worth one hair on the heads. . . ."

BLASTS FROM THE PAST

Domestic terror experts recalled a spate of eerily similar bombings in the 1970s, during the Vietnam War, in both Washington and New York City. The targets included the Capitol Building, the Pentagon, and offices of the New York City police.

In a March 2, 1971 incident, the Senate was bombed, very early in the morning. The device, which had been placed in a ground-floor bathroom, damaged seven rooms and shook the venerable structure's original brick archways.

Before the 1:32 a.m. detonation, an operator at the Capitol's switchboard got the following message: "This building will blow up in thirty minutes. You will get many calls like this, but this one is real." The voice went on: "Evacuate the building. This is in protest of the Nixon involvement in Laos." The reference was to President Nixon's "incursion" of US forces into Laos against Communist military "sanctuaries," or safe havens.

Some days after the attack, the Weather Underground, a radical leftist group, claimed responsibility. Its statement read: "We have attacked the Capitol . . . a monument to U.S. domination over the planet. Our plans can be as creative and indigenous as the bamboo booby traps of the Vietnamese." The bombing and the statement seemed to presage the 1983 attack and communique.

Security in 1971 was soft. Guards didn't check the packages or purses of visitors to the Building. In the aftermath, Congress spent $4 million on preventative measures, and almost doubled the number of Capitol police.

On May 19, 1972, a bomb went off at 12:40 a.m. in a women's restroom at the Pentagon, in its Air Force sector. Computer tapes containing classified data were severely damaged. No persons were injured. The bombers announced the attack was to retaliate for the US bombing and mining of North Vietnam. The date of May 19 was significant, as it was the birthday of North Vietnamese Communist chief Ho Chi Minh and of Latin American revolutionary Che Guevara. The Weather Underground's co-founder, William "Bill" Ayers, later recalled that "the bomb that rocked the Pentagon was itsy-bitsy—weighing close to two pounds—it caused 'tens of thousands of dollars' of damage. The operation cost under $500, and no one was killed or even hurt."

In 1974, a Weather Underground–related group published a Marxist manifesto, "Prairie Fire." It was titled after a quote by Chinese Communist dictator Mao Zedong, that "a single spark can set a prairie fire." The document called for a mass movement led by a violent, clandestine cluster of true believers.

Its authors included Ayers and wife Bernadine Dohrn. Like Ayers, Dohrn had worked for a branch of Students for a Democratic Society (SDS), a hard-left, antiwar organization. That group came out of the tumultuous civil rights, Black Power, and especially, anti–Vietnam War protests of the 1960s. Formed in 1960 by college socialists, SDS later organized more disruptive protests, and eventually violent acts against the military and municipal police. (In 1995, Ayers and Dohrn, with controversy resulting, would host at their Chicago home a fundraiser for future senator and president Barack Obama.)

Another of the manifesto's authors was a New Yorker named Kathy Boudin. Born in 1943, Boudin was raised in Manhattan's bohemian district of Greenwich Village. As a child, she attended a progressive school, The Little Red School House. Her father Leonard was a leading civil liberties attorney. During the 1950s Cold War, the FBI revoked his passport for suspected communist ties.

Thin, and with a mane of dark hair, in college she became an early member of SDS, and joined an SDS project that worked in impoverished African American and Hispanic communities. At the chaotic Democratic Party convention protests of 1968, Boudin was arrested. With others of the most radical SDS members, she joined the Weather Underground. Police arrested the young woman again in 1969, for vandalism at Chicago's Days of Rage street actions, in which demonstrators attacked police, whom they dubbed "pigs," and smashed store windows. It almost seemed a presage of Antifa.

The 1970s Weather Underground attacks continued. At around 1:00 a.m. on January 29, 1975, a bomb exploded in a men's room on the third floor of the State Department, in Foggy Bottom, DC. The bomb damaged some twenty offices. With the building mostly empty, there were no casualties. The group claiming responsibility denounced the Department's Agency for International Development for funding the anti-Communist South Vietnamese government. During this period other bombings took place in New York, including one at a police station.

In reaction, federal and local authorities cracked down hard on the Weather Underground and arrested many of its leaders.

However, those collared got a big break, one that stemmed back to 1971. A group called the Citizens' Commission to Investigate the FBI had broken into an FBI office in Pennsylvania. It made off with documents exposing the Agency's COINTELPRO program.

The agents in COINTELPRO employed break-ins, wiretaps, and other surveillance to keep track of and harass suspected subversives in groups such as SDS, the Weathermen, and the Black Liberation Army, a more violent offshoot of the Black Panthers. But it also went after mainstream organizations and individuals, including civil rights groups, labor unions, and the Rev. Martin Luther King Jr. The program partly inspired the Watergate break-in. (See the chapter on that scandal.)

After examining the document trove of the Citizens' Commission, the Supreme Court declared unconstitutional such government surveillance conducted without a court order. Much of the evidence against the Weather Underground detainees was thrown out. Prosecutors dropped most of the serious charges, and most of the radical leaders ended up with light sentences. A chastened FBI Director Hoover shut down COINTELPRO.

WOMEN OF THE UNDERGROUND

Remarkably, the people who helped plan and execute the 1970s bombings were closely linked to those who attacked the Capitol Building and Navy Yard in the 1980s. Indeed, they were associated with some of the most bizarre and violent incidents of an era of turmoil, which included a bomber without hands and a murderous armored-car robbery.

As remarkably, the group responsible for the latter bombings was largely made up of women: radical femmes who formed the May 19th Communist Organization. According to author William Rosenau, its ten or so leaders formed America's first female-dominated terrorist group.

A number of these women were eventually arrested for the 1983 Capitol Building attack and other bombings. They included: Judith Alice Clark; Susan Lisa Rosenberg; Marilyn Buck; Linda Sue Evans; Elizabeth

Anna Duke; Laura Whitehorn; and Kathy Boudin, the coauthor of the extremist manifesto.

A Bombing Gone Awry

Accidental explosions are an occupational hazard for bombers. Kathy Boudin found this out in a notorious incident in Greenwich Village, on March 6, 1970.

At a townhouse near Washington Square, five Weather Underground members were making explosives. Their goal was to blow up a military post in New Jersey, and a library at New York's Columbia University. Ex-SDS and Weatherman leader Mark Rudd recalled the "comrades were building pipe bombs packed with dynamite and nails, destined for a dance of non-commissioned officers and their dates at Fort Dix, New Jersey that night."

But one of the devices went off mistakenly. Three of the bomb makers were killed. The explosion caved in much of the building.

A survivor was Boudin. At the time of the detonation, she was taking a shower. Naked, Boudin rushed away from the ruins of the house, and disappeared. She would spend the next decade in Mexico, California, and Massachusetts, where she did menial labor such as picking grapes and cleaning houses. She stayed in contact with the other extremists and helped pen "Prairie Fire."

After the Washington Square disaster, the Weather Underground decided to explode their bombs very late at night, after everyone had left a building. The aim was "to send a message," without injuring people if possible. The group's later iteration followed that rule.

In 1975, the Vietnam War ended, and by the late 1970s the antiwar movements it fueled had fizzled out. Most ardent protestors made their peace with society and pursued normal lives. A few hardened radicals stayed underground, however, and engaged in violent, covert acts. Some linked up to another radical group, the John Brown Anti-Klan Committee.

Hooking Up with the Mad Bomber

In the late 1970s, several women who would be in on the 1983 Senate bomb plot aided one of the most blood-soaked terrorists in American history: Willie "No Hands" Morales.

One of his enablers was Marilyn Jean Buck, born in 1947, the fine-featured daughter of an Episcopal Church cleric. Marilyn attended college at a hotbed of 1960s radicalism, the University of California at Berkeley, as well as at her hometown University of Texas at Austin, where she joined SDS. She later linked up with the Black Liberation Army, as its lone Caucasian. In 1977, she escaped prison authorities while serving a sentence for firearms violations and went underground.

The East Harlem–bred Morales was the chief bombmaker for FALN, a pro–Puerto Rican independence group. FALN stands for Fuerzas Armadas de Liberación Nacional Puertorriqueña. In 1974-75, FALN staged bombings in Washington, Chicago, and in Manhattan—on Wall Street, Rockefeller Center, and Park Avenue. In the most notorious attack, its operatives set off a ten-pound bomb in New York's Revolutionary War-era Fraunces Tavern, killing four business executives.

But disaster struck the twenty-eight-year-old Morales one evening in July 1978, as he worked on a time bomb in his apartment in Queens, New York. His detonator was a watch, and it seems he mistakenly set the minute hand instead of the hour hand. As a result, as he was working on the bomb, it went off. The explosion shattered his jaw, gouged out an eye, and blew off his lips, as well as nine of his ten fingers. Thus his resulting nickname, "No Hands." As he waited for emergency personnel to arrive, Morales turned on his stove, hoping a gas explosion would kill any arriving police.

Sentenced to ninety-nine years in prison, the maimed bomber was moved for medical reasons to Manhattan's Bellevue Hospital. On May 21, 1979, Morales manipulated wire cutters with the stumps of his hands and sliced through the mesh of his third-floor cell window. He lowered himself out of the window with a rope fashioned from elastic bandages. The makeshift cord snapped, and he plummeted forty feet to the ground, smashing off an air-conditioner along the way. On the ground, he was met by a gang of over two dozen enablers, including members of FALN, the Black Liberation Army—and the May 19th group. They placed him into a cherry picker, yes, a cherry picker, for his escape. Directing him to a safe house in New Jersey was Marilyn Buck.

WILLIAM "GUILLERMO" MORALES

Unlawful Flight to Avoid Prosecution - Escape

DESCRIPTION

Aliases: Willie Morales, Guillermo Morales

Date(s) of Birth Used: February 7, 1950   **Place of Birth:** New York, New York

Hair: Gray   **Eyes:** Brown

Height: 5'10"   **Weight:** 170 pounds

Sex: Male   **Race:** White (Hispanic)

Occupation: Morales has worked as an airline reservation agent, assistant teacher, laboratory technician, lifeguard, and photographer.   **Nationality:** American

Scars and Marks: Morales has scars on the right side of his chin and over both eyebrows. He has no fingers on either hand and may wear prosthetics. The remaining portion of his hands are severely scarred. Morales has minimal vision in his left eye.   **NCIC:** W159237450

REWARD

The FBI is offering a reward of up to $100,000 for information leading to the arrest of William "Guillermo" Morales.

REMARKS

Morales speaks both English and Spanish. He is known to wear glasses and may have a beard. Although he grew up in New York, Morales is thought to have lived in Cuba since June of 1988.

CAUTION

William "Guillermo" Morales was an explosives expert/bomb maker for the FALN (Fuerzas Armadas Liberacion Nacional), an extremist organization advocating for Puerto Rican independence through acts of violence. The group, active in the 1970s and early 1980s, is credited with committing more than 100 bombings that caused several deaths, multiple injuries, and millions of dollars in damage.

On July 12, 1978, Morales was working on a bomb at a house in East Elmhurst, New York, when it exploded prematurely. Morales was severely injured, taken to a hospital, and arrested. Due to his injuries, Morales was held at the Bellevue Hospital prison ward in New York City until his potential transfer to federal prison. Morales escaped from Bellevue Hospital and fled to Mexico, where he was captured in May of 1983. He was imprisoned in Mexico, but eventually handed over to Cuban authorities and is believed to still be in that country.

A 1980s-era, mostly female terror group had links to the notorious 1970s bomber Willie "No Hands" Morales, as well as to the Senate bombing of 1971.

No Hands made his way to Mexico. There he was in a shootout in which two of his colleagues and a policeman were killed. After just five years in a Mexican prison, he was released. He made his way to Cuba, where Fidel Castro offered him sanctuary. As of 2021, he still resided in Havana, and was still on the FBI's Most Wanted List.

A Murderous Heist

In 1979, the year after No Hands almost blew himself to death, the radical women put out their own manifesto, "The Principles of Unity of the May 19th Communist Organization." They pledged alliance to Marxist-Leninism, and to their own brand of it, one that highlighted race and sex. The document foresaw the racial rhetoric of a future time, as it rejected "white-skin privilege," stating: "We, white women, say NO to amerika where white is a badge of acceptance of daily murder." (The radicals of the time spelled America with a "k" to give it a seemingly German-Nazi twist.) It was almost a presage of Black Lives Matter.

The most violent crime in which May 19 members took part was the 1981 Brinks armored car robbery, in Nanuet, New York. Involved in the murderous theft were Marilyn Buck, Kathy Boudin, and Judith Clark. Also conspiring in the plot were Elizabeth Duke and Susan Lisa Rosenberg.

Rosenberg, born in New York in 1955, was the daughter of a dentist and a theater promoter. By age twelve, she was marching in civil rights protests. By fourteen, she was a member of a high-school SDS club. The slender young woman sported an Afro, and in 1976 traveled to Cuba with the pro-Castro Venceremos ("We Shall Conquer") Brigade of like-minded Americans. Back in New York, she worked as a drug counselor at Lincoln Hospital in the South Bronx. There she came under the wing of Mutulu "Doc" Shakur, the former Jeral Wayne Williams. Linked to the Black Panthers, and their Latino brethren the Young Lords, Shakur was involved with the Republic of New Africa group. It aimed to set up a black homeland in the long-ago slave states of the Deep South.

If the name Shakur sounds familiar, it's because Mutulu was the stepdad of rap superstar and convicted felon Tupac Shakur. Tupac, after selling millions of recordings, and convicted of multiple assault charges, was shot to death in 1996.

Mutulu Shakur was the mastermind of the Brinks heist, conducted by his African-American gang. Known as "The Family," it was allied with the Black Liberation Army. His group, a mix of gangsters and extremists, employed educated, innocuous-seeming Caucasian women. They were given such tasks as renting safe houses, making fake IDs, and transporting wanted criminals and illicit goods. One such accomplice was the blue-eyed Duke, born in a small Texas town in 1940. In college, she'd been a sorority sister with a beehive hairdo.

Although the Brinks robbers made off with $1.6 million, the armored-car caper degenerated into an orgy of blood.

Outside a mall where Brinks guards were carrying bags of cash to their armored car, the robbers struck. Alighting from their Chevy van, and wielding shotguns and an M-16, they gunned to death one guard and wounded two others, including forty-eight-year-old Joseph Trombino. (Incredibly, Trombino, "the world's unluckiest man," would recover from his wounds and then, as a Brinks guard, survive the initial 1993 attack on the World Trade Towers, then die there during the September 11, 2001 attacks.)

The thieves transferred their loot and themselves into Judith Clark's Honda and into Boudin's rented U-Haul truck. The latter had joined the caper as a driver after leaving her two-month-old son Chesa with a babysitter.

The robbers and their accomplices took off as cops throughout the county scrambled to intercept. Four New Jersey policemen pulled the truck and the Honda over at a thruway entrance. Boudin talked with the police, who were confused at finding a white woman at the wheel, when they had been alerted the robbery was by black men. As she tried to allay their suspicions, six heavily armed gang members, guns blazing, stormed out of the truck. They killed two of the cops, one of them execution-style, and wounded another. Some got into the Honda and roared away. Boudin fled on foot, and a corrections officer who happened by detained her. (Boudin was tried, pleaded guilty, and got a twenty-year prison sentence.)

Marilyn Buck, another getaway driver, panicked when she encountered police. She mistakenly shot herself in the knee with a pistol. Still, she managed to escape, and a thirty-five-year-old doctor, Alan Berkman, treated her wound at a terrorist safe house. (The radical Berkman may have helped "No Hands" Morales in his escape.) Authorities discovered an apartment Buck had rented that contained explosive materials and firearms.

Clark, armed with a 9mm pistol, drove the Honda away at high speed, crashed it, and was nabbed. Clark was sentenced to seventy-five years in jail, which ended a long stretch of radicalism. From an early age, Clark had rebelled against her communist parents—as too moderate. In 1950, her father moved their family to the Soviet Union, where he worked as a reporter for the US-based communist newspaper the *Daily Worker*. The parents returned to America after three years, soured on Stalinism and, later, on Soviet domination of Eastern Europe. They moved on to become highly accomplished professionals. The mother in effect invented the political "exit poll" for the Daniel Yankelovich firm, while her father helped found the socialist, yet anti-Castro, magazine *Dissent*.

Their daughter went in the other direction. She remembered, "I would be the 'keeper of the flame'." Early on, her path paralleled the other radicals. At age fifteen, Clark walked in a march to end segregation. In 1969 at the University of Chicago, she joined SDS. She helped take over administrators' offices during an antiwar protest and was kicked out of the school. Unrepentant, the five-foot, three-inches tall Clark took part in the "Days of Rage" clash with Chicago police.

Following a brief jail term, Clark joined WITCH, the Women's International Terrorist Conspiracy from Hell. In the late 1960s, she and her sister WITCHes literarily put the hex on such symbols of capitalism and consumerism as the New York Stock Exchange.

After the Brinks debacle, the remaining members of May 19th stayed deep underground, only to emerge two years later with the Capitol Building and other capital city bombings.

Investigations, Arrests, and Foiled Plans

After the later bombings, a nationwide "womanhunt" led to the arrest of the remnants of May 19th. In November 1984, New Jersey police found Rosenberg and a male May 19th member loading high explosives into a U-Haul trailer from a storage space. Inside it were shotguns, rifles, detonators, and hundreds of pounds of explosives. The following spring, the FBI nabbed May 19th's Laura Whitehorn at a Baltimore apartment complex. In Whitehorn's lodging, agents found boxes of surveillance photographs and detailed notes of the Old Executive Office Building, which is the locale of the National Security Council next to the White House, as well as the US Naval Academy.

The FBI tracked Buck out of Baltimore; she led them to Linda Sue Evans. Born in 1947, Evans had been a student demonstrator at Michigan State University. She joined SDS at age twenty, and in 1969 traveled with other anti–Vietnam War leaders to Hanoi, the capital of North Vietnam. There, as part of a propaganda campaign, she accepted the release of three US prisoners of war. At one point she embraced a Viet Cong antiaircraft gun while wishing that "an American plane would come over." Back in the States, she was part of the Days of Rage. Authorities arrested both Evans and Buck; both had loaded pistols on them. Duke and Berkman were hauled in a few days later in Pennsylvania.

The detentions may have come just in time, for May 19th had shifted tactics. It was planning attacks aimed at killing people, as well as damaging high-profile buildings. Police officers and ranking national security officials, including former Nixon secretary of state Henry Kissinger, were among those considered for assassination. As Rosenberg later wrote in a poem: "our dreams will be the shell casings/that pierce the enemy. . . ."

Convictions and Pardons

Following her arrest in 1985, Duke eluded authorities after jumping bail that had been bonded by two of her family members. As of 2021, she was believed to be still on the lam with another May 19th member, Donna Joan Borup. The two women have been referred to as a real-life "Thelma and Louise."

In 1988, the federal government indicted members of May 19th for the Capitol Building, Navy Yard, and Fort McNair bombings. They included Buck, Duke, Evans, Rosenberg, Whitehorn, and Berkman.

In 1990, at the E. Barrett Prettyman Federal Courthouse, Evans was sentenced to five years in prison on top of a previous sentence of thirty-five years for illegal gun purchases. The judge of the Federal District

Court for the case was Harold H. Greene, who'd succeeded Judge John Sirica of Watergate fame, and who'd presided over the 1979 Hanafi terrorist attack on DC's City Hall.

Whitehorn got a twenty-year prison sentence. Paroled in 1999, she remained unrepentant, and took to lecturing at colleges. "I don't really even care that much," she stated, "whether people think I'm a terrorist or not."

In January 2001, as he was leaving office, President Bill Clinton, with controversy, pardoned Evans and Rosenberg. They had both served sixteen years of their forty- and fifty-eight-year sentences, respectively.

Boudin was paroled in 2003. While she was in prison, her son Chesa Boudin, the toddler she left off before the Brinks robbery, was raised by Bill Ayers and Bernadine Dohrn, the coauthors of the "Prairie Fire" manifesto. In 2020, Chesa Boudin was elected the attorney general of San Francisco.

Buck received long prison sentences from both her participation in the 1980s Washington bombings and the Brinks robbery. She died of cancer in 2010. Clark, formerly of WITCH, was paroled in 2019, after New York governor Andrew Cuomo had commuted part of her sentence three years before.

The violent femmes had run their violent course. Their 1983 bombing of the Senate makes up—with the related 1971 bombing, and the 1915 bombing by Eric Muenter—the three such explosive events in the long history of the Capitol.

CHAPTER THIRTY

Panic and the Fourth Plane: September 11th in the Capitol Building

9/11 Anniversary Tree, south grounds of the Capitol Building

(MUCH OF THIS CHAPTER IS DERIVED FROM THE BOOK, *THE ONLY PLANE in the Sky: An Oral History of 9/11*, by Garrett M. Graff.)

The weather that morning was exhilarating: 70 degrees, with clear, sparkling late-summer skies of "cobalt blue."

THE INITIAL ATTACK, AND A TERRORIST SYMPATHIZER

For many of the five thousand legislators, staffers, and administrative employees arriving, or already working in and around the Capitol Building, the mood soon turned to mild concern. Many of the offices had televisions, and many of the TVs were tuned to breaking news reports. A plane had flown into one of the World Trade Center towers in New York City at 8:46 a.m. The assumption was it was a small private airplane.

But at least one congressman, a former US Marines pilot, and a famous former astronaut, was less sanguine.

"Did you see that?" said Ohio Democrat Sen. John Glenn to the Senate majority leader, Democrat Tom Daschle of South Dakota. "A 'pilot' flew into the World Trade Center. Pilots don't fly into buildings. That wasn't a pilot."

In the top-floor meeting room of the House Intelligence Committee, Republican Rep. Porter Goss and Democrat Sen. Bob Graham, both of

Florida, were having breakfast with Lt. Gen. Mahmud Ahmed, the thirty-six-year-old director of Pakistan's intelligence agency, the ISI.

The two congressmen had met with Ahmed in Pakistan the week before. They were dismayed at his public support for Taliban leader mullah Mohammed Omar, according to author Garrett Graff. The Taliban were providing sanctuary for Osama bin Laden, the al-Qaeda terrorist leader behind the horrific 1998 attacks on the US embassies in Kenya and Tanzania, which killed 224 and wounded over four thousand. Goss and Graham had invited Ahmed to Washington for further consultations.

THE SECOND AND THIRD STRIKES

As they talked and sipped coffee, a staff member informed Goss that a second plane, a jetliner, had smashed into the second tower.

"Ahmed turned absolutely ashen," Goss recalled.

Along with the shock of learning the news, of an evident terror attack, and an instinctual dread that the Capitol Building in which he was sitting might be the target of the next plane to strike, Ahmed had another fear. Of being exposed for his complicity in it all.

As ISI chief, he'd been quietly supporting al-Qaeda in Afghanistan. More to the point, he'd personally urged terrorists to wire $100,000 to the terrorist cell in Hamburg, Germany, led by Mohammed Atta. Atta was the pilot of the first hijacked plane that struck the World Trade Center.

Minutes before, the House sergeant-at-arms, Wilson "Bill" Livingood, was in the office of the House Speaker, Republican Rep. Dennis Hastert of Illinois. Livingood was briefing the Speaker about the first plane to hit the Towers. The television was on in the room. It wasn't thought to be a big deal, remembered Hastert's press secretary, John Feehery.

Then those in the meeting saw the video of a second aircraft hitting the second tower. "Everybody was numb," recalled Tish Schwartz, a clerk for the House Judiciary Committee. "Oh my God," she thought, "what's going on?"

Around the same time, one of the Speaker's security detail looked out the office window to across the Potomac. "Look!" he shouted. He'd spotted "the column of smoke rising in the distance from the Pentagon," recalled Brian Gunderson, chief of staff for the majority leader, Republican Richard Armey of Texas. The Speaker's meeting broke up.

Hastert tried to contact Vice President Richard B. Cheney at the White House. Throughout the day, with President George W. Bush aboard Air Force One—"the only plane in the sky"—Cheney was in charge of the federal government's response to the attacks. The Speaker kept trying to call Cheney on a secure phone but couldn't get through. Then he saw the light flashing on his regular office phone, and figured it was Cheney reaching him. Hastert remembered picking it up, and hearing the voice of a man shouting, "What are you guys doing up there on Capitol Hill . . . taxes are too high . . . [there's] pollution all over the country!! . . ." It was an angry constituent, unaware of the attacks.

At about 9:45 a.m., Hastert was looking out his window toward the Pentagon when Representative Goss, fresh from his meeting with Ahmed, rushed in. They agreed the Capitol Building had to be evacuated. But first Hastert wanted to quickly convene, then close, the House session slated to open at 10:00 a.m., with a short prayer for deliverance.

THE RUSH TO THE EXITS

When Goss and Hastert went onto the floor of the House, recalled Goss, "I turned around to say something to the Speaker," but the Speaker had disappeared. Moments before, Hastert, a stocky man, felt himself whisked through the air. Two security personnel had each taken one of his arms and carried him hurriedly out of the building. Hastert blurted, "What's going on?"

"We think there's a fourth plane," one of the men answered, "and we think it's headed for the Capitol."

In a corridor, a House clerk, Eve Butler-Gee, saw "coming at me, was this entire wave of blue uniforms. It looked like thousands of them, all coming straight at me."

It was the Capitol Police, racing to every hall and room in the building, banging on doors, telling everyone to leave immediately. "Everybody out!" they yelled. "I was really scared," remembered House page Julia Rogers. "You could see the fear on their faces and in their eyes." At the same time, the building's fire alarm blared. As there was no formal evacuation plan, the police and the alarms had to do.

On the House floor, the lawmakers readied for the shortest session in House history. But first, the prayer. Guest chaplain Father Gerard "Gerry" Creedon of Arlington, Virginia, discarded his prepared entreaty on Mexican immigration. Goss ordered him: "I don't care what your prayer is, as long as it's brief." Creedon scribbled out a new invocation on the shoulder of the House chaplain, Rev. Dan Coughlin of Illinois. Then he hurriedly read it out. The session was declared closed. There followed a "mad scramble," recalled Sen. Daschle, the majority leader, with members, staff, and office workers "literally running out of the Capitol Building."

Outside, those fleeing saw a news crew scrambling to point its camera at the Capitol dome—to capture the moment, which some thought imminent, of a jetliner smashing into it. Others saw a slightly built female page struggling to push a big cart full of American flags, which members hand out to constituents. Recalled fellow page Tyler Rogers, "She was like, 'I can't leave these. I couldn't ditch' these."

Republican congressman Mike Ferguson of New Jersey rushed outside to near the Supreme Court Building. He and others paused in shock when they heard a loud roar. They feared a bomb had gone off nearby. Then they broke into a run. Other piercing sounds were heard later. They turned out to be the sonic booms of fighter planes scrambled to ward off, or shoot down, unauthorized aircraft approaching the capital.

After their hasty retreat, few members knew where to go or what to do. Some tried their cellphones, but the wireless connections were overloaded. Some had working Blackberry phones, but in their haste had left them in their offices.

Many headed over to the Capitol Police building, blocks away at 119 D Street N.E. "The police pulled down the shades of the window," recalled Daschle, "which I thought was weird." Legislators waited in a line for a landline phone to call family members and aides. Disputes broke out on whether it was safe, even at a police station, to keep so many congressmen in one place. They finally agreed to head out to wherever they thought right.

Staff members and administrators, as they ran out of the Capitol, were told to put a lot of distance between themselves and their workplace. Some went running far down the National Mall. Several joked sardonically that, if explosions went off around them, they could jump into the Reflecting Pool for safety. Adding to the angst were false reports the State Department had been bombed.

HEROIC RESISTANCE
None yet realized that a band of heroes had quite possibly saved the Capitol Building and its employees. Some 166 miles to the northwest, the fourth hijacked airliner, United Flight 93, plunged into the earth at Shanksville, Pennsylvania, killing everyone on board. The passengers had learned from cellphone conversations with relatives about the attacks on the Trade Towers and the Pentagon. They realized with horror they were themselves on a suicide plane. Under the worst pressure imaginable, they debated what to do. After taking a vote, they decided to act.

Racing up the plane's aisle, they stormed the hijackers near the cockpit. They punched and pushed and wielded whatever makeshift weapons they could seize. According to the recovered flight recorder, recorded cell conversations, and the 9/11 Commission Report, they were likely on the verge of retaking the aircraft. The terrorists in the cockpit then decided to dive the jet into the ground.

NORAD, or the North American Aerospace Defense Command, was in charge of the fighter jets scrambled that day. NORAD later claimed its F-16 fighters were prepared to shoot down Flight 93 if it approached Washington. The 9/11 Report concluded this was unlikely.

Flight 93, after all, was only ten to twenty minutes flying time from the capital when it crashed. By the time NORAD was informed of the hijacking, it had between just six to sixteen minutes to execute a complex mission. Namely, get authorization for shooting down a civilian airliner, locate the position of the airliner, brief the pilots, and direct the pilots to the airliner's projected path.

Concluded the 9/11 Report: "We are sure that the nation owes a debt to the passengers of United 93. Their actions saved the lives of countless others and may have saved either the Capitol or the White House from destruction."

Based on interviews with captured planners of the September 11 attacks, the Capitol Building, not the Executive Mansion, was the likely target of Flight 93.

Designated Survivors

The rushed evacuation of Speaker Hastert was part of an emergency scheme called "continuity of leadership." Never before put into effect, it aimed to evacuate top leaders of Congress, especially those in the line of succession to be president, in the event the president or vice president were killed or incapacitated. As Speaker of the House, Hastert was second in the line of succession, the vice president being first. (In this context, it's interesting to note that Hastert had serious character issues. In 2016, he would be convicted of child molestation.)

Third in the line of succession is the longest-serving senator of the majority party, in this case Sen. Robert Byrd. (In this context, it's interesting to note Byrd had been an official of the Ku Klux Klan.) A complication on September 11 was Byrd was eighty-three years old and slow of foot. After the evacuation order, he was spotted limping to the exits. Further, he stopped to talk to reporters. Finally he was rushed outside.

For several hours, the Air Force's 1st Helicopter Squadron whisked away some leaders from the lawn on the west side of the Capitol. From that improvised helipad, protected by armored cars, they were flown to an "undisclosed location," a term that became famous.

Other leaders, for instance Hastert, were first taken to Andrews Air Force Base, Maryland, seven miles from the Capitol. After the two guards carried him from the House floor, recalled Hastert, "I was whisked down the elevator. The next thing I know, I'm in the back of a Suburban [SUV], headed to Andrews . . . this car was just going a hundred miles an hour. . . ."

The legislators were then flown to one of two locations. One was Mount Weather, an underground complex in Berryville, Virginia, sixty-five miles to the west. The second was Raven Rock, an emergency military operations center seventy-five miles to the north near Carroll Valley,

Pennsylvania. The underground complexes were built in the 1950s, during Cold War fears of nuclear attack, to allow the federal government to keep functioning in crises.

On their way to these facilities, the congressmen looked down on an eerily changed landscape, according to Graff. "We flew over Reagan National Airport," said Hastert, "and there's nothing moving on the tarmac," as every jetliner in the nation had been grounded. "I looked out the other side of the helicopter," the Speaker added, and "there were flames pouring out of the Pentagon building and blue-black smoke."

A Changed Capitol

Yet by the afternoon, the congressmen felt the danger to the Capitol Building had passed. Some were taking flack they had fled their posts in a time of danger. They thought they should go back, to express patriotism and defiance during an emergency.

On their return, they found a building transformed into an armed camp. Grim-looking men in dark uniforms and submachine guns prowled the grounds. Soon, ugly concrete blocks intended to block the vehicles of suicide bombers would appear at the Capitol, and in front of other federal institutions.

That evening, upwards of 150 legislators gathered on the east Capitol steps. Hastert and Daschle made brief remarks condemning the terrorists and calling for national unity. Then a lawmaker broke into "God Bless America," and the others joined in.

The following day, the State Department told General Ahmed that "you are either 100 percent with us or 100 percent against us." Ahmed promised cooperation, but on the same day he told the CIA that Taliban leader Mullah Omar was a man of peace.

The following month, under US pressure, Pakistan's president sacked Ahmed.

On May 2, 2011, a strike squad of Navy SEALs killed bin Laden, who'd been hiding for years in a compound in Abbottabad, Pakistan, within a thousand yards of Pakistan's main Military Academy.

On September 13, 2011, two days after the tenth anniversary of the attacks, a clutch of congressmen gathered on the south lawn of the

To mark the tenth anniversary of September 11, congressmen planted an oak tree on the southwest grounds of the Capitol. Valiant passengers aboard United Flight 93, flying over Pennsylvania, forced terrorist hijackers to crash their aircraft. The jetliner was probably en route to the Capitol Building.

Capitol. With ceremony, they planted a white oak tree, a symbol of strength and endurance, in the earth, in commemoration of the valiant passengers of United Flight 93, the band of Americans who put up the fiercest fight on that fateful day.

CHAPTER THIRTY-ONE

Continuity in Crisis: Another Wild Year Around Washington City

Albert Pike pedestal, 3rd and D Street, N.W., Judiciary Square

IT WAS A YEAR OF THOUSANDS OF PROTESTS, AND RIOTS IN OVER SEVenty cities, including the capital city. There, over an eight-month period, turmoil extended from Georgetown and the White House to the Capitol Building itself.

On June 19, 2020, protestors, or rioters, depending on one's view, gathered angrily around the statue of Albert Pike. Pike, who died in the District in 1891 at age eighty-one, was a leader of the Scottish Rite of freemasonry, part of the fraternal organization popularly known as the Masons. His pedestaled figure, dedicated with pomp before thousands in 1901, was just three blocks from the Capitol in Judiciary Square. And just one block east of the first "Lincoln Memorial," a less-known marble statue of the author of the Emancipation Proclamation, standing in front of architect George Hadfield's stately, original City Hall.

A PLACE OF PRIOR AND CURRENT DISPUTES

Judiciary Square has witnessed many events related to civil rights and liberties, and municipal mayhem. In 1835-36, abolitionist Reuben Crandall was tried there for possessing documents advocating abolition. The jury acquitted Crandall, thus striking a blow for freedom of speech. (See the chapter on the Snow Riot.) In 1848, Rep. Joshua Giddings had rushed to the nearby city jail to pledge legal help for the co-captains of the *Pearl* ship, who had tried to sail seventy-seven enslaved African Americans to freedom. In 1859, congressman and future Union general Daniel Sickles was tried at the old City Hall for killing DC District Attorney Philip Barton Key II, after he discovered Key was having an affair with his wife. And, after the Civil War, famed abolitionist and author Frederick Douglass kept an office a few blocks to the east.

Although relatively few had ever heard of the Pike statue, and fewer still visited it, by the 1990s some city officials were calling for its removal. (Conspiracy theorist Lyndon LaRouche led protests to cart the figure away, as LaRouche believed Pike had been both a Klansman and a Satanist.) More recently, the idea gained momentum as part of the movement to take down Confederate statues. During the Civil War, Pike had been for nine months a ranking rebel officer. Among the most prominent Pike critics was DC's longstanding, non-voting congresswoman, Eleanor Holmes Norton. (The eighty-three-year-old Norton had been

In 2020, a few blocks from the Capitol Building, rioters pulled down and set ablaze the statue of Albert Pike, Masonic leader, jurist, Confederate general, explorer, and defender of Native American rights.

tinged with scandal years before. In 1990, she paid almost $90,000 to the District government after not paying municipal income taxes, for eight consecutive years.)

On that warm June night in 2020, on the anniversary of the end of slavery in the United States, the enraged demonstrators placed a rope around the figure of Pike. They pulled hard at it, and harder, and it came toppling down. Next, they poured lighter fluid on the fallen figure, and set it ablaze. The statue was on National Park Service property, and the Service quickly carted away the remains, leaving a large vacant pedestal behind.

A MAN WITH A VARIED PAST

The iconoclasts who saw themselves striking a blow for the lives of the oppressed might have been surprised, and taken pause, at Albert Pike's background, which was marked by virtues as well as faults.

For instance, Pike was arguably one of the greatest defenders of the rights of Native Americans in American history.

And a lot more. Good things and bad. Pike was an explorer, poet, soldier, Masonic leader, reporter, and influential jurist.

He reached prominence in the 1830s for an astonishing, twelve-hundred-mile trek through the wild Taos region of what became New Mexico. Six-feet tall, weighing in at three hundred pounds, with a face covered by straggly dark hair, Albert Pike looked like the stereotype of a "mountain man" of the Old West. (He was unrelated to another, better-known western explorer, Zebulon Pike, for whom Pike's Peak is named.)

The recipient of a Harvard honorary degree, Pike was an author of well-known books of poetry, and also a member of the fraternal and professional organization the Odd Fellows, better known for its African-American chapters during the era of segregation.

In his later years, Pike was famous as the head of the Southern wing of a major, Scottish Rite branch of the Freemasons in the United States. (For centuries, due in part to their mysterious rituals, the Freemasons were accused of involvement in radical conspiracies.) In 1944, Pike's remains were transferred to its DC-based headquarters, the Persian-like

"House of the Temple" on 16th Street N.W. The grandiose, granite-and-marble-laden structure was the work of John Russell Pope, who also designed the National Archives, Constitution Hall, the Jefferson Memorial, and the National Gallery of Art.

An expert on the law, ancient and modern, Pike served as attorney for American Indians after possibly the worst single act done to them: the expulsion of the five "civilized tribes" of Cherokee, Chickasaw, and others from the Southeast United States to beyond the Mississippi. These were the Native American tribes the federal government, during the Andrew Jackson and Martin Van Buren Administrations, had forced out of the Southeastern United States to the Oklahoma Territory. Thousands perished along the way.

In the Mexican-American War, Pike commanded Arkansas volunteers as a captain with the US Army. When the Civil War erupted, Pike was zealous for secession. As part of it, he fought for and with the Indians, not in the courtroom, but on the battlefield. Many Native Americans leaned toward the South, for an obvious reason. The "blue belly" troops of the Union had for generations been in large measure responsible for pushing them off their ancestral lands. So they sided with a Confederacy that was at the same time denying the rights of enslaved African Americans. Yes, the Civil War has nuances to it, shades of gray, and blue.

As a brigadier general for the Confederacy, Pike commanded three cavalry regiments of Native American warriors. They won and lost battles. In their Arkansas campaigns, Pike's troops were accused of an ugly Indian tradition, of scalping their wounded opponents.

For someone tarred for his association with the Confederacy, Pike did not last long in his position. He was in active service for less than a year, and he tangled with Confederate bigwigs, who accused him of treason. The US government pardoned him one year after the war's conclusion.

Still, it's clear Pike was no Booker T. Washington when it came to ethnic tolerance. He stridently opposed abolition. He had joined—as did many future proponents of the Union and abolition—the nationalist Know-Nothing Party opposed to Irish- and German-Catholic immigrants.

Pike was a man, in sum, of many facets. Some historians view him as an intriguing character worthy of examination and debate, not deletion or cancellation. Moreover, the District of Columbia had called for the removal of his statue through a legal process, not through a violent, illegal act.

IRONIC ASSAULTS IN HISTORIC LOCALES

Far more tumult of this sort occurred throughout the capital's downtown during the 2020 Memorial Day Weekend. Memorial Day as a national holiday had been created through the efforts of Union army general John Logan, who is himself commemorated at the District's imposing Logan Circle. He sought a day of remembrance for the Union soldiers who'd fallen in the Civil War. The holiday had its origins in Decoration Day, which honored fallen soldiers, North and South.

The disturbances that weekend recalled the 1919 riots, when white soldiers attacked black civilians, who attacked back in return, and the horrific 1968 riots, of blacks in downtown neighborhoods, in the wake of Dr. Martin Luther King Jr.'s assassination. Over a dozen people were killed and over a thousand were wounded in the 1968 turmoil. Large sections of the city were devastated, and many neighborhoods did not recover until the twenty-first century. There was also the less destructive yet still unsettling Adams-Morgan riot involving Hispanics in 1991.

The most recent tumult, echoed around the country, was touched off by the death in police custody of an African-American man, George Floyd, in Minneapolis, Minnesota. An autopsy found that Floyd, who had been arrested in possession of several counterfeit $20 bills, had heart disease and his body contained methamphetamine and high levels of fentanyl. A video went wildly viral of a police officer detaining Floyd, who cried out about being choked, as the cop kept his knee on Floyd's neck for many minutes.

The incident fueled a longstanding debate, with many on one side angry over alleged police brutality, especially in poorer black neighborhoods. Another perspective stresses the causes of street crime and focuses on decades of ineffective welfare programs and public housing, the decline of two-parent households, failed public schools in the inner cities, as well as a lax, not overly stringent, approach to law enforcement. A related issue may be the relative lack of reporting on, and attention to, the far greater number of deaths and injuries in inner-city neighborhoods due to violent crimes unrelated to police actions.

On Memorial Day Weekend, in the wake of large-scale protests, major riots erupted in various cities, including Philadelphia, Los Angeles, and Washington. Violent turmoil would consume over 70 cities that year, leading to numerous deaths, and property damage well in excess of a billion dollars. Afterwards, murder rates soared nationwide.

One neighborhood in the District affected was Mt. Vernon Square, about a mile northwest of the Capitol. The intersection of L'Enfant's diagonal streets there, at 7th Street and K Street, N.W., long hosted a city marketplace. It was the Square where US Marines, led by longtime commandant Archibald Henderson, put down the race and religion riot of whites in 1857. The unrest was instigated by the Know-Nothings, who brought in a gang of thugs from Baltimore to attack citizens of Celtic and German descent lining up to vote on municipal Election Day. (See the chapter on the "Plug Uglies" riot.)

In 1903, the Scottish-American steel magnate and philanthropist, Andrew Carnegie, established a stately library at the Square for city residents. It was the District's first racially integrated place of learning. It now houses the headquarters and archives of one of the District's leading cultural resources, the Washington Historical Society. It frequently puts on exhibits of the African-American experience. In 2019, Apple spent $30 million to renovate the old Carnegie Library and to install one of its flagship stores.

Sadly, those rioting there on May 30 were unaware of the altruistic legacy of the place. Black vandals smashed the windows of the Apple emporium. Looters, some claiming to act against police malfeasance, stripped the place, carrying its fortune in merchandise off into the night.

Similar yet more widespread destruction played out in Georgetown, three miles down Pennsylvania Avenue from Capitol Hill. The neighborhood boasts icons of civil rights history in its historic core, along M Street and up Wisconsin Avenue. For example, the vicinity contained the workplace of Dr. Mary Edwards Walker. She was the first woman surgeon in the US Army, and the first woman to receive the Congressional Medal of Honor, for saving the lives of many wounded Union army soldiers. Across the street from her long-gone military hospital is the former home of Dr. James Fleet, one of the first African-American doctors. In the antebellum era, Fleet declined migration back to Liberia, the African nation established for "free men and women of color." Instead he decided to stay "in his own country," and thrived as a Georgetown entrepreneur. Just down M Street is the Old Stone House, owned by John Suter Jr. In his father's Georgetown waterfront tavern would gather President Washington, Secretary of State Jefferson, District planner Pierre L'Enfant, African-American astronomer Benjamin Banneker, and surveyor Andrew Ellicott. One of their aims: plan, survey, and map the new capital city.

Yet on May 31 and June 1, 2020 all the way from Rock Creek, on Georgetown's eastern edge, and up to Friendship Heights on upper Wisconsin Avenue near the Maryland border, local hooligans and criminals from out of town wreaked destruction. Dozens of shops were broken into and ransacked, including a popular Nike store, another Apple Store, and a pharmacy, its medical supplies pilfered during a pandemic. According to the *Washington Post*, authorities collared more than four hundred lawbreakers. Many were charged with robbery and rioting.

When the author visited Georgetown the day after, he found immigrant store owners and Latino workmen boarding up the windows of scores of enterprises, given their dismay over the city government's ability or willingness to protect them. Moreover, on the National Mall, curse-laden graffiti was found scrawled on the Lincoln Memorial, and on the National World War II Memorial—the latter a homage to the generation that vanquished the most racist regime in history, Nazi Germany, and its companion regime of ethnic atrocities, Imperial Japan.

An Angry Throng Breaches the Capitol: The Riot of 2021

NOTE: *This section was written soon after the events described and strove to reflect new information as it was reported.*

Both houses of Congress were in session that early afternoon of January 6, 2021, for the quadrennial, and almost always humdrum, task of certifying the results of the previous fall's presidential election. According to the official results, former vice president Joseph Robinette Biden Jr. had defeated President Donald John Trump, in the Electoral College by 306 to 232, as well as in the popular vote by 51 to 47 percent.

Informed of a Shocking Event

In the House chamber, eighty-year-old Democratic Speaker Nancy Pelosi, a seventeen-term congresswoman from San Francisco, presided from the Speaker's rostrum. Various congressmen and reporters lolled in the gallery above, watching the session.

In the Senate, sixty-one-year old Republican vice president Mike Pence presided. As part of the proceedings, a dozen Republican senators were planning to challenge the election results.

Suddenly, at 2:15 p.m., an official alerted Pelosi of a security breach in the Building. She left abruptly, giving her gavel to Rep. Jim McGovern of Massachusetts, and leaving a cellphone behind in her haste. Soon after, the session was suspended.

Republican Sen. James Lankford of Oklahoma was then speaking to the Senate. He paused, and an aide informed him that "protestors are in the building." To the sharp sound of a gavel, Republican Sen. Charles Grassley of Iowa intoned, "The Senate will stand in recess until the call of the Chair."

As onlookers checked their phones and wondered what was happening, officials whisked Pence and Pelosi to a "secure location."

Challenging an Election's Tallies

Several hours before, President Trump had begun addressing a crowd of tens of thousands of supporters, gathered outside the Ellipse south of the White House, in a "Stop the Steal" rally. Since the November 3 election, Trump and his supporters had alleged widespread voter fraud in the closely contested electoral "swing states," such as Georgia, Arizona, and Pennsylvania.

The president and his legal team, including former New York City mayor Rudy Giuliani, had alleged many voting "irregularities," including: failure to verify the identities of persons voting by mail and by absentee ballots; voting by non-citizens, the deceased, and out-of-state residents; inadequate monitoring of ballot counting; backdating of ballots; voter identification machines with weak accuracy settings; and statistically unusual jumps in voter tallies. Hundreds of witnesses presented affidavits swearing they'd seen electoral abuses. For several years, members of both parties had expressed concern about the reliability and growing use of electronic voting machines. Democrats dismissed the charges of fraud, particularly in regard to the widely employed Dominion Voting Systems. They asserted Biden's victory resulted from record-high voter turnout, particularly in the cities of the contested states.

Many of the disputes involved changes in voter laws in the states, enacted during the Covid-19 pandemic originating in China, to permit greater absentee and mail-in voting. Conservatives asserted the changes were illegal under Article II, Section 1 of the Constitution, which reserves election law changes to the state legislatures. However, on December 11, 2020, the Supreme Court rejected a lawsuit from Texas and eighteen other states to block the Electoral College results from four of the swing states.

Some of the president's advisors saw the congressional certification as their final chance of throwing the election back to the states, or to the House of Representatives. Trump had for weeks posted tweets calling for a massive turnout at the January 6 rally, in an apparent, last-ditch effort to pressure Congress. Oddly, he also put public pressure on his own vice president, Pence, to not certify the results, in his role as the president of the Senate. Before the rally, President Trump tweeted: "Mike Pence didn't have the courage to do what should have been done to protect our Country . . . giving States a chance to certify a corrected set of facts, not the fraudulent or inaccurate ones." Among many Republicans, libertarians, and others on the internet, accusations were rife the election had been stolen, and that civil strife threatened. Others thought, given the unlikelihood of Congress acting on the election results, Trump would have been wiser to "cut his losses" and focus on post-election Senate races in Georgia and on his own post-presidential role.

A Rally Peaceful, and a Riot Ugly

When the author bicycled through the host of demonstrators stretching up past the Washington Monument at the time of the president's speech, he found the mood typical of a "Trump rally": boisterous and partisan, but non-violent.

The speech, while mocking Democratic policies and boasting of administration accomplishments, stated in part: "All Vice President Pence has to do is send [the election] back to the states to recertify, and we become president . . . do nothing . . . then we are stuck with a president who lost the election by a lot. . . . We're just not going to let that happen. . . . We have come to demand that Congress . . . only count the electors who have been lawfully slated. I know that everyone here will soon be marching over to the Capitol building to peacefully and patriotically make your voices heard . . . we are going to try to give our Republicans the kind of pride and boldness that they need. . . ."

At the other end of the National Mall, a smaller but still substantial crowd of protestors, many with hats emblazoned with the Trump campaign slogan, "Make America Great Again" (MAGA), and brandishing American flags, gathered west of the Capitol Building's West Lawn, near the U.S. Grant and James Garfield statues. In front of them loomed the platforms and scaffolding for the presidential inauguration on January 20. To the surprise of some, despite the very large protest spilling onto the Mall, and the joint session of Congress for certifying the election, few Capitol Police or Metropolitan DC police were visible, and no National Guardsmen.

Around 1:00 p.m., about ten minutes before the end of the president's oration, numbers of men began breaking up the light-metal barricades near the Capitol. Fistfights among ruffians and policemen broke out, and the cops were overwhelmed. Some brawlers had come for a fight: They wore gas masks and helmets. Hundreds of demonstrators then surged trespassing onto the lawn next to the Capitol's façade. Shockingly, young men climbed atop the inauguration platforms, waving flags and shouting "U.S.A, U.S.A!" Many more followed them.

More police arrived, though some merely milled about, having gotten unclear or few instructions from their leadership. Evidently none used bullhorns to order the crowd to get off the grounds. Then the police fired tear gas into the trespassers, according to an eyewitness report in *The Federalist*. Some in the crowd were stunned and angered at this.

Pouring toward the grounds came another, larger mass, the thousands who walked down Pennsylvania and Constitution Avenues after Trump's speech. They streamed into and jammed up against the first crowd. At the same time, agitators near the grass screamed at people not to depart. "Forward!" several cried. "Do not retreat!" Various men wearing the insignia of right-wing groups were spotted.

Demonstrators rushed up the steps to the top of the Capitol's stately balustrade. Some, astonishingly, scaled its steep walls, or dangled from them. The police responded by firing more tear gas. Members of the crowd, ever larger, stayed put, or surged forward even more. A line of about dozen young men with helmets and camouflage attire was spied marching military-style toward the entrance to the Rotunda. Some people, some helmeted, began smashing open the Capitol Building's doorways. Policemen were battered with poles and fists, even as they were forbidden to use greater force, and lacked basic riot gear like helmets.

The Building Breached

Some of the police stood by; incredibly, some seemed to wave interlopers into the Building. Soon swarms of people were inside. It was the first time across 221 years of the Capitol's eventful history that a non-military horde had broken in. People shouted: "Who's House? Our House!" and "Stop the Steal!," or "Be respectful! or "Treason!" Demonstrators pushed back the police trying to contain them; cops pepper-sprayed them in return. Roughly eight hundred people illicitly entered the Building.

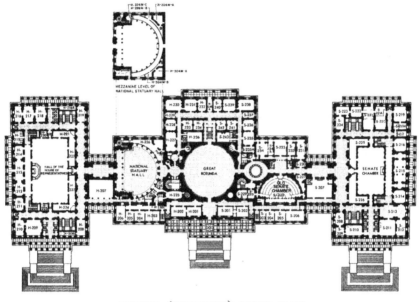

SECOND (PRINCIPAL) FLOOR PLAN

scale: ꜱ ꜱꜱ ꜱꜱ ꜱꜱ ꜱꜱ Feet
AS OF JUNE, 1997 NORTH ➜

In early 2021, in the twenty-second decade of its eventful existence, rioters broke into the Capitol Building's Rotunda, Statuary Hall, and House and Senate chambers, with a protestor shot to death and many police injured.

The behavior of the lawbreakers varied. One group treated its intrusion almost as a frat party, lolling about the hallowed Statuary Hall and the Rotunda, taking selfies or photos of the world-famous artwork, and were later largely charged with trespassing. Another group was combative, and broke into the offices of congressmen, including that of Majority Leader Steny Hoyer of Maryland and the House Speaker. They pushed documents off of desks onto carpets, even pilfered personal items. Some congressmen barricaded the doors to their offices and hid inside with staff.

Some intruders were very violent, and wielded bats and pipes. A group dragged a police officer down some stairs and beat him with a flagpole.

Surreally, a retired firefighter tossed a fire extinguisher at a clutch of police. According to a *Politico* photographer, police pepper-sprayed back a dozen rioters who'd pushed through an entranceway; they fell back down upon each other in a heap.

Many defenders of the Building rose to the occasion. One canny cop led rioters on a wild goose chase away from a Senate entrance. Employees from the Architect of the Capitol rushed to the roof to reverse the Building's airflow, aiding the removal of destructive chemical odors from tear gas and bear spray. Such employees recalled the intrepid clerks who spirited away valuable items from the Capitol prior to its destruction by the British in 1814.

The mayhem peaked at the entrance to the Speaker's Lobby, a hallway with access to the House. There, screaming rioters smashed the door's glass and wood. A few Capitol Police stood by without taking action. Then a tactical unit of four heavily armed police stepped warily up an adjacent stairwell. As they walked onto the landing, a shot rang out from the other side of the door. One of the intruders, thirty-five-year-old Air Force veteran Ashli Babbitt, was fatally shot by a policeman.

The House and Senate Besieged

In the congressional chambers, meantime, concern turned to fear and then to near panic. The scent of tear gas that police deployed in the Rotunda wafted in. In the House, staffers rushed to distribute gas masks to the hundred or so members, aides, and reporters trapped inside. According to *Politico*, Democrat Rep. Steve Cohen of Tennessee shouted to the Republicans, "Call Trump and tell him to call this off." A GOP lawmaker, referring to an issue stemming from the 2020 disorders, yelled back something like, "I bet you liberals are glad now you didn't defund the police." Officers rushed to safety the House Majority Leader, and seventy-nine-year-old House Majority Whip James Clyburn of South Carolina.

Rioters attempted to break into the House. Security men improvised by pushing a credenza across the doorway, then crouched behind it with pistols drawn. Cops helped members clamber over seats and railings to the exits. Police tersely exchanged words about which exit to take, for fear violent protestors might be outside.

In the Senate chamber, staffers locked the entrances. Lawmakers could hear the sound of the rioters in the halls outside. According to CBS, Minnesota Senator Amy Klobuchar cried out there had been gunfire in the Building. Eventually all congressmen were ushered to a "secure location."

But after their departure, interlopers broke into both houses of Congress, including some odd characters. In the Senate, an Arizona man bizarrely outfitted in buffalo horns and furs, and grasping a six-foot spear, briefly occupied the vice president's chair. Convinced he was an outer space alien, the disturbed fellow, a peyote user, left a note for Pence that read, "justice is coming." An Idahoan named Colt, after dangling from the balcony, also spent some time in Pence's seat. Intruders took pictures of themselves and their surroundings.

In the House, invaders pranced about the floor. A man in a ski cap made off with the Speaker's lectern, and later hoisted up his ill-gotten gain to his admirers. Rioters, some sporting military-style vests, also pushed their way into the Capitol Building from its east side, from the Portico where Lincoln had once appealed to "the better angels of our nature."

After a few hours, masses of police from various jurisdictions cleared the Building. A toll was compiled. Forty-two-year-old Capitol policeman Brian Sicknick was bear-sprayed by rioters, and died from heart disease the next day. Along with Babbitt, at least three demonstrators perished: two from heart disease (by natural causes), and another, who'd been trampled on at the riot, from an amphetamine overdose, according to DC's chief medical examiner. Over seventy Capitol Police and some sixty-five Metropolitan police were injured. In the days following the riot, a DC policeman and a Capitol policeman, the latter the son of a Senate sergeant-at-arms, committed suicide. Within four months of the disturbance, authorities had arrested about 440 alleged offenders, and charged over 400 (jailing many without trial). Federal officials indicted many members of the rightist Proud Boys group. (A Black Lives Matter activist was among those collared inside the Building.)

It could have been much, much worse. The more violent might have encountered members of Congress, with dire consequences. Fortunately, none of those who were arrested had firearms. The streams of intruders pacing up and down hallways and stairways could have stampeded, crushing many underfoot. On the night before the protest, and within several blocks of the Capitol, an unidentified person placed pipe bombs outside the Republican and Democratic National Committee offices. The twelve-inch-long explosives, which were discovered during the riot, were packed with gunpowder and flecks of metal.

Anarchists of Irony

In the Capitol's most honored places, the irony of the lawless stood out. At National Statuary Hall, instead of taking photos, the intruders might have reflected on the dangers of discord, and the virtues of comity. About them were figures of the president and vice president of the doomed

Confederacy, Virginia's Jefferson Davis and Georgia's Alexander Hamilton Stephens, as well as Missouri senator Thomas Hart Benton, who was nearly shot in the Senate during angry debates over the Compromise of 1850, a legislative attempt to stave off civil war. (See the chapter on Lincoln's lodging.) And Massachusetts senator Daniel Webster, famous in the antebellum era for his plea of, "Liberty and Union, now and forever, one and inseparable!"

The imposing Statuary Hall, formerly the meeting place of the House of Representatives, was penetrated by the rioters. It displays statues of noted historical figures from all the states.

And a symbol of reconciliation, in Alabama's Joseph Wheeler. The former Confederate general joined other former rebels in the Federal Army during the Spanish-American War. "Fighting Joe" was in charge of troops at Kettle Hill and San Juan Hill, where Theodore Roosevelt, with his western regiment of cowboys, Ivy Leaguers, and American Indians, marched into military glory. Attaining renown there as well was an all-black, all-American unit, the Buffalo Soldiers. It's said the elderly ex-Confederate, on seeing the Buffalo Soldiers charge up the rugged terrain, absentmindedly cried out, "Give them Yankees hell, boys, give 'em hell!"

In the grand Rotunda fashioned by Union general Montgomery Meigs, the intruders might have heeded exemplars of good conduct, and adherence to constitutional norms. Symbolized by Jonathan Trumbull's grand canvas of George Washington, depicted resigning his Army commission after the Revolution, signifying the primacy of civilian over military or arbitrary rule. Elsewhere about the Capitol were statues of Presidents Lincoln, Garfield, Reagan, and Jackson, who were either slain, wounded, or almost shot by assassins intent on ripping apart the body politic. The spirits of these figures, on witnessing the Capitol chaos, may have rolled in their graves.

An Aftermath of Another Impeachment

In the early hours of the morning following the riot, Congress was back in session for the vote certification. Six Republican senators who were planning to vote No switched their vote to Yes; the final tally was ninety-three to six. Biden was officially president-elect, the last obstacle cleared for his inauguration.

The House and its Speaker reacted immediately and angrily to the turmoil, placing the blame on President Trump. In addition, large social media platforms such as Twitter and Facebook suspended the accounts of the chief executive and other conservative figures. This led to concern about the impact of such bans on freedom of speech.

Speaker Pelosi stated: "We know that the president of the United States incited this insurrection, this armed rebellion, against our country." Republican House minority leader Kevin McCarthy of California responded: "A vote to impeach would further divide this nation...will further fan the flames, the partisan division."

Unlike the impeachments of Presidents Bill Clinton in 1998 and Andrew Johnson in 1868, the House held no hearings or investigations before its vote. On January 13, it acted to impeach, by a vote of 232 to 197, with ten Republicans joining all the Democrats.

A Senate trial followed, beginning on February 9, based on charges the former President had tried to block certification of the election results and incited the breach of the Capitol. Congressional Democrats asserted Trump had triggered an insurrection, while Trump termed the trial "the greatest witch hunt," and some Republicans doubted the constitutionality of trying someone already out of office.

The trial concluded after five days of presentations from the House impeachment managers, Trump's attorneys, and questions from senators. (In contrast, Johnson's trial lasted 10 weeks, and Clinton's five weeks.) The Senate voted against Trump, mostly along party lines, 57-43, short of the two-thirds majority required for a conviction.

It was the House's second impeachment of Trump, the first occurring thirteen months before. At issue then was a July 2020 phone call of President Trump's with Ukraine president Volodymyr Zelensky. In the conversation, Trump requested Zelensky cooperate with Giuliani and with his attorney general William Barr to look into the firing of a Ukrainian prosecutor who'd been investigating the Ukrainian energy firm Burisma. Hunter Biden, the son of then former Vice President Biden, had held a lucrative position with the company while his father, as vice president, was in charge of US anti-corruption policy on Ukraine. Republicans cried corruption, while Democrats shouted quid pro quo. Some wondered whether a phone conversation merited impeachment. Nonetheless, in December 2019, the House impeached Trump along party lines. In March 2020, the Senate voted almost entirely along party lines, fifty-one to forty-nine, to acquit.

The bitter back-and-forth between the president and Democrats dated back to the 2016 campaign, and the creation of a Russian dossier, filled with unfounded, salacious gossip about Trump. It was funded by ranking members of the Democratic Party and the presidential campaign of Hillary Clinton, the former first lady, ex–New York senator, and former secretary of state for President Obama. It led to a lengthy FBI inquiry, and an investigation by Special Prosecutor Robert Mueller, with no charges filed against Trump.

Letting One's Guard Down

Some placed the blame for the Capitol riot not on the chief executive, but on the rioters and instigators among the crowd—and on the Capitol's security. Soon the chief of the Capitol Police resigned, as did the House and Senate sergeants-at-arms, who are in charge of security at the congressional chambers. Despite a twenty-three-hundred-member force and a half-billion-dollar budget that is larger than many big city police departments, the Capitol's security, augmented by city police, failed to protect the sixty-three-acre Building and grounds complex.

Further, additional security resources might have been deployed at the Capitol, but weren't, even after portents of trouble emerged. In the weeks before the riot, during election protests outside the Supreme Court and Capitol Building, scuffles had broken out among Trump demonstrators and counter-demonstrators, with policemen injured and arrests being made. In the days before the January 6 demonstration, according to congressional testimony, the Capitol Police chief formally requested National Guard troops multiple times, but was turned down by Senate and House officials. According to the Associated Press, Capitol Building authorities turned aside Defense Department and Justice Department offers to add security personnel before the protest. (Trump himself later claimed he requested that thousands of National Guardsmen be on hand for the rally.)

Also prior to the "Stop the Steal" rally, New York City Police found signs that extremists with violent intent were traveling to Washington. It informed the federal terrorism task force, whose assessment was violence between groups on the right and the left was possible. However, neither the Capitol Police, municipal police, nor the FBI acted on the intelligence.

In addition, law enforcement seemed to pull its punches, in the wake of the nationwide 2020 riots, including the turmoil in Lafayette Square, when state and local officials and pressure groups chided police for supposed use of excessive force. It seems both Capitol and Defense Department officials were concerned about the "optics" of having the National Guard appear with police at the Capitol Building. Further, the police at the Capitol may have been caught off guard by the "Republican Riot," as the large number of well-attended Trump rallies across five years had been free of violence and vocal in their support of cops.

One almost wished that Francis Scott Key, or his son, the city's district attorneys of yore, had been around to call in the US Marines, as they did to quell the riots of 1835 and 1857. (See the chapters on those disorders.)

A veteran New England congressman commented on the protective measures for the Capitol Building: "I've always assumed there's a big red button that gets pushed, and everything is sealed and nobody gets anywhere. And that turns out not to be true."

After the breach of the Capitol, Congress mandated a striking show of force. Five thousand National Guard troops were stationed both inside and outside the Building. Soldiers in camouflaged fatigues bedded down amid the statues, historic paintings, and marbled corridors of the legislature, a jarring sight for the center of a democracy. For three months after the riot, a razor-wire fence ranging above seven feet high cordoned off several square miles around the Capitol Building, and walled off tourists, cyclists, and joggers.

The Capitol Riot ranks among the wildest events in the Building's more than two centuries of existence.

Injured Icons at President's Park

In 2020, the greatest outrage to historic sites and statues, especially those relating to civil rights and liberties, occurred in Lafayette Square, the "President's Park" across Pennsylvania Avenue from the White House.

On Memorial Day Weekend, May 29–June 1, the Square and its environs were the place of angry confrontations between protestors and rioters on the one hand, and federal Park Police and White House Secret Service agents on the other. Many in the downtown crowds were peaceful; others were not. Some hurled fireworks, bricks, and urine-filled bottles at law enforcement. Officers used pepper spray, smoke canisters, and "sting balls" in return. On that Saturday, crowds surged into the fenced-off Square. The Metropolitan Police made seventeen arrests that day, fourteen for rioting.

At one point, the Secret Service judged the White House itself was in danger. Agents took President Trump to a secure basement bunker for an hour, the first time that had happened since September 11. The Secret Service reported over ten of its agents and officers were hospitalized, out of about sixty injured. Some sixty-five US Park Police were hurt, and over twenty sent for medical treatment, according to the National Park Service and the Justice Department. Eleven DC policemen were hurt that Saturday. Authorities used police batons and tear gas to push out demonstrators. Some of the latter asserted they were unjustly attacked and injured by police.

Among those swarming through the Park were members of, or persons sympathetic to, Antifa and Black Lives Matter. Afterwards, city mayor Muriel Bowser named the portion of 16th Street directly north of the Square, Black Lives Matter Plaza. Countless cards and flowers were placed in the Plaza and on the gates of Lafayette Square in memory of Floyd and others who'd died in confrontations with police officers.

Black Lives Matter is an organization that states it is working against police killings and for social justice. Critics counter that several of its co-founders are Marxist, and that the organization frequently engages in street violence and in harassment of pedestrians. Antifa, a radical, self-proclaimed anti-fascist group, has participated in many assaults on police and reporters, and in lawless occupations of downtown districts in such cities as Portland and Seattle.

The sites the rioters damaged or defaced in Lafayette Square were many, and their actions highly ironic, given the stated, civil rights–related purpose of the protests. They included:

Stephen Decatur House—Navy Commodore Decatur was a hero of the Barbary Pirate wars of the early 1800s, waged in the Mediterranean Sea by Presidents Jefferson and Madison. The wars struck a crushing blow against the Pirates' slave trafficking in the Mediterranean and Atlantic Ocean. That baleful practice had for centuries consigned hundreds of thousands of Europeans and Africans to the auction block.

Baron von Steuben statue—Von Steuben was, according to some historians, a homosexual, a gay soldier who served in the court of Prussian emperor Frederick the Great. As a prince of the European Enlightenment, Frederick ended the laws of discrimination that barred Catholics and Jews from serving in universities and the professions. Von Steuben served, without pay, as the drillmaster for George Washington's patriot army, which ended the tyrannical reign of King George.

The Chamber of Commerce building—Formerly the site of the mansion of William Corcoran, who founded the Renwick & Corcoran galleries of art down and around the corner from the Square. Corcoran donated lavishly to schools and museums to help restore the Washington region after the War Between the States.

His house was later the residence of Massachusetts senator Daniel Webster, who may have helped secretly plan, along with the freed African-American servant and author Paul Jennings, a monumental slave escape. (See the chapter on Lincoln's lodging.)

The Kościuszko statue—Thaddeus Kościuszko was a Polish-Lithuanian engineer who built the original fortifications at West Point, later the site of the US Military Academy. He was one of the noble European officers, honored with statues in the Square, who came to America to help win its independence. He was a friend of Col. John Laurens of South Carolina, who called for forming regiments of black soldiers during the American Revolution. In his will, Kościuszko bequeathed his remaining life savings to purchase the freedom of American slaves.

The Cutts-Madison house—The stately home was the residence of Union navy commodore Charles Wilkes. Along with possibly serving as a real-life model for Captain Ahab of *Moby Dick*, Wilkes led a South Sea expedition whose scientific specimens helped lay the groundwork for the Smithsonian Institution. He was also one of the Union navy's most aggressive sea captains. Its naval blockade of the Confederacy, by ending the export of its cash crop of cotton, triggered the collapse of the South's economy and military, thus preserving the Union, and ending American slavery.

As its name attests, the townhouse was also the residence in retirement of President and First Lady James and Dolley Madison. Madison, the leading member of the first Congress, shepherded through the legislature the first ten amendments to his US Constitution. This Bill of Rights guaranteed freedom of speech and peaceful assembly, among many other privileges, for all Americans.

The Treasury Building—The Treasury Department was founded by that recent star of Broadway, Alexander Hamilton, a penniless immigrant from the West Indies who climbed to the top of the financial and political realms. He also co-founded, with Aaron Burr, of all people, the New York Manumission Society for the freeing of slaves in America's commercial hub.

Freedman's Bank—After the Civil War, the financial institution at this locale held the savings deposits of thousands of freed men and women. One of the Bank's presidents was Frederick Douglass who, along with condemning slavery and discrimination, was notable for his censure of lawless, self-destructive behavior.

Federal Circuit Court of Appeals—Site of the mansion of Lincoln's secretary of state William Seward. He was badly wounded there on the night of the president's assassination by one of John Wilkes Booth's conspirators. Booth was moved to murder by Lincoln's support of suffrage for blacks who'd served in the Union army. Before Seward's residence there, the house was the home of Commodore John Rodgers, a valiant commander of the Barbary Pirate wars; his son married the daughter of Union general Montgomery Meigs, the quartermaster, or chief provisioner, of Union forces and founder of Arlington National Cemetery.

The court's interior space contains an exact replica of a startling funeral sculpture that local author Henry Adams completed in 1891 for his deceased wife, Marian "Clover" Hooper Adams. Henry Adams was the grandson of abolitionist president John Quincy Adams who, in his later years as a congressman, ended the gag order forbidding discussion of slavery in the Capitol Building. He also defended the rebellious slaves in the Supreme Court case of the *Amistad* ship.

The Andrew Jackson Statue—On June 23, three weeks after Memorial Day, rioters attempted to topple the statue of the seventh president, before police stopped them. "Old Hickory" is depicted atop a horse during his overwhelming victory at the 1814 Battle of New Orleans. That War of 1812 fight ended the British Empire's hopes of regaining parts of the United States. It was made possible by plantation owner Jackson's astonishing deployment of troops from assorted backgrounds. His army included Creoles of Spanish ancestry, African-American "free men of color," who held the center of his line, Scotch-Irish frontiersmen from Tennessee and Kentucky, with their fearsome "long rifles," Native American scouts, and even French pirates, as well as regular US Army troops, many of English descent.

An inscription on the statue reads, "Our Federal Union, It Must Be Preserved." It was a toast Jackson pointedly spoke to South Carolina's John C. Calhoun, the apostle of nullification of federal laws, and defender of slavery, when Calhoun in 1832 threatened to take his state out of the Union. He backed down after Jackson threatened to march federal militia into Charleston and hang Calhoun by the nearest lamppost. Old Hickory undoubtedly had significant faults, but also strengths, seemingly making him a man worthy of study, not erasure.

The White House—The Executive Mansion escaped damage, despite the attempts of some rioters to climb its metal fence. Along with Benjamin Latrobe, of French and Germanic ancestry, and especially its Irish architect James Hoban, the place likely got a design assist from Jefferson, later the first person to reside for two terms in the President's House.

Though often maligned today on the issue of slavery, even in the University of Virginia he founded, the chief author of the Declaration of Independence in fact took many antislavery steps. As a young state legislator in Virginia, he pushed through a law on manumission, enabling owners to actually free their slaves in what was then the largest and most populous colony. As perhaps the most prominent federal legislator in the Articles of Confederation period of the 1780s, he authored the Jefferson Proviso of the Northwest Ordinance. The latter set rules for organizing all the territories and future states from Ohio to parts of Minnesota; the former banned slavery across that huge expanse. As president, he banned the infernal slave trade into America from Africa, after he launched the navy war that under his successor Madison defeated the Barbary Pirates. Indeed, Jefferson did more to restrict and reduce slavery than any American until Abraham Lincoln, and he did it, in America at least, without firing a shot.

St. John's Church—The "Church of the Presidents" was designed by the renowned Latrobe. Every chief executive since Madison has attended services there. They include: James Monroe, who more strictly enforced, through the US Navy, the slave trade ban; Lincoln, "the Great Emancipator"; and Lyndon Johnson, signer of the Civil Rights Act that consigned to oblivion the "Jim Crow" laws on segregation.

The venerable church suffered the most damage of any building, after arsonists set fire to its basement. If only a modern-day William Thornton had been on hand to thwart them, as that designer of the original Capitol Building had stopped British troops in 1814 from torching the Old Patent Office, today's magnificent National Portrait Gallery! (See the chapter on the British burning of Washington.)

Lafayette Statue—France's valiant Marquis de Lafayette spent his long life fighting for American independence and for liberty in Europe, in fact everywhere. He even set up a large farm in Central America for freed slaves. When Lafayette was buried in Paris in 1834, his son—George Washington Lafayette—poured soil onto his coffin that his father had collected from the American Revolutionary War battlefield of Bunker Hill.

So that the Marquis would rest forever—under the soil of a free people!

During the French Revolution, Lafayette tried to maintain democracy and civic order, until overwhelmed by the mobs instigating the Reign of Terror that consigned thousands of innocent people to the guillotine.

One wondered, as destructive chaos and insult to lovers of liberty and history took over his Square, whether Lafayette rolled in his grave.

The nation's capital, and especially its Capitol Building, have witnessed an extraordinary number of tumultuous events since Pierre L'Enfant began laying out the city in the 1790s. It has been the scene of bombings, foreign invasion, riots, bloody assaults, rowdy demonstrations, hangings, and duels to the death, and much more.

If its first 230-plus years are an indication, the District, Congress, and the Capitol Building face a future as tumultuous as its past.

SELECT BIBLIOGRAPHY

"100 Are in Hospital: Crowds Trample Men; Women Faint In Crush." *Washington Post*, March 4, 1913.

"5,000 Women March in a Woman's Suffrage Demonstration, Beset By Crowds." *New York Times*, March 4, 1913.

Ackerman, Kenneth D. *Dark Horse: The Surprise Election and Political Murder of James A. Garfield.* New York: Avalon Publishing, 2003.

Adams, Henry. *The Life of Albert Gallatin.* Philadelphia: J.B. Lippincott & Co., 1879. Vol. 3. Reprint. New York: Chelsea House, 1983.

Adams, Katherine H., and Michael L. Keene. *Alice Paul and the American Suffrage Campaign.* Urbana: University of Illinois Press, 2008.

Allen, William C. *U.S. Senate. History of the United States Capitol: A Chronicle of Design, Construction, and Politics.* 106th Congress, 2d sess., 2001. S. Doc. 106-29.

Ambrose, Stephen E. *Nothing Like It in the World: The Men Who Built the Transcontinental Railroad 1863–1869.* New York: Simon & Schuster, 2001.

Andrews, Evans. "Andrew Jackson Dodges an Assassination Attempt, 180 Years Ago." History.com. August 29, 2018. www.history.com/news/andrew-jackson-dodges-an-assassination-attempt-180-years-ago.

Architect of the Capitol. "9/11 Anniversary Tree." Retrieved January 2021. https://www.aoc.gov/explore-capitol-campus/art/9-11-anniversary-tree.

Architect of the Capitol. "The Statue of Freedom." Updated May 1, 2018. https://www.aoc.gov/art/other-statues/statue-freedom.

Architect of the Capitol. "Ulysses S. Grant Memorial," in *Preserving the Historic Buildings That Inspire Our Nation.* https://www.aoc.gov/explore-capitol-campus/art/ulysses-s-grant-memorial.

Arkansas Democrat Gazette. "Transcript of Speech by President Donald Trump on Jan. 6." (2021). https://www.arkansasonline.com/news/2021/jan/14/washington-post-transcript-of-speech-by-president/.

Arlington National Cemetery. "Pierre Charles L'Enfant." Retrieved November 2020. https://www.arlingtoncemetery.mil/Explore/Notable-Graves/Science-Technology-Engineering/Pierre-Charles-LEnfant.

Arnebeck, Bob. "Samuel Davidson for Sale." *DCSwamp* blog. March 21, 2011. http://dcswamp.blogspot.com/2011/03/samuel-davidson-for-sale.html.

Auricchio, Laura. *The Marquis: Lafayette Reconsidered.* New York: Knopf, 2014.

Bailey, Ronald. "Hail, Lafayette." *American History Magazine*, December 3, 2010.

Ball, Molly. "The Secret History of the Shadow Campaign That Saved the 2020 Election." *Time*. February 4, 2021.

Ballotpedia. "Impeachment of Donald Trump, 2021." https://ballotpedia.org/Impeach ment_of_Donald_Trump,_2021

Bank of America. "Custodian Who Saved Capital." Retrieved 2018. https://about .bankofamerica.com/en-us/our-story/custodian-who-saved-capital-hill.html.

"Battle of Washington." *Time*, August 8, 1932. http://content.time.com/time/ subscriber/printout/0,8816,744107,00.html.

BBC. "The Odd Objects Looted from Washington DC in 1814." August 29, 2014. https://www.bbc.com/news/blogs-magazine-monitor-28833238.

Beckert, Sven. *Empire of Cotton: A Global History*. New York: Vintage, 2015.

Bennett, Kevin. "Newark Congressman Once Tried to Shoot Sam Houston." *Newark Advocate*, September 14, 2016. https://www.newarkadvocate.com/story/news/ local/granville/2016/09/14/newark-congressman-tried-shoot-sam -houston/90278922/.

Bernstein, Carl, and Bob Woodward. *All the President's Men*. New York: Simon & Schuster, 1974.

Berg, Scott W. *Grand Avenues: The Story of Pierre Charles L'Enfant, the French Visionary Who Designed Washington, D.C.* New York: Vintage, Illustrated edition, 2008.

Blackman, Ann. *Wild Rose: Rose O'Neale Greenhow, Civil War Spy*. New York: Random House, 2005.

Blakemore, Erin. "The Largest Attempted Slave Escape in American History." History. com. August 23, 2017. https://www.history.com/news/the-largest-attempted -slave-escape-in-american-history.

Block, Eliana. "VERIFY: Yes, at least 150 local and federal officers were injured during the first week of protests in DC." June 11, 2020. https://www.wusa9.com/article/ news/verify/150-local-federal-officers-injured-during-dc-protests-verify/65 -8fdaf04e-df2e-47d0-abd6-a47017a699f8

Blum, Howard. *Dark Invasion: 1915: Germany's Secret War and the Hunt for the First Terrorist Cell in America*. New York: HarperCollins, 2014.

Brammer, Robert. "Love, Adultery, and Madness." Library of Congress. February 13, 2015. https://blogs.loc.gov/law/2015/02/love-adultery-and-madness/.

Brooks, Rebecca Beatrice. "Rose O'Neal Greenhow: Confederate Spy." *Civil War Saga* blog. October 3, 2012. http://civilwarsaga.com/rose-oneal-greenhow/.

Bruce, William Cabell. *John Randolph of Roanoke, 1773–1833*. New York, London: G. P. Putnam's Sons, 1922.

Bryan, Wilhemus Bogart. *A History of the National Capital from Its Foundation Through the Period of the Adoption of the Organic Act*. New York: The Macmillan Company, 1914.

Bryan, Wilhemus Bogart. "Hotels of Washington DC Prior to 1814." *American History and Genealogy Project (AHGP)*, speech originally from March 9, 1903.

Burrough, Bryan. *Days of Rage: America's Radical Underground, the FBI, and the Forgotten Age of Revolutionary Violence*. New York: Penguin, 2015.

Busfield, Roger M. "The Hermitage Walking Stick: First Challenge to Congressional Immunity." *Tennessee Historical Quarterly*, Vol. 21, no. 2 (1962): 122–30. www .jstor.org/stable/42621567.

Butterfield, Alexander. "Testimony of Alexander Porter Butterfield." *Testimony of Witnesses: Alexander Butterfield, Paul O'Brien, and Fred C. LaRue. Book I.* U.S. House of Representatives. 93d Cong., 2d sess. Washington, DC: US Government Printing Office, 1974.

Cannadine, David. *Mellon*. New York: Vintage Books, 2006.

Cassiday, G. "Capitol Bootlegger, Got First Rum Order From Dry." *Washington Post*, October 24, 1930, 1.

Cassiday, G. "Part of Cassiday's Rum Supply Stored in House Office Building." *Washington Post*, October 26, 1930, 1.

Cassiday, G. "Rum Buyers in Capitol Indicted as Law Violators by Cassiday." *Washington Post*, October 29, 1930, 1.

Castelucci, John. *Big Dance: The Untold Story of Weather-Man Kathy Boudin and the Terrorist Family That Committed the Brinks Robbery Murders*. New York: Dodd Mead, 1986.

Chernow, Ron. *Alexander Hamilton*. New York: Penguin Press, 2004.

Chernow, Ron. *Washington: A Life*. New York: Penguin Books, 2010.

Clark, James C. *The Murder of President James A. Garfield*. National Archives. Summer 1992. https://www.archives.gov/files/publications/prologue/1992/summer/ garfield.pdf.

Clarke, James W. *Defining Danger: American Assassins and the New Domestic Terrorists*. New Brunswick, NJ: Transaction Publishers, 2012.

"Climax of Folly: Coxey and Browne in the Role of Martyrs." *Washington Post*, May 2, 1894.

Columbia Historical Society. "Moore: Augustus Brevoort Woodward." *Records of the Columbia Historical Society*. Volumes 3-4. Washington, DC: Google Books.

Congressional Cemetery. "The Pearl." Washington, DC. https://congressionalcemetery .org/2019/02/14/the-pearl/.

Congressional Cemetery. Various personages. Washington, DC. https://congressional cemetery.org/.

Congressional Quarterly. "Terrorist Bomb Explosion Rocks Capitol." *CQ Almanac 1983*, 39th ed., 592–94. Washington, DC. Document ID: cqal83-1198381.

Conkling. A. R., ed. *The Life and Letters of Roscoe Conkling: Orator, Statesman, Advocate*. New York: Charles L. Webster & Company. 1889.

Conroy, Sarah Booth. "The Lives of the Lafayette Square Literati." *Washington Post*, June 10, 1990.

Cornell University. *Lafayette: Citizen of Two Worlds* website. 2006 exhibit. http://rmc .library.cornell.edu/lafayette/exhibition/english/introduction/index.html.

Costello, Matthew. "Paul Jennings: Slave, Freeman, and White House Memoirist." White House Historical Association. February 1, 2017.

"Coxey's March on Capitol Weirdest Parade in City's History: Coming of Jobless Army Was Dreaded By Residents Here." *Washington Post*, December 6, 1927.

Crawford, Jay Boyd. *The Credit Mobilier of America: Its Origin and History.* Boston: C. W. Calkins & Co., 1880.

Crouthhamel, James L. "James Watson Webb: Mercantile Editor." *New York History*, Vol. 41, no. 4 (October 1960), 400–422. Published by Fenimore Art Museum. https://www.jstor.org/stable/23153652?read-now=1&seq=8#page_scan_tab _contents.

Crowe, Mike. "One Man's Meat." *Fisherman's Voice*, Vol. 11, no. 1 (January 2006). www .fishermensvoice.com/archives/0106index.html.

Cultural Tourism DC. "Fifteenth Street Presbyterian Church, African American Heritage Trail." https://www.culturaltourismdc.org/portal/fifteenth-street-presbyterian -church-african-american-heritage-trail.

Cunningham, David. *There's Something Happening Here: The New Left, the Klan, and FBI Counterintelligence.* Berkeley: University of California Press, 2004.

Dean, John W. *The Nixon Defense: What He Knew and When He Knew It.* New York: Viking, 2014.

DeFerrari, John. "The Election Day Riot of 1857, Driven by Religious Intolerance." *Streets of Washington.* December 15, 2015. www.streetsofwashington .com/2015/12/the-election-day-riot-of-1857-driven-by.html?view=magazine.

DeFerrari, John. "Triumph and Tragedy at Decatur House." *Streets of Washington.* December 27, 2010. www.streetsofwashington.com/2010/12/triumph-and-tragedy -at-decatur-house.html#!/2010/12/triumph-and-tragedy-at-decatur-house.html.

Department of State, Office of the Historian. "Public Building West of the White House May 1801–August 1814." https://history.state.gov/departmenthistory/ buildings/section22.

Department of State, Office of the Historian. "The Trent Affair, 1861." Retrieved 2018. https://history.state.gov/milestones/1861-1865/trent-affair.

Diaz, Jaclyn. "Ex-Capitol Police Chief Says Requests for National Guard Denied 6 Times in Riots." NPR, WAMU. January 11, 2021.

Dickey, J. D. *Empire of Mud: The Secret History of Washington, DC.* Guilford, CT: Lyons Press, 2014.

Dickson, Paul, and Thomas B. Allen. *The Bonus Army: An American Epic.* New York: Walker & Company, 2004.

Dickson, Paul, and Thomas B. Allen. "Marching on History." *Smithsonian*, February 2003. https://www.smithsonianmag.com/history/marching-on-history -75797769/.

Dobbs, Michael. *Saboteurs: The Nazi Raid on America.* New York: Knopf Doubleday Publishing Group, 2005.

Dodd, Lynda G. "Parades, Pickets, and Prison: Alice Paul and the Virtues of Unruly Constitutional Citizenship." *Journal of Law & Politics*, Vol. 24, no. 4 (2008), 339–443.

Doyle, James. *Not Above the Law: The Battles of Watergate Prosecutors Cox and Jaworski.* New York: William Morrow and Company, 1977.

Duke University. Rose O'Neal Greenhow Papers: An On-line Archival Collection. May 1996. https://library.duke.edu/rubenstein/scriptorium/greenhow/roseindex.html.

Dungan, Nicholas. *Gallatin: America's Swiss Founding Father.* New York: NYU Press, 2010.

Eldridge, Thomas R., et al. *The 9/11 Commission Report.* National Commission on Terrorist Attacks Upon the United States. Madison & Adams Press, 2018.

Ellis, Joseph J. *Founding Brothers.* New York: Knopf, 2000.

Encyclopedia Americana. "Crédit Mobilier of America." 1920. https://en.wikisource.org/wiki/The_Encyclopedia_Americana_(1920)/Cr%C3%A9dit_Mobilier_of_America.

Encyclopaedia Britannica. "Freedmen's Bank." https://www.britannica.com/topic/Freedmens-Bank#ref1223106.

Encyclopedia.com. "John Ericsson." *Dictionary of American History.* 2004.

Enriques, Peter R. "1800: America's First Explosive Election." *HistoryNet.* October 26, 2020. https://www.historynet.com/1800-americas-first-explosive-election.htm.

Eschner, Kate. "How the Trial and Death of Henry Wirz Shaped Post–Civil War America." *Smithsonian,* November 10, 2017.

"FBI Captures Eight Saboteurs Landed in US by Axis Subs: Spies Carried American Money, Elaborate Plans to Impede Progress of our War Effort." *Washington Post,* June 28, 1942.

Female Spies in the Civil War. "Rose Greenhow." April 14, 2015. https://civilwarfemalespies.wordpress.com/female-spies/rose-greenhow-2/.

Ferling, John. "Thomas Jefferson, Aaron Burr and the Election of 1800." *Smithsonian,* November 1, 2004. https://www.smithsonianmag.com/history/thomas-jefferson-aaron-burr-and-the-election-of-1800-131082359/.

Finney, John W. "Bomb in Capitol Causes Wide Damage." *New York Times,* March 2, 1971.

Fishman, Susan Hoffman. "The Escape of the Pearl: Teaching about Slavery with Primary Source Documents." https://www.questia.com/library/journal/1G1-108048792/the-escape-of-the-pearl-teaching-about-slavery-with.

Fitting, Peter. "Urban Planning/Utopian Dreaming: Le Corbusier's Chandigarh Today. *Utopian Studies,* Vol. 13, no. 1 (2002), 69–93.

Fleming, Thomas. "When Dolley Madison Took Command of the White House." *Smithsonian,* March 2010. Adapted from *The Intimate Lives of the Founding Fathers* by Thomas Fleming.

Flowers, R. Barri. *Murder of the U.S. Attorney: Congressman Sickles' Crime of Passion in 1859.* CreateSpace/Amazon, 2018.

Foner, Eric. *A Short History of Reconstruction, 1863–1877.* New York: HarperPerennial, 1990.

Forester, C. S. *The Age of Fighting Sail.* New York: Doubleday, 2000.

Forrett, Jeff. "The Notorious 'Yellow House' That Made Washington, D.C. a Slavery Capital." *Smithsonian,* July 22, 2020. https://www.smithsonianmag.com/history/how-yellow-house-helped-make-washington-dc-slavery-capital-180975378/.

Fowler, Glenn. "Breuer's Plan Fails to Mollify Tower Critics." *New York Times,* June 21, 1968.

Frank, Anne, Otto H. Frank, and Mirjam Pressler (eds.). *Het Achterhuis (The Diary of a Young Girl – The Definitive Edition)* (Dutch). Susan Massotty, trans. New York:

Doubleday, 1995. Originally published in 1947. https://www.annefrank.org/en/anne-frank/diary/complete-works-anne-frank/.

Freeman, Douglas S. *R. E. Lee, A Biography*. New York: Charles Scribner's Sons, 1934.

Freeman, Joanne. *Affairs of Honor*. New Haven: Yale University Press, 2001, xv–xviii, 182–86.

Funderburg, J. Anne. "Bootleggers and Beer Barons of the Prohibition Era." In *History, Art & Archives*, US House of Representatives. https://history.house .gov/Collection/Detail/30338?current_search_qs=%3FClassification%3D Photographs%26PreviousSearch%3DSearch%252cPhotographs%252c Date%26CurrentPage%3D8%26SortOrder%3DDate%26ResultType% 3DGrid%26Command%3D10.

Gatewood, Willard B., Jr. "John Francis Cook: Antebellum Black Presbyterian." *American Presbyterians*, Vol. 67 (Fall 1989).

Georgetowner. "When Dolley Madison Fled Georgetown and Beyond." August 7, 2014.

Getlin, Larry. "The Epic Legal Battle Lincoln Waged—Over a Bridge." *New York Post*, February 8, 2015. https://nypost.com/2015/02/08/the-epic-legal-battle-lincoln -waged-over-a-bridge/.

Ghosts of DC. "Rough-and-Tumble Lost Neighborhood of Murder Bay." https:// ghostsofdc.org/2012/03/29/washingtons-rough-and-tumble-lost-neighborhood -of-murder-bay/.

Glass, Andrew. "Gap on Key Watergate Tape Revealed: Nov. 21, 1973." *Politico*, November 20, 2016.

Glass, Andrew. "Reporter Fatally Shoots Ex-Lawmaker in U.S. Capitol." *Politico*, February 28, 2018. Derived from House of Representatives, *History, Art & Archives*. https://www.politico.com/story/2018/02/28/reporter-fatally-shoots-ex-lawmaker -in-us-capitol-feb-28-1890-423402.

Global News. "US Capitol Lockdown: Pro-Trump Rioters Storm Congress, Clash with Police." Video, January 6, 2021. https://www.youtube.com/watch?v=SocnM1l-HZB4.

Goff, Jenna. "How a Failed German Spy Mission Turned into J. Edgar Hoover's Big Break." *Boundary Stones*, WETA, June 10, 2015. https://blogs.weta.org/boundary stones/2015/06/10/how-failed-german-spy-mission-turned-j-edgar -hoover%E2%80%99s-big-break.

Goodrich, Frances, and Albert Hackett, screenwriters. *The Diary of Anne Frank* (film). Twentieth Century-Fox Film Corporation, based on *The Diary of a Young Girl*, 1959.

Gordon, John Steele. "The Freedman's Bank." *American Heritage*, Vol. 44, issue 8 (December 1993).

Gott, Kendall D. "Confrontation at Anacostia Flats: The Bonus Army of 1932." *The Land Warfare Papers*, a National Security Affairs Paper published on occasion by The Institute of Land Warfare Association of the United States Army, No. 63W, Arlington, VA, April 2007. https://www.ausa.org/sites/default/files/LWP-63 -Confrontation-at-Anacostia-Flats-The-Bonus-Army-of-1932.pdf.

Graff, Garrett M. *The Only Plane in the Sky: An Oral History of 9/11*. New York: Avid Reader Press/Simon & Schuster, 2020.

Graff, Garrett M. "What Happened on Capitol Hill on 9/11." *Time*, September 11, 2019. https://time.com/5673607/september-11-congress/.

Green, Fletcher M. "Duff Green, Militant Journalist of the Old School." *American Historical Review*, Vol. 52, no. 2 (January 1947), 247–64. Published by Oxford University Press on behalf of the American Historical Association. https://www.jstor.org/stable/1841273?seq=1.

Greenhow, Rose O'Neal. *My Imprisonment and the First Year of Abolition Rule at Washington*. Whitefish, MT: Kessinger Publishing, 2007. Originally published in 1863.

Grinspan, Jon. "How a Ragtag Band of Reformers Organized the First Protest March on Washington, D.C." *Smithsonian*, May 1, 2014. https://www.smithsonianmag.com/smithsonian-institution/how-ragtag-band-reformers-organized-first-protest-march-washington-dc-180951270/.

Guillermoprieto, Alma. "Bomb Shatters Navy Yard Officers Club." *Washington Post*, April 21, 1984. https://www.washingtonpost.com/archive/local/1984/04/21/bomb-shatters-navy-yard-officers-club/44f34d4d-321a-4788-a25c-0888183273f2/.

Guiteau's Confession: The Garfield Assassination: A Full History of this Cruel Crime. Philadelphia: Old Franklin Publishing, 1881.

Gustaitis, Joseph. "Coxey's Army." *American History Illustrated*, March/April 1994, 39–45. www.angelfire.com/hi2/drme/coxey1894.html.

Hansen, Stephen A. *A History of Dupont Circle: Center of High Society in the Capital.* Mount Pleasant, SC: History Press, 2014.

Harkness, Robert H. "Dr. William B. Magruder." *Records of the Columbia Historical Society*, Vol. 16. Washington, DC: Columbia Historical Society, December 17, 1912.

Harrold, Stanley C., Jr. "The Pearl Affair: The Washington Riot of 1848." *Records of the Columbia Historical Society*, Vol. 50 (1980), 140–60. Published by Historical Society of Washington, DC. https://www.jstor.org/stable/40067813?read-now=1&seq=10#page_scan_tab_contents.

Harrold, Stanley C., Jr. *Subversives: Antislavery Community in Washington, D.C., 1828–1865.* Baton Rouge: Louisiana State University Press, 2003, 108–11.

Heidler, David S., and Jeanne T. Heidler. *Henry Clay: The Essential American.* New York: Random House Publishing Group, 2010.

Hickman, Kennedy. "War of 1812: Commodore Stephen Decatur." Thoughtco.com, November 7, 2017.

HistoryNet. "War Watchers at Bull Run During America's Civil War." June 6, 2006. http://www.historynet.com/war-watchers-at-bull-run-during-americas-civil-war.htm.

HistoryNet. "World War II: German Saboteurs Invade America in 1942." Retrieved September 2020. https://www.historynet.com/world-war-ii-german-saboteurs-invade-america-in-1942.htm.

History Things. "The Life of Revolutionary Marquis de Lafayette." October 18, 2016. http://historythings.com/life-revolutionary-marquis-de-lafayette-part-three/.

Hollmuller, Anne. "A 'Most Awful and Most Lamentable Catastrophe': The Explosion on the USS *Princeton*." *Boundary Stones*, WETA, April 25, 2018. https://blogs.

weta.org/boundarystones/2018/04/25/most-awful-and-most-lamentable-catastrophe-explosion-uss-princeton.

Holmes, Oliver W. "The Colonial Taverns of Georgetown." Washington, DC: Columbia Historical Society, 1951.

Hoopes, Roy. "It Was Bad Last Time Too: The Crédit Mobilier Scandal of 1872." *American Heritage*, Vol. 42, issue 1 (February/March 1991).

Hutzler, Alexandra. "Police Officer Brian Sicknick Died of Natural Causes." *Newsweek*. April 19, 2021.

Inks, Casey. "A Pair of Dueling Rifles Reveal Their Story." *American History Museum*, March 14, 2016. https://americanhistory.si.edu/blog/pair-dueling-rifles-reveal-their-story.

Kramer, Neil S. "The Trial of Reuben Crandall." *Records of the Columbia Historical Society*, Vol. 50 (1980): 123–39. Accessed December 2020. http://www.jstor.org/stable/40067812.

Jacobs, Jane. *A History of Dupont Circle: Center of High Society in the Capital.* New York: Vintage, 1961.

Jennings, Paul. *A Colored Man's Reminiscences of James Madison.* Brooklyn: George C. Beadle, 1865. Electronic Edition, University of North Carolina at Chapel Hill. https://docsouth.unc.edu/neh/jennings/jennings.html.

Johnson II, William Page. "Mosby's Fairfax Court House Raid March 9, 1863." *Fare Facs Gazette*, Vol. 10, issue 1 (Winter 2013). https://www.historicfairfax.org/wp-content/uploads/2012/05/HFCI1001-2013.pdf.

Jones, Mark. "A Congressional Beating: Sam Houston and William Stanbery." *Boundary Stones*, WETA, January 9, 2013. http://blogs.weta.org/boundarystones/2013/01/09/congressional-beating-sam-houston-and-william-stanbery.

Jones, Mark. "Red Summer Race Riot in Washington, 1919." *Washington Post*, April 18, 2017.

Jones, Mark. "Terrorism Hits Home in 1915: U.S. Capitol Bombing." *Boundary Stones*, WETA, June 22, 2015. https://boundarystones.weta.org/2015/06/22/terrorism-hits-home-1915-us-capitol-bombing.

Jusserand, Jean Jules. *With Americans of Past and Present Days.* (Pierre L'Enfant). New York: C. Scribner, 1916.

Kanon, Tom. *Tennesseans at War, 1812–1815.* Tuscaloosa: University of Alabama Press, 2014.

Kelly, John. "From Peacemaker to Widowmaker." *Washington Post*, October 25, 2014.

Kelly, John. "John Kelly's Washington: Congress Winks at Prohibition in Bootlegger's Tale." *Washington Post*, April 27, 2009.

Keneally, Thomas. *American Scoundrel: The Life of the Notorious Civil War General Dan Sickles.* New York: Doubleday, 2002.

Kessler, Ronald. *In the President's Secret Service: Behind the Scenes with Agents in the Line of Fire and the Presidents They Protect.* New York: Crown, 2009.

Khan, Saliqa. "Protestors, Police, Tear Gas, Looting." WUSA9, May 31, 2020. https://www.wusa9.com/article/news/local/dc/protesters-police-tear-gas-flames-damage-looting-the-aftermath-of-saturdays-justice-for-george-floyd-protests/65-37f183ba-2d89-421d-8edd-24b9b00502bc.

King, Gilbert. "Sabotage in New York Harbor." *Smithsonian*, November 1, 2011.

King, Gilbert. "The Stalking of the President." *Smithsonian*, January 7, 2012. https:// www.smithsonianmag.com/history/the-stalking-of-the-president-20724161/.

King, Gilbert. "War and Peace of Mind for Ulysses S. Grant." *Smithsonian*, January 16, 2013. https://www.smithsonianmag.com/history/war-and-peace-of-mind-for -ulysses-s-grant-1882227/.

Klotter, James C. "Sex, Scandal, and Suffrage in the Gilded Age." *The Historian: A Journal of History*, Vol. 42, no. 2 (February 1980), 225–43.

Kratz, Jesse. "Rescue of the Papers of State During the Burning of Washington." White House Historical Association. *White House History* no. 35 (Summer 2014).

Langeveld, Dirk. "James Brooks: Out of Stock." *The Downfall Dictionary*, January 9, 2010. http://downfalldictionary.blogspot.com/2010/01/james-brooks.html.

Langeveld, Dirk. "William Stanbery: Taking a Licking." *The Downfall Dictionary*, May 20, 2009. https://downfalldictionary.blogspot.com/2009/05/william-stanbery -taking-licking.html.

Langley, Julia. "Shrady and Casey, Ulysses S. Grant Memorial." Khan Academy. https:// www.khanacademy.org/humanities/art-americas/us-art-19c/us-19c-arch-sculp -photo/a/shrady-and-casey-ulysses-s-grant-memorial.

Laurence, Kenneth. *Duff Green and the United States' Telegraph, 1826–1837*. College of William & Mary–Arts & Sciences, Dissertations, 1981. https://scholarworks. wm.edu/cgi/viewcontent.cgi?article=3580&context=etd.

Lee, Antoinette J. *Architects to the Nation: The Rise and Decline of the Supervising Architect's Office*. Oxford: Oxford University Press, 2000.

Leepson, Marc. *What So Proudly We Hailed: Francis Scott Key, a Life*. New York: Palgrave Macmillan, 2014.

Levitt, Saul. *The Andersonville Trial* (play). New York: Random House, 1960. Originally dramatized in 1959.

Levitt, Saul. *The Andersonville Trial* (television adaptation of the play). PBS, 1970.

Levy, Gabrielle. "Anne Frank Memorial Tree Planted on Capitol Hill." UPI, April 30, 2014. https://www.upi.com/Top_News/US/2014/04/30/Anne-Frank-memorial -tree-planted-on-Capitol-Hill/1461398890821/.

Lewis, Charles Lee. *Famous American Naval Officers*. Boston: L.C. Page & Company, Inc., 1924.

Lewis, Nancy, and Rosa Michnya. "Bomb Explodes at Fort McNair, Blowing Out War College Window." *Washington Post*, April 27, 1983. https://www.washingtonpost. com/archive/local/1983/04/27/bomb-explodes-at-fort-mcnair-blowing-out-war -college-window/3211abfb-51e9-4ac8-822b-714c9811a1aa/.

Lewis, Tom. *Washington: A History of Our National City*. New York: Basic Books, 2015.

Library of Congress. "Marching for the Vote: Remembering the Woman Suffrage Parade of 1913." In *American Women: Topical Essays*. https://guides.loc.gov/ american-women-essays/marching-for-the-vote.

Liddy, G. Gordon. *Will: The Autobiography of G. Gordon Liddy*. New York: St. Martins, 1991.

Linder, Douglas O. "Andersonville Prison (Henry Wirz) Trial (1865)." *Famous Trials*. Retrieved December 2020. https://www.famous-trials.com/andersonville.

Lineberry, Cate. "The Wild Rose of Washington." *New York Times*, August 22, 2011.

Lockhart, Paul. *The Drillmaster of Valley Forge: The Baron de Steuben and the Making of the American Army*. Washington, DC: Smithsonian, 2008.

Lockwood, John. "The Curious Case of the Theft of the Pope's Stone 150 Years Ago." Aleteia.org, Newsmax, April 21, 2015. https://www.newsmax.com/US/Popes-Stone-stolen-Washington-Monument-Know-Nothings/2015/04/21/id/639920/.

Louisiana State Exhibit Museum. "Battle of New Orleans." http://laexhibitmuseum.org/historic-objects/battle-of-new-orleans/.

Mac Donald, Heather. *The War on Cops: How the New Attack on Law and Order Makes Everyone Less Safe*. New York: Encounter Books, 2016.

Mackenzie, Alexander Slidell. *Life of Stephen Decatur: A Commodore in the Navy of the United States*. Boston: C. C. Little and J. Brown, 1846.

MacMahon, Edward B., and Leonard Curry. *Medical Cover-Ups in the White House*. Washington, DC: Farragut, 1987.

MacNeil, Neil, and Richard A. Baker. *The American Senate: An Insider's History*. Oxford: Oxford University Press, 2013.

Madigan, Andrew. "The Pair of American Politicians Who Fought the 19th Century's Silliest Duel." AtlasObscura.com, January 8, 2016. https://www.atlasobscura.com/articles/the-pair-of-american-politicians-who-fought-the-19th-centurys-silliest-duel.

Madison, James, Alexander Hamilton, and John Jay. *The Federalist Papers*. New York: Penguin Books, 1987.

Mann, Ted, et al. "Lawmakers Were Feet and Seconds Away from Confrontation with the Mob in the Capitol." *Wall Street Journal*, January 12, 2021. https://www.wsj.com/articles/lawmakers-were-feet-and-seconds-away-from-confrontation-with-the-mob-in-the-capitol-11610481854?mod=newsviewer_click.

Marszalek, John F. *The Petticoat Affair*. Baton Rouge: Louisiana State University Press, 1997.

Marx, Rudolph, M.D. "The Health of the President: Andrew Jackson." HealthGuidance.org. https://www.healthguidance.org/entry/8908/1/the-health-of-the-president-andrew-jackson.html.

McCullough, David. *The Greater Journey: Americans in Paris*. New York: Simon & Schuster, 2011.

McElroy, John. *Andersonville: A Story of Rebel Military Prisons*. Toledo, OH: D. R. Locke, 1897.

McKee, Bradford. "The Battle for Pep-O-Mint Plaza." *Washington City Paper*, May 22–28, 1998.

McMurry, Donald L. *Coxey's Army: A Study in Industrial Unrest, 1893–1898*. Boston: Little, Brown & Co., 1929. Reissued 1968.

Melton, Tracy Matthew. *Hanging Henry Gambrill: The Violent Career of Baltimore's Plug Uglies, 1854–1860*. Baltimore: The Press at The Maryland Historical Society, 2005.

Merchant, Nomaan, and Colleen Long. "Police Command Structure Crumbled Fast during Capitol Riot." Associated Press, January 18, 2021.

Merry, Robert W. *A Country of Vast Designs: James K. Polk, the Mexican War, and the Conquest of the American Continent*. New York: Simon & Schuster, 2009.

Meteor, Julius. "The Burning of the USS *Philadelphia*." *Naval History Blog*, US Naval Institute, February 18, 2015. https://www.navalhistory.org/2015/02/18/the-burning-of-the-uss-philadelphia.

Metropolitan Police Department. "Richard Sylvester." DC.gov. https://mpdc.dc.gov/biography/richard-sylvester.

Miles, Ellen. "Gilbert Stuart Paints George Washington." National Portrait Gallery, February 19, 2016.

Miles, Nathania A. Branch, Monday M. Miles, and Ryan Quick. *Prince George's County and the Civil War: Life on the Border*. San Francisco, CA: The History Press Library Editions, Google Books, 2013.

Millard, Candice. *Destiny of the Republic: A Tale of Madness, Medicine and the Murder of a President*. New York: Doubleday, 2011.

Miller, David W. *Second Only to Grant: Quartermaster General Montgomery C. Meigs*. Shippensburg, PA: White Mane Books, 2000.

Mitchell, Alison, and Katharine Q. Seelye. "A Day of Terror: Congress; Horror Knows No Party As Lawmakers Huddle." *New York Times*, September 12, 2001. https://www.nytimes.com/2001/09/12/us/a-day-of-terror-congress-horror-knows-no-party-as-lawmakers-huddle.html.

Mitchell, Robert. "A Hungry Congressman Didn't Get the Breakfast He Ordered. So He Shot the Waiter." *Washington Post*, June 23, 2018. https://www.washington-post.com/news/retropolis/wp/2018/06/23/a-hungry-congressman-didnt-get-the-breakfast-he-ordered-so-he-shot-the-waiter/.

Mitchell, Robert B. "James Garfield's Greatest Fear: Being Stained by the Credit Mobilier Corruption Scandal." *HistoryNet*, October 27, 2020. https://www.historynet.com/james-garfields-greatest-fear-credit-mobilier-corruption-scandal.htm.

Morley, Jefferson. *Snow-Storm in August: Washington City, Francis Scott Key, and the Forgotten Race Riot of 1835*. New York: Nan Talese/Doubleday, 2012.

Morley, Jefferson. "The 'Snow Riot'." *Washington Post*, February 6, 2005. https://www.washingtonpost.com/archive/lifestyle/magazine/2005/02/06/the-snow-riot/0514ba84-54dd-46ac-851c-ff74856fcef4/.

Morris, Sylvia Jukes. "The Historian and the Hostess." *Washington Post*, December 25, 1983.

Mosby, John Singleton. *The Memoirs of Colonel John S. Mosby. Documenting the American South*. Electronic Edition. University of North Carolina. https://docsouth.unc.edu/fpn/mosby/mosby.html.

Moser, Edward P. "Brave Man, Bad Advisors." (Grant Administration). In *The Two-Term Jinx: How Most Second-Term Presidents Stumble, and Why Some Succeed* (Vol. 1). CreateSpace/Amazon, 2016.

Moser, Edward P. "The Biggest Slave Escape in American History." In *The White House's Unruly Neighborhood: Crime, Scandal and Intrigue in the History of Lafayette Square*. Jefferson, NC: McFarland & Company, Inc., 2020.

Moser, Edward P. "The Burning of the White House, and the Rescue of Its Riches." In *The White House's Unruly Neighborhood: Crime, Scandal and Intrigue in the History of Lafayette Square*. Jefferson, NC: McFarland & Company, Inc., 2020.

Moser, Edward P. "The Cunning Craft of a Deadly Spy." In *The White House's Unruly Neighborhood: Crime, Scandal and Intrigue in the History of Lafayette Square*. Jefferson, NC: McFarland & Company, Inc., 2020.

Moser, Edward P. "A Duel Between the Oddest and Most Famous of Congress." In *The White House's Unruly Neighborhood: Crime, Scandal and Intrigue in the History of Lafayette Square*. Jefferson, NC: McFarland & Company, Inc., 2020.

Moser, Edward P. "A Wartime Tavern Keeper's Unwanted Guests." In *The White House's Unruly Neighborhood: Crime, Scandal and Intrigue in the History of Lafayette Square*. Jefferson, NC: McFarland & Company, Inc., 2020.

Moser, Edward P. "The Entrepreneur and the Ingénue." (Roscoe Conklin). In *The White House's Unruly Neighborhood: Crime, Scandal and Intrigue in the History of Lafayette Square*. Jefferson, NC: McFarland & Company, Inc., 2020.

Moser, Edward P. "Murder Bay and Hooker's Division." In *The White House's Unruly Neighborhood: Crime, Scandal and Intrigue in the History of Lafayette Square*. Jefferson, NC: McFarland & Company, Inc., 2020.

Moser, Edward P. "The Most Criminally Inept Family in Military History." In *The White House's Unruly Neighborhood: Crime, Scandal and Intrigue in the History of Lafayette Square*. Jefferson, NC: McFarland & Company, Inc., 2020.

Moser, Edward P. "Frederick Douglass: Ride to Freedom." In *A Patriot's A to Z of America*. Nashville: Turner Publishing, 2011.

Moser, Edward P. "Victory at New Orleans: Old Hickory's Motley Crew." In *A Patriot's A to Z of America*. Nashville: Turner Publishing, 2011.

Moser, Edward P. Lafayette Square Tour of Scandal, Assassination, and Spies. "Capitol Hill Tour." https://www.meetup.com/Washarea-Discovery-Hikes/.

Moser, Edward P. Lafayette Square Tour of Scandal, Assassination, and Spies. "Congressional Cemetery Tour; Capitol Hill Tour." https://www.meetup.com/Washarea-Discovery-Hikes/.

Moser, Edward P. Lafayette Square Tour of Scandal, Assassination, and Spies. "Georgetown Tour; the Tyler House." https://www.meetup.com/Lafayette-Sq-Tours-of-Scandal-Assassination-Spies-Meetup/.

Moser, Edward P. Lafayette Square Tour of Scandal, Assassination, and Spies. "The Potent Potables Mayflower Hotel and Environs Tour." https://www.meetup.com/Washarea-Discovery-Hikes/.

Moser, Edward P. "A Rebound from War-Time Devastation: James Madison, 1813–1817." In *The Two-Term Jinx: How Most Second-Term Presidents Stumble, and Why Some Succeed* (Vol.1). CreateSpace/Amazon, 2016.

Moser, Edward P. "Second-Term Misfortune after a Four-Year Pause: Grover Cleveland, 1893–1897." In *The Two-Term Jinx: How Most Second-Term Presidents Stumble, and Why Some Succeed* (Vol. 1). CreateSpace/Amazon, 2016.

Moskowitz, Daniel B. "Nazi Saboteurs at the Supreme Court." *World War II* magazine, July/August 2014.

National Archives. *Founders Online.* "Thomas Jefferson to Pierre Charles L'Enfant, 27 February 1792." https://founders.archives.gov/documents/Hamil-
ton/01-11-02-0061. (Original source: *The Papers of Alexander Hamilton*, Vol.
11, February 1792–June 1792, 50–51, Harold C. Syrett, ed. New York: Columbia
University Press, 1966.)

National Archives. *Founders Online.* "To George Washington from Pierre L'Enfant, 21
November 1791." https://founders.archives.gov/documents/Washington/
05-09-02-0124. (Original source: *The Papers of George Washington*, Presidential
Series, vol. 9, 23 September 1791–29 February 1792, 219–25, Mark A. Mastrom-
arino, ed. Charlottesville: University Press of Virginia, 2000.)

National Archives. *Founders Online.* "To Thomas Jefferson from James McGurk," on or
before 19 April 1802. https://founders.archives.gov/documents/Jefferson/
01-37-02-0224.

National Archives. "Greenhow, Rose O'Neal," (1817–1864), "People Description."
Accessed February 5, 2013.

National Museum of American History. Moniz, Amanda B. "Why a Social Activist
Opposed Woman Suffrage." https://americanhistory.si.edu/blog/why-social
-activist-opposed-woman-suffrage.

National Park Service. "The Acquisition of Canada This Year Will Be a Mere Matter of
Marching." https://www.nps.gov/articles/a-mere-matter-of-marching.htm.

National Park Service. *Andersonville National Historic Site Georgia.* https://www.nps.gov/
ande/index.htm.

National Park Service. "Myth: The Mystery of Felix de la Baume." April 14, 2015.
https://www.nps.gov/ande/learn/historyculture/felixdelabaume.htm.

National Park Service. "The Prison Camp at Andersonville." History E-Library.
Retrieved July 2020. https://www.nps.gov/parkhistory/online_books/civil_war
_series/5/sec1.htm.

Naval History and Heritage Command. "The Defense and Burning of Washington in
1814: Naval Documents of the War of 1812." September 7, 2017. https://www
.history.navy.mil/research/library/online-reading-room/title-list-alphabetically/d/
the-defense-and-burning-of-washington-in-1814-naval-documents-of-the
-war-of-1812.html.

Naval History Blog. "The Trent Affair and the Indomitable Captain Charles Wilkes."
November 7, 2013. https://www.navalhistory.org/2013/11/07/the-trent-affair
-and-the-indomitable-captain-charles-wilkes.

New England Historical Society. "Baron von Steuben Shows the Army a Bayonet Is
Not a Grilling Tool." 2018. www.newenglandhistoricalsociety.com/baron-von
-steuben-shows-the-army-a-bayonet-is-not-a-grilling-tool/.

New England Historical Society. "Remembering Jonathan Cilley, the Reluctant Maine
Duelist." Retrieved July 2020. https://www.newenglandhistoricalsociety.com/
remembering-jonathan-cilley-the-reluctant-maine-duelist/.

Nilsson, Jeff. "Beatings, Brawls, and Lawmaking: Mayhem in Congress." *Saturday
Evening Post*, December 4, 2010. https://www.saturdayeveningpost.com/2010/12/
beatings-brawls-lawmaking-mayhem-congress/.

Noel, Francis Regis, and Margaret Brent Downing. *The Court-house of the District of Columbia*. Washington, DC: Judd & Detweiler, Inc. 1919, Google Books.

Northup, Solomon. *Twelve Years a Slave*. CreateSpace, 2018. Originally published in 1853.

NPR. "Failed Escape Sheds New Light on D.C. Slavery." May 9, 2007. https://www .npr.org/templates/story/story.php?storyId=10103500.

O'Brien, Greg. "Choctaw Recruits Fight with the U.S. Army." National Park Service. https://www.nps.gov/articles/choctaw-indians-and-the-battle-of-new-orleans .htm.

O'Brien, John. "Lincoln and the Abolitionists at the Sprigg House." *Lincoln in Washington*. October 31, 2012. http://www.lincolninwashington.com/2012/10/31/lincoln -and-the-abolitionists-at-the-sprigg-house/

O'Connor, John. "I'm the Guy They Called Deep Throat." *Vanity Fair*, July 2005.

O'Harrow, Robert, Jr. "Montgomery Meigs's Vital Influence on the Civil War—and Washington." *Washington Post Magazine*, July 1, 2011.

"One Nazi Who Informed On Others Gets Life Term, Second 30 Years; Doomed Six Are Given Scant Notice: Six Nazi Spies Die In Electric Chair." *Washington Post*, August 9, 1942.

"Other Government Buildings: Old Capitol Prison." *Mr. Lincoln's White House*. The Lehrman Institute. www.mrlincolnswhitehouse.org/washington/other-government -buildings/government-buildings-old-capitol-prison/.

O'Toole, Patricia. *Five of Hearts: An Intimate Portrait of Henry Adams and His Friends*. New York: Harmony/Crown, 1990.

Overby, Peter. "A Historic Killing in the Capitol Building." NPR, *Morning Edition*, February 19, 2007. https://www.npr.org/templates/story/story.php?story Id=7447550.

Pacanins, Gonzalo. "When the Klan Descended on Washington." *Boundary Stones*, WETA, December 11, 2019.

Parkinson, Hilary. "Suffrage and Suffering at the 1913 March." March 1, 2013. National Archives. https://prologue.blogs.archives.gov/2013/03/01/suffrage-and-suffering -at-the-1913-march/.

Park View, D.C. "Washington's Original Monument to Baron von Steuben." Retrieved June 2018. https://parkviewdc.com/2014/01/14/washingtons-original-monument -to-baron-von-steuben/.

Paterson Friends of the Great Falls. "S.U.M. Society for Establishing Useful Manufac- tures." Great Falls/S.U.M. National Historic Landmark District. http://paterson greatfalls.org/sum.html. 2020.

Paullin, Charles Oscar. *Commodore John Rodgers: Captain*. Cleveland: The Arthur H. Clark Company, 1910.

Paynter, John H. "The Fugitives of the Pearl" (excerpt). *Journal of Negro History*, July 1, 1916. From HU ArchivesNet, Howard University.

Paxson, Frederic Logan, Allen Johnson, and Dumas Malone, eds. *Dictionary of American Biography; Conkling, Roscoe*. New York: Charles Scribner's Sons, 1930.

PBS. "People & Events: Oakes Ames (1804–1873)." *American Experience*, 1999–2003. www.shoppbs.pbs.org/wgbh/amex/tcrr/peopleevents/p_ames.html.

Peck, Garrett. *Prohibition in Washington, D.C. How Dry We Weren't.* Charleston, SC: History Press, 2011.

Peskin, Allan. *Garfield: A Biography.* Kent, OH: Kent State University Press, 1978.

Philbrick, Nathaniel. *Sea of Glory: America's Voyage of Discovery, The U.S. Exploring Expedition, 1838–1842.* New York: Viking, 2003.

Pierce, J. Kingston. "Andrew Jackson: The Petticoat Affair—Scandal in Jackson's White House." *American History Magazine,* June 12, 2006.

Pinkerton, Allan. *A Spy of the Rebellion: Being a True History of the Spy System of the United States Army.* Whitefish, MT: Kessinger Publishing, LLC, 2010. Originally published in 1883.

Pitch, Anthony. *The Burning of Washington: The British Invasion of 1814.* Annapolis: Naval Institute Press, 1998.

Pitch, Anthony. "The Burning of Washington." White House Historical Association, *White House History* IV, Fall 1998.

Pohl, Robert. *TheHillIsHome.com.* "Lost Capitol Hill: The Caldwell House." November 15, 2010.

Pohl, Robert. *TheHillIsHome.com.* "Lost Capitol Hill: Slave Traders in the Hill." May 15, 2017.

Pohl, Robert. "Presidents on Capitol Hill." *HillRag.com.* November 5, 2013. http://www.capitalcommunitynews.com/content/presidents-capitol-hill-0.

Pohl, Robert S. *Urban Legends & Historic Lore of Washington.* Mt. Pleasant, SC: History Press Library Editions, 2013.

Pohl, Robert S. *Wicked Capitol Hill: An Unruly History of Behaving Badly.* San Francisco, CA: The History Press, 2012.

Politico Magazine. "'Is This Really Happening?': The Siege of Congress, Seen From the Inside." January 7, 2021.

Poole, Robert M. *On Hallowed Ground: The Story of Arlington National Cemetery.* London: Walker Books, 2009.

Presidential History Blog. "Kate Sprague and Roscoe Conkling: Beauty and the Boss." June 8, 2015. https://featherfoster.wordpress.com/2015/06/08/kate-sprague-and-roscoe-conkling-beauty-and-the-boss/.

Press, Donald E. "South of the Avenue: From Murder Bay to the Federal Triangle." *Records of the Columbia Historical Society,* Vol. 51, 1984. Washington, DC.

Puleo, Stephen. *The Caning: The Assault That Drove America to Civil War.* Yardley, PA: Westholme Publishing LLC, 2012.

Ramage, James A. *Gray Ghost: The Life of Col. John Singleton Mosby.* Lexington: University Press of Kentucky, 2009.

Ramsay, Jack C., Jr. *Jean Laffite: Prince of Pirates.* Burnet, TX: Eakin Press, 1996.

Remini, Robert V. *The House.* New York: HarperCollins Publishers Inc., 2006.

Remini, Robert V. *The Life of Andrew Jackson.* New York: HarperPerennial, 1988.

Reynolds, Brad. "The Worst Leaders in History: General William H. Winder." WarfareHistoryNetwork. September 18, 2018. http://warfarehistorynetwork.com/daily/military-history/the-worst-leaders-in-history-general-william-h-winder/.

Ricks, Mary Kay. *Escape on the Pearl.* New York: HarperCollins, 2009.

Ricks, Mary Kay. "Escape on the Pearl." *Washington Post*, August 12, 1998.

Roig-Franzia, Manuel. "A Terrorist in the House." *Washington Post*, February 22, 2002. https://www.washingtonpost.com/archive/lifestyle/magazine/2004/02/22/a-terrorist-in-the-house/293c52cd-8794-47bd-9960-9c7a871e009c/.

Romero, Melissa. "Before Jewelers' Row, There Was Robert Morris' Foiled McMansion." August 15, 2016. https://philly.curbed.com/2016/8/15/12481486/robert-morris-folly-mansion-jewelers-row-philadelphia.

Rosenau, William. "The Dark History of America's First Female Terrorist Group." *Politico*, May 3, 2020. https://www.politico.com/news/magazine/2020/05/03/us-history-first-women-terrorist-group-191037.

Rosenau, William. *Tonight We Bombed the US Capitol: The Explosive Story of May 19, America's First Female Terrorist Group.* New York: Atria Books/Simon & Schuster, 2020.

Rothman, Joshua. "When Bigotry Paraded Through the Streets." *The Atlantic*, December 4, 2016. https://www.theatlantic.com/politics/archive/2016/12/second-klan/509468/.

Russell, Daniel E. "The Day Morgan Was Shot.". *Glen Cove Heritage*. Retrieved August 2020. https://www.glencoveheritage.com/legacy_site/morganshooting.pdf.

Sawyer, Lemuel. *A Biography of John Randolph, of Roanoke.* New York: Burgess, Stringer & Co., 1844.

Schuster, Hannah. "'From Sadness to Empathy to Anger'." *DCist*, May 31, 2020. https://dcist.com/story/20/05/31/d-c-wakes-up-to-broken-glass-graffiti-after-intense-night-of-protests/.

Schwantes, Carlos A. *Coxey's Army: An American Odyssey.* Lincoln: University of Nebraska Press, 1985.

Schwarz, Frederic D. "The Klan on Parade." *New American*, July/August 2000.

Scott, Pamela. *Capital Engineers: The U.S. Army Corps of Engineers in the Development of Washington, D.C., 1790–2004.* Office of History Headquarters, US Army Corps of Engineers, Alexandria, VA, 2011. https://www.publications.usace.army.mil/Portals/76/Publications/EngineerPamphlets/EP_870-1-67_2011.pdf.

Segers, Grace. "Inside the Senate chambers as lawmakers evacuated and rioters stormed the Capitol." CBS News. January 7, 2021.

Sharp, John G. "Alethia 'Lethe' Browning Tanner." *Washington D.C. Genealogy Trails*. http://genealogytrails.com/washdc/biographies/bio6.html.

Shaw, Benjamin. "Fire and Rain: The Storm That Changed D.C. History." *Boundary Stones*, WETA, July 30, 2015. https://blogs.weta.org/boundarystones/2015/07/30/fire-and-rain-storm-changed-dc-history.

Shilts, Randy. *Conduct Unbecoming: Gays and Lesbians in the U.S. Military.* New York: St. Martin's Press, 1993.

Shiner, Michael. *The Diary of Michael Shiner Relating to the History of the Washington Navy Yard 1813–1869.* Transcribed with Introduction and Notes by John G. Sharp (12 October 2007). http://www.ibiblio.org/hyperwar/NHC/shiner/shiner_diary.htm.

Sickles, Daniel Edgar, and Felix Gregory De Fontaine. *Trial of the Hon. Daniel E. Sickles for Shooting Philip Barton Key.* New York: R.M. De Witt, 1859.

Singman, Brook. "Trump Slams His VP, Says Pence 'Didn't Have the Courage' to Decertify Results of Presidential Election." *FoxNews*, January 6, 2021.

Smith, Margaret Bayard. *The First Forty Years of Washington Society*. New York: Scribner's, 1906.

Smithsonian Institution. "Henry Merwin Shrady Papers, 1901–1972." *Archives of American Art*. https://www.aaa.si.edu/collections/henry-merwin-shrady-papers-9404.

Snow, Peter. *When Britain Burned the White House: The 1814 Invasion of Washington*. New York: Thomas Dunne, 2014.

Sotos, John, MD (Doctor Zebra). "Health and Medical History of President Andrew Jackson." *Medical History of U.S. Presidents*. www.doctorzebra.com/prez/.

South Dakota State University. "Undocumented Volcano Contributed to Extremely Cold Decade from 1810–1819." *ScienceDaily*, December 7, 2009. www.science daily.com/releases/2009/12/091205105844.htm.

Stahr, Walter. *Seward: Lincoln's Indispensable Man*. New York: Simon & Schuster, 2012. First edition.

Stewart, David O. *Madison's Gift: Five Partnerships That Built America*. New York: Simon & Schuster, 2015.

Story, Joseph. "The United States, Appellants, v. The Libellants and Claimants of the Schooner Amistad, Her Tackle, Apparel, and Furniture, Together With Her Cargo, and the Africans Mentioned and Described in the Several Libels and Claims, Appellees." Supreme Court of the United States, 40 U.S. 518; 10 L. Ed. 826 (January 1841 Term), Cornell University Law School.

Stowe, Harriet Ward Beecher. *Uncle Tom's Cabin*. Originally published in 1852.

Sumner, Charles. "The Crime Against Kansas." Speech, May 19, 1856, US Senate. Full text, https://www.senate.gov/artandhistory/history/resources/pdf/CrimeAgainst KSSpeech.pdf.

Swain, Claudia. "The Disappearing Corpse of D.C.'s First Murderer." *Boundary Stones*, WETA, June 8, 2016. https://blogs.weta.org/boundarystones/2016/06/08/disap pearing-corpse-dcs-first-murderer.

Swain, Craig. *The Historical Marker Database*. "William L. Chaplin Arrested!" October 25, 2017. Erected by National Underground Railroad–Network to Freedom. https://www.hmdb.org/marker.asp?marker=109230.

Taylor, David A. "The Inside Story of How a Nazi Plot to Sabotage the U.S. War Effort Was Foiled." *Smithsonian*, June 26, 2017, updated. https://www.smith sonianmag.com/history/inside-story-how-nazi-plot-sabotage-us-war-effort-was -foiled-180959594/.

Thorburn, Mark. "Charles Kincaid Trial: 1891." Encyclopedia.com. https://www .encyclopedia.com/law/law-magazines/charles-kincaid-trial-1891.

Thornton, Willis. "The Day They Burned The Capitol." *American Heritage*, Vol. 6, issue 1 (December 1954). https://www.americanheritage.com/day-they-burned-capitol.

Topham, Washington. "Northern Liberty Market." *Records of the Columbia Historical Society*, Vol. 24, March 16, 1920. Washington, DC: Google Books.

Tucker, Spencer. *Stephen Decatur: A Life Most Bold and Daring*. Annapolis, MD: Naval Institute Press, 2004.

Umana, Jose. "DC Protestors Topple, Burn Statue of Confederate General Albert Pike." WTOPNews, June 20, 2020. https://wtop.com/dc/2020/06/protesters-tear-down -albert-pike-statue-in-dc/.

University of Washington Libraries, Special Collections. "The Crusaders Map and Report Regarding Prohibition Sent to Senator Wesley Jones, 1932." https:// digitalcollections.lib.washington.edu/digital/collection/pioneerlife/id/19764/.

US Capitol Historical Society. *The Capitol Dome: Examining the War of 1812*. Vol. 51, no. 3 (Fall 2014). https://uschs.org/wp-content/uploads/2012/07/USCHS -Capitol-Dome-2014-Fall-1-30.pdf.

US Congress. Joint Committee on Printing. *Biographical Directory of the United States Congress 1774–2005*. Washington, DC: 2005. https://www.govinfo.gov/content/ pkg/GPO-CDOC-108hdoc222/pdf/GPO-CDOC-108hdoc222.pdf.

US Department of the Interior. National Park Service. "National Registry of Historical Places Inventory–Nomination Form." Ames Monument. https://npgallery.nps. gov/NRHP/GetAsset/NRHP/72001296_text.

US House of Representatives. "A Fatal Duel Between Members in 1838." https:// history.house.gov/Historical-Highlights/1800-1850/A-fatal-duel-between-Mem- bers-in-1838/.

US House of Representatives. "Timeline of 1954 Shooting Events." *History, Art & Archives*. Retrieved June 2020. http://history.house.gov/Exhibitions-and -Publications/1954-Shooting/Essays/Timeline/.

US Marine Corps University. "Colonel and Brevet Brigadier General Archibald Henderson, USMC (Deceased)." https://www.usmcu.edu/Research/ Marine-Corps-History-Division/People/Whos-Who-in-Marine-Corps-History/ Gagnon-Ingram/Colonel-Archibald-Henderson/.

US News Staff. "Watergate and the White House: The 'Third-Rate Burglary' That Toppled a President." *U.S. News & World Report*, August 8, 2014.

US Senate. "Bomb Rocks Capitol." July 2, 1915. http://www.senate.gov/artandhistory/ history/minute/Bomb_Rocks_Capitol.htm.

US Senate. "James Patterson Expulsion Case (Crédit Mobilier Scandal)." US Senate Historical Office. *United States Senate Election, Expulsion and Censure Cases: 1793–1990*. Washington: Government Printing Office, 1995. https://www.senate .gov/artandhistory/history/common/expulsion_cases/064JamesPatterson_expul- sion.htm.

US Senate. "Schuyler Colfax, 17th Vice President (1869–1873)." Retrieved December 24, 2020. https://www.senate.gov/about/officers-staff/vice-president/VP_Schuyler _Colfax.htm.

US Senate. Senate Committee on Rules and Administration and the Senate Homeland Security and Government Affairs Committee. "Written Testimony of USCP Former Chief of Police Steven A. Sund." February 23, 2021. https://www.rules .senate.gov/imo/media/doc/Testimony_Sund.pdf.

US Senate. Senate Select Committee on Presidential Campaign Activities (The Water- gate Committee). US Senate Historical Office, Washington, DC. https://www .senate.gov/about/powers-procedures/investigations/watergate.htm4.

"USS Enterprise." *Dictionary of American Naval Fighting Ships.* Department of the Navy–Naval Historical Center, January 29, 2004.

Verell, Nancy. "Aaron Burr." Monticello.org, March 30, 2015. https://www.monticello.org/site/research-and-collections/aaron-burr.

Von Eckardt, Wolf. "Breuer's New HEW: Fine Designs, Dollar Signs." *Washington Post*, May 13, 1972.

Washington D.C. Genealogy Trails. "The Metropolitan Police Department, District of Columbia: Law, Crime and Policing in the District 1790–1900." Retrieved September 2020. http://genealogytrails.com/washdc/lawsprisons/historyofpolicedept.html.

Washington, DC Metropolitan Police. "The Washington D.C. Metropolitan Police Department 1800–1860." www.dcmetropolicecollector.com/1800-1860.html.

Weather Underground. Washington, DC: US Government Printing Office, 1975.

Weather Underground Organization. *Prairie Fire: The Politics of Revolutionary Anti-Imperialism: the Political Statement of the Weather Underground.* San Francisco: Communications Co., 1975. https://archive.org/details/PrairieFireThePolitics OfRevolutionaryAnti-imperialismThePolitical.

Weaver, John D. "Bonus March." *American Heritage*, Vol. 14, issue 4 (June 1963). https://www.americanheritage.com/bonus-march.

Wheeler, Linda. "The Day It Poured." *Washington Post*, February 27, 1994.

White, Richard. *Railroaded: The Transcontinentals and the Making of Modern America.* New York: W.W. Norton, 2011.

"White-Robed Klan Cheered on March in Nation's Capital." *Washington Post*, August 9, 1925.

Wikipedia. "1954 United States Capitol Shooting." https://en.wikipedia.org/wiki/1954_United_States_Capitol_shooting.

Wikipedia. "Albert Pike." Retrieved July 2020. https://en.wikipedia.org/wiki/Albert_Pike.

Wikipedia. "Anne Frank." https://en.wikipedia.org/wiki/Anne_Frank.

Wikipedia. "Caning of Charles Sumner" and "Charles Sumner." https://en.wikipedia.org/wiki/Caning_of_Charles_Sumner.

Williamson, James Joseph. *Prison Life in the Old Capitol and Reminiscences of the Civil War.* Farmington Hills: Gale. 2010. Originally published in 1911.

Winkle, Kenneth J. *Lincoln's Citadel.* New York: W. W. Norton & Company, 2013.

Wise, Henry A. "Henry A. Wise's Account of the Duel." *The Cilley Pages.* From the *Saturday Evening Post*, June 2, 1906.

Witcover, Jules. *Sabotage at Black Tom: Imperial Germany's Secret War in America, 1914–1917.* Chapel Hill, NC: Algonquin Books of Chapel Hill, 1989.

Wood, Gordon. *Empire of Liberty: A History of the Early Republic, 1789-1815.* Oxford: Oxford University Press. 2009.

Wolfe, Tom. *From Bauhaus to Our House.* London: Picador, 1998.

"Women's Beauty, Grace, and Art Bewilder the Capital: Miles of Fluttering Femininity Present Entrancing Suffrage Appeal." *Washington Post*, March 4, 1913.

Wood, Margaret. "A Duel with Rifles." July 17, 2013, Library of Congress. https://blogs.loc.gov/law/2013/07/a-duel-with-rifles/.

Zahniser, J. D. and Amelia R. Fry. *Alice Paul: Claiming Power.* Oxford and New York: Oxford University Press, 2014.

INDEX